Better Homes and Gardens
BIGGEST BOOK OF CASSEROLES

Meredith® Books
Des Moines, Iowa

BIGGEST BOOK OF CASSEROLES

Editor: Tricia Laning
Project Editor and Indexer: Spectrum Communication Services, Inc.
Writer: Cynthia Pearson
Contributing Designer: Joyce DeWitt
Cover Designer: Daniel Pelavin
Copy Chief: Terri Fredrickson
Publishing Operations Manager: Karen Schirm
Edit and Design Production Coordinator: Mary Lee Gavin
Editorial Assistant: Cheryl Eckert
Book Production Managers: Pam Kvitne, Marjorie J. Schenkelberg, Rick von Holdt, Mark Weaver
Contributing Copy Editor: Susan Oliver Watson
Contributing Proofreaders: Judith Stern Friedman, Gretchen Kauffman, Susan J. Kling
Test Kitchen Director: Lynn Blanchard
Test Kitchen Product Supervisor: Marilyn Cornelius
Test Kitchen Home Economists: Marilyn Cornelius; Juliana Hale; Laura Harms, R.D.; Jennifer Kalinowski, R.D.; Maryellyn Krantz;
    Jill Moberly; Dianna Nolin; Colleen Weeden; Lori Wilson; Charles Worthington

Meredith® Books
Executive Director, Editorial: Gregory H. Kayko
Executive Director, Design: Matt Strelecki
Senior Editor/Group Manager: Jan Miller
Marketing Product Manager: Gina Rickert

Publisher and Editor in Chief: James D. Blume
Editorial Director: Linda Raglan Cunningham
Executive Director, Marketing: Jeffrey B. Myers
Executive Director, New Business Development: Todd M. Davis
Executive Director, Sales: Ken Zagor
Director, Operations: George A. Susral
Director, Production: Douglas M. Johnston
Business Director: Jim Leonar

Vice President and General Manager: Douglas J. Guendel

Better Homes and Gardens® Magazine
Editor in Chief: Karol DeWulf Nickell
Deputy Editor, Food and Entertaining: Nancy Hopkins

Meredith Publishing Group
President: Jack Griffin
Executive Vice President: Bob Mate

Meredith Corporation
Chairman and Chief Executive Officer: William T. Kerr
President and Chief Operating Officer: Stephen M. Lacy

In Memoriam: E. T. Meredith III (1933-2003)

Our Better Homes and Gardens® Test Kitchen seal on the back cover of this book assures you that every recipe in *Biggest Book of Casseroles* has been tested in the Better Homes and Gardens® Test Kitchen. This means that each recipe is practical and reliable, and meets our high standards of taste appeal. We guarantee your satisfaction with this book for as long as you own it.

All of us at Meredith® Books are dedicated to providing you with the information and ideas you need to create delicious foods. We welcome your comments and suggestions. Write to us at: Meredith Books, Cookbook Editorial Department, 1716 Locust St., Des Moines, IA 50309-3023.

If you would like to purchase any of our cooking, crafts, gardening, home improvement, or home decorating and design books, check wherever quality books are sold. Or visit us at: bhgbooks.com

TABLE OF CONTENTS

INTRODUCTION

We're falling in love again with casseroles, and why not?

Casseroles offer much, much more than they require. Slide a casserole into a hot oven and you'll be coaxing rich, luscious flavor from a medley of ingredients such as meat, poultry, fish, eggs, vegetables, and cheeses, blended with broth, milk, sauce, or soup. These ingredients add up to a whole that's much greater than the sum of its parts. At the same time, you'll be filling the kitchen with tantalizing aromas and heightening the anticipation of a delectable dish at the table—all of which elevates a casserole from mere food to an all-out sensory pleasure.

On a practical note—whether they're for dinner, brunch, or breakfast or sweet varieties made for dessert—casseroles often can be made ahead, leaving you free to do other things while they bake. You can prepare a casserole today, then slip it in the oven tomorrow to bake during your postwork gym session or while you're running kids to after-school activities. Make a few casseroles for the freezer—when you're in the mood—and pull one out later to bake and enjoy.

Casseroles are entertaining assets too. Want to invite friends for supper tonight or tomorrow? Pull a favorite casserole from the cold hold and you're on your way. How about dessert? Assemble a crisp or cobbler and instead of fussing over its preparation, you can be visiting with friends and family while it bakes. The smell of a warm dessert will delight everyone, including you.

Preparing food "en casserole" dates back several hundred years, and it's a method practiced nearly worldwide. While casseroles are sometimes considered old-fashioned, here's the bottom line: Casseroles are what you make of them—and it's easy to make them well. With the *Biggest Book of Casseroles* on your side, you can make an endless variety of casseroles to suit yourself, family, and friends. Chop or shred the ingredients yourself or enjoy the ease of ready-to-use fruits, vegetables, and sauces. Either way, you can make memorable meals happen—and they will be oh so good.

Enjoy!

STOCK THE PANTRY

Keep your kitchen stocked with basics and you'll never be too many ingredients away from what you need for a casserole. Use this list as a starter; add or delete as your casserole choices require.

Produce
- Garlic
  (fresh or bottled, minced)
- Lemons and limes
  (fresh or bottled juice)
- Onions
- Potatoes

Dairy
- Butter and/or margarine
- Cheeses
  (grated, sliced, or chunk)
- Eggs
- Milk
- Sour cream

Frozen
- Precut vegetables
- Vegetable mixtures
- Frozen fruits

Shelf & Canned Goods
- Beans *(dried or canned)*
- Bouillon cubes and/or base
  (beef, chicken, or vegetable)
- Bread crumbs
- Broth
  (chicken, beef, or vegetable)
- Canned cream soups
  (chicken, mushroom, or celery)
- Canned meats

- Honey
- Flour
- Nuts
  (almonds, pecans, walnuts, peanuts, or other favorites)
- Olives
- Pasta, dried *(various shapes)*
- Pimientos
- Rice *(white, brown, or wild)*
- Tomatoes
  (whole, diced, stewed)
- Tomato paste
- Tomato sauce

Oils, Condiments & Seasonings
- Cooking oil
  (vegetable, olive, or specialty)
- Herbs and spices
- Hot sauce
- Mayonnaise
- Mustard
  (yellow, brown, Dijon-style, or specialty)
- Soy sauce
- Worcestershire sauce

Favorite Ethnic Ingredients
List the ones you buy often, perhaps jalapeño peppers, salsa, taco seasoning, hoisin sauce, or water chestnuts.

CHILLY BASICS

A hot, delicious meal—when you've barely had time to turn on the oven—is a huge reward for a little effort spent ahead of time. First, check to see if your cold holds—your refrigerator and freezer —are working properly. They're your allies in maintaining food quality and safety.

Refrigerator temperature check
Place a refrigerator thermometer in the fridge overnight to check the temperature. Or put an instant-read thermometer in a glass of water and set it in the middle of the fridge space. Five to 8 hours later, check the temperature. It should be between 34°F and 40°F. If it's not, adjust the temperature control and recheck the next day.

Freezer temperature check
Slip a freezer thermometer between frozen food containers. Five to 8 hours later it should read 0°F or colder. If it's not, adjust and recheck in 5 to 8 hours.

CASSEROLE ACCOMPANIMENTS MADE EASY

Your casserole's the star of the table. Layered or mixed ingredients melded in the oven produce a virtual symphony of flavors, so simple is best for side dishes. Simple serve-alongs also are quick and easy on the cook. Choose items to complement your casserole's flavors and contents—match cool to hot, tangy to spicy, sweet to savory, simple to complex. Here are some suggestions:

- Sliced apples or pears
  (toss with lemon juice to prevent browning)
- Citrus fruit sections
- Sliced fresh vegetables
- Steamed or grilled vegetables
- Yogurt
- Mixed greens
- Chewy bread *(sourdough, whole wheat, or specialty)*
- Corn bread
- Rice
- Pasta
- Beans
- Hard-cooked egg slices

Similarly, side-dish casseroles can play a supporting role next to easy (or purchased) baked chicken, roasted meats, or sliced cold cuts.

Busy Cook's Tip:
Carry ingredient lists for your favorite casseroles with you *(in your purse, glove compartment, or PDA)* so you can pick up ingredients on a whim.

MAKE-AHEAD SAVVY

Try these approaches to filling your freezer with casseroles for busy times.

Make Two

When you're making one of your favorite casseroles, make a second one for the freezer while you're at it. Doubling the recipe will hardly, if at all, increase your preparation or cleanup time.

Swap

Team up with friends to stock each other's freezers with favorites. Use the Make Two (or Three) tip but swap the spares with your friends.

Indulge

When the mood or opportunity strikes, spend an afternoon or evening preparing casseroles. Make a favorite or two and an intriguing new one just for fun. No rush! Put on your favorite tunes and enjoy your kitchen creativity.

Tip: A stocked pantry shortens the shopping list for such sessions.

Batch Tasks

Lay out your recipes and combine similar tasks. Do all your veggie chopping at once, dividing amounts for each recipe into small cups or bowls. Brown any meats in separate pans simultaneously.

SPEED THE CHILL

Whether you're making a dish that's headed for the fridge or freezer, keep your food safe by cooling it quickly after cooking. Chilling quickly reduces the opportunity for harmful bacteria to grow. What's more, a fast chill reduces the likelihood of large ice crystals forming that can interfere with your casserole's flavor and texture. These tips help:

– Chill the cooked food quickly in the refrigerator. If you're going to divide it in half or into serving portions, divvy it up prior to the first chill down to hasten the release of heat.

– Once a casserole is cooled, tightly wrap and seal it. Then store it in the refrigerator or freezer. If you plan to freeze a casserole in several portions, it's best to arrange the containers in a single layer for faster freezing. You can stack the goods once frozen.

No-Dish Casserole Freezing Method:

This technique is handy for tucking some casseroles – baked or unbaked—into the freezer while keeping your cookware free for other uses.

– Line a greased casserole with a sheet of heavy-duty foil. (For casseroles with acidic ingredients, see below.) Make sure it is long and wide enough to fold and seal over the finished casserole.

– Assemble the casserole in the dish.

– Freeze the casserole unbaked or bake it according to the recipe.

– If you do bake the casserole, cool it quickly.

– Wrap the casserole by bringing the foil edges together over the food, fold the edges down, and seal so that the foil cradles the food.

– Freeze until firm.

– Remove the frozen casserole from dish; place it in a freezer bag or wrap it with another tight wrap of foil to seal out air.

– Label the casserole with the date as well as the finishing or baking instructions.

To thaw the casserole for serving, slip the wrapped food into its original dish. Thaw overnight in the refrigerator. Then reheat or bake.

Acidic Ingredients?

Casseroles that contain acidic ingredients, such as tomatoes or lemon juice, will need to be frozen in casseroles lined with plastic wrap. Their acidic nature reacts with aluminum foil, giving the finished dish an off flavor. For these casseroles, line the dish with freezer-safe plastic wrap before adding the food. Then overwrap it in foil. For baking, remove the plastic wrap and use the foil for a cover.

CASSEROLE-FREEZING TIPS:

– Use frozen casseroles within two months for best results.

– Hold the cheese, bacon, and crumb toppings if you're going to freeze a casserole (or leave it in the fridge overnight). Otherwise they'll become soggy or dry out. Freeze or refrigerate the toppings in separate airtight packages; label and attach them to the casserole with freezer tape.

– Avoid freezing casseroles that feature pasta, potatoes, or rice. These tend to lose texture after freezing. Similarly, avoid freezing casseroles that include cottage or ricotta cheese, sour cream, or mayonnaise.

DO THE THAW?

If time or cookware allows, you can slide a frozen casserole straight from the freezer into a preheated oven. If you do, make sure that you're using freezer-to-oven-capable cookware and that your schedule allows the additional bake time required. If not, thaw frozen casseroles safely in the fridge overnight. You can bake your from-the-freezer casserole at the temperature suggested in the recipe, but you'll need up to twice as much time in the oven. Check the casserole several times near the end of baking. Look for sauce bubbling at the edges and a hot center (at least 165°F).

Tip: Allow at least 10 minutes for your oven to fully preheat before baking your casserole.

Tip: For a crisp browned top, bake your casserole uncovered for the last third of baking.

REHEATING

The casserole you baked yesterday and chilled to serve today should be reheated in the oven at 325°F. The time will depend on the original baking time; start checking at about 45 minutes.

You also can reheat a few leftover portions, lightly covered, in the microwave oven on 70% power. Though the micro-cooking time will depend on the amount and type of food being warmed, start with 5 minutes and then check every 3 minutes thereafter.

Tip: If the food seems dry, add a little broth or sauce to the dish to rehydrate.

CASSEROLE COOKWARE

You've got options! Casserole dishes are deep, round, or oval ovenproof vessels with lids that are available in a variety of materials and price points. While all casserole dishes are ovenproof, they vary (by material and manufacturer) in their flexibility for use in the microwave oven, on the range top, and in the freezer. They also vary in their capability of going directly from freezer to oven—and then into the dishwasher. Choose cookware that meets your needs.

Tip: Slip a colorful pocket file or portfolio in your baking dish cupboard. Use it to keep product literature about your cookware handy for quick reference. Or look for cookware with dimensions and usage limitations stamped on the underside.

WHAT WILL YOU NEED?

Stock your kitchen with several covered casserole dishes in various sizes (1-, 2-, and 3-quart). For backup, make sure you have a few baking dishes in the 2-quart and 3-quart sizes.

As you explore making and serving casseroles, no doubt you'll find a dish size that you use so frequently you'll want to have two or three on the shelf. Ovenproof glass or ceramic casseroles are an affordable, useful investment, so add them when you can.

Ovenproof Glassware $

An excellent, versatile choice that can go nearly anywhere in the kitchen but on the range top. Available in clear and tinted glass that can be slipped into fitted baskets, cozies, and insulated totes.

Ovenproof Ceramic $–$$

You'll find this option in many styles; it's popular, versatile cookware similar to ovenproof glassware.

Handcrafted Ceramic $$

Beautiful on the table or buffet, these artful works are often ovenproof but not to the same degree as commercially produced pieces. Use

FOR FOIL, WRAPS, BAGS & PLASTIC CONTAINERS CHOOSE HEAVY-DUTY FREEZER GRADES

Don't let a bad wrap undo your make-ahead efforts in the freezer. When preparing make-aheads and leftovers for a stay in the freezer, protect them well using freezer-grade products. The difference in their performance is worth the extra cost, and it adds up in preventing moisture loss and protecting the texture and flavor of your food. Choose heavy-duty rather than regular aluminum foil, as well as freezer-grade plastic wrap and self-sealing bags. For leftovers, choose plastic freezer-grade containers sized to match the food portion as closely as possible.

them, but know their limits. (Keep the product information in a cupboard file for reference!) Imported pottery can have lead in its glaze which makes it unsafe for food preparation. Ask before making a purchase.

Anodized Aluminum, Lined Copper, Enameled Cast Iron $$$

Heavier and much more expensive than regular cookware, these dish materials can be used on the range top. That's handy for browning items prior to assembling a casserole—though the savings in cleanup may not justify the extra expense. Because these varieties aren't microwave-safe and may not be dishwasher-safe, they're best chosen by seasoned cooks as specialty items.

CASSEROLE SIZES & SUBSTITUTIONS

If a recipe calls for a casserole size that's not on your shelves, use a baking or soufflé dish as described below. Aluminum foil can stand in for a lid.

When choosing a dish for a casserole, volume (quart capacity) matters most, but so do height and width. Dimensions and volume often are stamped on the bottom of the most popular varieties.

Tip: If in doubt as to the size, fill the dish with water to within an inch of the top and measure the water to determine the volume.

Casserole size	Alternate
1-quart	6-inch soufflé
1½-quart	7-inch soufflé
2-quart	8-inch soufflé
	2-quart square baking dish
2½-quart	9-inch soufflé
	2-quart rectangular baking dish
3-quart	3-quart rectangular baking dish

If you must substitute a metal pan for a glass dish, the casserole will cook slower. Increase the oven temp by 25 degrees to compensate.

ABOUT YOUR SINK AND FAUCET

Standard sink features can be your friend or foe when it comes to simplifying kitchen life. You know this if you've ever struggled to fill, rinse, or wash an oversize pot, pan, or skillet in a standard two-bowl kitchen sink beneath a low-profile faucet. If you're thinking about remodeling your kitchen, an upgraded sink and faucet can make your life easier. Consider swapping a standard double-bowl sink with a style featuring a small prep sink on one side (that drains to the garbage disposal) and an oversize bowl on the other side—extra deep if possible—to allow for handling larger equipment. Make your life easier yet with a tall faucet—goosenecks come in a variety of designs that won't get in your way as you lift equipment from the sink.

SUPPORTING GEAR

Adapt this list to your own preferences. For instance, if you rely on peeled, precut veggies and bottled minced garlic—or simply enjoy chopping—you won't need a food processor or garlic press. It's also handy to have at least two or a few of some of the items listed so there's no need to stop to wash your lone teaspoon measure in the middle of a recipe. Multiples are more handy than pricey, so stock up.

- Bowls (various sizes)
- Colander
- Cutting boards (polypropylene or wood—for safety's sake, reserve one exclusively for use with raw meat or poultry)
- Dutch oven (4- or 6-quart)
- Food processor or other cutting appliances
- Garlic press
- Grater (box-style, rotary, or microplane)
- Large spoons for mixing
- Liquid measuring cups (1-, 2-, and 4-cup)
- Measuring cup sets
- Measuring spoon sets
- Oven mitts
- Protective hot pads and trivets (Nonskid flexible silicone pads handle high temps [675°F] and are terrific for keeping hot dishes from sliding. They are also dishwasher-safe.)
- Saucepans (large and small)
- Slope-sided large skillet
- Small cups or bowls to hold measured ingredients
- Spatulas
- Zester for cutting citrus peel

BREAKFAST
& BRUNCH

1

Scrambled eggs, ham, and vegetables in a creamy cheese sauce—if anything can make you look forward to getting out of bed on a weekend morning, this is it. Toasted English muffins are easy serve-alongs.

OVEN-STYLE EGGS & HAM

PREP:

30 minutes

CHILL:

4 to 24 hours

BAKE:

45 minutes

OVEN:

350°F

MAKES:

6 servings

5   eggs

⅛   teaspoon salt

2   tablespoons butter

1   tablespoon all-purpose flour

⅛   teaspoon black pepper

¾   cup milk

¾   cup cut-up process Gruyère or Swiss cheese (3 ounces)

1   teaspoon yellow mustard

1   16-ounce package desired frozen loose-pack vegetable mix, such as corn, broccoli, and red sweet peppers

3   ounces cooked ham, cut into bite-size strips (about ½ cup)

¼   cup shredded process Gruyère or Swiss cheese (1 ounce)

1 In a medium bowl beat eggs and salt together. In a 10-inch skillet melt 1 tablespoon of the butter over medium heat; pour in egg mixture. Cook, without stirring, until mixture begins to set on bottom and around edge.

2 With a spatula or large spoon, lift and fold the partially cooked eggs so the uncooked portion flows underneath. Continue cooking over medium heat for 2 to 3 minutes or until eggs are cooked through but are still glossy and moist. Remove from heat immediately; set aside.

3 For sauce, in a large saucepan melt the remaining 1 tablespoon butter over medium heat. Stir in flour and pepper. Add milk all at once. Cook and stir until mixture is thickened and bubbly. Add the ¾ cup cheese and the mustard, stirring until cheese melts.

4 Stir in frozen vegetables and ham; gently fold in cooked eggs. Transfer mixture to a 3-quart rectangular baking dish. Cover and chill for at least 4 hours or up to 24 hours.

5 Bake, covered, in a 350°F oven for 45 to 50 minutes or until heated through, stirring gently after 15 minutes. Stir gently again before serving. Sprinkle with the ¼ cup cheese.

Nutrition Facts per serving: 261 cal., 15 g total fat (7 g sat. fat), 214 mg chol., 500 mg sodium, 13 g carbo., 2 g fiber, 15 g pro.

Gruyère cheese and a touch of pear or apple and raisins add sophistication to this traditional brunch dish. Yet at its heart, this recipe retains its rustic, homey appeal.

HAM & CHEESE STRATA

2	tablespoons butter, softened (optional)
8	½-inch-thick slices cinnamon-raisin bread or rustic white bread
6	ounces thinly sliced ham
¼	cup finely chopped onion (½ medium)
1	small pear or tart apple, peeled, cored, and chopped
1	cup shredded sharp cheddar or Gruyère cheese (4 ounces)
2	cups milk
4	eggs
1½	teaspoons Dijon-style mustard
½	teaspoon Worcestershire sauce
¼	teaspoon black pepper

PREP:
30 minutes
CHILL:
2 to 24 hours
BAKE:
45 minutes
OVEN:
350°F
MAKES:
6 servings

1 If desired, lightly butter 1 side of each bread slice with the 2 tablespoons softened butter. Top buttered sides of 4 bread slices evenly with ham; top ham with another slice of bread, buttered side down. Quarter each sandwich to form 4 triangles. Arrange triangles, point sides up, in a buttered 2-quart square baking dish. Sprinkle onion, pear or apple, and cheese over triangles.

2 In a medium bowl, whisk together milk, eggs, mustard, Worcestershire sauce, and pepper. Carefully pour over triangles in dish. Cover and chill for at least 2 hours or up to 24 hours.

3 Bake, covered, in a 350°F oven for 20 minutes. Uncover. Bake about 25 minutes more or until puffed and golden and a knife inserted near the center comes out clean.

Nutrition Facts per serving: 542 cal., 19 g total fat (10 g sat. fat), 194 mg chol., 631 mg sodium, 70 g carbo., 7 g fiber, 26 g pro.

For this one-pot casserole, you don't have to precook the macaroni. Instead, it cooks up perfectly in the oven, along with the rest of the ingredients.

STIR & BAKE HAM CASSEROLE

PREP:

10 minutes

BAKE:

55 minutes

OVEN:

375°F

MAKES:

4 servings

1   10¾-ounce can condensed cream of celery soup

1¼   cups milk

1   4½-ounce jar (drained weight) sliced mushrooms, drained

1   tablespoon dried minced onion

2   cups diced cooked ham (10 ounces)

1   cup dried elbow macaroni

    Dash black pepper

½   cup shredded American or cheddar cheese (2 ounces)

1 In a lightly greased 1½-quart casserole combine soup, milk, mushrooms, and onion. Add ham, macaroni, and pepper. Mix well.

2 Bake, covered, in a 375°F oven for 30 minutes; stir well (mixture may appear curdled). Cover and bake for 20 to 30 minutes more or until macaroni is tender. Uncover; sprinkle with cheese. Bake, uncovered, for 5 minutes more.

Nutrition Facts per serving: 393 cal., 18 g total fat (8 g sat. fat), 59 mg chol., 1,837 mg sodium, 34 g carbo., 2 g fiber, 23 g pro.

Panko is Japanese-style bread crumbs, which are coarser than American bread crumbs. You can find them in Asian food stores or in the ethnic section of your supermarket.

ASPARAGUS-HAM BAKE

1	10¾-ounce can condensed cream of asparagus soup
¾	cup milk
2	cups cubed cooked ham (about 10 ounces)
2	cups cooked white rice
1	9-ounce package frozen cut asparagus, thawed
½	cup shredded Swiss cheese (2 ounces)
¼	cup finely chopped onion
½	cup panko (Japanese-style) bread crumbs
2	tablespoons butter, melted

PREP:
25 minutes
BAKE:
40 minutes
STAND:
10 minutes
OVEN:
375°F
MAKES:
6 servings

1 In a large bowl combine soup and milk. Add ham, rice, asparagus, cheese, and onion. Spoon ham mixture into an ungreased 2-quart square baking dish.

2 In a small bowl combine bread crumbs and butter; sprinkle over ham mixture. Bake, uncovered, in a 375°F oven for 40 to 45 minutes or until heated through and lightly browned. Let stand for 10 minutes before serving.

Nutrition Facts per serving: 306 cal., 14 g total fat (7 g sat. fat), 50 mg chol., 1,056 mg sodium, 28 g carbo., 2 g fiber, 16 g pro.

Just as a slice of cheddar cheese complements a piece of apple pie, this apple, cheese, and ham combination flows together seamlessly.

HAM-APPLE-CHEDDAR CASSEROLE

PREP:

20 minutes

BAKE:

35 minutes

OVEN:

350°F

MAKES:

6 servings

3	cups frozen loose-pack diced hash brown potatoes, thawed
1	large red apple, cored and chopped
1	teaspoon dried sage, crushed
1	tablespoon butter
1	cup diced cooked ham (5 ounces)
1½	cups milk
4	eggs
¾	cup shredded cheddar cheese (3 ounces)
¼	teaspoon salt

1 Press thawed potatoes between paper towels to remove moisture; set aside. In a small saucepan cook apple and sage in hot butter over medium heat until tender. Remove from heat. Combine apple mixture, potatoes, and ham in a lightly greased 2-quart square baking dish.

2 In a medium bowl whisk together milk, eggs, cheese, and salt. Pour egg mixture over potato mixture in dish. (Do not stir.) Bake, uncovered, in a 350°F oven for 35 to 40 minutes or until a knife inserted near the center comes out clean.

Nutrition Facts per serving: 374 cal., 22 g total fat (10 g sat. fat), 179 mg chol., 595 mg sodium, 29 g carbo., 2 g fiber, 16 g pro.

This casserole is similar to a strata but relies on seasoned croutons as a shortcut. That means the bread has already been cubed for you!

SAUSAGE BREAKFAST CASSEROLE

1½   pounds bulk pork sausage or Italian sausage

2½   cups seasoned croutons

2   cups shredded cheddar cheese (8 ounces)

2½   cups milk

4   eggs

¾   teaspoon dry mustard

1   10¾-ounce can condensed cream of mushroom soup

½   cup milk

1 In a large skillet cook sausage over medium heat until brown; drain.

2 Spread croutons evenly in bottom of a lightly greased 3-quart rectangular baking dish. Sprinkle 1 cup of the cheese over croutons. Top with sausage.

3 In a large bowl whisk together the 2½ cups milk, the eggs, and dry mustard. Pour over layers in dish. In a small bowl combine soup and the ½ cup milk. Spoon soup mixture evenly over mixture in dish. Cover and chill for at least 2 hours or up to 24 hours.

4 Bake, uncovered, in a 325°F oven for 45 minutes. Sprinkle with remaining 1 cup cheese. Bake for 5 to 10 minutes more or until a knife inserted near the center comes out clean. Let stand for 10 minutes before serving.

Nutrition Facts per serving: 472 cal., 35 g total fat (15 g sat. fat), 154 mg chol., 883 mg sodium, 14 g carbo., 1 g fiber, 20 g pro.

PREP:
25 minutes

CHILL:
2 to 24 hours

BAKE:
50 minutes

STAND:
10 minutes

OVEN:
325°F

MAKES:
10 servings

Strata is the ultimate make-ahead brunch dish, leaving you time to relax before guests arrive.

CHEDDAR, HAM & BROCCOLI STRATA

PREP:

20 minutes

CHILL:

2 to 24 hours

BAKE:

1 hour

STAND:

10 minutes

OVEN:

325°F

MAKES:

6 servings

1　cup broccoli florets

1　8-ounce loaf French bread, cut into ½-inch cubes (5 cups)

2　cups shredded cheddar cheese (8 ounces)

1　cup cubed cooked ham (5 ounces)

1¾　cups milk

3　eggs

2　tablespoons finely chopped onion

1　teaspoon dry mustard

　Dash black pepper

1　In a 1-quart microwave-safe casserole dish combine broccoli florets and 1 tablespoon water. Microwave, covered, on 100% power (high) for 2 to 3 minutes or until crisp-tender; drain well. (Or cook broccoli, covered, in a small amount of boiling water for 4 to 6 minutes or until crisp-tender; drain well.) Set aside.

2　Layer half of the bread cubes in a greased 2-quart square baking dish. Top with cheese, ham, and broccoli. Top with the remaining bread cubes. In a medium bowl whisk together milk, eggs, onion, mustard, and pepper. Pour evenly over layers in dish. Cover and chill for 2 to 24 hours.

3　Bake, uncovered, in a 325°F oven about 1 hour or until a knife inserted near the center comes out clean. Let stand for 10 minutes before serving.

Nutrition Facts per serving: 377 cal., 20 g total fat (11 g sat. fat), 165 mg chol., 886 mg sodium, 25 g carbo., 2 g fiber, 24 g pro.

Hard-cooked eggs, hash browns, and ham are at the heart of this brunch dish. Layer the bread cubes, meat, and cheese up to two days ahead, cover, and store in the refrigerator.

BREAKFAST CASSEROLE

7	slices white bread
2	tablespoons butter, softened
2	cups diced cooked ham (10 ounces), cooked sausage, or crumbled crisp-cooked bacon
2	cups shredded cheddar cheese (8 ounces)
3	cups milk
6	eggs
1	teaspoon dry mustard
¼	teaspoon black pepper

1 Spread 1 side of each bread slice with butter. Cut bread into ½-inch cubes. Arrange bread cubes evenly in a greased 2-quart rectangular baking dish. Top with meat and 1 cup of the cheese.

2 In a medium bowl whisk together milk, eggs, mustard, and pepper. Pour egg mixture over bread mixture in dish. Cover and chill at least 8 hours or overnight.

3 Bake, uncovered, in a 350°F oven for 35 minutes. Sprinkle with remaining 1 cup cheese. Bake about 10 minutes more or until a knife inserted near the center comes out clean. Let stand for 10 minutes before serving.

Nutrition Facts per serving: 485 cal., 29 g total fat (15 g sat. fat), 300 mg chol., 1,256 mg sodium, 21 g carbo., 1 g fiber, 33 g pro.

PREP:

20 minutes

CHILL:

8 hours or overnight

BAKE:

45 minutes

STAND:

10 minutes

OVEN:

350°F

MAKES:

6 to 8 servings

The classic combo of bagels, lox, and cream cheese takes center stage in this beguiling brunch entrée.

LOX-STYLE STRATA

PREP:

30 minutes

CHILL:

4 to 24 hours

BAKE:

45 minutes

STAND:

10 minutes

OVEN:

350°F

MAKES:

12 servings

4	to 6 plain bagels, cut into bite-size pieces (8 cups)
1	3-ounce package thinly sliced smoked salmon (lox-style), cut into small pieces
2	3-ounce packages cream cheese, cut into ½-inch pieces
¼	cup finely diced red onion
4	teaspoons dried chives, crushed
2	cups milk
8	eggs
1	cup cottage cheese
½	teaspoon dried dillweed, crushed
¼	teaspoon black pepper

1 In a lightly greased 3-quart rectangular baking dish spread half of the bagel pieces. Top with salmon, cream cheese, onion, and chives. Spread remaining bagel pieces over all.

2 In a large bowl whisk together milk, eggs, cottage cheese, dillweed, and pepper. Pour over layers in dish, pressing lightly to thoroughly moisten the bagel pieces. Cover and chill for 4 to 24 hours.

3 Bake, uncovered, in a 350°F oven for 45 to 50 minutes or until set and edges are puffed and golden. Let stand for 10 minutes before serving.

Nutrition Facts per serving: 212 cal., 11 g total fat (5 g sat. fat), 164 mg chol., 447 mg sodium, 16 g carbo., 1 g fiber, 13 g pro.

Now you can have Reuben sandwiches for breakfast—or any time of day, for that matter—with this easy one-dish strata. Make it up to 24 hours ahead and chill until ready to bake.

REUBEN BREAKFAST STRATA

8	slices rye bread, cubed (6 cups)
12	ounces sliced deli corned beef, chopped
1½	cups shredded Swiss cheese (6 ounces)
8	eggs
1¼	cups milk
½	cup bottled Thousand Island salad dressing
½	teaspoon caraway seeds
½	teaspoon dry mustard
½	teaspoon salt

PREP:
20 minutes

CHILL:
2 to 24 hours

BAKE:
40 minutes

STAND:
10 minutes

OVEN:
350°F

MAKES:
6 servings

1 In a large bowl combine bread cubes, corned beef, and 1 cup of the cheese. Spread bread mixture in a greased 3-quart rectangular baking dish.

2 In a medium bowl whisk together eggs, milk, salad dressing, caraway seeds, dry mustard, and salt. Pour egg mixture over bread mixture in dish, pressing lightly to thoroughly moisten the bread. Cover and chill for 2 to 24 hours.

3 Sprinkle with remaining ½ cup cheese. Bake, uncovered, in a 350°F oven for 40 to 45 minutes or until a knife inserted near the center comes out clean. Let stand for 10 minutes before serving.

Nutrition Facts per serving: 561 cal., 35 g total fat (12 g sat. fat), 373 mg chol., 1,469 mg sodium, 28 g carbo., 3 g fiber, 32 g pro.

Similar to an old-fashioned "hobo's breakfast," this quick meal marries a host of morning favorites into one delectable combination.

MEAT & POTATO BREAKFAST BAKE

PREP:

20 minutes

BAKE:

45 minutes

STAND:

10 minutes

OVEN:

350°F

MAKES:

6 servings

8   ounces bulk pork sausage

6   slices bacon, chopped

2   cups frozen loose-pack diced hash brown potatoes

12 eggs

¾   cup milk

1   tablespoon yellow mustard, Dijon-style mustard, or coarse-grain brown mustard

¼   teaspoon black pepper

½   cup shredded cheddar cheese (2 ounces)

1 In a large skillet cook sausage and bacon over medium heat until bacon is crisp and sausage is brown; drain. Place frozen potatoes and sausage mixture in a lightly greased 2-quart square baking dish; set aside.

2 In a large bowl whisk together eggs, milk, mustard, and pepper. Pour egg mixture over potato mixture in dish.

3 Bake, uncovered, in a 350°F oven about 45 minutes or until a knife inserted near the center comes out clean. Sprinkle with cheese. Let stand for 10 minutes before serving.

Nutrition Facts per serving: 408 cal., 26 g total fat (10 g sat. fat), 465 mg chol., 582 mg sodium, 16 g carbo., 1 g fiber, 24 g pro.

This homey breakfast-style dish is delicious for supper too. Whip it up in the morning, refrigerate during the day, and pop it in the oven when you get home. Then relax before dinner!

FARMER'S CASSEROLE

3	cups frozen shredded hash brown potatoes
¾	cup shredded Monterey Jack cheese with jalapeño peppers or shredded cheddar cheese (3 ounces)
1	cup diced cooked ham or Canadian-style bacon (5 ounces)
¼	cup sliced green onions (2)
1½	cups milk or one 12-ounce can evaporated milk
4	eggs
⅛	teaspoon salt
⅛	teaspoon black pepper

PREP:
25 minutes
BAKE:
40 minutes
STAND:
5 minutes
OVEN:
350°F
MAKES:
6 servings

1 Arrange frozen potatoes evenly in the bottom of a lightly greased 2-quart square baking dish. Sprinkle with cheese, ham or Canadian-style bacon, and green onions.

2 In a medium bowl whisk together milk, eggs, salt, and pepper. Pour egg mixture over potato mixture in dish.

3 Bake, uncovered, in a 350°F oven for 40 to 45 minutes or until a knife inserted near the center comes out clean. Let stand for 5 minutes before serving.

FARMER'S CASSEROLE FOR 12: Prepare as above, except double all ingredients and use a 3-quart rectangular baking dish. Bake, uncovered, for 45 to 55 minutes or until a knife inserted near the center comes out clean. Let stand for 5 minutes before serving. Makes 12 servings.

MAKE-AHEAD DIRECTIONS: Assemble as directed. Cover and chill unbaked casserole up to 24 hours. Bake, uncovered, in a 350°F oven for 50 to 55 minutes or until a knife inserted near the center comes out clean. Let stand for 5 minutes before serving.

Nutrition Facts per serving: 265 cal., 12 g total fat (6 g sat. fat), 175 mg chol., 590 mg sodium, 23 g carbo., 2 g fiber, 17 g pro.

Excellent for melting, Swiss cheese takes potato dishes to a creamier level. This recipe is the perfect example. If you like, sprinkle a few extra chunks on top before popping this casserole into the oven.

SWISS-POTATO BREAKFAST CASSEROLE

PREP:

25 minutes

BAKE:

35 minutes

OVEN:

350°F

MAKES:

6 servings

1	pound tiny new potatoes, cut into $\frac{1}{4}$-inch slices
$\frac{1}{3}$	cup thinly sliced leek
$\frac{3}{4}$	cup diced cooked ham ($3\frac{1}{2}$ ounces)
3	ounces Swiss cheese, cut into small pieces
$1\frac{1}{4}$	cups milk
1	tablespoon all-purpose flour
3	eggs
$\frac{1}{2}$	teaspoon dried thyme, crushed
$\frac{1}{4}$	teaspoon salt
$\frac{1}{4}$	teaspoon black pepper

1 In a large saucepan cook potatoes in a small amount of boiling lightly salted water about 10 minutes or just until tender, adding leek during the last 5 minutes of cooking. Drain.

2 In a lightly greased 2-quart rectangular baking dish arrange cooked potatoes and leek. Top with ham and cheese.

3 In a medium bowl stir milk into flour until smooth. Whisk in eggs, thyme, salt, and pepper. Pour the egg mixture over layers in dish.

4 Bake, uncovered, in a 350°F oven for 35 to 40 minutes or until a knife inserted near the center comes out clean. Serve immediately.

Nutrition Facts per serving: 207 cal., 9 g total fat (4 g sat. fat), 132 mg chol., 409 mg sodium, 18 g carbo., 2 g fiber, 13 g pro.

This one's perfect for a holiday or bridal shower brunch. Serve it with a salad of the freshest, most colorful in-season fruits you can find.

SPINACH BREAKFAST CASSEROLE

1	pound bulk pork sausage
4	cups seasoned croutons
1	10-ounce package frozen chopped spinach, thawed and drained well
½	cup coarsely shredded carrot
2	cups milk
4	eggs
1	10¾-ounce can condensed cream of mushroom soup
1	4-ounce can (drained weight) sliced mushrooms, drained
1	cup shredded cheddar cheese (4 ounces)
1	cup shredded Monterey Jack cheese (4 ounces)
¼	teaspoon dry mustard
	Shredded cheddar and/or Monterey Jack cheese (optional)

PREP:
30 minutes

CHILL:
8 to 24 hours

BAKE:
55 minutes

STAND:
10 minutes

OVEN:
325°F

MAKES:
12 servings

1 In a large skillet cook sausage over medium heat until brown; drain. Spread croutons evenly in the bottom of an ungreased 3-quart rectangular baking dish. Spread sausage over croutons. Top with spinach and carrot.

2 In a medium bowl whisk together milk, eggs, and soup. Stir in mushrooms, the 1 cup cheddar cheese, the 1 cup Monterey Jack cheese, and dry mustard until well mixed. Pour over layers in dish. Cover and chill for 8 to 24 hours.

3 Bake, uncovered, in a 325°F oven for 45 minutes. If desired, sprinkle with additional cheese. Bake about 10 minutes more or until edges are bubbly and center is heated through. Let stand for 10 minutes before serving.

Nutrition Facts per serving: 346 cal., 24 g total fat (10 g sat. fat), 115 mg chol., 754 mg sodium, 15 g carbo., 2 g fiber, 15 g pro.

Pork sausage, cheese, chiles, and eggs top English muffin halves for an easy make-ahead strata.

ALL-IN-ONE BREAKFAST

PREP:

25 minutes

CHILL:

overnight

BAKE:

35 minutes

STAND:

10 minutes

OVEN:

375°F

MAKES:

12 servings

6   English muffins, split

1   pound bulk pork sausage

12   eggs

1   8-ounce carton dairy sour cream

1   4$\frac{1}{2}$-ounce can chopped green chiles, drained

1   cup shredded cheddar cheese (4 ounces)

1 Arrange muffin halves in the bottom of a greased 3-quart rectangular baking dish, overlapping as necessary to make them fit; set aside.

2 In a large skillet cook sausage over medium heat until brown; drain. In a large bowl beat eggs lightly with a whisk. Add the sausage, sour cream, and chiles; whisk until combined. Pour egg mixture over muffins in dish, pressing lightly to thoroughly moisten the muffins. Sprinkle with cheese. Cover and chill overnight.

3 Bake, uncovered, in a 375°F oven for 35 to 40 minutes or until set. Let stand for 10 minutes before serving.

Nutrition Facts per serving: 336 cal., 23 g total fat (9 g sat. fat), 257 mg chol., 538 mg sodium, 15 g carbo., 1 g fiber, 17 g pro.

This cheesy casserole is rich and satisfying. Serve it with warm-from-the-oven corn bread and roasted red potatoes on the side.

MUSHROOM & EGG CASSEROLE

4	slices prosciutto (about 1½ ounces) or bacon, chopped
⅔	cup thinly sliced green onions (8)
1	tablespoon butter
1	pound fresh shiitake* and/or button mushrooms, sliced
8	eggs
1	cup milk
⅛	teaspoon black pepper
2½	cups shredded Monterey Jack or cheddar cheese (10 ounces)

1 In a large skillet cook prosciutto or bacon over medium heat until crisp; drain. Set aside.

2 Wipe pan clean. In same skillet cook green onions in butter over medium heat for 2 to 3 minutes. Add mushrooms; cook for 2 to 3 minutes more. Remove from heat.

3 In a large bowl whisk together eggs, milk, and pepper. Stir in cheese and the mushroom mixture. Pour egg mixture into a greased 2-quart rectangular baking dish.

4 Bake, uncovered, in a 350°F oven for 35 to 40 minutes or until puffed and a knife inserted near the center comes out clean. Let stand for 10 minutes before serving.

*NOTE: Remove and discard the tough stems from the shiitake mushrooms before slicing them.

Nutrition Facts per serving: 367 cal., 24 g total fat (13 g sat. fat), 336 mg chol., 544 mg sodium, 14 g carbo., 2 g fiber, 24 g pro.

PREP:
20 minutes
BAKE:
35 minutes
STAND:
10 minutes
OVEN:
350°F
MAKES:
6 servings

Your family or brunch guests will feel truly treated to something special when they dive into this spicy and warm breakfast. The Cajun Sauce adds a particularly fresh, tasty kick.

EGG CASSEROLE WITH CAJUN SAUCE

PREP:

20 minutes

BAKE:

40 minutes

STAND:

10 minutes

OVEN:

325°F

MAKES:

6 servings

2   cups plain croutons

1   cup shredded Monterey Jack cheese (4 ounces)

2   cups milk

4   eggs

1   teaspoon yellow mustard

  Dash black pepper

1   recipe Cajun Sauce

1 In a greased 2-quart square baking dish combine croutons and cheese; set aside. In a medium bowl whisk together milk, eggs, mustard, and pepper. Pour egg mixture over croutons and cheese in dish.

2 Bake, uncovered, in a 325°F oven about 40 minutes or until a knife inserted near the center comes out clean. Meanwhile, prepare Cajun Sauce. Let casserole stand for 10 minutes before serving. Serve with Cajun Sauce.

CAJUN SAUCE: In a medium saucepan combine one 14½-ounce can diced tomatoes with green pepper and onion, undrained; 1 teaspoon Cajun seasoning; 1 teaspoon sugar; and dash black pepper. Bring to boiling; reduce heat. Simmer, uncovered, about 10 minutes or until mixture is slightly thickened and reduced to 1¼ cups. Stir in ¼ cup sliced pimiento-stuffed green olives; heat through. Makes 1½ cups.

Nutrition Facts per serving: 234 cal., 12 g total fat (6 g sat. fat), 165 mg chol., 588 mg sodium, 18 g carbo., 1 g fiber, 13 g pro.

This brunch dish does great-grandma's casserole one better by including herbs, sharp cheddar cheese, and plenty of crisp-cooked bacon. Serve it with hash browns, fresh fruit, and orange juice for a complete meal.

HERBED EGG & CHEESE CASSEROLE

¼	cup butter
¼	cup all-purpose flour
¼	teaspoon dried thyme, crushed
¼	teaspoon dried basil, crushed
¼	teaspoon dried marjoram, crushed
1	12-ounce can (1½ cups) evaporated milk or 1⅓ cups half-and-half or light cream
⅔	cup milk
2	cups shredded sharp cheddar cheese (8 ounces)
18	eggs, hard-cooked and thinly sliced
8	ounces bacon, crisp-cooked, drained, and crumbled
4	teaspoons dried parsley flakes, crushed
1	cup fine dry bread crumbs
¼	cup butter, melted

PREP:
20 minutes
BAKE:
25 minutes
OVEN:
350°F
MAKES:
12 servings

1 In a medium saucepan melt ¼ cup butter over medium heat. Stir in flour, thyme, basil, and marjoram. Stir in evaporated milk and milk all at once. Cook and stir until thickened and bubbly. Remove from heat. Gradually add cheese to milk mixture, stirring after each addition until cheese is melted. Set aside.

2 Layer half of the sliced eggs, half of the bacon, and half of the parsley in a lightly greased 3-quart rectangular baking dish. Pour half of the cheese mixture over all. Repeat layers, ending with cheese mixture.

3 In small bowl combine bread crumbs and ¼ cup melted butter; sprinkle over casserole. Bake, uncovered, in a 350°F oven for 25 to 30 minutes or until heated through.

Nutrition Facts per serving: 372 cal., 27 g total fat (13 g sat. fat), 374 mg chol., 472 mg sodium, 13 g carbo., 0 g fiber, 20 g pro.

Easier than many egg casseroles, this dish is a great way to serve eggs to a crowd.

CHEESE & MUSHROOM EGG CASSEROLE

PREP:

25 minutes

BAKE:

20 minutes

OVEN:

350°F

MAKES:

10 servings

16	eggs
1	cup milk
2	tablespoons butter
3	cups sliced fresh mushrooms (8 ounces)
½	cup thinly sliced green onions (4)
1	10¾-ounce can condensed cream of broccoli or cream of asparagus soup
¼	cup milk
1	cup shredded Monterey Jack cheese (4 ounces)
¼	cup grated Parmesan cheese

1 In a large bowl whisk together eggs and the 1 cup milk. In a large nonstick skillet melt 1 tablespoon of the butter over medium heat. Add half of the egg mixture. Cook over medium heat, without stirring, until mixture begins to set on the bottom and around the edge.

2 With a spatula or a large spoon, lift and fold the partially cooked egg mixture so the uncooked portion flows underneath. Continue cooking over medium heat for 2 to 3 minutes or until egg mixture is cooked through but is still glossy and moist. Remove from heat immediately.

3 Transfer scrambled eggs to a greased 3-quart rectangular baking dish. Scramble remaining eggs with remaining 1 tablespoon butter; remove from heat immediately. Transfer to the baking dish.

4 In the same nonstick skillet cook mushrooms and green onions over medium heat until tender. Stir in soup and the ¼ cup milk. Stir in Monterey Jack cheese and Parmesan cheese. Spread mixture over eggs in dish.

5 Bake, covered, in a 350°F oven about 20 minutes or until heated through.

Nutrition Facts per serving: 239 cal., 17 g total fat (8 g sat. fat), 361 mg chol., 435 mg sodium, 6 g carbo., 1 g fiber, 16 g pro.

Herbs, onions, and cheese dress up sliced potatoes for breakfast or brunch and fill the kitchen with tantalizing aromas. Serve this hearty combo with scrambled eggs, fresh fruit, and cinnamon rolls.

HEARTY POTATO & SAUSAGE CASSEROLE

3	large, long white potatoes (about 1½ pounds), peeled and sliced ¼ inch thick (about 5 cups)
2	cups chopped onions
3	tablespoons butter
1	tablespoon dried parsley flakes, crushed
½	teaspoon garlic salt
½	teaspoon black pepper
½	teaspoon dried thyme, crushed
½	teaspoon dried sage, crushed
¼	teaspoon dried rosemary, crushed
16	to 18 ounces bulk pork sausage
2	cups shredded Swiss cheese (8 ounces) or 8 ounces Swiss cheese slices

PREP:
40 minutes
BAKE:
20 minutes
OVEN:
350°F
MAKES:
8 servings

1 In a large saucepan cook the potatoes in boiling lightly salted water for 12 to 15 minutes or just until tender. Drain.

2 In a large heavy skillet cook potatoes and onions in butter over medium-high heat until potatoes are light brown, turning often. Add parsley, garlic salt, pepper, thyme, sage, and rosemary; toss lightly. Spoon mixture into an ungreased 3-quart rectangular baking dish.

3 In the same skillet cook sausage over medium-low heat until brown; drain. Spread the cooked sausage over potato mixture. Sprinkle evenly with shredded cheese or arrange cheese slices on top.

4 Bake, uncovered, in a 350°F oven for 20 to 25 minutes or until heated through.

Nutrition Facts per serving: 423 cal., 29 g total fat (13 g sat. fat), 76 mg chol., 549 mg sodium, 24 g carbo., 2 g fiber, 16 g pro.

Can any combination of potatoes and cheese go wrong? In this version, smoked Gouda and provolone cheeses add a gourmet touch to this rich and creamy hash brown brunch dish.

SMOKY HASH BROWN BAKE

PREP:

20 minutes

BAKE:

1 hour 10 minutes

STAND:

10 minutes

OVEN:

350°F

MAKES:

12 servings

1   10¾-ounce can condensed cream of chicken with herbs soup

¾   cup milk

1   28-ounce package frozen loose-pack diced hash brown potatoes with onion and peppers, thawed

1   cup finely shredded smoked Gouda cheese (4 ounces)

1   cup finely shredded provolone cheese (4 ounces)

1   8-ounce package cream cheese, cut into cubes

2   teaspoons dried chives, crushed

½   teaspoon black pepper

1 In a very large bowl combine soup and milk. Stir in potatoes, Gouda cheese, ½ cup of the provolone cheese, the cream cheese, chives, and pepper. Spoon into a greased 2-quart casserole.

2 Bake, covered, in a 350°F oven for 40 minutes. Uncover and stir mixture. Sprinkle with remaining ½ cup provolone cheese. Bake, uncovered, about 30 minutes more or until top is golden and potatoes are tender. Let stand for 10 minutes before serving.

Nutrition Facts per serving: 199 cal., 13 g total fat (8 g sat. fat), 38 mg chol., 488 mg sodium, 14 g carbo., 1 g fiber, 7 g pro.

Taco flavors turn this meat-and-potato bake into a taste fiesta. It's perfect for anyone who has a hearty appetite, from teens to tailgaters.

MEXICALI POTATO BRUNCH BAKE

6	eggs
3	cups refrigerated shredded hash brown potatoes
1	7-ounce package maple brown-and-serve sausage links, sliced
1	cup shredded Monterey Jack cheese with jalapeño peppers (4 ounces)
¼	cup milk
⅛	teaspoon salt
⅛	teaspoon black pepper
1	tablespoon butter
½	cup purchased salsa

PREP:
25 minutes
BAKE:
25 minutes
STAND:
5 minutes
OVEN:
375°F
MAKES:
6 servings

1 In a large bowl beat 2 of the eggs. Stir in potatoes, sausage, and ½ cup of the cheese. Spread mixture into a greased 2-quart square baking dish.

2 In a medium bowl whisk together remaining 4 eggs, milk, salt, and pepper. In a medium skillet melt butter over medium heat; pour in egg mixture. Cook over medium heat, without stirring, until mixture begins to set on the bottom and around edge.

3 With a spatula or a large spoon, lift and fold the partially cooked egg mixture so the uncooked portion flows underneath. Continue cooking over medium heat for 2 to 3 minutes or until egg mixture is cooked through but is still glossy and moist. Spoon eggs evenly over potato mixture in dish. Top with salsa and the remaining ½ cup cheese.

4 Bake, covered, in a 375°F oven about 25 minutes or until heated through and cheese is melted. Let stand for 5 minutes before serving.

MAKE-AHEAD DIRECTIONS: Assemble casserole as directed; cover and chill unbaked casserole up to 24 hours. Bake, covered, in a 375°F oven for 45 to 50 minutes or until heated through and cheese is melted. Let stand for 5 minutes before serving.

Nutrition Facts per serving: 390 cal., 27 g total fat (11 g sat. fat), 263 mg chol., 751 mg sodium, 19 g carbo., 1 g fiber, 19 g pro.

This breakfast casserole is both delicious and convenient—you can assemble it up to 24 hours ahead.

EGG & POTATO CASSEROLE

PREP:

15 minutes

BAKE:

25 minutes

STAND:

5 minutes

OVEN:

350°F

MAKES:

4 servings

1⅓ cups frozen loose-pack diced hash brown potatoes
with onion and peppers

⅔ cup frozen loose-pack cut broccoli or frozen cut asparagus

¼ cup diced Canadian-style bacon or cooked ham (2½ ounces)

¼ cup milk

4 teaspoons all-purpose flour

5 eggs

½ cup shredded cheddar cheese (2 ounces)

1 teaspoon dried basil, crushed

½ teaspoon salt

¼ teaspoon black pepper

1 Arrange frozen potatoes and broccoli or asparagus evenly in the bottom of a lightly greased 2-quart square baking dish. Top with Canadian bacon or ham. In a medium bowl gradually stir milk into flour. Whisk in eggs, ¼ cup of the cheese, the basil, salt, and pepper. Pour egg mixture over vegetables in dish.

2 Bake, uncovered, in a 350°F oven for 25 to 30 minutes or until a knife inserted near the center comes out clean. Sprinkle with the remaining ¼ cup cheese. Let stand for 5 minutes before serving.

Nutrition Facts per serving: 327 cal., 19 g total fat (6 g sat. fat), 286 mg chol., 807 mg sodium, 23 g carbo., 3 g fiber, 17 g pro.

This ever-favorite cheesy hash brown casserole has starred on potluck tables for years. Ham transforms it into a crowd-pleasing breakfast dish.

HASH BROWN CASSEROLE

1   16-ounce carton dairy sour cream

1   10¾-ounce can condensed cream of chicken soup

1   32-ounce package frozen loose-pack diced hash brown potatoes

2   cups diced cooked ham (10 ounces)

2   cups cubed American cheese (8 ounces)

½   cup chopped onion

¼   teaspoon black pepper

2   cups crushed cornflakes

⅓   cup butter, melted

PREP:

20 minutes

CHILL:

8 to 24 hours

BAKE:

50 minutes

OVEN:

350°F

MAKES:

12 servings

1 In a very large bowl combine sour cream and soup. Stir in frozen potatoes, ham, cheese, onion, and pepper. Spread the mixture into the bottom of an ungreased 3-quart rectangular baking dish. Cover and chill for 8 to 24 hours.

2 In a small bowl combine cornflakes and melted butter. Sprinkle over the potato mixture. Bake, uncovered, in a 350°F oven for 50 to 55 minutes or until hot in center and bubbly around edges.

Nutrition Facts per serving: 388 cal., 24 g total fat (14 g sat. fat), 64 mg chol., 968 mg sodium, 31 g carbo., 1 g fiber, 13 g pro.

Family and friends will rave about the tropical fruits and nuts in this breakfast medley. Serve it with your favorite eggs and thickly sliced toasted brioche or multigrain bread.

TROPICAL BREAKFAST AMBROSIA

PREP:
25 minutes

BAKE:
30 minutes

OVEN:
350°F

MAKES:
8 to 10 side-dish servings

1 medium fresh pineapple, peeled, cored, and cut into bite-size pieces (about 4½ cups)

1 11-ounce can mandarin oranges, drained

1 medium mango, peeled, seeded, and cut into ½-inch pieces

1 cup frozen unsweetened pitted dark sweet cherries, thawed

2 tablespoons amaretto (optional)

2 medium bananas, cut into ½-inch slices

1 cup flaked coconut

½ cup chopped macadamia nuts or sliced almonds

1 In a large bowl combine pineapple, oranges, mango, cherries, and, if desired, amaretto; transfer to an ungreased 3-quart casserole.

2 Bake, uncovered, in a 350°F oven for 15 minutes. Stir in bananas. Sprinkle with coconut and macadamia nuts. Bake for 15 minutes more or until fruit is heated through and coconut and nuts are golden. Serve warm, spooning some of the liquid in bottom of casserole over fruit.

Nutrition Facts per serving: 241 cal., 12 g total fat (6 g sat. fat), 0 mg chol., 71 mg sodium, 36 g carbo., 5 g fiber, 3 g pro.

Hot, hearty oatmeal stars in this sweet bake infused with dried apricots, tart cherries, golden raisins, and, of course, brown sugar.

FRUIT & NUT BAKED OATMEAL

1¾	cups milk
2	tablespoons butter
1	cup regular rolled oats
⅓	cup snipped dried apricots
⅓	cup dried tart cherries
⅓	cup golden raisins
5	tablespoons packed brown sugar
½	teaspoon vanilla
¼	teaspoon salt
½	cup coarsely chopped walnuts or pecans
	Milk (optional)

PREP:
15 minutes
BAKE:
20 minutes
OVEN:
350°F
MAKES:
4 servings

1 In a medium saucepan bring the 1¾ cups milk and the butter to boiling. Slowly stir in oats. Stir in apricots, cherries, raisins, 3 tablespoons of the brown sugar, the vanilla, and salt. Cook and stir for 1 minute. Pour into a lightly greased 1½-quart casserole.

2 Bake, uncovered, in a 350°F oven for 15 minutes. Sprinkle with the remaining 2 tablespoons brown sugar and the nuts. Bake about 5 minutes more or until bubbly. Cool slightly. If desired, serve the warm oatmeal with additional milk.

Nutrition Facts per serving: 471 cal., 20 g total fat (5 g sat. fat), 25 mg chol., 250 mg sodium, 67 g carbo., 6 g fiber, 11 g pro.

Tender, cinnamon-spiced fruit and golden granola will be tempting warmers on cold mornings.

FRUIT & GRANOLA BREAKFAST BAKE

PREP:

25 minutes

BAKE:

40 minutes

OVEN:

350°F

MAKES:

6 side-dish servings

3	medium apples, peeled and cut into bite-size pieces
3	medium pears, peeled and cut into bite-size pieces
⅓	cup dried tart cherries
⅓	cup apple butter
¼	cup apple juice
½	teaspoon ground cinnamon
1	cup low-fat granola cereal

1 In an ungreased 2-quart rectangular baking dish combine apples, pears, and cherries. In a small bowl whisk together apple butter, apple juice, and cinnamon. Pour mixture over fruit in dish and toss to combine.

2 Bake, covered, in a 350°F oven for 30 minutes. Uncover; stir fruit mixture. Sprinkle with granola and bake, uncovered, for 10 to 15 minutes more or until top is golden and fruit is tender. Serve warm.

Nutrition Facts per serving: 257 cal., 1 g total fat (0 g sat. fat), 0 mg chol., 49 mg sodium, 62 g carbo., 6 g fiber, 2 g pro.

Blintzes are a Jewish-American favorite. This one-dish wonder makes preparing them easy by combining all the classic ingredients—cream cheese, sour cream, and cottage cheese—into two easy-pour layers.

ORANGE BLINTZ CASSEROLE

6	eggs
2	egg whites
1½	cups dairy sour cream
2	teaspoons finely shredded orange peel
½	cup orange juice
¼	cup butter, softened
1	cup all-purpose flour
½	cup sugar
2	teaspoons baking powder
2	cups cottage cheese
1	8-ounce package cream cheese, softened
2	egg yolks
2	tablespoons sugar
2	teaspoons vanilla
½	cup orange marmalade, melted

PREP:
25 minutes
BAKE:
45 minutes
COOL:
30 minutes
OVEN:
350°F
MAKES:
12 to 15 servings

1 For batter, in a blender or food processor combine eggs, egg whites, sour cream, orange peel, orange juice, and butter. Cover; blend or process until smooth. Add flour, sugar, and baking powder. Cover; blend or process until smooth. Transfer to a medium bowl; set aside. Rinse blender container or food processor bowl.

2 For filling, in the blender or food processor combine cottage cheese, cream cheese, egg yolks, sugar, and vanilla. Cover; blend or process until smooth. Pour about 2 cups of the batter into a greased 3-quart rectangular baking dish. Spoon filling over batter in dish. Swirl filling into batter with a knife. Pour remaining batter evenly over mixture in dish.

3 Bake, uncovered, in a 350°F oven about 45 minutes or until puffed and lightly golden. Cool for 30 minutes on a wire rack (edges may fall during cooling). Drizzle with melted marmalade.

Nutrition Facts per serving: 357 cal., 21 g total fat (12 g sat. fat), 221 mg chol., 325 mg sodium, 30 g carbo., 0 g fiber, 12 g pro.

A crunchy, pralinelike layer tops this easy, make-ahead brunch dish. The recipe features pieces of sausage patties tucked into a raisin-bread strata.

MORNING PECAN CASSEROLE

PREP:

25 minutes

CHILL:

8 hours or overnight

BAKE:

45 minutes

STAND:

15 minutes

OVEN:

350°F

MAKES:

10 servings

1	7-ounce package brown-and-serve sausage patties
12	slices raisin bread, cubed (about 8 cups)
3	cups milk
6	eggs
1	teaspoon vanilla
¼	teaspoon ground nutmeg
¼	teaspoon ground cinnamon
1	cup coarsely chopped pecans
½	cup packed brown sugar
¼	cup butter, softened
2	tablespoons pure maple syrup or maple-flavored syrup

1 Brown the sausage patties according to package directions. Cut patties into bite-size pieces. Spread bread cubes in bottom of a lightly greased 3-quart rectangular baking dish. Top with sausage pieces.

2 In a large bowl whisk together milk, eggs, vanilla, nutmeg, and cinnamon. Pour over bread and sausage, pressing lightly to thoroughly moisten the bread. Cover and chill for 8 hours or overnight.

3 For topping, in a small bowl combine pecans, brown sugar, butter, and maple syrup. Drop by teaspoonfuls over top of egg mixture.

4 Bake, uncovered, in a 350°F oven for 45 to 50 minutes or until a knife inserted near the center comes out clean. Let stand for 15 minutes before serving.

Nutrition Facts per serving: 408 cal., 24 g total fat (7 g sat. fat), 162 mg chol., 386 mg sodium, 36 g carbo., 2 g fiber, 14 g pro.

For the waffle lovers in your clan, this layered breakfast bake will likely become a new favorite. Serve it with fresh fruit for a colorful complement.

WAFFLE BREAKFAST CASSEROLE

1	pound bulk pork sausage
6	frozen waffles, toasted and cubed
1	cup shredded cheddar cheese (4 ounces)
2	cups milk
6	eggs
1	teaspoon dry mustard
1/8	teaspoon black pepper
	Pure maple syrup or maple-flavored syrup (optional)

1 In a large skillet cook sausage over medium heat until brown; drain.

2 Arrange half of the cubed waffles in a lightly greased 2-quart rectangular baking dish. Top with half of the sausage and 1/3 cup of the cheese. Repeat layers.

3 In a large bowl whisk together milk, eggs, dry mustard, and pepper. Pour over layers in dish. Cover and chill for 4 to 24 hours.

4 Bake, uncovered, in a 350°F oven for 50 to 60 minutes or until a knife inserted near the center comes out clean. Sprinkle with the remaining 1/3 cup cheese. Let stand for 10 minutes. If desired, drizzle with maple syrup.

Nutrition Facts per serving: 413 cal., 28 g total fat (12 g sat. fat), 217 mg chol., 668 mg sodium, 15 g carbo., 1 g fiber, 19 g pro.

PREP:
15 minutes

CHILL:
4 to 24 hours

BAKE:
50 minutes

STAND:
10 minutes

OVEN:
350°F

MAKES:
8 servings

Brioche is a French bread creation rich with butter and eggs that's shaped with a fluted base and a jaunty top knot. Look for it in your supermarket's bakery section or substitute another sweet bread.

RICH AMARETTO BRIOCHE BAKE

PREP:

20 minutes

CHILL:

4 to 24 hours

BAKE:

40 minutes

STAND:

15 minutes

OVEN:

350°F

MAKES:

8 servings

1   cup packed brown sugar

⅓   cup butter

¼   cup amaretto

2   tablespoons light-colored corn syrup

1   12-ounce loaf brioche or other sweet bread, cut into 9 slices

2   cups half-and-half, light cream, or milk

4   eggs

1½   teaspoons vanilla

½   teaspoon salt

¼   teaspoon ground nutmeg or cardamom

1 In a medium saucepan combine brown sugar, butter, amaretto, and corn syrup; cook and stir until mixture comes to boiling. Boil, uncovered, for 1 minute. Pour into a lightly greased 3-quart rectangular baking dish.

2 Arrange bread slices over brown sugar mixture. In a medium bowl whisk together half-and-half, eggs, vanilla, salt, and nutmeg. Pour over bread, pressing lightly to thoroughly moisten the bread. Cover and chill for 4 to 24 hours.

3 Bake, uncovered, in a 350°F oven for 40 to 45 minutes or until top is brown and a knife inserted near the center comes out clean. Let stand for 15 minutes before serving. Invert servings onto plates to serve.

Nutrition Facts per serving: 483 cal., 23 g total fat (10 g sat. fat), 189 mg chol., 450 mg sodium, 57 g carbo., 1 g fiber, 9 g pro.

Light and fluffy, this orange-scented strata is reminiscent of baked cinnamon-raisin French toast.

CITRUS RAISIN STRATA

10	slices cinnamon-raisin bread
2	cups half-and-half or light cream
3	eggs
⅔	cup sugar
1½	teaspoons finely shredded orange peel
1	teaspoon vanilla
	Vanilla yogurt (optional)

1 Tear bread into bite-size pieces. Spread torn bread in a greased 2-quart square baking dish. In a medium bowl whisk together half-and-half, eggs, sugar, orange peel, and vanilla. Pour over bread in baking dish.

2 Bake, uncovered, in a 350°F oven about 45 minutes or until a knife inserted near the center comes out clean. Let stand for 15 minutes before serving. If desired, serve with vanilla yogurt.

Nutrition Facts per serving: 345 cal., 14 g total fat (7 g sat. fat), 136 mg chol., 233 mg sodium, 48 g carbo., 2 g fiber, 9 g pro.

PREP:
10 minutes
BAKE:
45 minutes
STAND:
15 minutes
OVEN:
350°F
MAKES:
6 servings

Blueberries, almonds, and brown sugar surround dense Italian bread for a warming brunch bake.

BERRY FRENCH TOAST BAKE

PREP:

30 minutes

CHILL:

8 to 24 hours

BAKE:

40 minutes

STAND:

10 minutes

OVEN:

350°F

MAKES:

8 servings

12	ounces Italian bread, cut into 8 slices (about 1 inch thick)
2½	cups half-and-half or light cream
5	eggs
⅔	cup packed brown sugar
1	teaspoon vanilla
½	teaspoon ground nutmeg
2	cups fresh blueberries and/or raspberries
1	cup sliced almonds, lightly toasted
¼	cup packed brown sugar
¼	cup butter, melted

1 Arrange bread slices on the bottom of a lightly greased 3-quart rectangular baking dish, overlapping as necessary to fit bread.

2 In a large mixing bowl whisk together half-and-half, eggs, the ⅔ cup brown sugar, vanilla, and nutmeg. Carefully pour over bread in dish, pressing lightly to thoroughly moisten the bread. Cover and chill for 8 to 24 hours*.

3 Sprinkle berries and almonds over bread mixture. In a small bowl combine the ¼ cup brown sugar and melted butter. Drizzle over the fruit.

4 Bake, uncovered, in a 350°F oven about 40 minutes or until bubbly around edges and center is set. Let stand for 10 minutes before serving.

*NOTE: **If using a dense Italian bread, turn slices over once halfway through chilling.**

Nutrition Facts per serving: 525 cal., 28 g total fat (10 g sat. fat), 176 mg chol., 377 mg sodium, 57 g carbo., 5 g fiber, 14 g pro.

Rouse the sleepyheads in your family with this breakfast. Substitute strawberries, raspberries, or your favorite fruit for the blueberries to achieve a personalized twist.

FRENCH TOAST CASSEROLE

12	slices white bread, cut into ½-inch cubes (about 8 cups) and dried*
2	8-ounce packages cream cheese, cut into ¾-inch cubes
1	cup frozen blueberries
12	eggs
2	cups milk
½	cup pure maple syrup or maple-flavored syrup
	Blueberry-flavored, pure maple, or maple-flavored syrup

PREP:
20 minutes
CHILL:
2 to 24 hours
BAKE:
50 minutes
STAND:
10 minutes
OVEN:
375°F
MAKES:
8 servings

1 Spread half of the bread cubes evenly in bottom of a lightly greased 3-quart rectangular baking dish. Sprinkle cream cheese and blueberries over bread cubes. Arrange remaining bread cubes over cheese and berries.

2 In a large bowl whisk together eggs, milk, and the ½ cup maple syrup. Carefully pour over the bread mixture in dish. Cover and chill for 2 to 24 hours.

3 Bake, covered, in a 375°F oven for 25 minutes. Uncover and bake about 25 minutes more or until the top is puffed and golden and a knife inserted near the center comes out clean. Let stand for 10 minutes before serving. Serve warm with desired syrup.

*NOTE: **To dry bread cubes, spread cubes in a 15×10×1-inch baking pan. Bake in a 300°F oven for 10 to 15 minutes or until dry, stirring twice. Cool. (Bread cubes will continue to dry and crisp as they cool.) Or let bread cubes stand, loosely covered, at room temperature for 8 to 12 hours.**

Nutrition Facts per serving: 608 cal., 30 g total fat (16 g sat. fat), 386 mg chol., 497 mg sodium, 66 g carbo., 1 g fiber, 19 g pro.

For a delightful breakfast kissed with a touch of fancy, serve this layered French toast with a mix of fresh melon balls.

STRAWBERRIES & CREAM FRENCH TOAST

PREP:

40 minutes

CHILL:

2 to 24 hours

BAKE:

55 minutes

STAND:

10 minutes

OVEN:

300°F/350°F

MAKES:

8 servings

12   slices white bread, cut into ½-inch cubes (about 8 cups)

 1   8-ounce package cream cheese, cut into ¾-inch cubes

12   eggs

 2   cups milk

½   cup maple syrup or maple-flavored syrup

 2   cups coarsely chopped fresh or frozen strawberries, thawed
     Sifted powdered sugar
     Maple syrup or maple-flavored syrup (optional)

1 Arrange bread cubes in a single layer in a 15½×10½×2-inch baking pan. Bake in a 300°F oven for 10 to 15 minutes or until bread cubes are dry, stirring twice; cool. (Bread will continue to dry and crisp as it cools.) Or let bread stand, loosely covered, at room temperature for 8 to 12 hours.

2 Spread half of the dried bread cubes evenly in a lightly greased 3-quart rectangular baking dish. Sprinkle cream cheese over bread cubes. Arrange remaining bread cubes over cream cheese.

3 In a large mixing bowl whisk together eggs, milk, and the ½ cup maple syrup. Carefully pour over bread mixture in dish, pressing lightly to thoroughly moisten the bread. Cover and chill for 2 to 24 hours.

4 Bake, covered, in a 350°F oven for 25 minutes. Uncover and bake for 30 to 40 minutes more or until the top is puffed and golden and a knife inserted near the center comes out clean. Let stand for 10 minutes before serving. Sprinkle with strawberries and sift powdered sugar on the top. If desired, serve warm with maple syrup.

Nutrition Facts per serving: 409 cal., 20 g total fat (9 g sat. fat), 353 mg chol., 475 mg sodium, 41 g carbo., 2 g fiber, 17 g pro.

BREAD

No kneading is required for this yeast bread—it will rise right in the baking dish.

DILLY BREAD

PREP:
15 minutes

RISE:
50 minutes

BAKE:
25 minutes

OVEN:
375°F

MAKES:
1 loaf (8 servings)

2 cups all-purpose flour
1 package active dry yeast
2 teaspoons dillseeds
¼ teaspoon baking soda
2 tablespoons finely chopped onion
1 tablespoon butter
1 cup cream-style cottage cheese
¼ cup water
2 tablespoons sugar
½ teaspoon salt
1 egg

1 In a large mixing bowl combine ¾ cup of the flour, the yeast, dillseeds, and baking soda. Set aside.

2 In a medium saucepan cook onion in butter over medium heat until tender. Add cottage cheese, the water, sugar, and salt to onion mixture; heat and stir just until warm (120°F to 130°F). Add to flour mixture along with egg. Beat with an electric mixer on low speed for 30 seconds, scraping side of bowl constantly. Beat on high speed for 3 minutes. Using a wooden spoon, stir in the remaining 1¼ cups flour.

3 Spoon batter into a well-greased 1½-quart casserole or 9-inch round baking pan, spreading to edges. Cover and let rise in warm place until nearly double in size (50 to 60 minutes).

4 Bake, uncovered, in a 375°F oven about 25 minutes or until golden. (If necessary, cover with foil during the last 10 minutes of baking to prevent overbrowning.) Immediately remove from casserole. Serve warm, or cool on a wire rack.

Nutrition Facts per serving: 171 cal., 4 g total fat (1 g sat. fat), 31 mg chol., 305 mg sodium, 27 g carbo., 1 g fiber, 8 g pro.

This speedy yeast bread rises just once and requires no kneading. It's heavenly with a pork or beef roast.

CARAWAY BATTER BREAD

2	cups all-purpose flour
1	package active dry yeast
½	cup water
½	cup cream-style cottage cheese
1	tablespoon sugar
1	tablespoon caraway seeds or dillseeds
1	tablespoon butter
1	teaspoon dried minced onion
1	teaspoon salt
1	egg
½	cup toasted wheat germ

PREP:
15 minutes
RISE:
50 minutes
BAKE:
25 minutes
OVEN:
375°F
MAKES:
1 loaf (8 servings)

1 In a large mixing bowl combine 1 cup of the flour and the yeast; set aside.

2 In a medium saucepan heat and stir the water, cottage cheese, sugar, caraway seeds, butter, dried onion, and salt over medium heat just until warm (120°F to 130°F) and butter almost melts. Add to flour mixture along with egg. Beat with an electric mixer on low to medium speed for 30 seconds, scraping side of bowl constantly. Beat on high speed for 3 minutes. Using a wooden spoon, stir in wheat germ and the remaining 1 cup flour (batter will be stiff).

3 Spoon batter into a greased 1-quart casserole or 9-inch round baking pan, spreading to edges. Cover and let rise in a warm place until nearly double in size (50 to 60 minutes).

4 Bake, uncovered, in a 375°F oven for 25 to 30 minutes or until golden. Immediately remove from casserole. Serve warm, or cool on a wire rack.

Nutrition Facts per serving: 185 cal., 4 g total fat (2 g sat. fat), 33 mg chol., 369 mg sodium, 30 g carbo., 2 g fiber, 8 g pro.

Cottage cheese creates a wonderful moist texture in this well-seasoned bread that complements any soup or salad.

PEPPER & FENNEL BATTER BREAD

PREP:

15 minutes

RISE:

50 minutes

BAKE:

25 minutes

OVEN:

375°F

MAKES:

1 loaf (8 servings)

2	cups all-purpose flour
1	package active dry yeast
½	cup water
½	cup cream-style cottage cheese
1	tablespoon sugar
1	tablespoon butter
1	to 2 teaspoons fennel seeds, crushed
1	to 1½ teaspoons coarsely ground black pepper
1	teaspoon dried minced onion
½	teaspoon salt
1	egg
½	cup toasted wheat germ

1 In a large mixing bowl combine 1 cup of the flour and the yeast; set aside.

2 In a medium saucepan heat and stir the water, cottage cheese, sugar, butter, fennel seeds, pepper, dried onion, and salt over medium heat just until warm (120°F to 130°F) and butter almost melts. Add to flour mixture along with egg. Beat with an electric mixer on low to medium speed for 30 seconds, scraping side of bowl constantly. Beat on high speed for 3 minutes. Using a wooden spoon, stir in wheat germ and the remaining 1 cup flour (batter will be stiff).

3 Spoon batter into a greased 1-quart casserole or 9-inch round baking pan, spreading to edges. Cover and let rise in a warm place until nearly double in size (50 to 60 minutes).

4 Bake, uncovered, in a 375°F oven for 25 to 30 minutes or until bread sounds hollow when lightly tapped. (If necessary, cover with foil during the last 10 minutes of baking to prevent overbrowning.) Immediately remove from casserole. Serve warm, or cool on a wire rack.

Nutrition Facts per serving: 178 cal., 4 g total fat (2 g sat. fat), 32 mg chol., 220 mg sodium, 28 g carbo., 2 g fiber, 8 g pro.

Muffin cups make this bread super easy to serve. Team it with a piping hot pot of red or white chili for your next football party.

CHIVE BATTER ROLLS

1	tablespoon yellow cornmeal
2	cups all-purpose flour
1	package quick-rising active dry yeast
¼	teaspoon black pepper
1	cup milk
2	tablespoons sugar
3	tablespoons butter
½	teaspoon salt
1	egg
⅓	cup yellow cornmeal
3	tablespoons dried chives, crushed

1 Sprinkle bottoms of 12 greased 2½-inch muffin cups evenly with the 1 tablespoon cornmeal; set aside. In a large mixing bowl combine 1¼ cups of the flour, the yeast, and pepper; set aside.

2 In a small saucepan heat and stir milk, sugar, butter, and salt over medium heat just until warm (120°F to 130°F) and butter almost melts. Add to flour mixture along with egg. Beat with an electric mixer on low to medium speed for 30 seconds, scraping side of bowl constantly. Beat on high speed for 3 minutes. Using a wooden spoon, stir in the ⅓ cup cornmeal and the chives. Stir in remaining ¾ cup flour (batter will be soft and sticky). Cover and let rest in a warm place for 10 minutes.

3 Spoon batter into prepared muffin cups. Cover loosely and let rise in a warm place for 20 minutes.

4 Bake, uncovered, in a 350°F oven about 18 minutes or until rolls sound hollow when lightly tapped. Cool in muffin cups for 5 minutes; loosen edges and remove from muffin cups. Serve warm.

Nutrition Facts per roll: 140 cal., 4 g total fat (2 g sat. fat), 28 mg chol., 144 mg sodium, 21 g carbo., 1 g fiber, 4 g pro.

PREP:
30 minutes
STAND:
10 minutes
RISE:
20 minutes
BAKE:
18 minutes
COOL:
5 minutes
OVEN:
350°F
MAKES:
12 rolls

Batter breads have all the home-baked goodness of a tricky yeast bread—with none of the fuss. Cheddar cheese makes this one extra flavorful.

CHEDDAR BATTER BREAD

PREP:

15 minutes

RISE:

20 minutes

BAKE:

40 minutes

OVEN:

350°F

MAKES:

1 loaf (16 slices)

1 tablespoon yellow cornmeal

2 cups all-purpose flour

1 package quick-rising active dry yeast

¼ teaspoon onion powder

¼ teaspoon black pepper

1 cup milk

2 tablespoons sugar

2 tablespoons butter

½ teaspoon salt

1 egg

¾ cup shredded cheddar cheese (3 ounces)

½ cup yellow cornmeal

1 Grease the bottom and ½ inch up the sides of an 8×4×2-inch loaf pan. Sprinkle with the 1 tablespoon cornmeal; set aside. In a large mixing bowl combine 1½ cups of the flour, the yeast, onion powder, and pepper; set aside.

2 In a small saucepan heat and stir milk, sugar, butter, and salt over medium heat just until warm (120°F to 130°F) and butter almost melts. Add to flour mixture along with egg. Beat with an electric mixer on low to medium speed for 30 seconds, scraping side of bowl constantly. Beat on high speed for 3 minutes. Using a wooden spoon, stir in cheese and the ½ cup cornmeal. Stir in remaining ½ cup flour (batter will be soft and sticky).

3 Spread batter evenly into prepared pan. Cover and let rise in a warm place until nearly double in size (about 20 minutes).

4 Bake, uncovered, in a 350°F oven about 40 minutes or until bread sounds hollow when lightly tapped. (If necessary, cover with foil during the last 15 minutes of baking to prevent overbrowning.) Immediately remove from pan. Serve warm, or cool on a wire rack.

Nutrition Facts per serving: 124 cal., 4 g total fat (2 g sat. fat), 24 mg chol., 129 mg sodium, 17 g carbo., 1 g fiber, 4 g pro.

While the origins of Sally Lunn bread are unknown, this ring-shaped bread was served slathered in clotted cream alongside tea during colonial times. Bring it to your table when you're looking for a rich, slightly sweet yeast bread.

SALLY LUNN BREAD

3	cups all-purpose flour
1	package active dry yeast
1	cup milk
3	tablespoons sugar
3	tablespoons butter
½	teaspoon salt
2	eggs

1 In a large mixing bowl combine 1½ cups of the flour and the yeast. Set aside.

2 In a small saucepan, heat and stir milk, sugar, butter, and salt over medium heat just until warm (120°F to 130°F) and butter almost melts. Add to flour mixture along with eggs. Beat with an electric mixer on low to medium speed for 30 seconds, scraping side of bowl constantly. Beat on high speed for 3 minutes. Using a wooden spoon, stir in remaining flour (batter will be stiff). Cover and let rise in a warm place until nearly double in size (about 1 hour).

3 Using a wooden spoon, stir batter down. Spread batter evenly into a lightly greased 7- to 8-cup tube pan or Turk's head mold. Cover and let rise in a warm place until nearly double in size (about 35 minutes).

4 Bake, uncovered, in a 375°F oven for 20 minutes. Cover with foil. Bake about 20 minutes more or until bread sounds hollow when lightly tapped. Immediately remove from pan. Serve warm, or cool on a wire rack.

Nutrition Facts per serving: 201 cal., 5 g total fat (2 g sat. fat), 54 mg chol., 169 mg sodium, 31 g carbo., 1 g fiber, 6 g pro.

PREP:
20 minutes

RISE:
1 hour + 35 minutes

BAKE:
40 minutes

OVEN:
375°F

MAKES:
1 loaf (10 servings)

Traditional spoon bread was an 18th-century favorite. This spicy version will become a "hot item" on your table too.

JALAPEÑO-JACK SPOON BREAD

PREP:
15 minutes
STAND:
20 minutes
BAKE:
45 minutes
COOL:
20 minutes
OVEN:
350°F
MAKES:
8 to 10 servings

3	egg whites
2	cups milk
1½	cups yellow cornmeal
2	cups shredded Monterey Jack cheese with jalapeño peppers (8 ounces)
1	14¾-ounce can cream-style corn
⅓	cup finely chopped red sweet pepper
3	egg yolks
½	teaspoon salt
	Purchased salsa (optional)
	Dairy sour cream (optional)

1 Allow egg whites to stand at room temperature for 20 minutes. Meanwhile, in a large saucepan combine milk and cornmeal. Cook, stirring constantly, over medium heat about 5 minutes or until mixture is very thick and pulls away from the side of the pan. Remove from heat.

2 In a medium bowl combine 1½ cups of the cheese, the corn, sweet pepper, egg yolks, and salt. Stir into cornmeal mixture. Set aside.

3 In a medium mixing bowl beat egg whites with an electric mixer on high speed until stiff peaks form (tips stand straight). Stir about one-third of the beaten egg whites into cornmeal mixture. Gently fold remaining beaten egg whites into cornmeal mixture. Spoon mixture into a greased 2-quart casserole (dish will be full).

4 Bake, uncovered, in a 350°F oven for 45 to 50 minutes or until a knife inserted near the center comes out clean. Top evenly with remaining ½ cup cheese. Cool on a wire rack about 20 minutes before serving. If desired, serve with salsa and sour cream.

Nutrition Facts per serving: 295 cal., 12 g total fat (7 g sat. fat), 107 mg chol., 498 mg sodium, 33 g carbo., 3 g fiber, 14 g pro.

Some like it hot, and others do not! For a punch of pepper, use Monterey Jack cheese with jalapeño peppers in place of the cheddar cheese.

CHEDDAR SPOON BREAD

4	egg whites
1½	cups milk
½	cup cornmeal
2	cups shredded cheddar cheese or Monterey Jack cheese (8 ounces)
1	tablespoon butter
1½	teaspoons baking powder
1	teaspoon sugar
¼	teaspoon salt
4	egg yolks

PREP:
25 minutes
STAND:
20 minutes
BAKE:
45 minutes
OVEN:
325°F
MAKES:
8 servings

1 Allow egg whites to stand at room temperature for 20 minutes. Meanwhile, in a large saucepan combine milk and cornmeal. Cook, stirring constantly, over medium heat about 5 minutes or until mixture is very thick and pulls away from the side of the pan. Remove from heat. Add cheese, butter, baking powder, sugar, and salt; stir until cheese melts.

2 Add egg yolks, one at a time, to cornmeal mixture, stirring after each addition just until combined (mixture will be thick). Set aside.

3 In a large mixing bowl beat egg whites with an electric mixer on high speed until stiff peaks form (tips stand straight). Stir about one-third of the beaten egg whites into cornmeal mixture. Gently fold remaining beaten egg whites into cornmeal mixture until combined. Spoon mixture into an ungreased 2-quart casserole or soufflé dish.

4 Bake, uncovered, in a 325°F oven for 45 to 50 minutes or until a knife inserted near the center comes out clean. Serve immediately.

Nutrition Facts per serving: 221 cal., 14 g total fat (8 g sat. fat), 143 mg chol., 393 mg sodium, 10 g carbo., 1 g fiber, 12 g pro.

Havarti is a Danish cheese now widely available in supermarkets. Its mild yet tangy flavor complements the creaminess of this side dish.

COUNTRY SPOON BREAD

PREP:
20 minutes

STAND:
20 minutes

BAKE:
55 minutes

OVEN:
350°F

MAKES:
8 servings

3	egg whites
2	cups milk
1½	cups yellow cornmeal
1	cup cream-style cottage cheese with chives
¾	cup shredded Havarti cheese with dill* (3 ounces)
1	8½-ounce can cream-style corn
3	egg yolks
½	teaspoon salt

① Allow egg whites to stand at room temperature for 20 minutes. Meanwhile, in a large saucepan combine milk and cornmeal. Cook, stirring constantly, over medium heat about 5 minutes or until mixture is very thick and pulls away from the side of the pan. Remove from heat.

② In a medium bowl combine cottage cheese, cheese, corn, egg yolks, and salt. Stir into cornmeal mixture. Set aside.

③ In a medium mixing bowl beat egg whites with an electric mixer on high speed until stiff peaks form (tips stand straight). Stir about one-third of the beaten egg whites into the cornmeal mixture. Gently fold remaining beaten egg whites into cornmeal mixture. Spoon mixture into a greased 2-quart casserole.

④ Bake, uncovered, in 350°F oven for 55 to 60 minutes or until a knife inserted near the center comes out clean. Serve immediately.

***NOTE:** If you like, substitute ¾ cup regular plain cheese and ¼ teaspoon dried dillweed for the Havarti cheese with dill.**

Nutrition Facts per serving: 245 cal., 9 g total fat (2 g sat. fat), 99 mg chol., 443 mg sodium, 29 g carbo., 2 g fiber, 13 g pro.

Don't forget the spoons! Although spoon bread is technically a bread, usually it's soft enough that it must be served and eaten with a spoon.

ZUCCHINI SPOON BREAD

3	cups shredded zucchini
1	8¼-ounce package corn muffin mix
1⅓	cups shredded Italian-style or Mexican-style cheese blend
4	eggs
½	cup cooking oil
½	cup finely chopped onion
¼	cup buttermilk or sour milk*
½	teaspoon Italian seasoning blend, crushed
	Dash bottled hot pepper sauce
⅔	cup chopped almonds

PREP:
20 minutes

BAKE:
35 minutes

OVEN:
350°F

MAKES:
8 to 10 servings

1 In a large bowl combine zucchini, muffin mix, 1 cup of the cheese, the eggs, oil, onion, buttermilk, Italian seasoning, and hot pepper sauce. Spoon into a greased 2- to 2½-quart casserole. Sprinkle with almonds and remaining ⅓ cup cheese.

2 Bake, uncovered, in a 350°F oven about 35 minutes or until a knife inserted near the center comes out clean. To serve, spoon warm mixture onto plates.

*NOTE: To make ¼ cup sour milk, place 1 teaspoon lemon juice or vinegar in a glass measuring cup. Add enough milk to make ¼ cup liquid; stir. Let the mixture stand for 5 minutes before using.

Nutrition Facts per serving: 416 cal., 30 g total fat (6 g sat. fat), 120 mg chol., 382 mg sodium, 26 g carbo., 2 g fiber, 13 g pro.

This version of spoon bread calls for sweet figs and corn—warm and comforting flavors that pair well with a meaty main dish.

CORN & FIG SPOON BREAD

PREP:

35 minutes

STAND:

20 minutes

BAKE:

45 minutes

OVEN:

375°F

MAKES:

8 servings

3	egg whites
½	cup chopped dried figs
½	cup apple juice
2	cups milk
1½	cups buttermilk or sour milk*
1¼	cups yellow cornmeal
1	tablespoon sugar
1	teaspoon salt
1½	cups frozen whole kernel corn, thawed
¼	cup butter, cut up
3	egg yolks
1	teaspoon baking powder

1 Allow egg whites to stand at room temperature for 20 minutes. Meanwhile, in a small saucepan combine figs and apple juice. Bring just to boiling; remove from heat. Set aside.

2 In a large saucepan combine milk, buttermilk, cornmeal, sugar, and salt. Cook and stir over medium heat for 10 to 15 minutes or until mixture is very thick and just comes to a boil. Remove from heat. Stir in corn, butter, and the fig-apple juice mixture.

3 In a small bowl whisk together egg yolks and baking powder. Gradually stir 1 cup of the hot cornmeal mixture into the yolk mixture. Return mixture to saucepan. In a medium mixing bowl beat the egg whites with an electric mixer on high speed until stiff peaks form (tips stand straight). Stir about one-third of the beaten egg whites into the cornmeal mixture. Gently fold remaining beaten egg whites into cornmeal mixture. Spoon mixture into a lightly greased 2½-quart casserole.

4 Bake, uncovered, in a 375°F oven about 45 minutes or until a knife inserted near the center comes out clean.

*NOTE: To make 1½ cups sour milk, place 4½ teaspoons lemon juice or vinegar in a glass measuring cup. Add enough milk to make 1½ cups liquid; stir. Let the mixture stand for 5 minutes before using.

Nutrition Facts per serving: 279 cal., 10 g total fat (5 g sat. fat), 100 mg chol., 468 mg sodium, 40 g carbo., 4 g fiber, 9 g pro.

The onion adds a pungent flavor to this bread, while the poppy seeds add a nutty, crunchy texture. Serve it with a brothy soup or any hearty meal.

ONION-CHEESE SUPPER BREAD

½	cup chopped onion (1 medium)
2	tablespoons butter
½	cup milk
1	egg
1½	cups packaged biscuit mix
1	cup shredded American cheese or cheddar cheese (4 ounces)
2	teaspoons poppy seeds

PREP:
15 minutes
BAKE:
20 minutes
OVEN:
400°F
MAKES:
8 servings

1 In a small skillet cook onion in 1 tablespoon of the butter over medium heat until tender.

2 In a medium bowl whisk together milk and egg. Add biscuit mix; stir just until moistened. Add the chopped onion, ½ cup of the cheese, and 1 teaspoon of the poppy seeds to biscuit mix mixture. Spread batter into a greased 8-inch round baking pan. Sprinkle with the remaining 1 teaspoon poppy seeds. Melt remaining 1 tablespoon butter; drizzle over batter in pan.

3 Bake, uncovered, in a 400°F oven for 10 minutes. Sprinkle top with remaining ½ cup cheese. Bake about 10 minutes more or until a wooden toothpick inserted near the center comes out clean. Serve warm.

Nutrition Facts per serving: 202 cal., 12 g total fat (6 g sat. fat), 49 mg chol., 528 mg sodium, 16 g carbo., 1 g fiber, 6 g pro.

In Ireland, it's a rare meal that isn't accompanied by rounds of soda bread. Each warm, thick slice makes a delectable platter for butter and honey or marmalade.

IRISH SODA BREAD

PREP:

15 minutes

BAKE:

50 minutes

COOL:

30 minutes

OVEN:

350°F

MAKES:

1 loaf (12 servings)

4	cups all-purpose flour
¼	cup sugar
1	teaspoon salt
1	teaspoon baking powder
1	teaspoon baking soda
½	cup shortening
1	cup raisins
1	tablespoon caraway seeds
1⅓	cups buttermilk or sour milk*
1	egg
1	tablespoon butter, melted

1 In a large bowl combine flour, sugar, salt, baking powder, and baking soda. Using a pastry blender, cut in shortening until mixture resembles fine crumbs. Stir in raisins and caraway seeds. Make a well in the center of the dry mixture.

2 In a small bowl whisk together buttermilk and egg. Add to dry mixture. Stir just until all is moistened. On a lightly floured surface, gently knead dough 10 to 12 times or until smooth. Place dough in a greased 9-inch round baking pan. Pat dough gently until dough reaches side of pan. Using a sharp knife, cut an "X" in the top of the dough about ½ inch deep.

3 Bake, uncovered, in a 350°F oven about 50 minutes or until a wooden toothpick inserted near the center comes out clean and dough in the "X" appears dry. Remove bread from pan and place on a wire rack. Brush top of bread with melted butter. Cool for 30 to 40 minutes on wire rack. Serve bread warm.

*NOTE: To make 1⅓ cups sour milk, place 4 teaspoons lemon juice or vinegar in a glass measuring cup. Add enough milk to make 1⅓ cups liquid; stir. Let the mixture stand for 5 minutes before using.

Nutrition Facts per serving: 305 cal., 10 g total fat (3 g sat. fat), 21 mg chol., 378 mg sodium, 47 g carbo., 2 g fiber, 6 g pro.

Broccoli and cheddar cheese add color and nutrients without overwhelming the sweet taste of this corn bread.

BROCCOLI CORN BREAD

1   8½-ounce package corn muffin mix

3   eggs

2   cups shredded cheddar cheese (8 ounces)

1   10-ounce package frozen chopped broccoli, thawed and drained well

½   cup chopped onion

1 In a large bowl combine muffin mix and eggs. Stir in cheese, broccoli, and onion. Spoon into a greased 2-quart square baking dish.

2 Bake, uncovered, in a 350°F oven about 30 minutes or until a wooden toothpick inserted near the center comes out clean. Serve warm.

Nutrition Facts per serving: 184 cal., 10 g total fat (4 g sat. fat), 73 mg chol., 278 mg sodium, 16 g carbo., 1 g fiber, 8 g pro.

PREP:
10 minutes
BAKE:
30 minutes
OVEN:
350°F
MAKES:
12 servings

This bread packs a load of different sensations that will delight your palate—gritty corn from the cornmeal, nutty from the cumin, and tangy from the buttermilk.

LOADED BUTTERMILK-CUMIN CORN BREAD

PREP:

15 minutes

BAKE:

20 minutes

OVEN:

400°F

MAKES:

9 servings

1	cup whole wheat flour or all-purpose flour
1	cup yellow cornmeal
3	to 4 tablespoons sugar
2	teaspoons baking powder
¾	teaspoon salt
¾	teaspoon ground cumin
¼	teaspoon baking soda
¼	teaspoon crushed red pepper
1	cup buttermilk or sour milk*
2	eggs
¼	cup butter, melted
½	cup frozen whole kernel corn, thawed
4	brown-and-serve sausage patties, chopped (⅔ cup)

1 In a large bowl combine flour, cornmeal, sugar, baking powder, salt, cumin, baking soda, and crushed red pepper; set aside.

2 In medium bowl whisk together buttermilk, eggs, and butter. Add egg mixture all at once to flour mixture. Stir just until moistened. Fold in corn and sausage. Spoon batter into a lightly greased 2-quart square baking dish.

3 Bake, uncovered, in a 400°F oven for 20 to 25 minutes or until a wooden toothpick inserted near the center comes out clean. Serve warm.

*NOTE: **To make 1 cup sour milk, place 1 tablespoon lemon juice or vinegar in a glass measuring cup. Add enough milk to make 1 cup liquid; stir. Let the mixture stand for 5 minutes before using.**

Nutrition Facts per serving: 278 cal., 14 g total fat (6 g sat. fat), 81 mg chol., 528 mg sodium, 29 g carbo., 3 g fiber, 10 g pro.

Cut this crispy, golden treat into bite-size pieces and serve with warm spaghetti sauce as predinner breadsticks. It's sure to be a favorite of the little ones around the house.

PARMESAN-OLIVE BREAD

2	cups all-purpose flour
1	package active dry yeast
²⁄₃	cup warm water (120°F to 130°F)
1	egg
1	tablespoon butter, melted
1	tablespoon sugar
½	teaspoon salt
1	cup shredded Parmesan cheese (4 ounces)
½	cup chopped, pitted kalamata olives
	Olive oil

PREP:
15 minutes

RISE:
45 minutes

BAKE:
25 minutes

OVEN:
375°F

MAKES:
1 loaf (12 servings)

1 In a medium mixing bowl combine 1 cup of the flour and the yeast. Add the water, egg, butter, sugar, and salt. Beat with an electric mixer on low speed for 30 seconds, scraping side of bowl constantly. Beat on high speed for 3 minutes. Using a wooden spoon, stir in remaining 1 cup flour, ³⁄₄ cup of the Parmesan cheese, and olives (dough will be stiff).

2 Spoon batter into a well-greased 1½-quart casserole. Cover and let rise in a warm place until nearly double in size (45 to 60 minutes).

3 Brush top of dough with olive oil and sprinkle with remaining ¼ cup cheese. Bake, uncovered, in a 375°F oven for 25 to 30 minutes or until bread sounds hollow when lightly tapped and cheese is golden. Remove from casserole and cool completely on a wire rack.

Nutrition Facts per serving: 138 cal., 5 g total fat (2 g sat. fat), 27 mg chol., 334 mg sodium, 17 g carbo., 1 g fiber, 6 g pro.

This bread is a close cousin of focaccia bread, so it's a natural to slice and make into sandwiches with fresh-cut deli meats and cheeses.

ROSEMARY CASSEROLE BREAD

PREP:

20 minutes

RISE:

25 minutes

BAKE:

30 minutes

OVEN:

375°F

MAKES:

1 loaf (12 servings)

3   cups all-purpose flour

1   package quick-rising active dry yeast

½   teaspoon dried rosemary, crushed

1   cup lukewarm water (120°F to 130°F)

1   egg

1   tablespoon butter, melted

1   tablespoon sugar

½   teaspoon salt

     Olive oil

¼   teaspoon dried rosemary, crushed

1 In a medium mixing bowl combine 1½ cups of the flour, the yeast, and the ½ teaspoon rosemary. Add the water, egg, butter, sugar, and salt. Beat with an electric mixer on low speed for 30 seconds, scraping side of bowl constantly. Beat on high speed for 3 minutes. Using a wooden spoon, stir in the remaining 1½ cups flour (batter will be stiff).

2 Spoon batter into a well-greased 1½-quart casserole. Cover and let rise in a warm place until nearly double in size (25 to 30 minutes).

3 Brush top of dough with olive oil and sprinkle with the ¼ teaspoon rosemary. Bake, uncovered, in a 375°F oven for 30 to 35 minutes or until bread sounds hollow when lightly tapped. Remove from casserole and cool completely on a wire rack.

Nutrition Facts per serving: 129 cal., 2 g total fat (1 g sat. fat), 20 mg chol., 111 mg sodium, 23 g carbo., 1 g fiber, 4 g pro.

DESSERT

This dessert is for chocolate lovers! It offers a hefty dose of chocolate topped with cinnamon cream. Just before dinner, put this dish in the oven and it's ready to serve at dessert time.

CHOCOLATE BREAD PUDDING

PREP:
30 minutes
BAKE:
45 minutes
COOL:
20 minutes
OVEN:
350°F
MAKES:
9 servings

5½	cups white bread cubes, dried*
6	ounces bittersweet or semisweet chocolate, chopped
3	cups whipping cream
¾	cup granulated sugar
3	eggs
3	egg yolks
⅛	teaspoon salt
3	ounces bittersweet or semisweet chocolate, chopped
½	cup whipping cream
2	tablespoons powdered sugar
½	teaspoon ground cinnamon

1 In a buttered 2-quart square baking dish toss together bread cubes and the 6 ounces chocolate; set aside. In a medium saucepan bring the 3 cups whipping cream to boiling over medium heat. Meanwhile, in a medium bowl whisk together granulated sugar, eggs, egg yolks, and salt. Slowly whisk 1 cup of hot cream into egg mixture. Whisk hot egg mixture back into cream in saucepan. Cook for 1 to 2 minutes over medium-low heat until sugar dissolves. Add the 3 ounces chocolate, stirring until melted. Pour over bread mixture in baking dish, stirring carefully until well coated.

2 Place baking dish in a large roasting pan. (Make sure there is at least 1 inch of space between the baking dish and the sides of the roasting pan.) Pour enough hot water into roasting pan to reach halfway up sides of baking dish. Bake, uncovered, in a 350°F oven for 45 to 55 minutes or until center is set. Remove pudding from water bath and cool for 20 minutes on a wire rack.

3 For cinnamon cream, in a medium mixing bowl beat the ½ cup whipping cream, the powdered sugar, and cinnamon with an electric mixer on medium speed until soft peaks form (tips curl). Spoon over each serving of pudding.

*NOTE: **To dry bread cubes, spread cubes in a 15×10×1-inch baking pan. Bake in a 300°F oven for 10 to 15 minutes or until bread cubes are dry, stirring once. Cool. (Bread cubes will continue to dry and crisp as they cool.) Or let bread cubes stand, loosely covered, at room temperature for 8 to 12 hours.**

Nutrition Facts per serving: 629 cal., 48 g total fat (29 g sat. fat), 267 mg chol., 247 mg sodium, 48 g carbo., 3 g fiber, 8 g pro.

Bring any evening to a sweet ending with this special dessert. The sweet apples and tart cherries complement each other deliciously.

CHERRY-APPLE BREAD PUDDING

9   slices firm-textured white bread

3   tablespoons butter, softened

3   medium Golden Delicious apples, peeled and very thinly sliced

2   tablespoons lemon juice

½   cup dried tart red cherries

3   cups milk

6   eggs

½   cup sugar

PREP:
25 minutes
BAKE:
45 minutes
COOL:
30 minutes
OVEN:
350°F
MAKES:
8 to 10 servings

1 Lightly butter 1 side of the bread slices; cut bread into quarters. Arrange half of the bread pieces, buttered sides down, in an ungreased 3-quart rectangular baking dish.

2 Toss together apples and lemon juice. Sprinkle apple-lemon juice mixture and cherries over bread in baking dish. Top with remaining bread pieces, buttered sides up. Whisk together milk, eggs, and sugar. Pour egg mixture over bread in dish, pressing lightly to thoroughly moisten the bread.

3 Bake, uncovered, in a 350°F oven for 45 to 50 minutes or until a knife inserted near the center comes out clean. Cool for 30 minutes on a wire rack. Serve warm.

Nutrition Facts per serving: 315 cal., 11 g total fat (5 g sat. fat), 178 mg chol., 270 mg sodium, 45 g carbo., 2 g fiber, 10 g pro.

If you don't have homemade biscuits to use in this pudding, refrigerated biscuits work just as well.

BISCUIT BREAD PUDDING

PREP:

30 minutes

STAND:

10 minutes

BAKE:

35 minutes

OVEN:

350°F

MAKES:

8 servings

1¾ cups sugar

1 12-ounce can (1½ cups) evaporated milk

4 slightly beaten eggs

¼ cup butter, melted

1 teaspoon vanilla

½ teaspoon ground cinnamon

½ teaspoon ground nutmeg

6 cups coarsely crumbled homemade buttermilk biscuits*
(8 to 10 biscuits)

1 recipe Lemon Sauce

1 In a large bowl whisk together sugar, evaporated milk, eggs, melted butter, vanilla, cinnamon, and nutmeg. Place crumbled biscuits into a greased 2-quart rectangular baking dish. Pour egg mixture over biscuits in dish, pressing lightly to thoroughly moisten the biscuits. Let stand for 10 minutes.

2 Bake, uncovered, in a 350°F oven about 35 minutes or until a knife inserted near the center comes out clean. Serve warm with Lemon Sauce.

LEMON SAUCE: In a medium saucepan whisk together 1 egg, 2 tablespoons water, and 2 tablespoons lemon juice. Add ½ cup sugar and ¼ cup butter, cut up. Cook and stir over medium-low heat until mixture is thickened and just bubbly around edges. If desired, strain sauce. Serve warm. Store in the refrigerator. Makes about 2 cups.

***NOTE:** Use homemade biscuits or 1 package refrigerated large Southern-style biscuits, baked according to package directions.

Nutrition Facts per serving: 610 cal., 29 g total fat (12 g sat. fat), 178 mg chol., 405 mg sodium, 79 g carbo., 1 g fiber, 10 g pro.

This recipe updates an old favorite by replacing regular bread with croissants and adding mashed banana to the creamy custard mixture.

BANANA-PECAN STREUSEL BREAD PUDDING

1	12-ounce can (1½ cups) evaporated milk
1⅓	cups mashed ripe bananas (4 medium)
3	eggs
½	cup granulated sugar
1	tablespoon vanilla
1	teaspoon ground cinnamon
¼	to ½ teaspoon almond extract
2	large croissants, cut or torn into 1-inch pieces (4 cups)
¼	cup packed brown sugar
2	tablespoons all-purpose flour
1	tablespoon butter, melted
1	teaspoon ground cinnamon
½	cup chopped pecans
	Whipped cream or ice cream (optional)

PREP:
20 minutes
BAKE:
40 minutes
STAND:
30 minutes
OVEN:
350°F
MAKES:
10 to 12 servings

1 In a medium bowl whisk together evaporated milk, bananas, eggs, granulated sugar, vanilla, 1 teaspoon cinnamon, and the almond extract. Place croissant pieces in a lightly greased 2-quart rectangular baking dish. Pour egg mixture over croissants in dish, pressing lightly to thoroughly moisten the croissants.

2 In a small bowl combine brown sugar, flour, melted butter, and 1 teaspoon cinnamon. Stir in pecans. Sprinkle over croissant mixture.

3 Bake, uncovered, in a 350°F oven for 40 to 45 minutes or until a knife inserted near the center comes out clean. Let stand for 30 minutes. Serve warm. If desired, top with whipped cream or ice cream.

Nutrition Facts per serving: 280 cal., 12 g total fat (6 g sat. fat), 96 mg chol., 141 mg sodium, 38 g carbo., 1 g fiber, 7 g pro.

The luscious caramel sauce makes this fruity bread pudding almost impossible to resist.

CRANBERRY BREAD PUDDING

PREP:

20 minutes

BAKE:

1 hour

OVEN:

325°F

MAKES:

6 servings

2 cups milk

4 eggs

¾ cup granulated sugar

½ cup half-and-half or light cream

1 teaspoon ground cinnamon

1 teaspoon vanilla

8 ounces Vienna bread or challah, cut into 1-inch cubes (about 8 cups) and dried*

¾ cup dried cranberries

1 recipe Caramel-Orange Sauce

1 In a medium bowl whisk together milk, eggs, sugar, half-and-half, cinnamon, and vanilla.

2 In a very large bowl combine the dry bread cubes and cranberries. Pour milk mixture over bread cube mixture. Stir until bread has soaked up all the milk mixture. Transfer bread cube mixture to a heavily greased 2-quart square baking dish.

3 Bake, uncovered, in a 325°F oven about 1 hour or until a knife inserted near the center comes out clean. Cool slightly. Serve warm with Caramel-Orange Sauce.

CARAMEL-ORANGE SAUCE: In a heavy medium saucepan combine ⅓ cup butter or margarine, ⅓ cup granulated sugar, ⅓ cup packed brown sugar, and ⅓ cup whipping cream. Cook and stir over medium-high heat until mixture boils. Stir in ⅓ cup coarsely chopped pecans, toasted; 1 tablespoon orange liqueur; and 1 teaspoon vanilla. Serve immediately.

MAKE·AHEAD DIRECTIONS: Prepare the Carmel-Orange Sauce up to 3 days ahead. Let it cool. Cover and store in the refrigerator. Reheat just before serving.

***NOTE: To dry bread cubes, spread cubes in a 15×10×1-inch baking pan. Bake in a 300°F oven for 10 to 15 minutes or until bread cubes are dry, stirring once. Cool. (Bread cubes will continue to dry and crisp as they cool.) Or let bread cubes stand, loosely covered, at room temperature for 8 to 12 hours.**

Nutrition Facts per serving: 639 cal., 28 g total fat (14 g sat. fat), 202 mg chol., 442 mg sodium, 86 g carbo., 3 g fiber, 12 g pro.

Take advantage of the summer harvest of blueberries with this simple crisp.
A scoop of vanilla ice cream adds to the dessert's perfection.

BLUEBERRY CRISP

4	teaspoons all-purpose flour
1	tablespoon granulated sugar
3	cups fresh or frozen blueberries
2	tablespoons lemon juice
⅔	cup packed brown sugar
½	cup all-purpose flour
½	cup quick-cooking rolled oats
¾	teaspoon ground cinnamon
⅓	cup cold butter

PREP:
20 minutes
BAKE:
30 minutes
OVEN:
375°F
MAKES:
4 to 6 servings

1 In a large bowl combine the 4 teaspoons flour and the granulated sugar. Add blueberries and lemon juice; toss gently to combine. Spread berry mixture evenly in a lightly greased 2-quart square baking dish; set aside.

2 For topping, combine brown sugar, the ½ cup flour, the oats, and cinnamon. Using a pastry blender, cut in cold butter until mixture resembles coarse crumbs. Sprinkle topping evenly over berries.

3 Bake, uncovered, in a 375°F oven about 30 minutes or until topping is golden and edges are bubbly. Serve warm.

Nutrition Facts per serving: 458 cal., 17 g total fat (8 g sat. fat), 43 mg chol., 132 mg sodium, 74 g carbo., 7 g fiber, 4 g pro.

For this tasty crisp update, the freezer section at your grocery store is your friend. Just pick out your favorite frozen pound cake and dress it up with blackberries or another favorite berry.

BLACKBERRY & POUND CAKE CRISP

PREP:
25 minutes

BAKE:
45 minutes

COOL:
15 minutes

OVEN:
350°F

MAKES:
6 servings

1	10¾-ounce frozen pound cake, thawed
1	cup all-purpose flour
¾	cup packed brown sugar
½	teaspoon ground cinnamon
¼	teaspoon salt
⅓	cup cold butter, cut up
1	cup whipping cream
2	tablespoons all-purpose flour
2	tablespoons granulated sugar
4	cups fresh or frozen blackberries

1 Cut pound cake into ½-inch slices. Place slices on a baking sheet. Broil about 4 inches from the heat about 1 minute per side or until slices are lightly toasted. (Watch carefully so they do not burn.) Cut the toasted slices into fourths. Arrange pieces in the bottom of a lightly greased 2-quart rectangular baking dish. Set aside.

2 For topping, in a medium bowl combine the 1 cup flour, the brown sugar, cinnamon, and salt. Using a pastry blender, cut in cold butter until the mixture resembles coarse crumbs. Set aside.

3 In a large bowl whisk together whipping cream, the 2 tablespoons flour, and granulated sugar until combined. Fold in blackberries. Spread the blackberry mixture over pound cake layer. Sprinkle topping over blackberry mixture.

4 Bake, uncovered, in a 350°F oven for 45 to 50 minutes or until topping is golden and edges are bubbly. Cool on a wire rack for 15 minutes. Serve warm.

Nutrition Facts per serving: 526 cal., 28 g total fat (16 g sat. fat), 105 mg chol., 315 mg sodium, 66 g carbo., 5 g fiber, 5 g pro.

If you want to savor summer's fresh flavors in the winter, make this simple crisp with frozen fruit.

PEACH MELBA CRISP

5	cups sliced, peeled peaches or frozen unsweetened peach slices, thawed (do not drain)
2½	teaspoons cornstarch
1	10-ounce package frozen red raspberries in syrup, thawed
1½	cups plain granola
⅔	cup flaked or shredded coconut
3	tablespoons butter, melted
	Vanilla or cinnamon-flavored ice cream (optional)

PREP:
20 minutes
BAKE:
40 minutes
OVEN:
350°F
MAKES:
6 servings

1 Place peaches in an ungreased 2-quart square baking dish. Sprinkle with cornstarch and toss gently to coat.

2 If desired, press the undrained raspberries through a sieve; discard seeds. Spoon raspberries over the peaches. Bake, uncovered, in a 350°F oven for 20 minutes.

3 Meanwhile, in a medium bowl combine granola, coconut, and melted butter. Stir partially cooked peach mixture gently. Sprinkle granola mixture over peaches. Bake for 20 to 25 minutes more or until topping is golden and edges are bubbly. Serve warm. If desired, serve with ice cream.

Nutrition Facts per serving: 462 cal., 16 g total fat (7 g sat. fat), 16 mg chol., 81 mg sodium, 80 g carbo., 10 g fiber, 5 g pro.

Savory cheddar cheese adds to the chewy topping of this ginger-scented dessert.

CHEESY APPLE CRISP

PREP:

20 minutes

BAKE:

35 minutes

OVEN:

375°F

MAKES:

4 servings

3	cups sliced, peeled apples
3	tablespoons all-purpose flour
¼	cup water or apple juice
¼	cup rolled oats
¼	cup packed brown sugar
¼	teaspoon ground ginger
2	tablespoons butter, softened
½	cup shredded cheddar cheese (2 ounces)
¼	cup chopped pecans, walnuts, or almonds
	Vanilla ice cream, half-and-half, or light cream (optional)

1 In a medium bowl toss apples with 1 tablespoon of the flour. Place mixture into an ungreased 1-quart casserole. Pour the water over apples.

2 For topping, in a small bowl combine remaining 2 tablespoons flour, the oats, brown sugar, and ginger. Stir in softened butter until crumbly. Stir in cheese and pecans. Sprinkle topping over apples.

3 Bake, uncovered, in a 375°F oven about 35 minutes or until topping is golden and edges are bubbly. Serve warm. If desired, serve with ice cream, half-and-half, or light cream.

Nutrition Facts per serving: 311 cal., 16 g total fat (7 g sat. fat), 31 mg chol., 139 mg sodium, 38 g carbo., 4 g fiber, 6 g pro.

After a meal of pork chops or steak, there's nothing more delicious than this crunchy fruit dessert topped with a scoop of French vanilla ice cream.

GINGER-PEAR-ALMOND CRISP

1	pound pears, peeled, cored, and sliced
¼	cup dried cranberries
2	tablespoons orange juice or water
1	tablespoon finely chopped crystallized ginger or ¼ teaspoon ground ginger
½	teaspoon ground cinnamon
½	teaspoon vanilla
⅓	cup quick-cooking rolled oats
¼	cup packed brown sugar
2	tablespoons all-purpose flour
2	tablespoons butter, melted
2	tablespoons sliced almonds
	Vanilla ice cream (optional)
	Coarsely chopped crystallized ginger (optional)

PREP:
15 minutes

BAKE:
20 minutes

OVEN:
375°F

MAKES:
4 servings

1 In a medium bowl combine pears, cranberries, orange juice, the finely chopped ginger, cinnamon, and vanilla. Spoon mixture into an ungreased 1-quart casserole.

2 In a small bowl combine oats, brown sugar, and flour. Stir in melted butter. Sprinkle oat mixture and almonds over pear mixture.

3 Bake, uncovered, in a 375°F oven for 20 to 25 minutes or until pears are tender and almonds are golden brown. Serve warm. If desired, top with ice cream and additional crystallized ginger.

Nutrition Facts per serving: 275 cal., 9 g total fat (3 g sat. fat), 16 mg chol., 52 mg sodium, 40 g carbo., 5 g fiber, 3 g pro

The name says it all—just choose your favorite fruit and you'll enjoy a hot-from-the-oven treat in less than an hour.

EASY FRUIT CRISP

PREP:

20 minutes

BAKE:

30 minutes

OVEN:

350°F

MAKES:

6 servings

5   cups peeled and sliced fresh apples, pears, or peaches, or frozen unsweetened peach slices, thawed

¼   cup dried cherries, cranberries, or mixed dried fruit bits

2   tablespoons sugar

1½   cups granola

3   tablespoons butter, melted

Vanilla ice cream (optional)

1 Place the sliced fruit and dried fruit into an ungreased 2-quart square baking dish; sprinkle with sugar. Combine the granola and melted butter; sprinkle over fruit.

2 Bake, uncovered, in a 350°F oven for 30 to 35 minutes or until fruit is tender. If desired, serve warm with ice cream.

Nutrition Facts per serving: 306 cal., 13 g total fat (5 g sat. fat), 16 mg chol., 66 mg sodium, 46 g carbo., 5 g fiber, 3 g pro.

Sliced, peeled pears make an equally delicious stand-in for the cooking apples.

APPLE CRUMBLE

6	cups sliced, peeled Granny Smith apples
¼	cup granulated sugar
¼	teaspoon ground cinnamon
1	tablespoon lemon juice
½	cup rolled oats
½	cup packed brown sugar
¼	cup all-purpose flour
1	teaspoon ground cinnamon
¼	teaspoon ground nutmeg
¼	cup cold butter
	Vanilla ice cream (optional)

PREP:
20 minutes
BAKE:
40 minutes
OVEN:
350°F
MAKES:
6 servings

1 In a large bowl toss apples with granulated sugar, the ¼ teaspoon cinnamon, and the lemon juice. Transfer to a lightly greased 2-quart square baking dish.

2 In a medium bowl combine oats, brown sugar, flour, the 1 teaspoon cinnamon, and the nutmeg. Using a pastry blender, cut in the cold butter until mixture resembles coarse crumbs. Sprinkle over apples in dish.

3 Bake, uncovered, in a 350°F oven for 40 to 45 minutes or until topping is golden and edges are bubbly. Serve warm. If desired, top with vanilla ice cream.

Nutrition Facts per serving: 285 cal., 9 g total fat (4 g sat. fat), 22 mg chol., 67 mg sodium, 52 g carbo., 4 g fiber, 2 g pro.

Tart and sweet combine in this crumbly, delicious dessert. Rhubarb provides the tangy tart and pineapple lends the sweetness.

RHUBARB-PINEAPPLE CRUMBLE

PREP:

10 minutes

STAND:

1 hour

BAKE:

45 minutes

OVEN:

350°F

MAKES:

6 to 8 servings

7	cups fresh or frozen rhubarb, cut into 1-inch pieces
1	8-ounce can pineapple tidbits (juice pack), drained
1	cup packed brown sugar
2	tablespoons cornstarch
2	teaspoons finely shredded lemon peel
⅔	cup all-purpose flour
¼	cup packed brown sugar
1	tablespoon granulated sugar
1	tablespoon chopped crystallized ginger
	Dash salt
3	tablespoons cold butter
	Whipped cream (optional)
	Chopped crystallized ginger (optional)

1 Thaw rhubarb, if frozen; drain well. In a large bowl combine rhubarb, pineapple, and the 1 cup brown sugar. Let stand for 1 hour. Drain mixture, reserving juices. Set fruit aside.

2 If necessary, add water to reserved fruit juices to equal ⅔ cup liquid. Place juices in a small saucepan. Stir in cornstarch. Cook and stir over medium heat until thickened and bubbly. Remove from heat. Stir into fruit and stir in lemon peel. Spoon into an ungreased 2-quart square baking dish; set aside.

3 In a small bowl combine flour, the ¼ cup brown sugar, the granulated sugar, the 1 tablespoon ginger, and salt. Using a pastry blender, cut in cold butter until mixture resembles coarse crumbs. Sprinkle over fruit.

4 Bake, uncovered, in a 350°F oven for 45 to 50 minutes or until topping is golden and edges are bubbly. Serve warm. If desired, top with whipped cream and additional ginger.

Nutrition Facts per serving: 362 cal., 7 g total fat (3 g sat. fat), 16 mg chol., 93 mg sodium, 76 g carbo., 4 g fiber, 3 g pro.

If you want an ice cream topper for this cranberry-infused crumble, break away from traditional vanilla—try a scoop of ginger ice cream instead.

PEACH OF A CRUMBLE

⅓ cup granulated sugar

2 tablespoons all-purpose flour

1 tablespoon cornstarch

5 cups sliced, peeled peaches or frozen unsweetened peach slices, thawed (do not drain)

1½ cups fresh or frozen cranberries

¼ cup butter, melted

1 tablespoon lemon juice

¾ cup all-purpose flour

½ cup packed brown sugar

¼ teaspoon baking powder

¼ teaspoon baking soda

⅛ teaspoon salt

3 tablespoons cold butter

¼ cup sliced almonds

PREP:
30 minutes
BAKE:
40 minutes
OVEN:
375°F
MAKES:
8 servings

1 In a large bowl combine granulated sugar, the 2 tablespoons flour, and the cornstarch. Add peaches and cranberries; toss gently to coat. Stir in melted butter and lemon juice. Spread peach mixture into an ungreased 2-quart square baking dish. Set aside.

2 For topping, in a small bowl combine the ¾ cup flour, the brown sugar, baking powder, baking soda, and salt. Using a pastry blender, cut in the cold butter until mixture resembles coarse crumbs. Sprinkle topping and almonds over fruit in dish.

3 Bake, uncovered, in a 375°F oven about 40 minutes or until topping is golden and edges are bubbly. Serve warm.

Nutrition Facts per serving: 307 cal., 13 g total fat (7 g sat. fat), 29 mg chol., 203 mg sodium, 47 g carbo., 4 g fiber, 3 g pro.

For the crowning glory, top each serving of this captivating crunch with a spoonful of whipped cream laced with your favorite fruit-flavored liqueur.

RHUBARB CRUNCH

PREP:

15 minutes

BAKE:

1 hour

COOL:

30 minutes

OVEN:

350°F

MAKES:

9 servings

1	cup all-purpose flour
1	cup quick-cooking rolled oats
1	cup packed brown sugar
1	teaspoon ground cinnamon
½	cup cold butter
4	cups diced fresh or frozen rhubarb
1	cup granulated sugar
2	tablespoons cornstarch
1	cup water
1	teaspoon vanilla
	Few drops red food coloring (optional)
	Whipped cream or vanilla ice cream (optional)

1 In a large bowl combine flour, oats, brown sugar, and cinnamon. Using a pastry blender, cut in cold butter until mixture resembles fine crumbs. Press half of the mixture into bottom of a lightly greased 2-quart square baking dish. Sprinkle rhubarb evenly over crust; set aside.

2 In a small saucepan combine granulated sugar and cornstarch; add the water. Cook and stir over medium heat until mixture is thickened and bubbly. Stir in vanilla and, if desired, red food coloring. Pour over rhubarb. Sprinkle with remaining crumb mixture.

3 Bake, uncovered, in a 350°F oven for 1 hour or until topping is golden and edges are bubbly. Cool for 30 minutes. Serve warm. If desired, top with whipped cream or ice cream.

Nutrition Facts per serving: 379 cal., 12 g total fat (7 g sat. fat), 29 mg chol., 124 mg sodium, 67 g carbo., 3 g fiber, 4 g pro.

Pecan-swirled biscuits make a tasty topping for this juicy, crowd-pleasing cobbler.

PEACH-PRALINE COBBLER

¾	cup packed brown sugar
¼	cup butter, melted
1½	cups chopped pecans
8	cups sliced, peeled peaches or frozen unsweetened peaches, thawed (do not drain)
1	cup granulated sugar
1	cup water
2	tablespoons cornstarch
1	teaspoon ground cinnamon
¾	cup milk
2	teaspoons lemon juice
2¼	cups all-purpose flour
2	teaspoons granulated sugar
2	teaspoons baking powder
½	teaspoon baking soda
½	teaspoon salt
½	cup shortening
	Half-and-half or light cream (optional)

PREP:
25 minutes
BAKE:
25 minutes
OVEN:
400°F
MAKES:
12 servings

1 For pecan filling, combine brown sugar and melted butter. Add pecans; toss to mix. Set aside.

2 In a Dutch oven combine peaches, the 1 cup granulated sugar, the water, cornstarch, and cinnamon. Cook and stir over medium heat until mixture is thickened and bubbly. Keep warm.

3 Combine milk and lemon juice; set aside. In a large bowl combine flour, the 2 teaspoons granulated sugar, the baking powder, baking soda, and salt. Using a pastry blender, cut in shortening until mixture resembles coarse crumbs. Make a well in the center; add milk mixture. Stir just until dough clings together.

4 On a lightly floured surface, knead dough gently for 10 to 12 strokes. Roll dough into a 12×8-inch rectangle; spread pecan filling over dough. Roll dough up from one of the long sides. Cut roll into twelve 1-inch slices.

5 Transfer hot peach mixture to an ungreased 3-quart rectangular baking dish. Place pecan roll slices, cut sides down, on top of the hot peach mixture. Bake, uncovered, in a 400°F oven about 25 minutes or until topping is golden. Serve warm. If desired, serve with half-and-half.

Nutrition Facts per serving: 511 cal., 23 g total fat (6 g sat. fat), 12 mg chol., 272 mg sodium, 76 g carbo., 7 g fiber, 6 g pro.

Rice pudding is a favorite dessert throughout Scandinavia. Tradition calls for a whole almond to be buried in the pudding—whoever finds it will be blessed with good luck.

CHRISTMAS RICE PUDDING

PREP:

30 minutes

BAKE:

1 hour 15 minutes

COOL:

10 minutes

OVEN:

325°F

MAKES:

8 to 10 servings

1½	cups water
½	teaspoon salt
¾	cup short grain or medium grain rice
2	cups half-and-half or light cream
1½	cups milk
⅔	cup sugar
2	beaten eggs
1	tablespoon butter, melted
½	teaspoon ground cardamom
1	whole almond, shelled
1	recipe Raspberry Sauce

1 In a medium saucepan bring the water and salt to boiling. Stir in rice; reduce heat. Cover and simmer for 12 to 15 minutes or until the rice has absorbed the water (rice still will be slightly crunchy).

2 In a large bowl combine the cooked rice, half-and-half, milk, sugar, eggs, melted butter, and cardamom. Transfer mixture to a buttered 2-quart casserole. Hide the almond in the pudding.

3 Place casserole in a large baking pan. (Make sure there is at least 1 inch of space between the casserole and the sides of the baking pan.) Pour boiling water into baking pan to reach halfway up sides of casserole.

4 Bake, uncovered, in a 325°F oven for 1 hour. Stir mixture. Bake for 15 minutes more. Remove casserole from water bath. Stir mixture once more. (Pudding should have a creamy texture.) Set aside to cool slightly.

5 Serve rice pudding warm with warm Raspberry Sauce.

RASPBERRY SAUCE: In a medium saucepan combine 2 tablespoons cornstarch and 2 tablespoons sugar. Stir in 1½ cups cranberry-raspberry juice and 1 teaspoon lemon juice. Cook and stir over medium heat until sauce is thickened and bubbly. Cook and stir for 2 minutes more. Remove from heat. Cover surface of sauce with plastic wrap; cool slightly without stirring.

Nutrition Facts per serving: 437 cal., 26 g total fat (16 g sat. fat), 143 mg chol., 230 mg sodium, 47 g carbo., 1 g fiber, 6 g pro.

Everyone will clamor for this rice pudding, which only gets better with a light drizzle of the Molasses-Chocolate Sauce.

INCREDIBLE RICE PUDDING

2	cups half-and-half, light cream, or whole milk
4	eggs
1/3	cup sugar
1/4	cup unsweetened cocoa powder
1	teaspoon vanilla
1	cup cooked white rice, cooled
4	ounces semisweet chocolate, chopped
1	recipe Molasses-Chocolate Sauce

PREP:

20 minutes

BAKE:

1 hour

OVEN:

325°F

MAKES:

6 to 8 servings

1 In a large bowl whisk together half-and-half, eggs, sugar, cocoa powder, and vanilla. Stir in rice and chocolate. Pour custard mixture into a 1½- or 2-quart casserole. Place dish in a 13×9×2-inch baking pan set on an oven rack. Carefully pour 1 inch of boiling water into baking pan.

2 Bake, uncovered, in a 325°F oven for 60 to 65 minutes or until a knife inserted near center comes out clean.

3 Serve rice pudding warm with warm Molasses-Chocolate Sauce.

MOLASSES-CHOCOLATE SAUCE: In a small saucepan combine ¼ cup packed brown sugar and 1 tablespoon cornstarch. Stir in ⅓ cup water, 2 tablespoons chocolate-flavored syrup, and 1 tablespoon molasses. Cook and stir over medium-low heat for 2 minutes or until thickened and bubbly.

Nutrition Facts per serving: 401 cal., 19 g total fat (11 g sat. fat), 172 mg chol., 84 mg sodium, 52 g carbo., 1 g fiber, 10 g pro.

Dating back to colonial America, betties are baked puddings made of layers of sugared and spiced fruit and buttered bread crumbs or cubes. Serve this to guests with ice cream and wow them with your knowledge of its historic origins.

PEACH-BERRY BETTY

PREP:

20 minutes

BAKE:

25 minutes

OVEN:

375°F

MAKES:

6 servings

$\frac{1}{2}$	cup sugar
1	tablespoon all-purpose flour
$\frac{1}{2}$	teaspoon ground nutmeg
3	cups sliced, peeled fresh peaches or nectarines
2	cups fresh raspberries or blueberries
$\frac{1}{4}$	cup orange juice or water
4	cups soft bread cubes
$\frac{1}{4}$	cup flaked coconut
2	tablespoons butter, melted
$\frac{1}{8}$	teaspoon ground nutmeg

1 For filling, combine sugar, flour, and the $\frac{1}{2}$ teaspoon nutmeg. Add peaches and raspberries. Stir in orange juice. Add 2 cups of the bread cubes, tossing to mix. Transfer to an ungreased 2-quart square baking dish.

2 For topping, combine the remaining 2 cups bread cubes and the coconut. Combine the melted butter and the $\frac{1}{8}$ teaspoon nutmeg. Drizzle over bread cube mixture. Toss gently to coat. Sprinkle topping over peach mixture in dish.

3 Bake, uncovered, in a 375°F oven for 25 to 35 minutes or until fruit is tender and topping is golden.

Nutrition Facts per serving: 236 cal., 7 g total fat (4 g sat. fat), 11 mg chol., 186 mg sodium, 43 g carbo., 6 g fiber, 3 g pro.

Welcome the Yuletide season with this heartwarming gingerbread. Brandy-flavored whipped cream is a delectable topper for this dessert.

GINGERBREAD WITH BRANDY CREAM

¼ cup granulated sugar

1 egg

⅓ cup butter, melted

2¼ cups all-purpose flour

1 teaspoon baking powder

1 teaspoon ground ginger

1 teaspoon ground cinnamon

½ teaspoon baking soda

¼ teaspoon salt

¾ cup hot water

¼ cup molasses

¼ cup honey

1 recipe Brandy Cream or Sweetened Whipped Cream
   Ground nutmeg (optional)

PREP:
20 minutes
BAKE:
20 minutes
OVEN:
350°F
MAKES:
9 servings

1 In a large mixing bowl beat sugar and egg with an electric mixer on medium speed for 1 minute. Add melted butter and beat until combined. Set aside.

2 In a medium bowl combine flour, baking powder, ginger, cinnamon, baking soda, and salt. In a small bowl combine the hot water, molasses, and honey. Alternately add flour mixture and molasses mixture to egg mixture, beating after each addition just until combined. Pour batter into a lightly greased 2-quart square baking pan.

3 Bake, uncovered, in a 350°F oven for 20 to 25 minutes or until a wooden toothpick inserted near the center comes out clean. Serve warm with Brandy Cream or Sweetened Whipped Cream. If desired, sprinkle with nutmeg.

BRANDY CREAM: In a medium mixing bowl beat ¾ cup whipping cream, ¼ cup sifted powdered sugar, and 1 tablespoon brandy with an electric mixer on medium speed until soft peaks form (tips curl).

SWEETENED WHIPPED CREAM: Prepare Brandy Cream as directed, except omit brandy.

Nutrition Facts per servings: 336 cal., 15 g total fat (8 g sat. fat), 70 mg chol., 232 mg sodium, 45 g carbo., 1 g fiber, 4 g pro.

A fudgy cake sparked with cocoa and raspberries, this dessert will be a hit at home or a party. If serving a larger group, simply cut it into 12 small pieces.

RASPBERRY FUDGE PUDDING CAKE

PREP:

30 minutes

BAKE:

40 minutes

COOL:

1 hour

OVEN:

350°F

MAKES:

6 servings

2	10-ounce packages frozen red raspberries in syrup, thawed
½	cup all-purpose flour
1	tablespoon unsweetened cocoa powder
1	teaspoon baking powder
2	tablespoons butter, softened
½	cup packed brown sugar
1	teaspoon vanilla
¼	cup milk
⅓	cup packed brown sugar
2	tablespoons unsweetened cocoa powder
	Sweetened Vanilla Whipped Cream or vanilla ice cream (optional)

1 Drain thawed berries, reserving ¾ cup syrup. Set aside.

2 In a small bowl combine flour, the 1 tablespoon cocoa powder, and the baking powder; set aside. In a medium mixing bowl beat butter with an electric mixer on medium speed for 30 seconds. Add the ½ cup brown sugar and the vanilla; beat until well combined. Alternately add flour mixture and milk, beating until smooth after each addition.

3 Spread batter into a greased 2-quart square baking dish. Spoon drained raspberries over batter. Pour reserved raspberry syrup on top. Combine the ⅓ cup brown sugar and the 2 tablespoons cocoa powder; sprinkle evenly over batter.

4 Bake, uncovered, in a 350°F oven about 40 minutes or until a wooden toothpick inserted about ½ inch into the cake portion comes out clean. Cool about 1 hour on a wire rack. If desired, serve warm with Sweetened Vanilla Whipped Cream or ice cream.

Nutrition Facts per serving: 367 cal., 5 g total fat (2 g sat. fat), 12 mg chol., 114 mg sodium, 79 g carbo., 3 g fiber, 3 g pro.

SWEETENED VANILLA WHIPPED CREAM: In a medium mixing bowl beat ⅔ cup whipping cream, 2 tablespoons sugar, and 1 teaspoon vanilla with an electric mixer on medium speed until soft peaks form (tips curl).

This pumpkin pie-inspired dish is sure to be your family's new fall favorite.

HARVEST PUMPKIN COBBLER

1	15-ounce can pumpkin
1	5-ounce can ($\frac{2}{3}$ cup) evaporated milk
1	slightly beaten egg
$\frac{1}{3}$	cup granulated sugar
$\frac{1}{4}$	cup packed brown sugar
$1\frac{1}{2}$	teaspoons all-purpose flour
1	teaspoon pumpkin pie spice
$\frac{1}{8}$	teaspoon salt
$\frac{1}{2}$	cup all-purpose flour
$\frac{1}{2}$	cup granulated sugar
$1\frac{1}{2}$	teaspoons baking powder
$\frac{1}{8}$	teaspoon salt
$\frac{1}{2}$	cup milk
$\frac{1}{4}$	cup butter, melted
$\frac{1}{2}$	teaspoon vanilla

PREP:
25 minutes
BAKE:
45 minutes
OVEN:
350°F
MAKES:
6 to 8 servings

1 For filling, in a medium bowl combine pumpkin, evaporated milk, and egg. Add the $\frac{1}{3}$ cup granulated sugar, the brown sugar, the $1\frac{1}{2}$ teaspoons flour, the pumpkin pie spice, and $\frac{1}{8}$ teaspoon salt. Whisk lightly just until combined; set aside.

2 In a medium bowl combine the $\frac{1}{2}$ cup flour, the $\frac{1}{2}$ cup granulated sugar, the baking powder, and $\frac{1}{8}$ teaspoon salt. Stir in milk, 2 tablespoons of the melted butter, and the vanilla. Pour remaining 2 tablespoons melted butter into a 2-quart square baking dish, tilting dish to coat. Pour batter into dish, spreading evenly. Spoon pumpkin mixture on top.

3 Bake, uncovered, in a 350°F oven for 45 to 50 minutes or until top is golden. Serve warm.

Nutrition Facts per serving: 431 cal., 12 g total fat (6 g sat. fat), 65 mg chol., 269 mg sodium, 75 g carbo., 3 g fiber, 12 g pro.

A variety of flavors—polenta, pecans, apples, and brown sugar—spices this twist on a traditional apple cobbler. It's perfect as an after-dinner treat or as a brunch or breakfast dish.

POLENTA-PECAN APPLE COBBLER

PREP:
15 minutes

BAKE:
25 minutes

COOL:
30 minutes

OVEN:
375°F

MAKES:
6 servings

½	cup all-purpose flour
⅓	cup quick-cooking polenta mix or yellow cornmeal
2	tablespoons granulated sugar
1	teaspoon baking powder
½	teaspoon salt
3	tablespoons cold butter
½	cup chopped pecans
2	tablespoons packed brown sugar
½	teaspoon ground cinnamon
2	21-ounce cans apple pie filling
⅓	cup half-and-half or light cream
	Half-and-half or light cream (optional)

1 For topping, in a medium bowl combine flour, polenta mix, granulated sugar, baking powder, and salt. Using a pastry blender, cut in cold butter until mixture resembles coarse crumbs; set aside. In a small bowl combine pecans, brown sugar, and cinnamon; set aside.

2 In a medium saucepan heat apple pie filling over medium heat until bubbly, stirring frequently. Cover to keep warm; set aside. Add the ⅓ cup half-and-half to the flour mixture, stirring just until moistened.

3 Transfer hot apple pie filling to an ungreased 2-quart square baking dish. Using a spoon, immediately drop topping in small mounds onto filling. Sprinkle evenly with pecan mixture.

4 Bake, uncovered, in a 375°F oven about 25 minutes or until topping is golden. Cool about 30 minutes on a wire rack before serving. If desired, serve with half-and-half.

Nutrition Facts per serving: 441 cal., 15 g total fat (6 g sat. fat), 22 mg chol., 498 mg sodium, 77 g carbo., 4 g fiber, 4 g pro.

Mouthwatering mounds of cobbler raise the goodness of sweet peaches and tart cherries. This truly tasty summer dessert will disappear fast with a hefty scoop of ice cream!

CHERRY-PEACH COBBLER

1	cup all-purpose flour
2	tablespoons sugar
1½	teaspoons baking powder
¼	teaspoon ground nutmeg
2	tablespoons cold butter
½	cup sugar
4	teaspoons cornstarch
⅓	cup water
3	cups sliced, peeled peaches or frozen unsweetened peach slices, thawed (do not drain)
2	cups fresh or frozen unsweetened pitted tart red cherries
⅓	cup dairy sour cream
1	slightly beaten egg
	Ground nutmeg (optional)
	Ice cream (optional)

PREP:
35 minutes
BAKE:
20 minutes
COOL:
10 minutes
OVEN:
400°F
MAKES:
6 servings

1 For topping, in a medium bowl combine flour, the 2 tablespoons sugar, the baking powder, and the ¼ teaspoon nutmeg. Using a pastry blender, cut in cold butter until mixture resembles coarse crumbs. Set aside.

2 For filling, in a large saucepan combine the ½ cup sugar and the cornstarch. Stir in the water. Add peach slices and cherries. Cook and stir over medium heat until thickened and bubbly. Cover to keep warm; set aside.

3 Combine sour cream and egg. Add sour cream mixture to topping mixture, stirring just until moistened.

4 Transfer filling to an ungreased 2-quart square baking dish. Using a spoon, immediately drop topping mixture in 6 mounds directly onto filling.

5 Bake, uncovered, in a 400°F oven for 20 to 25 minutes or until topping is golden and a wooden toothpick inserted into topping comes out clean. Cool slightly. If desired, sprinkle with additional ground nutmeg and serve warm with ice cream.

Nutrition Facts per serving: 287 cal., 7 g total fat (4 g sat. fat), 51 mg chol., 108 mg sodium, 53 g carbo., 3 g fiber, 4 g pro.

A slump is an old-fashioned New England fruit dessert—usually berries topped with biscuit dough.

STRAWBERRY-RHUBARB SLUMP

PREP:

25 minutes

BAKE:

20 minutes

OVEN:

400°F

MAKES:

8 servings

4	cups fresh whole strawberries
4	cups fresh or frozen unsweetened sliced rhubarb
½	to ¾ cup granulated sugar
¼	cup water
2	tablespoons apple juice
1	tablespoon cornstarch
1	cup all-purpose flour
¼	cup granulated sugar
1	teaspoon baking powder
¼	teaspoon baking soda
¼	teaspoon salt
¼	cup cold butter
½	cup buttermilk or sour milk*
½	teaspoon almond extract
	Coarse sugar or granulated sugar

1 Halve any large strawberries. In a large skillet combine strawberries, rhubarb, the ½ cup granulated sugar, and the water. Bring to boiling; reduce heat. Cover and simmer for 10 minutes. Combine apple juice and cornstarch; add to fruit in skillet. Cook and stir until thickened and bubbly. Transfer mixture to an ungreased 2-quart baking dish; keep warm.

2 Meanwhile, for topping, in a medium bowl combine flour, the ¼ cup granulated sugar, the baking powder, baking soda, and salt. Using a pastry blender, cut in cold butter until mixture resembles coarse crumbs. Combine buttermilk and almond extract; add to flour mixture, stirring just until moistened. Using a spoon, immediately drop topping in 8 mounds onto filling.

3 Sprinkle top with coarse sugar. Bake, uncovered, in a 400°F oven about 20 minutes or until topping is golden. Serve warm.

*NOTE: To make ½ cup sour milk, place 1½ teaspoons lemon juice or vinegar into a glass measuring cup. Add enough milk to make ½ cup liquid; stir. Let the mixture stand for 5 minutes before using.

Nutrition Facts per serving: 229 cal., 7 g total fat (3 g sat. fat), 17 mg chol., 205 mg sodium, 41 g carbo., 3 g fiber, 3 g pro.

This cobblerlike fruit casserole saves you time. Instead of measuring oatmeal for the topping, all you have to do is open a package of instant oatmeal—all of the spices already have been added.

CRANBERRY-APPLE CASSEROLE

⅔ cup granulated sugar

2 tablespoons all-purpose flour

4 cups sliced, peeled apples

2 cups fresh or frozen cranberries

2 1.23-ounce envelopes instant oatmeal with cinnamon and spice

¾ cup chopped pecans

½ cup packed brown sugar

⅓ cup all-purpose flour

⅓ cup butter, melted

PREP:
20 minutes
BAKE:
45 minutes
OVEN:
350°F
MAKES:
8 servings

1 In a large bowl combine granulated sugar and the 2 tablespoons flour. Add apple slices and cranberries; toss to coat. Transfer the fruit mixture to an ungreased 2-quart casserole.

2 For topping, in a medium bowl combine oatmeal, pecans, brown sugar, and the ⅓ cup flour. Stir in melted butter until moistened. Sprinkle topping over fruit.

3 Bake, uncovered, in a 350°F oven about 45 minutes or until fruit is tender. If necessary, cover loosely with foil the last 10 minutes of baking to prevent overbrowning. Serve warm.

Nutrition Facts per serving: 372 cal., 16 g total fat (6 g sat. fat), 22 mg chol., 148 mg sodium, 58 g carbo., 4 g fiber, 3 g pro.

Dessert trends come and go, but a decadent, gooey, and chocolatey treat always is in style. This homespun pudding cake cousin combines two favorite flavors—chocolate and peanut butter.

CHOCOLATE-PEANUT BUTTER CASSEROLE

PREP:

15 minutes

BAKE:

35 minutes

OVEN:

350°F

MAKES:

6 servings

½ cup all-purpose flour

¾ cup sugar

¾ teaspoon baking powder

⅓ cup milk

1 tablespoon cooking oil

1 teaspoon vanilla

¼ cup peanut butter

⅓ cup semisweet chocolate pieces

¼ cup unsweetened cocoa powder

¾ cup boiling water

⅓ cup coarsely chopped honey-roasted peanuts

2 tablespoons crumbled chocolate graham crackers (optional)

   Whipped cream (optional)

1 In a medium bowl combine flour, ¼ cup of the sugar, and the baking powder. Add milk, oil, and vanilla. Whisk until smooth. Stir in peanut butter and chocolate pieces.

2 Pour batter into an ungreased 1-quart casserole. Set aside. In the same medium bowl combine the remaining ½ cup sugar and the cocoa powder. Gradually stir in the boiling water. Pour mixture over batter in casserole.

3 Bake, uncovered, in a 350°F oven for 35 to 40 minutes or until a wooden toothpick inserted into the cake portion comes out clean. Remove from oven; top with peanuts and, if desired, crumbled graham crackers. Serve warm. If desired, top with whipped cream.

Nutrition Facts per serving: 333 cal., 15 g total fat (3 g sat. fat), 1 mg chol., 170 mg sodium, 42 g carbo., 3 g fiber, 7 g pro.

FISH & SEAFOOD

This is is not your ordinary tuna casserole. Cheese, water chestnuts, red sweet peppers, and broccoli make it supreme!

BAKED TUNA SUPREME

PREP:

25 minutes

BAKE:

20 minutes

OVEN:

350°F

MAKES:

6 servings

1	10-ounce package frozen chopped broccoli
1	9-ounce can tuna, drained and flaked
1	8-ounce can sliced water chestnuts, drained
½	of a 7-ounce jar roasted red sweet peppers, drained and cut into strips (½ cup)
1	10¾-ounce can condensed cream of mushroom soup
4	ounces sharp process American cheese slices, torn
¼	cup milk
1	cup soft bread crumbs*
1	tablespoon butter, melted
¼	teaspoon dried dillweed

1 Cook broccoli according to package directions, except omit salt; drain. Arrange cooked broccoli in an ungreased 2-quart square baking dish. Top with tuna. Sprinkle evenly with water chestnuts and roasted sweet pepper strips.

2 In a medium saucepan combine soup, cheese, and milk; cook and stir over medium heat until cheese is melted. Pour over tuna mixture in dish. In a small bowl combine bread crumbs, melted butter, and dillweed; sprinkle over top.

3 Bake, uncovered, in a 350°F oven for 20 to 25 minutes or until heated through.

*NOTE: Use a blender or food processor to make fluffy soft bread crumbs. One slice yields ¾ cup crumbs.

Nutrition Facts per serving: 287 cal., 16 g total fat (7 g sat. fat), 42 mg chol., 869 mg sodium, 22 g carbo., 2 g fiber, 18 g pro.

You'll be amazed at how easy it is to turn a can of tuna into a colorful entrée.
Serve alongside a tossed green salad with a tart dressing for a pleasing contrast.

DEEP-DISH TUNA PIE

½	of an 11-ounce package piecrust mix (1⅓ cups)
1	cup chopped onion (1 large)
1	cup diced, peeled potato
1	10¾-ounce can condensed cream of mushroom soup
⅓	cup milk
⅓	cup grated Parmesan cheese
1	tablespoon lemon juice
¾	teaspoon dried dillweed
¼	teaspoon black pepper
1	16-ounce package frozen mixed vegetables
1	9-ounce can tuna (water pack), drained and broken into chunks

PREP:
25 minutes
BAKE:
40 minutes
OVEN:
400°F
MAKES:
6 servings

1 Prepare piecrust mix according to package directions, except do not roll out. Cover dough; set aside.

2 In a covered large skillet cook onion and potato in a small amount of boiling water about 7 minutes or until tender. Drain. Stir in soup, milk, Parmesan cheese, lemon juice, dillweed, and pepper. Cook and stir until bubbly. Gently stir in vegetables and tuna. Spoon mixture into an ungreased 2-quart casserole.

3 On a lightly floured surface, roll piecrust dough into a circle 2 inches larger than the diameter of the top of the casserole. Make several 1-inch slits near the center of the pastry. Center pastry over casserole, allowing pastry to hang over edge. Trim pastry ½ inch beyond edge of casserole. Turn pastry under; flute to the casserole edge, pressing gently.

4 Bake in a 400°F oven for 40 to 45 minutes or until crust is golden. Serve immediately.

Nutrition Facts per serving: 347 cal., 15 g total fat (5 g sat. fat), 23 mg chol., 834 mg sodium, 35 g carbo., 4 g fiber, 18 g pro.

A double dose of cheddar cheese plus green chiles and salsa give this creamy comfort food a Mexican twist.

CHEESY MEXICALI TUNA BAKE

PREP:

25 minutes

BAKE:

35 minutes

OVEN:

375°F

MAKES:

6 servings

2¼ cups dried medium noodles (about 5 ounces)

1 11-ounce can condensed nacho cheese soup

½ cup dairy sour cream

½ cup milk

1 4-ounce can diced green chile peppers, undrained

1 tablespoon dried minced onion

1 12-ounce can tuna (water pack), drained and flaked

½ cup shredded cheddar or Monterey Jack cheese (2 ounces)

1 cup coarsely broken nacho cheese-flavored tortilla chips or plain tortilla chips

   Purchased salsa

   Dairy sour cream

1 Cook noodles according to package directions; drain. Set aside.

2 In a large bowl combine soup, the ½ cup sour cream, and the milk. Stir in undrained chile peppers and dried onion. Fold in cooked noodles and tuna. Spoon into an ungreased 1½-quart casserole.

3 Bake, covered, in a 375°F oven for 30 minutes. Uncover. Sprinkle with cheese; top with chips. Bake, uncovered, for 5 to 10 minutes more or until heated through. Serve with salsa and additional sour cream.

Nutrition Facts per serving: 375 cal., 17 g total fat (9 g sat. fat), 77 mg chol., 810 mg sodium, 30 g carbo., 2 g fiber, 24 g pro.

For a faster version of the sauce, substitute a 10³/₄-ounce can condensed cream of mushroom soup mixed with ³/₄ cup milk.

TUNA-NOODLE CASSEROLE

3   cups dried medium noodles (4 ounces)
     or 1 cup dried elbow macaroni (3¹/₂ ounces)

¹/₂   cup soft bread crumbs*

1   tablespoon butter, melted

1   cup chopped celery

¹/₄   cup chopped onion

¹/₄   cup butter or margarine

¹/₄   cup all-purpose flour

¹/₂   teaspoon salt

¹/₂   teaspoon dry mustard

¹/₄   teaspoon black pepper

2   cups milk

1   9-ounce can tuna, drained and broken into chunks,
     or two 6-ounce cans skinless, boneless salmon, drained

1   cup cubed cheddar cheese (4 ounces)

¹/₄   cup chopped roasted red sweet pepper or pimiento

PREP:
25 minutes
BAKE:
20 minutes
OVEN:
375°F
MAKES:
4 servings

1 Cook noodles according to package directions; drain. Set aside. Meanwhile, combine bread crumbs and 1 tablespoon melted butter; set aside.

2 For sauce, in a medium saucepan cook celery and onion in the ¹/₄ cup butter until tender. Stir in flour, salt, dry mustard, and black pepper. Add milk all at once; cook and stir until slightly thickened and bubbly.

3 Combine sauce, tuna or salmon, cheese cubes, roasted sweet pepper or pimiento, and cooked noodles. Transfer to a 1¹/₂-quart casserole. Sprinkle with crumb mixture.

4 Bake, uncovered, in a 375°F oven for 20 to 25 minutes or until bubbly and topping is golden.

NOTE: Use a blender or food processor to make fluffy soft bread crumbs. One slice yields ³/₄ cup crumbs.

Nutrition Facts per serving: 588 cal., 34 g total fat (18 g sat. fat), 127 mg chol., 986 mg sodium, 37 g carbo., 2 g fiber, 34 g pro.

Here classic tuna-rice casserole gets an update with broccoli cheese soup and roasted red peppers. Squeeze lemon over the dish—it adds a nice zing, especially if you use the salmon option.

TUNA & RICE BAKE

PREP:

25 minutes

BAKE:

30 minutes

OVEN:

350°F

MAKES:

6 servings

1   10¾-ounce can condensed broccoli cheese soup

1   cup cooked white rice

¼   cup chopped bottled roasted red sweet pepper

2   teaspoons dried parsley flakes, crushed

4   beaten egg yolks

1   6-ounce can tuna or skinless, boneless salmon, drained and flaked

4   egg whites

Lemon wedges (optional)

1 In a medium saucepan combine soup, cooked rice, roasted sweet pepper, and parsley; cook and stir over medium heat until heated through. Remove from heat. Gradually stir into egg yolks. Fold in tuna or salmon; set aside.

2 In a large mixing bowl beat egg whites with an electric mixer on high speed until stiff peaks form (tips stand straight). Fold about 1 cup of the beaten egg whites into tuna mixture. Fold in remaining beaten whites. Spoon into an ungreased 2-quart casserole.

3 Bake, uncovered, in a 350°F oven for 30 to 35 minutes or until a knife inserted near the center comes out clean. Serve immediately. If desired, pass lemon wedges to squeeze over each serving.

Nutrition Facts per serving: 190 cal., 9 g total fat (3 g sat. fat), 151 mg chol., 507 mg sodium, 12 g carbo., 1 g fiber, 15 g pro.

This is not your mother's tuna-noodle casserole. Italian-style ingredients—artichoke hearts, dried tomatoes, olives, and mozzarella cheese—give it a worldly update.

MEDITERRANEAN TUNA CASSEROLE

4	ounces dried fettuccine, broken
¼	cup chopped onion
1	tablespoon butter
1	10¾-ounce can condensed cream of chicken soup
1	9- to 12-ounce can solid white tuna (water pack), drained and broken into chunks
1	8- to 9-ounce package frozen artichoke hearts, thawed and cut up
⅔	cup milk
½	cup shredded mozzarella cheese (2 ounces)
3	tablespoons oil-packed dried tomatoes, drained and snipped
3	tablespoons sliced pitted ripe olives
½	teaspoon dried thyme, crushed
3	tablespoons grated Parmesan cheese

PREP:
25 minutes
BAKE:
40 minutes
STAND:
10 minutes
OVEN:
350°F
MAKES:
6 servings

1 Cook fettuccine according to package directions; drain.

2 Meanwhile, in a large skillet cook onion in hot butter over medium heat until tender. Remove from heat. Stir in soup, tuna, artichoke hearts, milk, mozzarella cheese, dried tomatoes, olives, and thyme. Stir in cooked fettuccine. Transfer to a lightly greased 2-quart rectangular baking dish. Sprinkle with Parmesan cheese.

3 Bake, covered, in a 350°F oven for 20 minutes. Uncover and bake about 20 minutes more or until casserole is bubbly. Let stand for 10 minutes before serving.

MAKE-AHEAD DIRECTIONS: Assemble as directed. Cover unbaked casserole with plastic wrap and chill up to 24 hours. Remove plastic wrap and cover with foil. Bake in a 350°F oven for 35 minutes. Uncover and bake about 15 minutes more or until casserole is bubbly. Let stand for 10 minutes before serving.

Nutrition Facts per serving: 280 cal., 11 g total fat (5 g sat. fat), 37 mg chol., 732 mg sodium, 25 g carbo., 4 g fiber, 19 g pro.

Kids will love this biscuit-topped casserole, and so will the cook—it takes less than 50 minutes.

SURPRISE TUNA PIE

PREP:

25 minutes

BAKE:

15 minutes

OVEN:

425°F

MAKES:

4 servings

1	cup packaged biscuit mix
1/3	cup milk
1/2	cup 1/4-inch cubes or shredded process American cheese (2 ounces)
2	tablespoons butter
2	tablespoons all-purpose flour
1/4	teaspoon salt
	Dash black pepper
1 3/4	cups milk
1	teaspoon instant chicken bouillon granules
1	9-ounce can tuna, drained and flaked
1	10-ounce package frozen peas and carrots, thawed
1/3	cup chopped green sweet pepper
2	tablespoons chopped pimiento
2	tablespoons chopped onion

1 In a medium bowl combine biscuit mix and milk. Stir just until combined. Stir in cheese; set aside.

2 In a medium saucepan melt butter over medium heat. Stir in flour, salt, and black pepper. Add milk and bouillon granules all at once. Cook and stir until thickened and bubbly. Add tuna, peas and carrots, sweet pepper, pimiento, and onion. Bring mixture to boiling.

3 Transfer to a 2-quart casserole. Drop the biscuit mixture in 8 mounds onto hot tuna mixture. Bake in a 425°F oven for 15 to 20 minutes or until biscuits are golden.

Nutrition Facts per serving: 476 cal., 23 g total fat (9 g sat. fat), 51 mg chol., 1,334 mg sodium, 37 g carbo., 3 g fiber, 31 g pro.

A creamy tuna mixture bubbles underneath a hot biscuit topping for a satisfying supper.

TUNA WITH CHEESE BISCUITS

½   cup chopped onion

½   cup chopped green sweet pepper

3   tablespoons butter

1   10¾-ounce can condensed cream of chicken soup

1   cup milk

1   9-ounce can tuna, drained and flaked

2   teaspoons lemon juice

1   7¾-ounce package cheese-garlic or 3-cheese complete biscuit mix

PREP:
20 minutes
BAKE:
30 minutes
OVEN:
425°F
MAKES:
4 to 6 servings

1 In a large saucepan cook onion and sweet pepper in butter over medium heat until tender. Stir in soup and milk. Cook and stir until bubbly. Stir in tuna and lemon juice.

2 Transfer to an ungreased 1½-quart casserole. Bake, uncovered, in a 425°F oven for 15 minutes.

3 Meanwhile, prepare biscuit mix according to package directions. Drop batter in 6 mounds onto hot tuna mixture. Bake for 15 to 20 minutes more or until biscuits are golden and a wooden toothpick inserted in the center of a biscuit comes out clean.

Nutrition Facts per serving: 564 cal., 31 g total fat (12 g sat. fat), 46 mg chol., 1,470 mg sodium, 45 g carbo., 1 g fiber, 26 g pro.

Mmmm! You'll love the way refrigerated Alfredo sauce adds a creamy richness to this so easy casserole. Baking time is so short—you'll have more time to indulge!

TUNA ALFREDO CASSEROLE

PREP:

20 minutes

BAKE:

10 minutes

OVEN:

425°F

MAKES:

6 servings

3 cups dried rigatoni or penne pasta

1 10-ounce container refrigerated Alfredo or four-cheese pasta sauce, or 1¼ cups bottled Alfredo or four-cheese pasta sauce

3 tablespoons milk

2 tablespoons purchased dried tomato pesto

1 12-ounce can solid white tuna (water pack), drained and broken into chunks

¼ cup shredded Parmesan cheese (1 ounce)

1 Cook pasta according to package directions; drain. Return pasta to pan. Meanwhile, for sauce, in a medium bowl combine Alfredo sauce, milk, and pesto. Add sauce to cooked pasta, stirring gently to coat. Gently fold in tuna.

2 Transfer to an ungreased 2-quart baking dish. Sprinkle with cheese. Bake, uncovered, in a 425°F oven for 10 to 15 minutes or until heated through and cheese is just melted.

Nutrition Facts per serving: 453 cal., 24 g total fat (4 g sat. fat), 53 mg chol., 587 mg sodium, 35 g carbo., 2 g fiber, 24 g pro.

This casserole transcends the ho-hum, thanks to added richness from mayonnaise, flavor and color from roasted red sweet pepper, and an irresistible buttery crumb topping.

TUNA-MACARONI CASSEROLE

4	ounces dried small shell macaroni (1 cup)
1	10¾-ounce can condensed cream of onion soup
⅓	cup milk
¼	cup mayonnaise or salad dressing
½	teaspoon dry mustard
1	6-ounce can tuna, drained and flaked
1	cup shredded American or cheddar cheese (4 ounces)
½	cup chopped roasted red sweet pepper
¼	cup fine dry bread crumbs
1	tablespoon butter, melted
½	teaspoon paprika
	Snipped fresh parsley (optional)

PREP:
25 minutes
BAKE:
40 minutes
OVEN:
350°F
MAKES:
4 servings

1 Cook macaroni according to package directions; drain. In a large bowl combine soup, milk, mayonnaise, and mustard. Stir in tuna, cheese, and roasted sweet pepper. Gently fold in cooked macaroni. Transfer to an ungreased 1½-quart casserole.

2 In a small bowl combine bread crumbs, melted butter, and paprika; sprinkle over macaroni mixture.

3 Bake, uncovered, in a 350°F oven for 40 to 45 minutes or until heated through. If desired, sprinkle with parsley.

Nutrition Facts per serving: 498 cal., 29 g total fat (11 g sat. fat), 72 mg chol., 1,394 mg sodium, 36 g carbo., 2 g fiber, 23 g pro.

Captivating toppers, such as chutney, orange peel, coconut, and peanuts, add flavorful dimension to this Indian-style casserole.

BAKED SHRIMP CURRY

PREP:

30 minutes

BAKE:

15 minutes

OVEN:

400°F

MAKES:

4 servings

1   pound fresh or frozen cooked, peeled, and deveined medium shrimp

2   tablespoons butter

1   tablespoon all-purpose flour

1½ teaspoons curry powder

¼   teaspoon paprika

    Dash ground nutmeg

1   cup half-and-half, light cream, or milk

1   tablespoon dry sherry (optional)

1   teaspoon lemon juice

1   teaspoon grated fresh ginger

    Dash Worcestershire sauce

2   cups hot cooked white rice

    Chutney, finely shredded orange peel, flaked coconut, and/or chopped peanuts (optional)

1 Thaw shrimp, if frozen. Rinse shrimp; pat dry with paper towels. Set aside.

2 In a saucepan melt butter over medium heat. Stir in flour, curry powder, paprika, and nutmeg. Add half-and-half all at once. Cook and stir until thickened and bubbly. Cook and stir 1 minute more. Stir in shrimp, sherry (if desired), lemon juice, ginger, and Worcestershire sauce; heat through. Transfer to an ungreased 1-quart casserole.

3 Bake, uncovered, in a 400°F oven about 15 minutes or until bubbly and lightly browned. Serve with rice. If desired, pass chutney, orange peel, coconut, and/or peanuts.

Nutrition Facts per serving: 358 cal., 15 g total fat (9 g sat. fat), 260 mg chol., 342 mg sodium, 27 g carbo., 1 g fiber, 28 g pro.

Dried Italian seasoning is a real time-saver—measuring just one ingredient yields a windfall of herbs. Brands vary, but most include basil, oregano, thyme, and rosemary.

SHRIMP ITALIAN

4	ounces dried penne or gemelli pasta (about 1 cup)
8	ounces fresh or frozen cooked, peeled, and deveined medium shrimp
½	cup chopped onion (1 medium)
1	tablespoon butter
1	10¾-ounce can condensed cream of shrimp or cream of mushroom soup
⅔	cup half-and-half or light cream
1	4-ounce can (drained weight) sliced mushrooms, drained
⅓	cup grated Parmesan cheese
1	teaspoon dried Italian seasoning, crushed
3	tablespoons grated Parmesan cheese

1 Cook pasta according to package directions; drain. Set aside. Thaw shrimp, if frozen. Set aside.

2 In a medium saucepan cook onion in hot butter over medium heat until tender. Stir in shrimp, soup, half-and-half, mushrooms, the ⅓ cup Parmesan cheese, and the Italian seasoning. Stir in cooked pasta. Transfer to an ungreased 1½-quart casserole. Sprinkle with the 3 tablespoons Parmesan cheese.

3 Bake, uncovered, in a 350°F oven about 40 minutes or until heated through.

Nutrition Facts per serving: 365 cal., 16 g total fat (8 g sat. fat), 154 mg chol., 1,036 mg sodium, 32 g carbo., 3 g fiber, 23 g pro.

PREP:
25 minutes
BAKE:
40 minutes
OVEN:
350°F
MAKES:
4 to 6 servings

Stop by your supermarket's fish department or deli counter to find the cooked shrimp.

SHRIMP BAKE

PREP:

25 minutes

BAKE:

40 minutes

STAND:

5 minutes

OVEN:

350°F

MAKES:

6 servings

2/3   cup long grain rice

1   10¾-ounce can condensed cream of celery soup

1   10-ounce package frozen cut asparagus, thawed

8   ounces cooked, peeled, and deveined medium shrimp

1   8-ounce can sliced water chestnuts, drained

½   cup milk

1   tablespoon sliced green onion

½   teaspoon salt

½   teaspoon dried dillweed

1 Cook rice according to package directions. In a large bowl combine cooked rice, soup, asparagus, shrimp, water chestnuts, milk, green onion, salt, and dillweed. Transfer to an ungreased 1½-quart casserole.

2 Bake, covered, in a 350°F oven for 40 to 45 minutes or until heated through. Let stand for 5 minutes before serving.

Nutrition Facts per serving: 232 cal., 6 g total fat (1 g sat. fat), 77 mg chol., 683 mg sodium, 34 g carbo., 2 g fiber, 13 g pro.

This hearty stuffing bake is your ticket to stretching twelve ounces of shrimp to feed four.

SHRIMP & STUFFING BAKE

12	ounces fresh or frozen peeled and deveined medium shrimp
½	cup chopped celery (1 stalk)
½	cup chopped onion (1 medium)
2	tablespoons butter
1	10¾-ounce can condensed cream of shrimp or cream of celery soup
¼	cup milk
½	teaspoon ground sage
¼	teaspoon dried thyme, crushed
	Dash black pepper
2	beaten eggs
4	cups dry French bread cubes*

PREP:
30 minutes
BAKE:
45 minutes
STAND:
10 minutes
OVEN:
350°F
MAKES:
4 servings

1 Thaw shrimp, if frozen. Rinse shrimp; pat dry with paper towels. In a large saucepan cook shrimp in a large amount of boiling water for 1 to 3 minutes or just until shrimp turn opaque. Drain well; set aside.

2 In same saucepan cook celery and onion in hot butter over medium heat until tender. Stir in soup, milk, sage, thyme, and pepper. Add eggs; mix well. Fold in dry bread cubes and cooked shrimp. Transfer to an ungreased 1½-quart casserole.

3 Bake, covered, in a 350°F oven for 30 minutes. Uncover; bake about 15 minutes more or until set in center. Let stand, covered, for 10 minutes before serving.

*NOTE: **To dry the bread cubes, spread cubes in a 15×10×1-inch baking pan. Bake in a 300°F oven for 10 to 15 minutes or until bread cubes are dry, stirring twice. Cool. (Bread cubes will continue to dry and crisp as they cool.) Or let bread cubes stand, loosely covered, at room temperature for 8 to 12 hours.**

Nutrition Facts per serving: 375 cal., 15 g total fat (7 g sat. fat), 263 mg chol., 1,099 mg sodium, 32 g carbo., 2 g fiber, 27 g pro.

Be sure to use bay scallops to make these luscious cheese-sauced enchiladas. They don't water-out as much as sea scallops and their meat is more succulent.

BAYSIDE ENCHILADAS

PREP:

30 minutes

BAKE:

30 minutes

STAND:

10 minutes

OVEN:

350°F

MAKES:

6 servings

½   pound fresh or frozen medium shrimp in shells

½   pound fresh or frozen bay scallops

1   8-ounce carton dairy sour cream

½   cup purchased salsa

2   cups shredded Monterey Jack cheese (8 ounces)

6   7- to 8-inch flour tortillas

¼   cup cottage cheese

¼   cup milk

2   tablespoons grated Parmesan cheese

¼   cup sliced green onions (2)

¼   cup sliced pitted ripe olives

1 Thaw shrimp and scallops, if frozen. Peel and devein shrimp. Rinse shrimp and scallops; pat dry with paper towels. Set aside.

2 In a large bowl combine sour cream and salsa. Stir in shrimp, scallops, and 1 cup of the Monterey Jack cheese. Spoon about ½ cup of the shrimp mixture onto each tortilla near an edge; roll up. Place filled tortillas, seam sides down, in a lightly greased 3-quart rectangular baking dish; set aside.

3 In a blender or food processor, combine cottage cheese, milk, and Parmesan cheese. Cover and blend or process until nearly smooth (mixture will be thin). Pour mixture over filled tortillas in dish. Sprinkle with green onions and olives.

4 Bake, uncovered, in a 350°F oven for 25 minutes. Sprinkle with the remaining 1 cup Monterey Jack cheese. Bake for 5 minutes more or until cheese melts. Cover and let stand for 10 minutes before serving.

Nutrition Facts per serving: 404 cal., 24 g total fat (13 g sat. fat), 109 mg chol., 604 mg sodium, 20 g carbo., 1 g fiber, 27 g pro.

Salsa verde is "green salsa," which typically is based on tomatillos, green chiles, and cilantro. In this Mexican shrimp casserole, it provides the heat.

FIESTA TORTILLA-SHRIMP CASSEROLE

6	6-inch corn tortillas
1	cup purchased salsa verde
½	cup dairy sour cream
3	tablespoons all-purpose flour
4	teaspoons dried cilantro, crushed
1	12-ounce package frozen cooked, peeled, and deveined shrimp, thawed
1	cup frozen whole kernel corn
1	cup shredded Mexican Chihuahua or farmer cheese (4 ounces)
	Dairy sour cream (optional)
	Chopped tomato (optional)
	Jalapeño chile pepper, thinly sliced* (optional)

PREP:
20 minutes

BAKE:
45 minutes

OVEN:
350°F

MAKES:
4 servings

1 Cut 3 of the tortillas into 6 wedges each; place into the bottom of a lightly greased 2-quart square baking dish; set aside. Cut remaining tortillas into thin bite-size strips and place on a baking sheet; bake in a 350°F oven about 10 minutes or until crisp.

2 Meanwhile, combine salsa, the ½ cup sour cream, the flour, and cilantro. Stir in shrimp and corn. Spoon shrimp mixture over tortillas in dish.

3 Bake, uncovered, in a 350°F oven for 40 to 45 minutes or until heated through. Arrange baked tortilla pieces over casserole. Sprinkle with cheese. Bake for 5 minutes more. If desired, garnish with additional sour cream, tomato, and/or jalapeño pepper.

*NOTE: Because chile peppers contain volatile oils that can burn your skin and eyes, avoid direct contact with them as much as possible. When working with chile peppers, wear plastic or rubber gloves. If your bare hands do touch the peppers, wash your hands and nails well with soap and water.

Nutrition Facts per serving: 412 cal., 16 g total fat (9 g sat. fat), 207 mg chol., 575 mg sodium, 39 g carbo., 2 g fiber, 29 g pro.

In Italian, orzo means "barley," but it's actually a tiny, rice-shape pasta, slightly smaller than a pine nut. In this case, it makes a great stand-in for rice.

GREEK ORZO SHRIMP CASSEROLE

PREP:

30 minutes

BAKE:

45 minutes

STAND:

10 minutes

OVEN:

350°F

MAKES:

8 servings

12	ounces dried orzo pasta
1	pound fresh or frozen peeled and deveined medium shrimp
2	medium green and/or red sweet peppers, cut into bite-size strips
1	8-ounce package sliced fresh mushrooms
1/3	cup chopped onion (1 small)
1	clove garlic, minced
1	tablespoon olive oil
1	8-ounce package shredded Italian-style cheese blend (2 cups)
4	ounces feta or kasseri cheese, crumbled
1/2	cup chopped, pitted kalamata olives
1	26-ounce jar marinara sauce

1 Cook orzo according to package directions; drain. Set aside. Thaw shrimp, if frozen. Rinse shrimp; pat dry with paper towels. Set aside.

2 In a 12-inch skillet cook sweet peppers, mushrooms, onion, and garlic in hot oil over medium heat until peppers and onion are tender. Add shrimp and cook about 3 minutes or until shrimp turn opaque.

3 In a very large bowl combine shrimp mixture, cooked orzo, 1 1/2 cups of the Italian-style cheese, the feta cheese, and olives. Add marinara sauce and stir until well coated. Transfer mixture to an ungreased 3-quart rectangular baking dish.

4 Bake, covered, in a 350°F oven about 45 minutes or until mixture is heated through. Top with remaining 1/2 cup Italian-style cheese; let stand for 10 minutes before serving.

Nutrition Facts per serving: 428 cal., 17 g total fat (7 g sat. fat), 97 mg chol., 878 mg sodium, 44 g carbo., 4 g fiber, 26 g pro.

Creamy rice studded with shrimp, imbued with sherry, and sprinkled with almonds—this is really one of those "what's not to like?" casseroles.

SHRIMP NEW ORLEANS

½	cup chopped onion (1 medium)
¼	cup chopped green or red sweet pepper
2	tablespoons butter
12	ounces cooked, peeled, and deveined medium shrimp
2	cups cooked white rice
1	10¾-ounce can condensed cream of shrimp soup
½	cup half-and-half or light cream
2	tablespoons dry sherry
1	teaspoon lemon juice
¼	teaspoon salt
⅛	teaspoon cayenne pepper
3	tablespoons slivered almonds, toasted

PREP:
30 minutes
BAKE:
30 minutes
OVEN:
350°F
MAKES:
6 servings

1 In a medium saucepan cook onion and sweet pepper in hot butter over medium heat about 4 minutes or until tender. Remove from heat.

2 Stir in shrimp, cooked rice, soup, half-and-half, sherry, lemon juice, salt, and cayenne pepper. Transfer to an ungreased 2-quart square baking dish.

3 Bake, uncovered, in a 350°F oven about 30 minutes or until heated through. Sprinkle with almonds.

Nutrition Facts per serving: 290 cal., 13 g total fat (5 g sat. fat), 141 mg chol., 624 mg sodium, 23 g carbo., 1 g fiber, 19 g pro.

The rich, flavorful mix of onion, celery, and sweet pepper in this recipe is a hallmark of both Cajun and Creole cooking styles. The use of butter and the dish's overall creaminess, however, slants toward the more refined Creole style.

BAYOU SEAFOOD CASSEROLE

PREP:

1 hour

BAKE:

30 minutes

OVEN:

350°F

MAKES:

10 servings

1	pound fresh or frozen small shrimp in shells
1	pound fresh or frozen peeled, cooked crawfish tails*
½	cup butter
1	8-ounce package cream cheese
1	cup chopped onion (1 large)
1	cup sliced celery (2 stalks)
¾	cup chopped green sweet pepper (1 medium)
1	pound chunk-style imitation crabmeat, chopped
1	10¾-ounce can condensed cream of mushroom soup
1	4-ounce can (drained weight) mushroom stems and pieces, drained
6	cloves garlic, minced
½	to 1 teaspoon bottled hot pepper sauce
½	teaspoon dried thyme, crushed
½	teaspoon dried oregano, crushed
½	teaspoon dried basil, crushed
3	cups hot cooked white rice
¾	cup shredded sharp cheddar cheese (3 ounces)
½	cup fine dry bread crumbs

1 Thaw shrimp and crawfish, if frozen. Peel and devein shrimp. Rinse shrimp; pat dry with paper towels. Set aside. Set aside 2 tablespoons of the butter. In a small saucepan combine the remaining 6 tablespoons butter and the cream cheese. Heat over low heat until butter is melted and cream cheese is softened, stirring occasionally. Set aside.

2 In a Dutch oven melt the reserved 2 tablespoons butter over medium heat. Add onion, celery, and sweet pepper; cook and stir for 5 minutes. Add shrimp; cook and stir for 4 to 5 minutes more or until shrimp turn opaque. Stir in cream cheese mixture, crawfish, imitation crabmeat, soup, mushrooms, garlic, hot pepper sauce, thyme, oregano, and basil. Stir in cooked rice.

3 Transfer seafood mixture to an ungreased 3-quart rectangular baking dish. Sprinkle with cheese and bread crumbs. Bake, uncovered, in a 350°F oven about 30 minutes or until heated through.

*NOTE: If crawfish are not available, use 2 pounds imitation crabmeat.

Nutrition Facts per serving: 429 cal., 24 g total fat (14 g sat. fat), 178 mg chol., 1,077 mg sodium, 27 g carbo., 2 g fiber, 25 g pro.

Look for cooked, peeled, and deveined shrimp at the supermarket—either in the frozen food aisle or at the fish counter. If the shrimp are frozen, thaw them in the refrigerator before using.

TRIPLE SEAFOOD BAKE

2½	cups half-and-half, light cream, or milk
1	10¾-ounce can condensed cream of mushroom with roasted garlic soup
⅓	cup dry sherry
1⅓	cups uncooked instant rice
1	6½-ounce can minced clams, drained
1	6-ounce can crabmeat, drained
6	ounces cooked, peeled, and deveined medium shrimp, halved lengthwise
1	4-ounce can (drained weight) sliced mushrooms, drained
¼	cup sliced almonds
	Snipped fresh parsley (optional)

PREP:
25 minutes

BAKE:
40 minutes

OVEN:
350°F

MAKES:
5 or 6 servings

1 In a large saucepan combine half-and-half, soup, and sherry. Bring to boiling. Stir in rice, clams, crabmeat, shrimp, and mushrooms. Transfer to an ungreased 2-quart casserole. Sprinkle with almonds.

2 Bake, uncovered, in a 350°F oven about 40 minutes or until rice is tender. If desired, sprinkle with parsley before serving.

Nutrition Facts per serving: 476 cal., 20 g total fat (9 g sat. fat), 168 mg chol., 780 mg sodium, 37 g carbo., 2 g fiber, 32 g pro.

This hearty casserole features shrimp, imitation crabmeat, rice, and vegetables. It's especially good when served with a side of cocktail sauce.

SEAFOOD RICE CASSEROLE

PREP:

30 minutes

BAKE:

30 minutes

OVEN:

350°F

MAKES:

4 servings

6	ounces fresh or frozen cooked, peeled, and deveined shrimp
1½	cups sliced fresh mushrooms (4 ounces)
½	of a small onion, cut into thin wedges
¼	cup chopped green sweet pepper
2	teaspoons cooking oil
1¼	cups cooked white rice
½	of an 8-ounce can sliced water chestnuts, drained
½	cup mayonnaise or salad dressing
½	cup tomato juice
⅛	teaspoon salt
	Dash black pepper
½	of a 6- or 8-ounce package flake-style imitation crabmeat
¼	cup sliced almonds, toasted

1 Thaw shrimp, if frozen. In a large skillet cook mushrooms, onion, and sweet pepper in hot oil over medium heat about 5 minutes or until tender. In a very large bowl combine cooked vegetables, cooked rice, water chestnuts, mayonnaise, tomato juice, salt, and black pepper; mix well. Stir in shrimp and imitation crabmeat.

2 Transfer seafood mixture to an ungreased 1½-quart rectangular baking dish. Bake, covered, in a 350°F oven for 30 to 35 minutes or until bubbly. Sprinkle with almonds.

Nutrition Facts per serving: 419 cal., 30 g total fat (4 g sat. fat), 103 mg chol., 618 mg sodium, 24 g carbo., 2 g fiber, 17 g pro.

You'll relish the sweet, moist scallops in this dish—and the luscious sidekicks, including orzo, eggplant, onion, tomatoes, and sweet pepper.

MEDITERRANEAN SCALLOP CASSEROLE

½ cup dried orzo pasta

3 cups diced peeled eggplant (about 12 ounces)

½ cup chopped onion (1 medium)

½ cup chopped red sweet pepper (1 small)

4 cloves garlic, minced

1 tablespoon olive oil

1 14½-ounce can diced tomatoes, drained

1 8-ounce can tomato sauce

2 teaspoons dried basil, crushed

¼ teaspoon salt

¼ teaspoon black pepper

1 pound bay scallops

½ cup fine dry bread crumbs

¼ cup grated Parmesan cheese

2 tablespoons butter, melted

PREP:
30 minutes
BAKE:
20 minutes
OVEN:
350°F
MAKES:
4 servings

1 Cook orzo according to package directions; drain. Meanwhile, in a large nonstick skillet cook eggplant, onion, sweet pepper, and garlic in hot oil over medium heat about 4 minutes or until onion is tender. Stir in drained tomatoes, cooked orzo, tomato sauce, basil, salt, and black pepper; bring to boiling. Transfer orzo mixture to a lightly greased 2-quart casserole.

2 Rinse scallops; pat dry with paper towels. Place scallops evenly on top of orzo mixture. In a small bowl combine bread crumbs, Parmesan cheese, and melted butter. Sprinkle over scallops.

3 Bake, uncovered, in a 350°F oven for 20 to 25 minutes or until scallops turn opaque.

Nutrition Facts per serving: 407 cal., 13 g total fat (5 g sat. fat), 58 mg chol., 1,241 mg sodium, 44 g carbo., 5 g fiber, 28 g pro.

Tender asparagus and succulent crab are coated in rich, creamy mushroom sauce. Serve it with crusty artisan bread to soak up every bit.

CRAB & ASPARAGUS BAKE

PREP:

30 minutes

BAKE:

35 minutes

STAND:

10 minutes

OVEN:

400°F

MAKES:

6 servings

2	cups sliced fresh mushrooms (6 ounces)
½	cup finely chopped onion (1 medium)
2	tablespoons butter
2	tablespoons cornstarch
¼	teaspoon salt
⅛	teaspoon black pepper
1½	cups milk
1	pound fresh or frozen cooked crabmeat, thawed, drained, and cut into bite-size pieces, or two 8-ounce packages flake-style imitation crabmeat
2	10-ounce packages frozen asparagus cuts
¼	cup slivered almonds
¼	cup grated Parmesan cheese

1 In a large saucepan cook mushrooms and onion in butter over medium heat until onion is tender. Stir in cornstarch, salt, and pepper. Add milk all at once. Cook and stir until thickened and bubbly. Stir in crabmeat and frozen asparagus. Transfer crabmeat mixture to a 2-quart au gratin or rectangular baking dish.

2 In a small bowl combine almonds and Parmesan cheese. Sprinkle evenly over crabmeat mixture in dish.

3 Bake, uncovered, in a 400°F oven for 35 to 40 minutes or until bubbly and top is brown. Let stand for 10 minutes before serving.

Nutrition Facts per serving: 238 cal., 11 g total fat (4 g sat. fat), 94 mg chol., 424 mg sodium, 12 g carbo., 3 g fiber, 24 g pro.

Busy week ahead? Stock these five ingredients in your kitchen now and you'll be ready to make this incredibly satisfying casserole anytime.

CRAB & SPINACH PASTA WITH FONTINA

8	ounces dried bow tie pasta (3½ cups)
1	10-ounce package frozen chopped spinach, thawed and drained well
2	6- to 6½-ounce cans crabmeat, drained, flaked, and cartilage removed
1	26-ounce jar pasta sauce
1½	cups shredded fontina cheese (6 ounces)

1 Cook pasta according to package directions; drain. Meanwhile, in a medium bowl combine spinach and crabmeat.

2 Cover bottom of a 2-quart square baking dish with 1 cup of the sauce. Top with pasta. Top pasta evenly with crab mixture. Sprinkle with ¾ cup of the cheese. Top with remaining sauce. Sprinkle with remaining ¾ cup cheese.

3 Bake, uncovered, in a 375°F oven for 30 to 35 minutes or until sauce is bubbly around edges and cheese is slightly golden. Let stand for 10 minutes before serving.

Nutrition Facts per serving: 376 cal., 11 g total fat (6 g sat. fat), 83 mg chol., 1,061 mg sodium, 45 g carbo., 5 g fiber, 27 g pro.

PREP:
30 minutes
BAKE:
30 minutes
STAND:
10 minutes
OVEN:
375°F
MAKES:
6 servings

You can't go wrong with this creamy seafood-and-vegetable dish. The dusting of cracker crumbs and Parmesan cheese adds a delightfully crisp topping.

BAKED CRAB & BROCCOLI

PREP:

35 minutes

BAKE:

30 minutes

OVEN:

400°F

MAKES:

4 servings

2	cups frozen cut broccoli
1	8-ounce package flake-style imitation crabmeat
2	cups sliced fresh mushrooms (6 ounces)
1	clove garlic, minced
2	tablespoons butter
2	tablespoons all-purpose flour
1/2	teaspoon dried thyme, crushed
1/4	teaspoon salt
1/8	teaspoon black pepper
1	cup milk
1/2	cup shredded sharp cheddar cheese (2 ounces)
2	tablespoons grated Parmesan cheese
2	tablespoons finely crushed rich round crackers (5 crackers)

1 In a 1 1/2-quart au gratin or baking dish arrange frozen broccoli and imitation crabmeat. Set aside.

2 For sauce, in a medium saucepan cook mushrooms and garlic in butter over medium heat about 4 minutes or until mushrooms are tender. Stir in flour, thyme, salt, and pepper (mixture will be thick). Add milk all at once. Cook and stir until thickened and bubbly; remove from heat. Stir in cheddar cheese until melted. Pour sauce over broccoli and imitation crabmeat.

3 Bake, covered, in a 400°F oven for 20 minutes. In a small bowl combine Parmesan cheese and cracker crumbs. Sprinkle casserole evenly with crumb mixture. Bake, uncovered, about 10 minutes more or until bubbly around edges and heated through.

Nutrition Facts per serving: 278 cal., 15 g total fat (8 g sat. fat), 55 mg chol., 479 mg sodium, 18 g carbo., 3 g fiber, 20 g pro.

No need to make pastry for this potpie. Shards of phyllo dough top the creamy crab mixture and provide a crispy contrast in texture.

CRAB POTPIE

3	sheets frozen phyllo dough (14×9-inch rectangles), thawed
3	tablespoons butter, melted
	Paprika
1	cup chopped onion (1 large)
½	cup sliced celery (2 stalks)
3	tablespoons butter
¼	cup all-purpose flour
2	cups milk
3	6½-ounce cans lump crabmeat, drained, or three 6- to 8-ounce packages chunk- or flake-style imitation crabmeat
½	cup frozen peas
2	tablespoons dry sherry (optional)
¼	teaspoon dried tarragon or thyme, crushed
¼	teaspoon salt
¼	teaspoon black pepper

1 Unfold phyllo dough; remove 1 sheet of the phyllo dough. (As you work, cover the remaining phyllo dough with plastic wrap to prevent it from drying out.) Lightly brush dough with some of the 3 tablespoons melted butter; fold in half crosswise. Brush again with butter. Repeat with remaining phyllo sheets, brushing each sheet with some of the melted butter.

2 Stack the sheets on a baking sheet to make 6 layers. Brush top of stack with any remaining melted butter. Sprinkle with paprika. Bake in a 375°F oven for 8 to 10 minutes or until brown and crisp. Cool on baking sheet on a wire rack. Break stack into large shards; store in an airtight container until ready to serve.

3 In a large skillet cook onion and celery in the 3 tablespoons butter over medium heat for 2 to 3 minutes or just until tender. Add flour; cook and stir for 1 minute. Add milk all at once. Cook and stir until mixture begins to boil. Remove from heat; stir in crabmeat, peas, sherry (if desired), tarragon, salt, and pepper. Transfer crabmeat mixture to an ungreased 2-quart rectangular baking dish. Cover and refrigerate for at least 4 hours or up to 24 hours.

4 Bake, covered, in a 375°F oven for 25 to 30 minutes or until heated through. Serve topped with the phyllo shards.

Nutrition Facts per serving: 295 cal., 15 g total fat (9 g sat. fat), 121 mg chol., 619 mg sodium, 15 g carbo., 1 g fiber, 24 g pro.

PREP:
40 minutes

CHILL:
4 to 24 hours

BAKE:
25 minutes

OVEN:
375°F

MAKES:
6 servings

Many cooks will fondly remember this dish as quintessential ladies' luncheon fare.
More saucy and delicate than a typical casserole, it's terrific with crusty bread.

CRAB-MUSHROOM BAKE

PREP:

20 minutes

BAKE:

25 minutes

OVEN:

350°F

MAKES:

4 servings

½	cup finely chopped celery (1 stalk)
1	tablespoon butter
1	10¾-ounce can condensed cream of shrimp soup
¾	cup soft bread crumbs*
1	4-ounce can (drained weight) sliced mushrooms, drained
⅓	cup milk
2	tablespoons dry sherry
1	6½-ounce can pasteurized crabmeat, drained, or one 6½-ounce can crabmeat, drained, flaked, and cartilage removed
⅓	cup shredded Parmesan cheese (1½ ounces)
	Lemon wedges (optional)

1 In a medium saucepan cook celery in hot butter over medium heat until tender. Stir in soup, ½ cup of the bread crumbs, the mushrooms, milk, and sherry. Bring mixture just to boiling, stirring constantly. Stir in crabmeat. Transfer to an ungreased 9-inch pie plate.

2 In a small bowl combine the remaining ¼ cup bread crumbs and the Parmesan cheese. Sprinkle over crab mixture.

3 Bake, uncovered, in a 350°F oven about 25 minutes or until mixture is bubbly and top is golden. If desired, serve with lemon wedges.

*NOTE: Use a blender or food processor to make fluffy soft bread crumbs. One slice yields ¾ cup crumbs.

Nutrition Facts per serving: 276 cal., 10 g total fat (6 g sat. fat), 83 mg chol., 1,260 mg sodium, 26 g carbo., 2 g fiber, 17 g pro.

The rich and creamy lemon-wine sauce is a refreshing treatment for sweet sea scallops.

COQUILLES ST. JACQUES

½   cup soft bread crumbs*

¼   cup grated Parmesan cheese

1   teaspoon dried parsley flakes, crushed

⅛   teaspoon black pepper

5   tablespoons butter

1   pound sea scallops, halved crosswise

3   cups sliced fresh mushrooms (8 ounces)

1⅓   cups thinly sliced leeks (4)

2   cloves garlic, minced

¼   cup dry white wine

½   teaspoon salt

¾   cup whipping cream

2   teaspoons finely shredded lemon peel

PREP:
30 minutes
BAKE:
10 minutes
OVEN:
400°F
MAKES:
4 servings

1 In a small bowl combine bread crumbs, Parmesan cheese, parsley, and pepper. Melt 1 tablespoon of the butter; stir into bread crumb mixture until combined. Set aside.

2 Rinse scallops; pat dry with paper towels. In a large nonstick skillet melt 1 tablespoon of the remaining butter over medium heat. Add scallops and cook for 1 to 2 minutes per side or until brown. Transfer scallops to a colander using a slotted spoon; set aside. Drain liquid from skillet.

3 Melt remaining 3 tablespoons butter in the same skillet over medium heat. Add mushrooms, leeks, and garlic. Cook about 6 minutes or until mushrooms are tender, stirring occasionally. Add wine and salt; boil gently about 3 minutes or until liquid is evaporated. Add cream and lemon peel; bring to boiling. Reduce heat; boil gently for 3 to 5 minutes or until slightly thickened, stirring frequently.

4 Transfer scallops to an ungreased 2-quart square baking dish. Pour mushroom mixture over scallops. Sprinkle with bread crumb mixture. Bake in a 400°F oven for 10 to 15 minutes or until scallops turn opaque and top is brown.

*NOTE: **Use a blender or food processor to make fluffy soft bread crumbs. One slice yields ¾ cup crumbs.**

Nutrition Facts per serving: 473 cal., 35 g total fat (19 g sat. fat), 144 mg chol., 723 mg sodium, 14 g carbo., 1 g fiber, 25 g pro.

This seafood-filled lasagna brings together the best of all worlds—fresh asparagus, pasta, Brie cheese, and, of course, lobster. Served in bite-size portions, it makes a great appetizer.

LOBSTER LASAGNA

PREP:

50 minutes

BAKE:

25 minutes

STAND:

5 minutes

OVEN:

475°F/400°F

MAKES:

12 appetizer servings

1	pound fresh asparagus
1	tablespoon olive oil
4	ounces no-boil lasagna noodles
2	tablespoons butter
2	tablespoons all-purpose flour
¾	cup chicken broth
⅛	teaspoon ground white pepper
1	4½-ounce round Brie cheese, peeled and cubed
2	tablespoons dry sherry (optional)
1¼	cups chopped cooked lobster meat or one 6- or 8-ounce package flake-style imitation lobster
⅓	cup grated Parmesan cheese
½	cup chopped tomato (1 medium)

1 Snap off and discard woody bases from asparagus. If desired, scrape off scales. Cut asparagus into 2-inch pieces. Place in a 13×9×2-inch baking pan; toss with oil. Roast, uncovered, in a 475°F oven for 5 to 10 minutes or until crisp-tender; cool.

2 Meanwhile, separate lasagna noodles and soak in water for 15 minutes; drain. Reduce oven temperature to 400°F.

3 In a small saucepan melt butter over medium heat; stir in flour. Cook and stir about 2 minutes or until lightly browned. Stir in broth and white pepper; cook and stir until thickened and bubbly. Reduce heat to low. Stir in Brie cheese until melted. If desired, stir in sherry.

4 Place one-third of the lasagna noodles into the bottom of a greased 2-quart square baking dish, folding or trimming as necessary to fit. Top with ⅓ cup of the Brie cheese sauce, half of the asparagus, half of the lobster, and some of the Parmesan cheese. Repeat layers.

5 Top with remaining one-third lasagna noodles, the tomato, remaining Brie cheese sauce, and remaining Parmesan. Bake, covered, for 20 minutes. Uncover and bake for 5 to 10 minutes more or until bubbly. Let stand 5 minutes before serving.

Nutrition Facts per serving: 136 cal., 7 g total fat (4 g sat. fat), 32 mg chol., 247 mg sodium, 9 g carbo., 0 g fiber, 8 g pro.

These manicotti shells are packed with lobster! Another time, try them with crab.

LOBSTER MANICOTTI

12	dried manicotti shells
1	tablespoon butter
1	tablespoon all-purpose flour
1¼	cups milk
1	8-ounce tub cream cheese with chive and onion
¼	cup grated Romano or Parmesan cheese
12	ounces chopped cooked lobster or chunk-style imitation lobster (about 2⅔ cups)
1	10-ounce package frozen chopped broccoli, thawed and drained well
½	of a 7-ounce jar roasted red sweet peppers, drained and chopped, or one 4-ounce jar diced pimiento, drained
¼	teaspoon black pepper
	Paprika

PREP:
45 minutes
BAKE:
30 minutes
OVEN:
350°F
MAKES:
6 servings

1 Cook the manicotti shells according to package directions. Drain; rinse with cold water. Drain again.

2 Meanwhile, for sauce, in a medium saucepan melt butter over medium heat. Add flour and stir until combined. Add 1 cup of the milk. Cook and stir over medium heat until mixture is thickened and bubbly. Turn heat to low. Gradually add cream cheese, stirring until smooth. Stir in Romano cheese.

3 For filling, in a medium bowl combine ¾ cup of the sauce, the lobster, broccoli, roasted sweet peppers, and black pepper. Using a small spoon, carefully fill each manicotti shell with about ⅓ cup of the filling. Arrange the filled shells in an ungreased 3-quart rectangular baking dish. Stir the remaining ¼ cup milk into the remaining sauce. Pour over the shells. Sprinkle with paprika.

4 Bake, covered, in a 350°F oven for 30 to 40 minutes or until heated through.

Nutrition Facts per serving: 386 cal., 17 g total fat (11 g sat. fat), 90 mg chol., 471 mg sodium, 34 g carbo., 2 g fiber, 21 g pro.

This spicy dish is a favorite way for folks in Louisiana to fix crawfish when it's in season.

CRAWFISH FETTUCCINE

PREP:

25 minutes

BAKE:

20 minutes

OVEN:

350°F

MAKES:

6 servings

12	ounces fresh or frozen peeled crawfish tails
12	ounces dried fettuccine, broken
¾	cup coarsely chopped green sweet pepper (1 medium)
½	cup chopped onion (1 medium)
2	cloves garlic, minced
3	tablespoons butter
2	tablespoons all-purpose flour
¼	to ½ teaspoon cayenne pepper
¼	teaspoon salt
1½	cups half-and-half, light cream, or milk
1	cup shredded American cheese (4 ounces)
2	teaspoons dried parsley flakes, crushed
¼	cup grated Parmesan cheese

1 Thaw crawfish tails, if frozen. Rinse crawfish tails; pat dry with paper towels. Set aside. Cook fettuccine according to package directions; drain. Return to pan; set aside.

2 Meanwhile, in a large saucepan or skillet cook sweet pepper, onion, and garlic in butter over medium heat about 5 minutes or until tender. Stir in flour, cayenne pepper, and salt. Add half-and-half all at once. Cook and stir until thickened and bubbly. Add American cheese, stirring until melted. Remove from heat. Stir in crawfish tails and parsley. Pour sauce over fettuccine in pan, tossing gently to coat.

3 Spread crawfish mixture evenly in an ungreased 3-quart baking dish. Sprinkle with Parmesan cheese. Bake, covered, in a 350°F oven for 20 to 25 minutes or until heated through.

Nutrition Facts per serving: 506 cal., 21 g total fat (13 g sat. fat), 170 mg chol., 646 mg sodium, 50 g carbo., 2 g fiber, 27 g pro.

A seafood lover's favorite! Mustardy Dijon sauce adds a clean, sharp flavor to this casserole infused with three types of seafood.

SEAFOOD-STUFFED SOLE

6	4- to 6-ounce fresh or frozen sole or cod fillets, cut ½ inch thick
8	ounces fresh or frozen cooked, peeled, and deveined shrimp, coarsely chopped
½	cup thinly sliced green onions (4)
½	cup chopped celery (2 stalks)
2	cloves garlic, minced
6	tablespoons butter
¾	cup fine dry bread crumbs
1	6½-ounce can crabmeat, drained, flaked, and cartilage removed
¼	teaspoon cayenne pepper
	Salt
	Black pepper
½	cup dairy sour cream
1	tablespoon all-purpose flour
1	tablespoon Dijon-style mustard
⅛	teaspoon dried thyme, crushed
½	cup chicken broth

PREP:
30 minutes
BAKE:
20 minutes
OVEN:
400°F
MAKES:
6 servings

1 Thaw fish and shrimp, if frozen. Rinse fish; pat dry with paper towels. Set aside. In a large skillet cook green onions, celery, and garlic in 2 tablespoons of the butter over medium heat until tender. Stir in bread crumbs, shrimp, remaining 4 tablespoons butter, the crabmeat, and cayenne pepper. Season to taste with salt and black pepper.

2 For Dijon sauce, in a small saucepan combine sour cream, flour, mustard, and thyme. Add broth, stirring until well mixed. Cook and stir over medium heat until mixture is thickened and bubbly. Cook and stir for 1 minute more.

3 Place about 2 tablespoons of the stuffing mixture on a short side of each fish fillet; roll up fish around stuffing. Press remaining stuffing evenly into a lightly greased 2-quart square baking dish. Arrange fish fillets, seam sides down, on stuffing in baking dish. Pour sauce over fish.

4 Bake, uncovered, in a 400°F oven about 20 minutes or until fish flakes easily when tested with a fork.

Nutrition Facts per serving: 366 cal., 18 g total fat (9 g sat. fat), 189 mg chol., 903 mg sodium, 13 g carbo., 1 g fiber, 38 g pro.

How do you make 6 ounces of smoked salmon serve six? Bake it with pasta and a Gouda cheese sauce.

SMOKED GOUDA-SALMON BAKE

PREP:

30 minutes

BAKE:

30 minutes

OVEN:

350°F

MAKES:

6 servings

1	9-ounce package refrigerated linguine or spinach fettuccine
1	6-ounce piece smoked salmon, flaked, with skin and bones removed
⅓	cup finely chopped onion (1 small)
1	tablespoon butter
1½	cups milk
6	ounces reduced-fat cream cheese (Neufchâtel), cubed and softened
1	cup finely shredded smoked Gouda cheese (4 ounces)
1	teaspoon dried chives, crushed
½	teaspoon coarsely ground black pepper

1 Cook linguine according to package directions; drain. Transfer linguine to a lightly greased 2-quart rectangular baking dish. Snip noodles a few times with scissors to cut into shorter lengths. Sprinkle with smoked salmon.

2 In a medium saucepan cook onion in hot butter over medium heat until tender. Stir in milk, cream cheese, and Gouda cheese. Cook and stir until melted. Stir in chives and pepper. Pour sauce over salmon.

3 Bake, covered, in a 350°F oven about 30 minutes or until fish is heated through.

Nutrition Facts per serving: 340 cal., 17 g total fat (10 g sat. fat), 99 mg chol., 699 mg sodium, 28 g carbo., 1 g fiber, 19 g pro.

Snapper is available fresh all year, but its peak season is summer. Stop by your supermarket's fish department or deli counter to pick up some.

MUSHROOM-DILL BAKED SNAPPER

2	pounds fresh or frozen skinless red snapper fillets
	Salt
	Black pepper
5	tablespoons butter
4	cups sliced fresh mushrooms (about 10 ounces)
1	cup chopped red onion (1 large)
2	cloves garlic, minced
1	cup whipping cream
½	cup white wine
2	tablespoons Dijon-style mustard
1	teaspoon dried dillweed
1	10-ounce package frozen chopped spinach, thawed and drained well
¾	cup fine dry bread crumbs
¾	cup grated Parmesan cheese

PREP:
40 minutes
BAKE:
25 minutes
OVEN:
375°F
MAKES:
6 to 8 servings

1 Thaw fish, if frozen. Rinse fish; pat dry with paper towels. Cut fish fillets into 6 to 8 portions and place in a greased 3-quart rectangular baking dish. Sprinkle with salt and pepper. Set aside.

2 In a very large skillet melt 3 tablespoons of the butter over medium heat. Add mushrooms, onion, and garlic. Cook about 10 minutes or until mushrooms are tender. Add cream and wine. Bring to boiling. Boil gently about 30 minutes or until mixture is reduced to about 1½ cups (mixture will thicken slightly). Stir in mustard and dillweed. Stir in spinach. Pour mushroom mixture over fish in dish.

3 Melt remaining 2 tablespoons butter. Stir in bread crumbs and Parmesan cheese. Sprinkle over mushroom mixture.

4 Bake, uncovered, in a 375°F oven for 25 to 30 minutes or until fish flakes easily when tested with a fork.

Nutrition Facts per serving: 544 cal., 33 g total fat (17 g sat. fat), 146 mg chol., 968 mg sodium, 19 g carbo., 3 g fiber, 43 g pro.

A generous Parmesan cheese topping and decadent Dijon sauce are luscious atop tender fish.

CREAMY SEA BASS

PREP:

20 minutes

BAKE:

20 minutes

OVEN:

450°F

MAKES:

6 servings

1½ pounds fresh or frozen sea bass or other white fish fillets, ½ inch thick

½ of an 8-ounce tub cream cheese with chive and onion

2 tablespoons mayonnaise or salad dressing

1 tablespoon milk

1 teaspoon lemon juice

1 teaspoon Dijon-style mustard

¾ cup soft bread crumbs*

¼ cup grated Parmesan cheese

4 teaspoons dried parsley flakes, crushed

½ teaspoon paprika

1 Thaw fish, if frozen. Rinse fish; pat dry with paper towels. If necessary, cut fillets into 6 portions. Arrange fillets in a single layer in an ungreased 2-quart square baking dish. Set aside.

2 In a small bowl combine cream cheese, mayonnaise, milk, lemon juice, and mustard. Spread cream cheese mixture over fillets. Bake in a 450°F oven for 10 minutes.

3 Meanwhile, combine bread crumbs, Parmesan cheese, parsley, and paprika; sprinkle over fillets. Bake, uncovered, about 10 minutes more or until crumbs are golden and fish flakes easily when tested with a fork.

MAKE-AHEAD DIRECTIONS: Prepare cream cheese mixture; cover and chill up to 4 hours. Prepare bread crumb mixture; cover and chill for up to 4 hours.

*NOTE: Use a blender or food processor to make fluffy soft bread crumbs. One slice yields ¾ cup crumbs.

Nutrition Facts per serving: 243 cal., 13 g total fat (6 g sat. fat), 71 mg chol., 300 mg sodium, 5 g carbo., 0 g fiber, 24 g pro.

If you plan to serve this casserole right after you assemble it, skip the chilling step and bake it in a 350°F oven for about 15 minutes or until heated through.

SALMON & EGGS BENEDICT

1	1⅛- or 0.9-ounce envelope hollandaise sauce mix
2	tablespoons capers, drained
½	teaspoon finely shredded lemon peel
3	English muffins, split and toasted
6	ounces thinly sliced, smoked salmon (lox-style) or Canadian-style bacon
6	eggs
¼	cup milk
⅛	teaspoon black pepper
2	tablespoons butter
¾	cup soft bread crumbs*
	Snipped fresh chives (optional)

PREP:
30 minutes

CHILL:
overnight

BAKE:
25 minutes

OVEN:
350°F

MAKES:
6 servings

1 Prepare sauce mix according to package directions (you should have about 1¼ cups). Stir in capers and lemon peel. Spread about ½ cup of the sauce over the bottom of an ungreased 2-quart rectangular baking dish. Cover remaining sauce and set aside. Arrange muffin halves, cut sides up, on top of sauce in dish. Divide salmon or Canadian bacon into six equal portions. Place salmon or bacon, folding as necessary, on top of each muffin half.

2 Whisk together eggs, milk, and pepper. In a large skillet melt 1 tablespoon of the butter over medium heat. Pour in egg mixture. Cook, without stirring, until mixture begins to set on the bottom and around the edge. Using a spatula or large spoon, lift and fold the partially cooked eggs so the uncooked portion flows underneath. Continue cooking for 2 to 3 minutes or until eggs are cooked through but are still glossy and moist. Spoon eggs evenly over muffin stacks. Spoon remaining sauce over eggs.

3 Melt remaining 1 tablespoon butter. Add bread crumbs, tossing lightly to coat. Cover and chill the egg dish and crumbs separately overnight.

4 Sprinkle muffin stacks with crumbs. Bake, uncovered, in a 350°F oven about 25 minutes or until heated through. If desired, sprinkle with chives.

*NOTE: Use a blender or food processor to make fluffy soft bread crumbs. One slice yields ¾ cup crumbs.

Nutrition Facts per serving: 244 cal., 11 g total fat (4 g sat. fat), 230 mg chol., 1,064 mg sodium, 20 g carbo., 1 g fiber, 14 g pro.

Couscous, a staple of North African cuisine, is really granular semolina. In this couscous casserole, the onion-apple mixture is a natural with the curry powder seasoning.

CURRIED HALIBUT & COUSCOUS CASSEROLE

PREP:

25 minutes

BAKE:

20 minutes

OVEN:

450°F

MAKES:

6 servings

1½ pounds fresh or frozen halibut steaks or cod fillets

1½ cups thinly sliced onion

1 tablespoon butter

1 to 2 teaspoons curry powder

1 large apple, cored and cut into thin wedges (1½ cups)

1 cup chopped roma tomatoes (2)

¼ teaspoon salt

⅛ teaspoon black pepper

1 10-ounce package couscous

2½ cups chicken broth

Salt

Black pepper

Chutney (optional)

1 Thaw fish, if frozen. Rinse fish; pat dry with paper towels. If necessary, cut into 6 portions. Set aside.

2 In a large skillet cook onion in hot butter over medium heat about 5 minutes or until tender. Stir in curry powder. Remove skillet from heat. Stir in apple, tomatoes, the ¼ teaspoon salt, and the ⅛ teaspoon pepper. Set aside.

3 In an ungreased 3-quart rectangular baking dish combine couscous and broth. Arrange fish on top in a single layer. Sprinkle with additional salt and pepper. Top evenly with onion-apple mixture.

4 Bake, covered, in a 450°F oven for 20 to 25 minutes or until fish flakes easily when tested with a fork. If desired, serve with chutney.

Nutrition Facts per serving: 358 cal., 5 g total fat (1 g sat. fat), 42 mg chol., 612 mg sodium, 45 g carbo., 4 g fiber, 31 g pro.

MEAT

Serve tortilla chips alongside to dip into this taco-flavored hot dish.

MEXICAN BISCUIT CASSEROLE

PREP:

30 minutes

BAKE:

20 minutes

STAND:

5 minutes

OVEN:

350°F

MAKES:

6 servings

1½	pounds lean ground beef
1	1¼-ounce package taco seasoning mix
¾	cup water
1	15½- to 16-ounce can kidney beans. undrained
1	11-ounce can whole kernel corn with sweet peppers, drained
2	cups packaged biscuit mix
⅔	cup milk
1	cup shredded cheddar cheese (4 ounces)

1 In a large skillet cook ground beef over medium heat until brown; drain. Add taco seasoning mix, the water, undrained kidney beans, and the drained corn; bring to boiling. Meanwhile, combine biscuit mix and milk; stir until moistened.

2 Transfer meat mixture to an ungreased 2-quart rectangular baking dish. Top with cheese. Drop biscuit mixture in mounds onto top of hot meat mixture.

3 Bake, uncovered, in a 350°F oven about 20 minutes or until a wooden toothpick inserted into center of a biscuit comes out clean. Let stand for 5 minutes before serving.

Nutrition Facts per serving: 554 cal., 24 g total fat (10 g sat. fat), 93 mg chol., 1,736 mg sodium, 52 g carbo., 6 g fiber, 34 g pro.

Golden raisins add a hint of sweetness to this fiery casserole. You may want to adjust the amount of jalapeño pepper for a dish the whole family will enjoy.

CORN PIE IN GROUND BEEF CRUST

1	cup chopped onion (1 medium)
½	cup chopped celery (1 stalk)
½	cup chopped red or green sweet pepper
2	tablespoons finely chopped, seeded jalapeño chile pepper*
6	cloves garlic, minced
1	tablespoon olive oil
1	14½-ounce can diced tomatoes, drained
½	cup golden raisins
1	tablespoon chili powder
1	teaspoon ground cumin
½	teaspoon salt
½	teaspoon crushed red pepper
1	pound lean ground beef
¼	cup fine dry bread crumbs
2	slightly beaten eggs
½	cup milk
1	tablespoon all-purpose flour
¼	teaspoon salt
2¾	cups fresh or frozen whole kernel corn, thawed and drained
¼	cup thinly sliced green onions (2)

PREP:
30 minutes
BAKE:
40 minutes
STAND:
10 minutes
OVEN:
350°F
MAKES:
6 servings

1 In a large skillet cook onion, celery, sweet pepper, jalapeño pepper, and garlic in hot oil over medium heat about 5 minutes or until tender. Remove from heat; drain. Stir in drained tomatoes, raisins, chili powder, cumin, the ½ teaspoon salt, and the crushed red pepper. In a large bowl combine ground beef, bread crumbs, and the onion-tomato mixture. Transfer to an ungreased 2-quart square baking dish, spreading evenly.

2 In the same bowl whisk together eggs, milk, flour, and the ¼ teaspoon salt. Stir in corn and green onions. Pour evenly over meat layer.

3 Bake, uncovered, in a 350°F oven about 40 minutes or until corn layer is just set and meat layer is no longer pink. Let stand for 10 minutes; cut into portions to serve.

*NOTE: Because hot chile peppers contain volatile oils that can burn your skin and eyes, avoid direct contact with chiles as much as possible. When working with chile peppers, wear plastic or rubber gloves. If your bare hands do touch the chile peppers, wash your hands well with soap and water.

Nutrition Facts per serving: 325 cal., 9 g total fat (3 g sat. fat), 116 mg chol., 545 mg sodium, 45 g carbo., 5 g fiber, 23 g pro.

This hot dish allows you to put wholesome food on your table even on busy weekdays. It calls for packaged foods that offer both convenience and homemade goodness.

CREAMY MEATBALL CASSEROLE

PREP:

15 minutes

BAKE:

1 hour

OVEN:

350°F

MAKES:

6 servings

1	10¾-ounce can condensed cream of mushroom or cream of onion soup
1	cup milk
½	cup dairy sour cream
½	teaspoon salt
⅛	teaspoon black pepper
32	frozen cooked meatballs (½ ounce each)
1	20-ounce package refrigerated red-skinned potato wedges
1	16-ounce package frozen stir-fry vegetables (any combination)

1 In a large bowl combine soup, milk, sour cream, salt, and pepper. Stir in meatballs, potato wedges, and vegetables. Transfer to an ungreased 3-quart rectangular baking dish.

2 Bake, covered, in a 350°F oven about 1 hour or until heated through.

Nutrition Facts per serving: 423 cal., 28 g total fat (12 g sat. fat), 37 mg chol., 1,291 mg sodium, 28 g carbo., 6 g fiber, 17 g pro.

It may look like lasagna, but it tastes like a Mexican marvel! This south-of-the-border dinner has layers of tortillas (no boiling noodles!), salsa-spiked tomato sauce (for extra zing), chiles, zucchini, and cheese.

ENCHILADA CASSEROLE

1	16-ounce jar mild salsa
½	pound ground beef
⅔	cup chopped poblano chile pepper, chopped* (1 medium)
½	cup chopped onion (1 medium)
2	cloves garlic, minced
2	cups coarsely chopped zucchini (1 medium)
¼	teaspoon salt
¼	teaspoon ground cumin
⅛	teaspoon cayenne pepper
2	cups crumbled feta cheese (8 ounces)
½	cup ricotta cheese
1	cup shredded Monterey Jack cheese (4 ounces)
8	6-inch corn tortillas

PREP:
45 minutes
BAKE:
40 minutes
STAND:
5 minutes
OVEN:
350°F
MAKES:
6 servings

1 Spread ⅓ cup of the salsa in the bottom of a lightly greased 2-quart rectangular baking dish; set aside. In a large skillet cook ground beef, poblano chile, onion, and garlic over medium-high heat until meat is brown and vegetables are tender; drain. Reserve ½ cup of the salsa; set aside. Stir remaining salsa, the zucchini, salt, cumin, and cayenne pepper into the meat mixture. Remove from heat; set aside.

2 In a medium bowl combine feta cheese, ricotta cheese and ½ cup of the Monterey Jack cheese.

3 Arrange 3 tortillas over salsa in baking dish, overlapping slightly to fit. Spread half of the meat mixture over tortillas. Spoon half of the cheese mixture over the meat mixture. Arrange 2 tortillas on top. Top with remaining meat mixture, cheese mixture, and remaining 3 tortillas. Spread with reserved ½ cup salsa. Cover loosely with foil.

4 Bake, covered, in a 350°F oven for 35 minutes. Top with remaining ½ cup Monterey Jack cheese. Bake, uncovered, about 5 minutes more or until cheese melts and edges are bubbly. Let stand for 5 minutes before serving.

*NOTE: **Because hot chile peppers contain volatile oils that can burn your skin and eyes, avoid direct contact with chiles as much as possible. When working with chile peppers, wear plastic or rubber gloves. If your bare hands do touch the chile peppers, wash your hands well with soap and water.**

Nutrition Facts per serving: 414 cal., 22 g total fat (13 g sat. fat), 84 mg chol., 1,212 mg sodium, 31 g carbo., 2 g fiber, 23 g pro.

A salsa-accented beef and corn filling bubbles underneath a hearty corn bread and cheese topping for a meat pie with Mexican flair.

BEEFY CORN BREAD CASSEROLE

PREP:

25 minutes

BAKE:

20 minutes

STAND:

5 minutes

OVEN:

375°F

MAKES:

6 servings

1   pound ground beef

½   cup frozen whole kernel corn

1   16-ounce jar salsa

1   10-ounce package corn bread mix
     or one 8½-ounce package corn muffin mix

1   cup shredded cheddar cheese (4 ounces)
     Snipped fresh cilantro (optional)

1 In a large skillet cook ground beef over medium heat until meat is brown; drain. Stir in frozen corn and 1½ cups of the salsa; heat through. Remove from heat; cover to keep warm.

2 Prepare corn bread batter according to package directions (do not bake). Spread half of the corn bread batter into a lightly greased 2-quart rectangular baking dish. Spoon meat mixture over batter; sprinkle with ½ cup of the cheese. Spoon remaining batter in mounds over cheese.

3 Bake, uncovered, in a 375°F oven about 20 minutes or until corn bread is golden. Sprinkle with remaining ½ cup cheese. Let stand for 5 minutes before serving. Serve with remaining salsa. If desired, garnish with cilantro.

Nutrition Facts per serving: 166 cal., 23 g total fat (9 g sat. fat), 104 mg chol., 1,101 mg sodium, 41 g carbo., 3 g fiber, 25 g pro.

This familiar favorite is warming, soothing, and oh so comforting! Try serving this creamy layered bake with mixed vegetables and dinner rolls for the perfect end to "one of those days."

HAMBURGER CHEESE HOT DISH

¾ pound lean ground beef

½ cup chopped onion (1 medium)

1 15-ounce can tomato sauce

1 teaspoon sugar

¼ teaspoon salt

¼ teaspoon garlic powder

¼ teaspoon black pepper

4 cups dried medium noodles (8 ounces)

1 cup cream-style cottage cheese

½ of an 8-ounce package cream cheese, softened

⅓ cup sliced green onions

¼ cup dairy sour cream

¼ cup chopped green sweet pepper

¼ cup grated or shredded Parmesan cheese

PREP:
30 minutes

BAKE:
45 minutes

OVEN:
350°F

MAKES:
6 servings

1 In a large skillet cook ground beef and onion over medium heat until meat is brown and onion is tender; drain. Stir in tomato sauce, sugar, salt, garlic powder, and black pepper. Remove from heat.

2 Meanwhile, cook noodles according to package directions; drain. Set aside. In a medium bowl combine cottage cheese, cream cheese, green onions, sour cream, and sweet pepper; set aside.

3 Spread half of the noodles in an ungreased 2-quart rectangular baking dish. Top with about half of the meat mixture. Top with the cottage cheese mixture. Top with remaining noodles and meat mixture. Sprinkle with Parmesan cheese.

4 Bake, covered, in a 350°F oven for 30 minutes. Uncover. Bake about 15 minutes more or until heated through.

Nutrition Facts per serving: 351 cal., 17 g total fat (9 g sat. fat), 92 mg chol., 700 mg sodium, 26 g carbo., 2 g fiber, 22 g pro.

Baked pasta is a surefire crowd-pleaser, especially when it's full of Italian meatballs, tangy pasta sauce, and luscious cheeses.

CHEESY ITALIAN MEATBALL CASSEROLE

PREP:
30 minutes

BAKE:
45 minutes

OVEN:
350°F

MAKES:
8 to 10 servings

16 ounces dried ziti or penne pasta

1 26-ounce jar tomato pasta sauce

1 16-ounce package Italian-style frozen cooked meatballs (32), thawed

1 15-ounce can Italian-style tomato sauce

1 15-ounce carton ricotta cheese

½ cup grated Parmesan cheese

2 cups shredded mozzarella cheese (8 ounces)

1 Cook pasta according to package directions; drain. Return to pan. Stir in pasta sauce, meatballs, and tomato sauce. Transfer to an ungreased 3-quart rectangular baking dish. Bake, covered, in a 350°F oven for 30 minutes.

2 Meanwhile, in a small bowl combine ricotta cheese and Parmesan cheese. Uncover pasta mixture and spoon ricotta mixture in mounds over pasta mixture. Cover loosely; bake about 10 minutes more or until heated through. Top with mozzarella cheese and bake, uncovered, for 5 minutes more.

Nutrition Facts per serving: 611 cal., 28 g total fat (14 g sat. fat), 86 mg chol., 1,441 mg sodium, 57 g carbo., 7 g fiber, 33 g pro.

Salsa and chile peppers brighten this beef and rice bake. Round out the menu with crusty bread.

BEEF & RICE CASSEROLE

1	pound ground beef or ground pork
1	cup chopped celery (2 stalks)
½	cup chopped onion (1 medium)
1¼	cups water
1	cup uncooked long grain rice
1	14½-ounce can diced tomatoes, undrained
1	cup purchased salsa
½	cup sliced pitted ripe olives
1	4½-ounce can diced green chile peppers, drained
1½	teaspoons instant beef bouillon granules
1	teaspoon chili powder
1	teaspoon Worcestershire sauce
¼	teaspoon black pepper
½	cup shredded cheddar cheese (2 ounces)

PREP:
30 minutes
BAKE:
45 minutes
STAND:
10 minutes
OVEN:
350°F
MAKES:
6 servings

1 In a large skillet cook ground beef, celery, and onion over medium heat until meat is brown and onion is tender; drain.

2 Stir in the water, rice, undrained tomatoes, the salsa, olives, chile peppers, bouillon granules, chili powder, Worcestershire sauce, and black pepper. Bring to boiling. Transfer to an ungreased 2-quart casserole.

3 Bake, covered, in a 350°F oven for 45 to 50 minutes or until rice is tender. Sprinkle with cheese. Let stand, covered, for 10 minutes before serving.

Nutrition Facts per serving: 348 cal., 14 g total fat (6 g sat. fat), 57 mg chol., 676 mg sodium, 33 g carbo., 2 g fiber, 20 g pro.

Corn, sweet pepper, pimiento, onion, and mushrooms add zip to old-fashioned beef and noodles.

BEEFY VEGETABLES & NOODLES

PREP:

35 minutes

BAKE:

30 minutes

OVEN:

350°F

MAKES:

6 servings

1	8-ounce package dried extra-wide noodles
1	pound lean ground beef or ground raw turkey
¾	cup coarsely chopped green sweet pepper (1 medium)
½	cup chopped onion (1 medium)
1	10¾-ounce can condensed golden mushroom soup
1	10-ounce package frozen whole kernel corn
1	cup chopped fresh mushrooms
½	of an 8-ounce package cream cheese, cut up
⅓	cup milk
1	2-ounce jar diced pimiento, drained
½	teaspoon salt
½	teaspoon dried marjoram, crushed
¼	teaspoon black pepper

1 Cook noodles according to package directions; drain. Rinse with cold water; drain well.

2 Meanwhile, in a 4-quart Dutch oven cook ground beef, sweet pepper, and onion over medium heat until meat is brown and vegetables are tender; drain. Stir in soup, corn, mushrooms, cream cheese, milk, pimiento, salt, marjoram, and black pepper. Heat and stir until cream cheese is melted. Gently stir in cooked noodles. Transfer to an ungreased 2-quart rectangular baking dish.

3 Bake, covered, in a 350°F oven for 30 to 35 minutes until heated through.

Nutrition Facts per serving: 416 cal., 18 g total fat (8 g sat. fat), 107 mg chol., 688 mg sodium, 41 g carbo., 3 g fiber, 23 g pro.

Kids and adults alike will love this casserole that's filled with all-American cheeseburger flavors.

CHEESEBURGER CASSEROLE

4	ounces dried penne pasta (2 cups)
1	pound ground beef or ground pork
½	cup chopped onion (1 medium)
1	clove garlic, minced
2	10¾-ounce cans condensed cheddar cheese soup
½	cup milk
1	teaspoon dried basil, crushed
⅛	teaspoon black pepper
1½	cups shredded Swiss or American cheese (6 ounces)
1	cup chopped tomatoes (2 medium)

PREP:
25 minutes
BAKE:
30 minutes
STAND:
10 minutes
OVEN:
375°F
MAKES:
6 servings

1 Cook pasta according to package directions; drain. Set aside. Meanwhile, in a large skillet cook ground beef, onion, and garlic until meat is brown and onion is tender; drain. Stir in soup, milk, basil, and pepper. Stir in cooked pasta and 1 cup of the cheese. Transfer to an ungreased 2-quart rectangular baking dish.

2 Bake, covered, in a 375°F oven for 30 to 35 minutes or until heated through. Sprinkle with remaining ½ cup cheese and the tomatoes. Let stand for 10 minutes before serving.

Nutrition Facts per serving: 519 cal., 34 g total fat (15 g sat. fat), 103 mg chol., 944 mg sodium, 32 g carbo., 2 g fiber, 28 g pro.

Wholesome, satisfying, and easy to prepare, this is basically a shepherd's pie. It's a classic winter warmer and perfect weeknight fare to bring your family together for a meaningful, enjoyable meal.

HAMBURGER PIE

PREP:

30 minutes

BAKE:

25 minutes

OVEN:

350°F

MAKES:

4 to 6 servings

1	recipe Mashed Potatoes
1	pound ground beef
½	cup chopped onion (1 medium)
2	cups loose-pack frozen green beans, thawed
1	10¾-ounce can condensed tomato soup
½	teaspoon salt
	Dash black pepper
½	cup shredded process American cheese (2 ounces) (optional)

1 Prepare Mashed Potatoes; set aside. In a large skillet cook ground beef and onion over medium heat until meat is brown and onion is tender; drain. Stir in beans, soup, salt, and pepper. Transfer to a greased 1½-quart baking dish.

2 Spoon Mashed Potatoes in mounds onto bean mixture. If desired, sprinkle cheese over the potatoes. Bake, uncovered, in a 350°F oven for 25 to 30 minutes or until mixture is bubbly and potatoes are golden.

MASHED POTATOES: Peel and quarter 1½ pounds (about 4 medium) baking potatoes. Cook, covered, in boiling lightly salted water to cover for 20 to 25 minutes or until tender; drain. Mash with a potato masher or beat with an electric mixer on low speed. Add 2 tablespoons butter. Season to taste with salt and black pepper. Gradually beat in enough milk (2 to 4 tablespoons) to make potatoes light and fluffy.

Nutrition Facts per serving: 457 cal., 22 g total fat (9 g sat. fat), 88 mg chol., 1,047 mg sodium, 40 g carbo., 4 g fiber, 27 g pro.

Serve this quick-to-fix bake with a variety of condiments so everyone can choose a mix of favorites.

CHEESEBURGER & FRIES CASSEROLE

2 pounds lean ground beef

1 10¾-ounce can condensed golden mushroom soup

1 10¾-ounce can condensed cheddar cheese soup

1 20-ounce package frozen fried crinkle-cut potatoes

Toppings (such as ketchup, pickles, mustard, and chopped tomato) (optional)

1 In a large skillet cook ground beef, half at a time, over medium heat until brown; drain. Place the cooked meat in an ungreased 3-quart rectangular baking dish. In a medium bowl combine the soups. Spread over meat in baking dish. Sprinkle potatoes over the top.

2 Bake, uncovered, in a 350°F oven for 45 to 55 minutes or until the fries are golden. If desired, serve with toppings.

Nutrition Facts per serving: 348 cal., 18 g total fat (6 g sat. fat), 78 mg chol., 654 mg sodium, 24 g carbo., 2 g fiber, 24 g pro.

PREP:
15 minutes

BAKE:
45 minutes

OVEN:
350°F

MAKES:
8 to 10 servings

If you're crunched for time, enlist the help of instant mashed potatoes for this dish. They're easy to prepare and will cut prep time in half.

PRAIRIE POTATO BAKE

PREP:

45 minutes

COOL:

1 hour

BAKE:

40 minutes

OVEN:

350°F

MAKES:

6 servings

1	recipe Old-Fashioned Mashed Potatoes
1½	pounds ground beef
½	cup chopped onion (1 medium)
¾	cup beef broth
¼	cup all-purpose flour
¼	teaspoon salt
⅛	teaspoon black pepper
1	10¾-ounce can condensed cream of mushroom soup
1	8-ounce carton dairy sour cream
6	ounces process cheese food, cut into six 1½-inch cubes
2	cups cornflakes, crushed

1 Prepare Mashed Potatoes; set aside to cool for 1 hour or until cool enough to handle.

2 In a large skillet cook ground beef and onion over medium heat until meat is brown and onion is tender; drain. In a small bowl combine broth, flour, salt, and pepper; mix well. Stir broth mixture into meat mixture. Cook and stir over medium heat until thickened and bubbly. Remove from heat. Stir in soup and sour cream. Transfer to an ungreased 3-quart casserole; set aside.

3 For potato topping, shape about ⅔ cup of the Mashed Potatoes into a ball. Make a hole in the center of ball; insert a cube of cheese into the hole, then reshape into a ball, enclosing the cheese. Repeat with remaining mashed potatoes and cheese cubes. Roll each ball in crushed cornflakes. Arrange potato balls on top of meat mixture in casserole.

4 Bake, uncovered, in a 350°F oven about 40 minutes or until bubbly and potatoes are heated through.

OLD-FASHIONED MASHED POTATOES: Peel and quarter 2 pounds (about 6 medium) baking potatoes. Cook, covered, in boiling lightly salted water to cover for 20 to 25 minutes or until tender; drain. Mash with a potato masher or beat with an electric mixer on low speed. Add ¼ cup butter. Season to taste with salt and black pepper. Gradually beat in enough milk (⅓ to ½ cup) to make potatoes light and fluffy.

Nutrition Facts per serving: 685 cal., 41 g total fat (21 g sat. fat), 130 mg chol., 1,157 mg sodium, 44 g carbo., 2 g fiber, 34 g pro.

Refrigerated corn bread twists make a quick crust for this hearty Tex–Mex pie.

CHILI-CORN BREAD PIE

¾	pound lean ground beef
½	cup chopped onion (1 medium)
½	cup coarsely chopped green sweet pepper (1 small)
1	15-ounce can chili beans with chili gravy or chili beans, undrained
1	8-ounce can tomato sauce
1	6-ounce can tomato paste
2	to 3 tablespoons chili powder
½	teaspoon ground cumin
½	teaspoon bottled hot pepper sauce
1	11½-ounce package (8) refrigerated corn bread twists
1	8-ounce carton dairy sour cream
2	tablespoons all-purpose flour
1	cup shredded cheddar cheese (4 ounces)
2	cups corn chips, coarsely crushed (about 1 cup)
	Chopped green sweet pepper (optional)

PREP:
35 minutes
BAKE:
30 minutes
STAND:
10 minutes
OVEN:
375°F
MAKES:
8 servings

1 In a large skillet cook ground beef, onion, and the ½ cup sweet pepper over medium heat until meat is brown and vegetables are tender; drain. Stir in undrained beans, the tomato sauce, tomato paste, chili powder, cumin, and hot pepper sauce. Bring to boiling; reduce heat. Simmer, uncovered, for 5 minutes, stirring frequently.

2 Meanwhile, for crust, unwrap and separate corn bread twists but do not uncoil. Arrange corn bread coils in a lightly greased 9- or 10-inch pie plate. Press onto the bottom and up side of plate, extending about ½ inch above edge of pie plate.

3 Spoon ground beef mixture into crust. In a small bowl combine sour cream and flour; spread evenly over ground beef mixture. Sprinkle with cheese and crushed corn chips. Place pie plate on a baking sheet.

4 Bake, uncovered, in a 375°F oven about 30 minutes or until heated through. Let stand for 10 minutes before serving. If desired, garnish with chopped sweet pepper.

Nutrition Facts per serving: 492 cal., 26 g total fat (11 g sat. fat), 54 mg chol., 753 mg sodium, 43 g carbo., 5 g fiber, 21 g pro.

Thrifty grandmothers of yesteryear called on casseroles like this one as a way to stretch 8 ounces of ground beef into a dinner for four. You can call on it as an easy way to satisfy a hungry family.

GRANDMA'S SPAGHETTI CASSEROLE

PREP:

30 minutes

BAKE:

45 minutes

OVEN:

350°F

MAKES:

4 to 6 servings

8 ounces dried spaghetti

½ pound ground beef

½ cup chopped onion (1 medium)

½ cup chopped green sweet pepper (1 small)

1 14½-ounce can diced tomatoes

1 10¾-ounce can condensed tomato soup

½ teaspoon black pepper

2 cups shredded cheddar cheese (8 ounces)

4 slices bacon, crisp-cooked, drained, and crumbled

1 Cook spaghetti according to package directions; drain. Set aside.

2 In a large skillet cook ground beef, onion, and sweet pepper over medium heat until meat is brown and vegetables are tender; drain. Stir in undrained tomatoes, the soup, and black pepper. Bring just to boiling. Stir in 1 cup of the cheese until melted.

3 Add cooked spaghetti and the bacon to beef mixture, tossing to combine. Transfer to a greased 2-quart casserole. Bake, covered, in a 350°F oven for 30 minutes. Sprinkle with remaining 1 cup cheese. Bake, uncovered, about 15 minutes more or until bubbly and heated through.

Nutrition Facts per serving: 675 cal., 31 g total fat (16 g sat. fat), 100 mg chol., 1,007 mg sodium, 61 g carbo., 3 g fiber, 35 g pro.

This casserole is a hit at family tables—especially when there are teenagers involved. By the way, it's easy enough for a teenager to make, so hand over this recipe to a budding cook and take the night off.

NACHO CASSEROLE

1	pound lean ground beef
½	cup chopped onion (1 medium)
1	15-ounce can pork and beans in tomato sauce
1	11-ounce can whole kernel corn with sweet peppers, drained
1	10¾-ounce can condensed tomato soup
1	4-ounce can diced green chile peppers, drained
2	teaspoons chili powder
2	cups shredded Monterey Jack cheese or Monterey Jack cheese with jalapeño peppers (8 ounces)
2	cups coarsely crushed tortilla chips

1 In a large skillet cook ground beef and onion over medium heat until meat is brown and onion is tender; drain. Stir in pork and beans, corn, soup, chile peppers, and chili powder. Transfer to an ungreased 2-quart rectangular baking dish.

2 Bake, covered, in a 350°F oven about 40 minutes or until heated through. Sprinkle with cheese and tortilla chips. Bake, uncovered, for 5 minutes more. Serve immediately.

Nutrition Facts per serving: 555 cal., 32 g total fat (14 g sat. fat), 94 mg chol., 1,194 mg sodium, 42 g carbo., 7 g fiber, 30 g pro.

PREP:
20 minutes
BAKE:
45 minutes
OVEN:
350°F
MAKES:
6 servings

Boost the zest—or bring it down—depending on the type of pasta sauce you buy for this hearty Italian dish. Choose from cheese-infused sauces to plain-Jane-but-delicious marinara.

ZESTY ITALIAN CRESCENT CASSEROLE

PREP:

20 minutes

BAKE:

20 minutes

OVEN:

375°F

MAKES:

8 servings

1	pound lean ground beef
¼	cup chopped onion
1	cup purchased spaghetti or pasta sauce
1½	cups shredded mozzarella or Monterey Jack cheese (6 ounces)
½	cup dairy sour cream
1	8-ounce package refrigerated crescent rolls
⅓	cup grated Parmesan cheese
2	tablespoons butter, melted

1 In a large skillet cook ground beef and onion over medium heat until meat is brown and onion is tender; drain. Stir in spaghetti sauce; heat through. Transfer to an ungreased 2-quart baking dish.

2 Meanwhile, in a small bowl combine mozzarella cheese and sour cream. Spoon cheese mixture over meat in baking dish.

3 Unroll crescent roll dough. Separate into triangles for a round casserole or press edges together and roll out slightly into a rectangle for a rectangular casserole. Place dough over the cheese in baking dish. Combine Parmesan cheese and melted butter. Brush over dough.

4 Bake, uncovered, in a 375°F oven for 20 to 25 minutes or until deep golden brown.

Nutrition Facts per serving: 286 cal., 12 g total fat (5 g sat. fat), 44 mg chol., 490 mg sodium, 22 g carbo., 2 g fiber, 21 g pro.

Your grandmother may have made Hot Tamale Pie—this recipe dates back to the 1940s and has been rated high with families ever since. Freshen it up with a little sour cream on top.

HOT TAMALE PIE

1½	pounds lean ground beef
1	cup chopped onion (1 large)
1	10¾-ounce can condensed tomato soup
1	8-ounce can tomato sauce
¾	cup frozen whole kernel corn
½	cup chopped pitted ripe olives
2	tablespoons chili powder
½	teaspoon black pepper
¾	cup yellow cornmeal
½	cup all-purpose flour
1	teaspoon baking powder
½	teaspoon baking soda
½	teaspoon salt
1	egg
1	cup buttermilk or sour milk*
2	tablespoons cooking oil
½	cup shredded cheddar cheese (2 ounces) (optional)

PREP:
30 minutes
BAKE:
20 minutes
OVEN:
425°F
MAKES:
6 to 8 servings

1 In a large skillet cook ground beef and onion over medium heat until meat is brown and onion is tender; drain. Stir in soup, tomato sauce, corn, olives, chili powder, and pepper. Bring just to boiling. Transfer to an ungreased 2-quart square baking dish; set aside.

2 In a medium bowl combine cornmeal, flour, baking powder, baking soda, and salt. In a small bowl whisk together egg, buttermilk, and oil. Add to cornmeal mixture; stir just until batter is smooth. If desired, fold in cheese. Spread over hot meat mixture.

3 Bake, uncovered, in a 425°F oven for 20 to 25 minutes or until golden.

*NOTE: To make 1 cup sour milk, place 1 tablespoon lemon juice or vinegar in a glass measuring cup. Add enough milk to make 1 cup liquid; stir. Let the mixture stand for 5 minutes before using.

Nutrition Facts per serving: 534 cal., 30 g total fat (10 g sat. fat), 119 mg chol., 1,138 mg sodium, 40 g carbo., 4 g fiber, 27 g pro.

Instant mashed potatoes are the key ingredient for the crusts. Add a salad for a satisfying meal.

DOUBLE-CRUST PIZZA CASSEROLE

PREP:
25 minutes

BAKE:
35 minutes

STAND:
5 minutes

OVEN:
425°F

MAKES:
12 servings

3	cups all-purpose flour
3	cups packaged instant mashed potatoes
2	cups milk
½	cup butter, melted
1	pound lean ground beef
¾	pound bulk Italian sausage
1	cup coarsely chopped onion (1 large)
1	8-ounce can tomato sauce
1	6-ounce can Italian-style tomato paste
½	of a 1.3- to 1.5-ounce package sloppy joe seasoning mix (about 2 tablespoons)
1	2¼-ounce can sliced ripe olives, drained (optional)
1	cup shredded mozzarella cheese (4 ounces)
1	tablespoon yellow cornmeal

1 For crust dough, combine flour, dried potatoes, milk, and melted butter; set aside. (Mixture will stiffen somewhat as it stands.)

2 For filling, in a large skillet cook ground beef, sausage, and onion over medium heat until meat is brown and onion is tender; drain. Stir in tomato sauce, tomato paste, seasoning mix, and, if desired, olives.

3 Using floured fingers, press half of the dough over the bottom and about 1½ inches up the sides of an ungreased 3-quart rectangular baking dish. Spread filling over crust; sprinkle with cheese. Between two large sheets of waxed paper, roll remaining dough to a 15×11-inch rectangle; remove top sheet and invert rolled dough over filling. Remove waxed paper. Trim edges as necessary. Turn edges of top crust under and seal to bottom crust. Sprinkle with cornmeal.

4 Bake, uncovered, in a 425°F oven about 35 minutes or until heated through and crust is golden brown. Let stand for 5 minutes before serving.

Nutrition Facts per serving: 456 cal., 23 g total fat (10 g sat. fat), 76 mg chol., 708 mg sodium, 41 g carbo., 2 g fiber, 19 g pro.

Pastitsio (pah-STEET-see-oh) is a Greek-style pasta casserole with a white sauce. Wow your guests or friends at a potluck with your talents in cooking ethnic fare.

PASTITSIO

1	pound lean ground beef
1	cup chopped onion (1 large)
1	8-ounce can tomato sauce
¼	cup dry white wine, beef broth, or water
⅛	teaspoon ground cinnamon
8	ounces dried penne pasta (4 cups)
¾	cup milk
4	slightly beaten eggs
¼	cup butter
2	tablespoons all-purpose flour
¼	teaspoon salt
⅛	teaspoon black pepper
1½	cups milk
1	cup shredded Kefalotiri, kasseri, or Romano cheese*

PREP:

45 minutes

BAKE:

30 minutes

STAND:

15 minutes

OVEN:

350°F

MAKES:

8 servings

1 For meat sauce, in a large skillet cook ground beef and onion over medium heat until meat is brown and onion is tender; drain. Stir in tomato sauce, wine, and cinnamon. Bring to boiling; reduce heat. Cover and simmer for 30 minutes, stirring occasionally. Set aside.

2 Meanwhile, cook pasta according to package directions; drain. In a large bowl toss cooked pasta with the ¾ cup milk, 2 of the eggs, and 2 tablespoons of the butter. Set aside.

3 For cream sauce, in a small saucepan melt the remaining 2 tablespoons butter over medium heat. Stir in flour, salt, and pepper until smooth. Gradually add the 1½ cups milk. Cook and stir until mixture is thickened and bubbly. Gradually stir hot mixture into the remaining 2 eggs. Set aside.

4 Spread half of the pasta mixture in a greased 3-quart rectangular baking dish. Top with meat sauce. Sprinkle with ⅓ cup of the cheese. Top with the remaining pasta mixture; sprinkle with another ⅓ cup of the cheese. Pour cream sauce over all; sprinkle with remaining ⅓ cup cheese.

5 Bake, covered, in a 350°F oven for 20 minutes. Uncover. Bake for 10 to 15 minutes more or until a knife inserted in center comes out clean. Let stand for 15 minutes before serving.

*NOTE: Kefalotiri and kasseri cheeses are both hard cheeses widely used in Greek cooking. They have sharp, salty flavors that are quite similar to Romano cheese, which you may find more readily in your supermarket.

Nutrition Facts per serving: 431 cal., 23 g total fat (12 g sat. fat), 178 mg chol., 537 mg sodium, 30 g carbo., 2 g fiber, 23 g pro.

Lovingly referred to as simply "the hot dish" in some parts of the country, this quintessential dish is hometown cooking at its best and will surely warm your soul.

HAMBURGER, POTATO & BEAN CASSEROLE

PREP:

30 minutes

BAKE:

55 minutes

STAND:

10 minutes

OVEN:

350°F

MAKES:

6 servings

1   pound lean ground beef

1   10¾-ounce can condensed golden mushroom soup

½   cup milk

1   teaspoon garlic salt

½   teaspoon black pepper

3   medium potatoes, peeled if desired, halved lengthwise, and sliced ¼ inch thick

1   medium onion, halved and sliced

1   15½-ounce can dark red kidney beans, rinsed and drained

1   4½-ounce can (drained weight) sliced mushrooms, drained

1   cup shredded cheddar cheese (4 ounces)

1 In a large skillet cook ground beef over medium heat until brown; drain. Set aside.

2 In a medium bowl combine soup, milk, garlic salt, and pepper; spread ⅓ cup of soup mixture into the bottom of an ungreased 3-quart rectangular baking dish. Top with half of each of the potatoes, the onion, beans, cooked beef, and mushrooms. Drizzle with half of the remaining soup mixture. Repeat layers, starting with potatoes and ending with remaining soup mixture.

3 Bake, covered, in 350°F oven for 55 to 60 minutes or until the potatoes are tender. Sprinkle with cheese. Let stand for 10 minutes before serving.

Nutrition Facts per serving: 364 cal., 15 g total fat (7 g sat. fat), 70 mg chol., 903 mg sodium, 32 g carbo., 6 g fiber, 27 g pro.

This stripped-down version of lasagna has no surprises, so it's perfect for kids. Enlist their help when preparing it. They'll love building the different layers.

KIDS' FAVORITE LASAGNA

¾	pound ground beef
2½	cups purchased spaghetti sauce
6	dried lasagna noodles (6 ounces)
1½	cups cottage cheese
1½	cups shredded mozzarella cheese (6 ounces)
2	tablespoons grated Parmesan cheese (optional)

1 In a large skillet cook ground beef over medium heat until brown; drain. Stir in 1½ cups of the spaghetti sauce.

2 Spread remaining spaghetti sauce into the bottom of an ungreased 2-quart rectangular baking dish. Place 2 uncooked noodles on sauce. Spread one-third of the meat mixture over noodles and ¾ cup of the cottage cheese over meat. Sprinkle ½ cup of the mozzarella cheese over cottage cheese. Repeat layers. Layer remaining noodles, meat mixture, and mozzarella cheese. (Layers will be high in the dish but will cook down.) If desired, sprinkle Parmesan cheese on top.

3 Bake, covered, in a 350°F oven about 1 hour or until heated through. Let stand for 15 minutes before serving.

Nutrition Facts per serving: 273 cal., 12 g total fat (6 g sat. fat), 63 mg chol., 632 mg sodium, 21 g carbo., 2 g fiber, 20 g pro.

PREP:
30 minutes
BAKE:
1 hour
STAND:
15 minutes
OVEN:
350°F
MAKES:
8 servings

This version of traditional beef and noodles uses vermicelli—very thin spaghetti noodles.

BEEF & NOODLE CASSEROLE

PREP:

15 minutes

BAKE:

30 minutes

STAND:

5 minutes

OVEN:

350°F

MAKES:

4 servings

1	pound ground beef
½	cup milk
½	of an 8-ounce tub cream cheese with chives and onion (½ cup)
½	cup shredded carrot (1 medium)
1	4.6-ounce package vermicelli with garlic and olive oil or one 4.8-ounce package angel hair pasta with herbs
1½	cups boiling water

1 In a large skillet cook ground beef over medium heat until brown; drain.

2 Meanwhile, in a greased 1½-quart casserole gradually whisk milk into cream cheese until smooth. Stir in carrot and seasoning packet from pasta mix. Stir in beef. Break pasta from pasta mix into 1-inch-long pieces; stir into meat mixture. Slowly pour the boiling water over meat mixture.

3 Bake, covered, in a 350°F oven for 30 to 35 minutes or until noodles are tender, stirring twice. Let stand, covered, for 5 minutes. Stir before serving.

Nutrition Facts per serving: 463 cal., 25 g total fat (13 g sat. fat), 101 mg chol., 619 mg sodium, 28 g carbo., 2 g fiber, 28 g pro.

This dish combines sweet pepper, mushrooms, and spinach with Italian flavors. What comes out is easy and tasty, and people can't get enough of it.

ITALIAN BEEF & SPINACH PIE

12	ounces lean ground beef
¾	cup chopped red and/or yellow sweet pepper (1 medium)
1	clove garlic, minced
1	cup water
1	6-ounce can Italian-style tomato paste
1	4-ounce can (drained weight) sliced mushrooms, drained
½	teaspoon dried Italian seasoning, crushed
1	10-ounce package frozen chopped spinach, thawed and drained well
¾	cup shredded mozzarella cheese (3 ounces)
⅔	cup light or regular ricotta cheese
½	teaspoon salt
1	baked 9-inch pastry shell*

PREP:
20 minutes
BAKE:
30 minutes
STAND:
10 minutes
OVEN:
350°F
MAKES:
8 servings

1 In a large skillet cook ground beef, sweet pepper, and garlic over medium heat until meat is brown and sweet pepper is tender; drain. Stir in the water, tomato paste, mushrooms, and Italian seasoning. Bring to boiling; reduce heat. Cover and simmer for 10 minutes.

2 Meanwhile, in a medium bowl combine spinach, ¼ cup of the mozzarella cheese, the ricotta cheese, and salt. Spoon spinach mixture into baked pastry shell. Top with meat mixture. Cover edge of pastry with foil to prevent overbrowning.

3 Bake in a 350°F oven for 30 to 35 minutes or until heated through. Sprinkle with remaining ½ cup mozzarella cheese. Let stand for 10 minutes before serving.

*NOTE: For a baked pastry shell, bake one 9-inch frozen unbaked deep-dish pastry shell according to package directions. Or prepare and bake 1 rolled refrigerated unbaked piecrust (¹/₂ of a 15-ounce package) according to package directions.

Nutrition Facts per serving: 237 cal., 12 g total fat (4 g sat. fat), 38 mg chol., 635 mg sodium, 16 g carbo., 2 g fiber, 15 g pro.

Tamales—which usually are only part of a Mexican dinner—star in this main-dish adaptation.

TAMALE PIE

PREP:

20 minutes

BAKE:

22 minutes

OVEN:

375°F

MAKES:

6 servings

1 8½-ounce package corn muffin mix

1 cup shredded cheddar cheese (4 ounces)

1 4-ounce can diced green chile peppers, drained

1 pound ground beef or bulk pork sausage

1 15-ounce can red kidney beans, rinsed and drained

1 10-ounce can enchilada sauce

   Dairy sour cream (optional)

1 Prepare muffin mix according to package directions (do not bake). Stir in ½ cup of the cheese and the chile peppers. Spread mixture into the bottom of a greased 2-quart rectangular baking dish.

2 Bake in a 375°F oven for 12 to 15 minutes or until a wooden toothpick inserted near the center comes out clean.

3 Meanwhile, in a large skillet cook ground beef over medium heat until brown; drain. Stir in beans and enchilada sauce. Spread meat mixture over baked corn muffin mixture.

4 Bake for 7 minutes more. Sprinkle with remaining ½ cup cheese. Bake about 3 minutes more or until cheese melts and mixture is heated through. To serve, cut into squares. If desired, serve with sour cream.

Nutrition Facts per serving: 464 cal., 21 g total fat (8 g sat. fat), 67 mg chol., 778 mg sodium, 44 g carbo., 4 g fiber, 27 g pro.

Most spaghetti pies use pasta as a crust. This luscious favorite is reversed so the spaghetti tops the meat. If you like, sprinkle with additional Parmesan cheese.

SPAGHETTI PIE

1	5-ounce can (²⁄₃ cup) evaporated milk
½	cup fine dry bread crumbs
⅓	cup chopped onion (1 small)
1	teaspoon salt
1	teaspoon dried Italian seasoning, crushed
¼	teaspoon black pepper
1	pound lean ground beef
4	ounces dried spaghetti
1	tablespoon butter
¼	cup grated Parmesan cheese
1	beaten egg
1	8-ounce can pizza sauce
1	cup shredded mozzarella cheese (4 ounces)

1 In a large bowl combine evaporated milk, bread crumbs, onion, salt, Italian seasoning, and pepper. Add ground beef and mix well. Spread beef mixture evenly over the bottom and up the side of an ungreased 9-inch pie plate. Bake, uncovered, in a 350°F oven about 30 minutes or until meat is brown and an instant-read thermometer inserted into center of meat registers 160°F. Carefully tilt pie plate and drain off fat.

2 Meanwhile, cook spaghetti according to package directions; drain. Return to pan. Add butter and stir until melted. Stir in Parmesan cheese and egg until spaghetti is coated.

3 Spoon half of the pizza sauce over the meat mixture in pie plate. Top with ½ cup of the mozzarella cheese and the spaghetti mixture. Spoon remaining pizza sauce over spaghetti layer; top with remaining ½ cup cheese. Bake, uncovered, about 20 minutes more or until pie is heated through. Let stand for 15 minutes before serving.

Nutrition Facts per serving: 373 cal., 17 g total fat (8 g sat. fat), 110 mg chol., 1,078 mg sodium, 28 g carbo., 2 g fiber, 26 g pro.

PREP:
20 minutes
BAKE:
50 minutes
STAND:
15 minutes
OVEN:
350°F
MAKES:
6 servings

Eggplant, ground beef, Italian seasoning, and an Italian-style cheese combo blend deliciously in this dinner-in-a-dish.

EGGPLANT & BEEF CASSEROLE

PREP:

50 minutes

BAKE:

30 minutes

STAND:

10 minutes

OVEN:

350°F

MAKES:

8 servings

¾ cup milk

1 egg

¾ cup all-purpose flour

½ teaspoon salt

¼ teaspoon black pepper

1 eggplant (1½ pounds), peeled and sliced ½ inch thick

3 tablespoons cooking oil

1 pound lean ground beef

1 cup chopped green sweet pepper (1 large)

¾ cup chopped onions (1½ medium)

1 15-ounce can tomato sauce

1 8-ounce can tomato sauce

1½ teaspoons dried Italian seasoning, crushed

2 cups shredded Italian-style cheese blend (8 ounces)

1 In a small bowl whisk together milk and egg. In a shallow dish combine flour, salt, and black pepper. Dip eggplant slices into egg mixture, then into flour mixture, turning to coat both sides. In a large skillet cook eggplant slices, several at a time, in hot oil over medium-high heat for 4 to 6 minutes or until golden, turning once. (If necessary, add more oil.) Drain on paper towels.

2 In a large skillet cook ground beef, sweet pepper, and onions over medium heat until meat is brown; drain. Stir in both cans of tomato sauce and Italian seasoning.

3 Layer half of the eggplant slices in a greased 3-quart rectangular baking dish, cutting slices to fit. Spread with half of the meat mixture; sprinkle with 1 cup of the cheese. Repeat layers.

4 Bake, covered, in a 350°F oven for 20 minutes. Uncover. Bake for 10 to 15 minutes more or until heated through. Let stand for 10 minutes before serving.

Nutrition Facts per serving: 340 cal., 19 g total fat (7 g sat. fat), 84 mg chol., 796 mg sodium, 23 g carbo., 4 g fiber, 22 g pro.

This robust Louisiana-style lasagna is a tasty combination of sausage and beef with traditional lasagna ingredients. Andouille sausage, a spicy smoked sausage, is perfect for this dish.

CREOLE LASAGNA

9	dried lasagna noodles (8 ounces)
½	pound cooked andouille sausage or smoked pork sausage links, halved lengthwise and sliced
½	pound lean ground beef
½	cup chopped celery (1 stalk)
⅓	cup chopped green sweet pepper
⅓	cup chopped onion (1 small)
2	cloves garlic, minced
1½	cups water
1	6-ounce can tomato paste
2	teaspoons sugar
¼	teaspoon cayenne pepper
8	ounces sliced mozzarella cheese
⅓	cup shredded Parmesan cheese (1½ ounces)

PREP:
35 minutes
BAKE:
30 minutes
STAND:
10 minutes
OVEN:
350°F
MAKES:
8 servings

1 Cook lasagna noodles according to package directions; drain. Rinse with cold water; drain well.

2 Meanwhile, for meat sauce, in a large saucepan cook sausage over medium-high heat until brown, stirring frequently. Remove sausage from saucepan. Drain fat from saucepan. In the same saucepan cook ground beef, celery, sweet pepper, onion, and garlic until meat is brown and vegetables are tender; drain. Stir in sausage, the water, tomato paste, sugar, and cayenne pepper. Bring to boiling; reduce heat. Cover and simmer for 15 minutes.

3 Arrange 4 of the lasagna noodles in a lightly greased 3-quart rectangular baking dish. Top with half of the meat sauce and half of the cheeses. Repeat layers with remaining noodles and remaining meat sauce.

4 Bake, covered, in a 350°F oven for 20 minutes. Top with remaining cheeses. Bake, uncovered, for 10 minutes more. Let stand for 10 minutes before serving.

Nutrition Facts per serving: 384 cal., 20 g total fat (9 g sat. fat), 63 mg chol., 615 mg sodium, 26 g carbo., 2 g fiber, 23 g pro.

This hearty casserole is the perfect dish to come home to after a long day. Consider it comfort food with a south-of-the-border twist.

BEAN & BEEF ENCHILADA CASSEROLE

PREP:

35 minutes

BAKE:

40 minutes

OVEN:

350°F

MAKES:

8 servings

8	ounces lean ground beef
½	cup chopped onion (1 medium)
1	teaspoon chili powder
½	teaspoon ground cumin
1	15-ounce can pinto beans, rinsed and drained
1	4-ounce can diced green chile peppers, undrained
1	8-ounce carton dairy sour cream
2	tablespoons all-purpose flour
¼	teaspoon garlic powder
8	6-inch corn tortillas
1	10-ounce can enchilada sauce
¾	cup shredded cheddar cheese (3 ounces)
	Fresh cilantro (optional)

1 In a large skillet cook the ground beef and onion over medium heat until meat is brown and onion is tender; drain. Stir in chili powder and cumin; cook and stir for 1 minute more. Stir in pinto beans and undrained chile peppers; set aside. In a small bowl combine sour cream, flour, and garlic powder; set aside.

2 Place 4 of the tortillas in the bottom of a lightly greased 2-quart rectangular baking dish, cutting to fit and overlapping as necessary. Top with half of the meat mixture, half of the sour cream mixture, and half of the enchilada sauce. Repeat layers.

3 Bake, covered, in a 350°F oven for 35 to 40 minutes or until heated through. Sprinkle with cheese. Bake, uncovered, about 5 minutes more or until cheese is melted. If desired, garnish with cilantro.

Nutrition Facts per serving: 298 cal., 14 g total fat (7 g sat. fat), 41 mg chol., 419 mg sodium, 30 g carbo., 4 g fiber, 14 g pro.

To lighten this recipe, you can use light sour cream dip, light cream cheese, and reduced-fat cheddar cheese and still enjoy the same satisfying results.

CREAMY LAYERED BEEF & PASTA BAKE

8	ounces dried rotini or elbow macaroni (2¾ cups)
1	pound lean ground beef
1	15-ounce can Italian-style tomato sauce
1	8-ounce container dairy sour cream chive dip
3	ounces cream cheese, softened
2	tablespoons milk
¾	cup shredded cheddar cheese and/or mozzarella cheese (3 ounces)
2	tablespoons sliced green onion (1) (optional)

PREP:
30 minutes
BAKE:
30 minutes
OVEN:
350°F
MAKES:
8 servings

1 Cook rotini according to package directions; drain. Meanwhile, in a large skillet cook ground beef over medium heat until brown; drain. Stir in tomato sauce. Bring to boiling; reduce heat. Simmer, uncovered, for 15 minutes, stirring occasionally.

2 In a small bowl combine dip, cream cheese, and milk. Layer beef mixture, cooked pasta, and dip mixture in a greased 2-quart rectangular baking dish.

3 Bake, covered, in a 350°F oven for 15 minutes. Sprinkle with cheese. Bake, uncovered, for 15 minutes more. If desired, top with green onion.

Nutrition Facts per serving: 354 cal., 19 g total fat (10 g sat. fat), 71 mg chol., 613 mg sodium, 28 g carbo., 2 g fiber, 19 g pro.

Traditionally, enchiladas are made with corn tortillas. This layered version uses flour tortillas and rich refried beans. Add Spanish rice for a complete meal.

ENCHILADA GRANDE CASSEROLE

PREP:

30 minutes

BAKE:

30 minutes

STAND:

10 minutes

OVEN:

350°F

MAKES:

8 to 10 servings

1	pound lean ground beef
1	16-ounce can refried beans
1	15-ounce can low-sodium tomato sauce
½	cup water
1	1⅜-ounce package enchilada sauce mix
8	7- to 8-inch flour tortillas
2	cups shredded cheddar cheese (8 ounces)
	Dairy sour cream (optional)
	Sliced green onions (optional)

1 In a large skillet cook ground beef over medium heat until brown; drain. Stir in refried beans, tomato sauce, the water, and enchilada sauce mix. Bring to boiling; reduce heat. Simmer, uncovered, for 15 minutes, stirring occasionally.

2 Arrange 4 tortillas in the bottom of a greased 3-quart rectangular baking dish, cutting to fit and overlapping as necessary. Spoon half of the meat mixture over tortillas in dish. Sprinkle with 1 cup of the cheese. Repeat layers with remaining 4 tortillas and meat mixture.

3 Bake, uncovered, in a 350°F oven for 20 minutes. Sprinkle with remaining 1 cup cheese. Bake, uncovered, about 10 minutes more or until heated through. Let stand for 10 minutes. If desired, top with sour cream and green onions.

Nutrition Facts per serving: 442 cal., 20 g total fat (10 g sat. fat), 60 mg chol., 1,227 mg sodium, 41 g carbo., 8 g fiber, 24 g pro.

Get extra mileage from 2 cups of leftover spaghetti sauce by using it in place of the sauce mix and tomato sauce. Because the family-style casserole has a biscuit-like top, you can skip serving bread.

POP-UP PIZZA CASSEROLE

1½	pounds ground beef
1	cup chopped onion (1 large)
1	cup chopped green sweet pepper (1 large)
1	clove garlic, minced
1	1.5-ounce envelope spaghetti sauce mix
½	teaspoon dried oregano, crushed
1	15-ounce can tomato sauce
½	cup water
1	cup milk
2	eggs
1	tablespoon cooking oil
1	cup all-purpose flour
½	teaspoon salt
1	cup shredded mozzarella cheese (4 ounces)
¼	cup grated Parmesan cheese

PREP:
30 minutes

BAKE:
25 minutes

OVEN:
400°F

MAKES:
9 servings

1 In a large skillet cook ground beef over medium heat until brown; drain. Stir in onion, sweet pepper, garlic, spaghetti sauce mix, and oregano. Add tomato sauce and the water. Cook and stir until mixture comes to boiling; reduce heat. Cover and simmer for 10 minutes.

2 Meanwhile, in a medium mixing bowl, beat milk, eggs, and oil with an electric mixer on medium speed for 1 minute. Add flour and salt; beat for 2 minutes more.

3 Transfer hot beef mixture to an ungreased 3-quart rectangular baking dish. Sprinkle with mozzarella cheese. Pour egg mixture evenly over top. Sprinkle with Parmesan cheese. Bake, uncovered, in a 400°F oven for 25 to 30 minutes or until puffed and golden brown. Serve immediately.

Nutrition Facts per serving: 392 cal., 24 g total fat (10 g sat. fat), 119 mg chol., 896 mg sodium, 22 g carbo., 2 g fiber, 22 g pro.

To make this dish heartier and spicier, add a can each of chili beans and chopped green chiles.

GUADALUPE SWEET PEPPER PIE

PREP:

25 minutes

BAKE:

30 minutes

OVEN:

375°F

MAKES:

8 to 10 servings

2¼ cups packaged biscuit mix

½ cup cold water

1 pound ground beef

1 8-ounce carton dairy sour cream

1 cup shredded cheddar cheese (4 ounces)

⅔ cup mayonnaise or salad dressing

2 tablespoons chopped onion

2 medium tomatoes, thinly sliced

¾ cup chopped green sweet pepper (1 medium)

Paprika

1 For crust, in a medium bowl combine biscuit mix and cold water until biscuit mix is moistened and a soft dough has formed. Press mixture into the bottom and ½ inch up the sides of a greased 3-quart rectangular baking dish. Bake in a 375°F oven about 12 minutes or until lightly browned.

2 Meanwhile, in a large skillet cook ground beef over medium heat until brown; drain. Set aside. In a medium bowl combine sour cream, cheese, mayonnaise, and onion. Set aside.

3 Sprinkle cooked ground beef over baked crust. Layer tomatoes over beef and sprinkle with sweet pepper. Spread sour cream mixture on top. Sprinkle with paprika.

4 Bake, uncovered, about 30 minutes or until bubbly around edges.

Nutrition Facts per serving: 561 cal., 43 g total fat (15 g sat. fat), 75 mg chol., 653 mg sodium, 26 g carbo., 1 g fiber, 17 g pro.

Canned items—diced tomatoes, mushrooms, olives, and cream of mushroom soup—drive this flavorful bake. Such timesavers make preparation that much easier.

SPAGHETTI BAKE

12	ounces dried spaghetti
1	pound lean ground beef
1	cup chopped onion (1 large)
1	cup chopped green sweet pepper (1 large)
1	28-ounce can diced tomatoes, undrained
1	4-ounce can (drained weight) sliced mushrooms, drained
1	2¼-ounce can sliced pitted ripe olives, drained
1½	teaspoons dried oregano, crushed
2	cups shredded cheddar cheese (8 ounces)
1	10¾-ounce can condensed cream of mushroom soup
¼	cup water
¼	cup grated Parmesan cheese

PREP:

25 minutes

BAKE:

30 minutes

OVEN:

350°F

MAKES:

8 servings

1 Cook spaghetti according to package directions; drain. Set aside. In a large skillet cook ground beef, onion, and sweet pepper over medium heat until meat is brown and vegetables are tender; drain. Stir in undrained tomatoes, the mushrooms, olives, and oregano. Bring to boiling; reduce heat. Simmer, uncovered, for 10 minutes.

2 Spread half of the cooked spaghetti into a greased 3-quart rectangular baking dish. Top with half of the beef mixture and 1 cup of the cheddar cheese; repeat layers. Combine soup and the water; spread over cheese. Sprinkle with Parmesan cheese. Bake, uncovered, in a 350°F oven for 30 minutes or until heated through.

Nutrition Facts per serving: 456 cal., 19 g total fat (9 g sat. fat), 68 mg chol., 797 mg sodium, 44 g carbo., 3 g fiber, 25 g pro.

Savor the comfort and taste of a homemade potpie without spending hours in the kitchen. Prepared pastry, refrigerated potatoes, and frozen vegetables make it easy!

EASY BEEF POTPIE

PREP:

15 minutes

BAKE:

18 minutes

STAND:

10 minutes

OVEN:

400°F

MAKES:

8 servings

½ of a 15-ounce package (1 crust) rolled refrigerated unbaked piecrust

1½ pounds lean ground beef

2 cups refrigerated diced potatoes with onions or frozen loose-pack diced hash brown potatoes with onions and peppers

2 cups loose-pack frozen mixed vegetables

1 15-ounce can Italian-style or regular tomato sauce

1 14½-ounce can Italian-style stewed tomatoes, undrained

2 teaspoons sesame seeds

1 Let refrigerated piecrust stand according to package directions. Meanwhile, in a large skillet cook ground beef over medium heat until brown; drain. Stir in potatoes, frozen mixed vegetables, tomato sauce, and undrained tomatoes. Bring to boiling; remove from heat. Transfer to an ungreased 3-quart rectangular baking dish, spreading evenly.

2 Unfold piecrust; cut into eight wedges. Place half of the wedges along one long side of the dish, with points toward center, overlapping wedges slightly at the base. Repeat with the remaining pastry wedges on opposite side. Sprinkle with sesame seeds.

3 Bake, uncovered, in a 400°F oven for 18 to 20 minutes or until pastry is golden brown. Let stand for 10 minutes before serving.

Nutrition Facts per serving: 342 cal., 16 g total fat (6 g sat. fat), 59 mg chol., 669 mg sodium, 32 g carbo., 3 g fiber, 19 g pro.

Improvise with this recipe the way you would with pizza. Substitute Italian sausage for the ground beef or stir drained, canned sliced mushrooms or ripe olives into the meat mixture, if you like.

UPSIDE-DOWN PIZZA CASSEROLE

1½ pounds lean ground beef

1 15-ounce can Italian-style tomato sauce

1½ cups shredded mozzarella cheese (6 ounces)

1 10-ounce package (10) refrigerated biscuits

1 In a large skillet cook ground beef over medium heat until brown; drain. Stir in tomato sauce; heat through. Transfer to an ungreased 2-quart rectangular baking dish. Sprinkle with cheese. Flatten each biscuit with your hands; arrange the biscuits on top of cheese.

2 Bake, uncovered, in a 400°F oven about 15 minutes or until biscuits are golden.

Nutrition Facts per small serving: 321 cal., 20 g total fat (8 g sat. fat), 58 mg chol., 551 mg sodium, 15 g carbo., 1 g fiber, 17 g pro.

PREP:
20 minutes

BAKE:
15 minutes

OVEN:
400°F

MAKES:
10 small or 5 large servings

This potpie has a wonderful, cooked-all-day flavor. It's hearty enough for the biggest of appetites!

DEEP-DISH STEAK & VEGETABLE PIE

PREP:

40 minutes

BAKE:

25 minutes

STAND:

10 minutes

OVEN:

400°F

MAKES:

8 servings

½   of a 15-ounce package rolled refrigerated unbaked piecrust (1 crust)

¾   cup beef broth

2   cloves garlic, minced

1   teaspoon dried marjoram, crushed

¼   teaspoon salt

¼   teaspoon black pepper

2   medium parsnips (about 10 ounces), peeled and cut into ½-inch pieces

¾   cup thinly sliced carrots (2 small)

½   cup chopped onion (1 medium)

1   cup half-and-half or light cream

¼   cup all-purpose flour

2   17-ounce packages refrigerated cooked beef roast with au jus, cut into ¾-inch pieces

¾   cup frozen peas

Half-and-half or light cream

1 Let refrigerated piecrust stand according to package directions.

2 In a large saucepan combine broth, garlic, marjoram, salt, and pepper; bring to boiling. Add parsnips, carrots, and onion. Reduce heat; simmer, covered, for 10 minutes.

3 Meanwhile, in a small bowl, combine the 1 cup half-and-half and the flour. Stir half-and-half mixture into vegetable mixture. Cook and stir until thickened and bubbly. Add the beef, juices from meat, and the peas. Heat through. Remove from heat; cover to keep warm.

4 On a lightly floured surface, roll piecrust into a circle 2 inches larger than the diameter of the top of a 2-quart casserole. Transfer the meat mixture to ungreased casserole. Center pastry on top of meat mixture. Trim pastry 1 inch beyond edge of the casserole. Turn pastry under and flute to edge of casserole. Prick pastry several times with a fork. (If desired, use pastry scraps to make small vegetable decorations.) Brush crust with additional half-and-half. (If using pastry decorations, place on crust and brush again with half-and-half.)

5 Bake, uncovered, in a 400°F oven for 25 to 30 minutes or until crust is golden brown. Let stand for 10 minutes before serving.

Nutrition Facts per serving: 387 cal., 19 g total fat (10 g sat. fat), 81 mg chol., 719 mg sodium, 30 g carbo., 3 g fiber, 26 g pro.

If your family enjoys Reubens, take note! Now you can enjoy all the wonderful flavors of the specialty in a casserole, without having to fuss making individual sandwiches.

INSTANT REUBEN CASSEROLE

6 slices rye bread, toasted

2 5- to 6-ounce packages sliced corned beef, chopped

1 14- to 16-ounce can sauerkraut, rinsed, drained, and snipped

1 10¾-ounce can condensed cream of celery soup

1 cup shredded Swiss cheese (4 ounces)

3 tablespoons bottled Thousand Island salad dressing

2 tablespoons water

1 tablespoon butter, melted

PREP:
25 minutes
BAKE:
35 minutes
OVEN:
375°F
MAKES:
6 servings

1 Cut 4 slices of the toasted bread into cubes. Toss bread cubes with corned beef; spread in the bottom of a greased 2-quart square baking dish.

2 In a medium bowl combine sauerkraut, soup, ½ cup of the Swiss cheese, the Thousand Island salad dressing, and the water; spoon over corned beef mixture. Tear remaining 2 slices bread and place in a food processor or blender. Cover and process or blend until coarse crumbs form. Toss crumbs with melted butter; sprinkle on top of sauerkraut mixture.

3 Bake, uncovered, in a 375°F oven about 30 minutes or until heated through. Sprinkle with remaining ½ cup cheese. Bake about 5 minutes more or until cheese is melted.

Nutrition Facts per serving: 301 cal., 15 g total fat (6 g sat. fat), 46 mg chol., 1,643 mg sodium, 24 g carbo., 4 g fiber, 19 g pro.

This one-dish dinner is a winner every time with the combination of pork, apples, and cheddar.

PORK & APPLE CASSEROLE

PREP:

25 minutes

BAKE:

30 minutes

OVEN:

400°F

MAKES:

6 servings

1   pound bulk pork sausage

1⅓   cups chopped cored apples (2 medium)

1⅓   cups packaged corn bread stuffing mix

1   tablespoon dried minced onion

1¼   cups apple juice or apple cider

2   eggs

½   cup shredded cheddar cheese (2 ounces)

1 In a large skillet cook sausage over medium heat until brown; drain. Stir in apples, stuffing mix, and dried onion. In a small bowl whisk together apple juice and eggs. Add to sausage mixture, tossing to coat. Transfer mixture to a greased 2-quart square baking dish.

2 Bake, covered, in a 400°F oven for 20 minutes. Stir stuffing mixture and sprinkle with cheese. Bake, uncovered, about 10 minutes more or until heated through.

Nutrition Facts per serving: 429 cal., 29 g total fat (11 g sat. fat), 138 mg chol., 776 mg sodium, 24 g carbo., 2 g fiber, 17 g pro.

Classic Reuben sandwich fixings—sauerkraut, Swiss cheese, and corned beef—with seasonings and croutons are layered in this tasty casserole.

REUBEN SANDWICH CASSEROLE

1	32-ounce jar sauerkraut, rinsed and drained
½	cup chopped onion (1 medium)
4	teaspoons dried parsley flakes, crushed
2	teaspoons caraway seeds
4	cups shredded Swiss cheese (1 pound)
1⅓	cups bottled Thousand Island salad dressing
12	ounces thinly sliced cooked corned beef, coarsely chopped
6	slices rye bread, cut into ½-inch cubes
¼	cup butter, melted

PREP:
20 minutes
BAKE:
35 minutes
OVEN:
375°F
MAKES:
8 to 10 servings

1 In a large bowl combine drained sauerkraut, onion, parsley, and caraway seeds. Spread sauerkraut mixture evenly into a 3-quart rectangular baking dish.

2 Top with 2 cups of the cheese, ⅔ cup of the salad dressing, and the corned beef. Top with the remaining ⅔ cup salad dressing and 2 cups cheese.

3 In a large bowl toss bread cubes in melted butter until coated. Sprinkle bread cubes over the top of the casserole. Bake, uncovered, in a 375°F oven about 35 minutes or until heated through and bread cubes are browned.

Nutrition Facts per serving: 596 cal., 45 g total fat (18 g sat. fat), 120 mg chol., 3,872 mg sodium, 22 g carbo., 10 g fiber, 26 g pro.

Cilantro, spices, and chile peppers give a Southwestern kick to this biscuit-topped pie.

SANTA FE PORK PIE

PREP:

25 minutes

BAKE:

15 minutes

OVEN:

425°F

MAKES:

6 servings

1⅓   cups chicken broth

3   medium potatoes, peeled and cut into ½-inch cubes

½   cup sliced celery (1 stalk)

4   cloves garlic, minced

2   teaspoons chili powder

1   teaspoon dried thyme, crushed

1   pound boneless pork loin, cut into ¾-inch cubes

2   tablespoons cooking oil

1   4-ounce can diced green chile peppers, drained

4   teaspoons dried cilantro, crushed

1   4½- to 6-ounce package (5 or 6) refrigerated biscuits

    Dairy sour cream (optional)

1 In a medium saucepan combine broth, potatoes, celery, and garlic. Bring to boiling; reduce heat. Cover and simmer for 8 to 10 minutes or until potatoes are nearly tender. Do not drain.

2 Meanwhile, for filling, in a medium bowl combine chili powder and thyme. Add pork cubes; toss to coat. In a large skillet cook pork, half at a time, in hot oil over medium heat for 4 to 5 minutes or until no longer pink; drain. Return all meat to skillet. Add potato mixture, chile peppers, and cilantro. Bring to boiling. Transfer to an ungreased 2-quart casserole.

3 Snip each biscuit into 4 pieces; arrange on top of hot mixture. Bake, uncovered, in a 425°F oven about 15 minutes or until biscuits are golden. If desired, top with sour cream.

Nutrition Facts per serving: 240 cal., 10 g total fat (2 g sat. fat), 45 mg chol., 388 mg sodium, 18 g carbo., 2 g fiber, 19 g pro.

You can certainly use leftover pork or ham from the Sunday roast for this rich dish—but whatever you do, don't call it "leftovers," as it's a luscious and lovely creation in itself.

PORK & SPINACH BAKE

1	10¾-ounce can condensed cream of chicken soup
¼	cup shredded Swiss cheese (1 ounce)
2	tablespoons mayonnaise or salad dressing
1	teaspoon lemon juice
½	teaspoon Worcestershire sauce
2	10-ounce packages frozen chopped spinach, thawed and drained well
1½	cups chopped cooked pork or ham (about 8 ounces)
1½	cups soft bread crumbs*
2	tablespoons butter, melted

PREP:
20 minutes
BAKE:
35 minutes
OVEN:
350°F
MAKES:
6 servings

1 In a small saucepan combine soup, cheese, mayonnaise, lemon juice, and Worcestershire sauce. Bring to boiling. Remove from heat. In a large bowl stir ¾ cup of the soup mixture into drained spinach.

2 Spread spinach mixture into an ungreased 2-quart square baking dish. Sprinkle pork over spinach mixture. Spoon remaining soup mixture over all. In a small bowl toss together bread crumbs and melted butter; sprinkle over soup mixture.

3 Bake, uncovered, in a 350°F oven about 35 minutes or until mixture is heated through.

*NOTE: Use a blender or food processor to make fluffy soft bread crumbs. One slice yields ¾ cup crumbs.

Nutrition Facts per serving: 254 cal., 16 g total fat (6 g sat. fat), 52 mg chol., 680 mg sodium, 11 g carbo., 3 g fiber, 16 g pro.

Here, the good old-fashioned pork chop-and-rice bake is reinvented with a new style of cream of mushroom soup—one that's been infused with roasted garlic. Serve it with buttered green beans—updated with chopped, toasted cashews if you're feeling adventuresome!

PORK CHOP & RICE BAKE

PREP:

25 minutes

BAKE:

35 minutes

STAND:

10 minutes

OVEN:

375°F

MAKES:

4 servings

4	pork rib chops, cut ½ inch thick (about 2 pounds total)
1	tablespoon cooking oil
	Black pepper
1	small onion, thinly sliced and separated into rings
1	10¾-ounce can condensed cream of mushroom with roasted garlic soup
¾	cup water
½	cup dry white wine
¾	cup uncooked long grain rice
1	4-ounce can (drained weight) sliced mushrooms, drained
1	teaspoon Worcestershire sauce
¼	teaspoon dried thyme, crushed
2	tablespoons snipped fresh parsley (optional)

1 In a large skillet cook pork chops in hot oil over medium heat until brown on both sides. Remove pork chops from skillet, reserving drippings. Season chops with pepper; set aside.

2 In the same skillet cook onion in drippings until tender; set aside. In a large bowl combine soup, the water, and wine; stir in rice, mushrooms, Worcestershire sauce, and thyme. Transfer to an ungreased 3-quart rectangular baking dish. Top with pork chops; spoon cooked onions over chops.

3 Bake, covered, in a 375°F oven for 35 to 40 minutes or until rice is tender and chops are done (160°F). Let stand, covered, for 10 minutes before serving. If desired, sprinkle with parsley.

Nutrition Facts per serving: 602 cal., 22 g total fat (7 g sat. fat), 124 mg chol., 735 mg sodium, 36 g carbo., 2 g fiber, 55 g pro.

Those handy, crispy canned onions that usually appear on green bean casseroles top off this meaty dish.

PORK CHOP CASSEROLE

8	boneless pork loin chops, cut about ¾ inch thick (about 2 pounds)
⅓	cup all-purpose flour
¼	teaspoon salt
¼	teaspoon black pepper
2	tablespoons cooking oil
1	10¾-ounce can condensed cream of mushroom soup
⅔	cup chicken broth
½	cup dairy sour cream
½	teaspoon ground ginger
½	teaspoon dried rosemary, crushed
1	2.8-ounce can french-fried onions
	Hot cooked noodles

PREP:
15 minutes
BAKE:
30 minutes
OVEN:
350°F
MAKES:
8 servings

1 Trim fat from pork chops. In a shallow dish combine flour, salt, and pepper. Dip pork chops into flour mixture, turning to coat both sides.

2 In a large skillet cook chops, half at a time, in hot oil over medium heat until brown on both sides. Remove from heat.

3 In a medium bowl combine soup, broth, sour cream, ginger, and rosemary. Stir in half of the onions. Transfer to an ungreased 3-quart rectangular baking dish. Top with chops.

4 Bake, covered, in a 350°F oven for 25 minutes. Sprinkle with remaining onions. Bake, uncovered, for 5 to 10 minutes more or until pork chops are done (160°F). Serve with hot cooked noodles.

Nutrition Facts per serving: 411 cal., 19 g total fat (5 g sat. fat), 95 mg chol., 536 mg sodium, 31 g carbo., 1 g fiber, 28 g pro.

Anyone who grew up in mid-20th-century America likely will have fond memories of this good old potato-and-pork chop oven meal! With refrigerated diced potatoes, this version simplifies the classic.

PORK CHOPS WITH SCALLOPED POTATOES

PREP:

20 minutes

BAKE:

40 minutes

OVEN:

350°F

MAKES:

4 servings

1	10¾-ounce can condensed cream of celery soup
1	cup milk
⅓	cup sliced green onions (3)
4	slices American cheese, torn (4 ounces)
1	20-ounce package refrigerated diced potatoes with onions
4	cooked smoked pork chops (1½ to 2 pounds)
⅛	teaspoon black pepper
2	tablespoons snipped fresh chives (optional)

1 In a medium saucepan combine soup, milk, and onions. Heat through over medium heat. Stir in cheese; cook and stir until cheese is melted. Remove from heat; set aside.

2 Arrange potatoes in a single layer in an ungreased 3-quart rectangular baking dish. Place pork chops on top of potatoes. Sprinkle chops with pepper. Pour soup mixture over chops and potatoes.

3 Bake, covered, in a 350°F oven about 40 minutes or until heated through. If desired, sprinkle with chives just before serving.

Nutrition Facts per serving: 541 cal., 23 g total fat (11 g sat. fat), 123 mg chol., 3,226 mg sodium, 39 g carbo., 4 g fiber, 43 g pro.

Precooked dinner entrées make fuss-free, simple meals in themselves. With just a few more ingredients, and not a lot of time, you can serve an entrée worthy of Sunday company.

PORK STUFFING CASSEROLE

1	10¾-ounce can condensed cream of mushroom with roasted garlic soup
2	eggs
1	6-ounce package chicken-flavored stuffing mix
1	cup water
¼	cup butter
1	17-ounce package refrigerated cooked pork au jus
¼	cup milk

PREP:
15 minutes
BAKE:
45 minutes
OVEN:
350°F
MAKES:
6 servings

1 In a large bowl whisk together half of the soup (a scant ⅔ cup) and eggs; stir in stuffing mix. In a small saucepan combine the water and butter; bring to boiling. Add to stuffing mixture; mix well. Set aside.

2 Chop pork, reserving juices. In a medium bowl combine remaining soup, the milk, and reserved meat juices; stir in pork. Spread into an ungreased 2-quart square baking dish. Spoon stuffing mixture evenly on top.

3 Bake, uncovered, in a 350°F oven about 45 minutes or until mixture is heated through.

Nutrition Facts per serving: 367 cal., 19 g total fat (8 g sat. fat), 142 mg chol., 1,229 mg sodium, 25 g carbo., 1 g fiber, 24 g pro.

Crisp rice cereal adds surprising flavor and texture to this bold, flavorful bake.

CHEESY SAUSAGE & RICE BAKE

PREP:

25 minutes

BAKE:

45 minutes

STAND:

10 minutes

OVEN:

325°F

MAKES:

6 servings

1   pound mild and/or hot bulk pork sausage

¼   cup chopped onion

3   cups crisp rice cereal

¾   cup cooked white rice

1   cup shredded cheddar cheese (4 ounces)

1   10¾-ounce can reduced-sodium condensed cream of celery soup

3   eggs

¼   cup milk

1½   teaspoons butter, melted

1 In a large skillet cook sausage and onion over medium heat until sausage is brown and onion is tender; drain. Set aside.

2 Meanwhile, in a large bowl combine 2½ cups of the cereal and the cooked rice. Spread rice mixture evenly into the bottom of a greased 2-quart square baking dish. Spoon sausage mixture over rice. Sprinkle with cheese.

3 In a medium bowl whisk together soup, eggs, and milk; carefully pour over layers in baking dish. Press down lightly with the back of a spoon to moisten all ingredients. Toss the remaining ½ cup cereal with the melted butter; sprinkle on top.

4 Bake, uncovered, in a 325°F oven for 45 to 50 minutes or until bubbly and golden brown. Let stand for 10 minutes before serving.

Nutrition Facts per serving: 490 cal., 33 g total fat (14 g sat. fat), 175 mg chol., 872 mg sodium, 24 g carbo., 0 g fiber, 19 g pro.

A corn muffin mix provides a super-simple topper for this wholesome sausage-bean bake.

CORN BREAD-TOPPED SAUSAGE BAKE

1	8½-ounce package corn muffin mix
½	cup chopped carrot (1 medium)
¼	cup chopped onion
¼	cup chopped green sweet pepper
¼	cup chopped celery
2	tablespoons cooking oil
1	11½-ounce can condensed bean with bacon soup
¾	cup milk
2	teaspoons yellow mustard
1	pound cooked smoked Polish sausage, sliced

PREP:
25 minutes
BAKE:
20 minutes
OVEN:
425°F
MAKES:
6 servings

1 Prepare muffin mix according to package directions (do not bake); set aside.

2 In a medium saucepan cook carrot, onion, sweet pepper, and celery in hot oil over medium heat until tender. Stir in soup, milk, and mustard; stir in sausage. Heat and stir until bubbly. Transfer to an ungreased 2-quart rectangular baking dish. Spoon muffin batter over hot mixture.

3 Bake, uncovered, in a 425°F oven for 20 to 25 minutes or until a wooden toothpick inserted into muffin mixture comes out clean.

Nutrition Facts per serving: 562 cal., 34 g total fat (11 g sat. fat), 94 mg chol., 1,566 mg sodium, 43 g carbo., 6 g fiber, 20 g pro.

This sausage-filled casserole will taste great as the cold weather starts to hit. A Waldorf salad makes a terrific serve-along.

CHEESY BRAT CASSEROLE

PREP:

20 minutes

BAKE:

45 minutes

OVEN:

350°F

MAKES:

6 servings

1   pound cooked bratwurst or Polish sausage, cut into ½-inch slices

4   medium potatoes (about 1¼ pounds), cooked, peeled, and cubed

1   10-ounce package frozen cut green beans, thawed

1   10¾-ounce can reduced-fat and reduced-sodium condensed cream of mushroom soup

1   cup shredded cheddar cheese (4 ounces)

⅓   cup finely chopped onion (1 small)

1 In a large bowl combine bratwurst, potatoes, green beans, soup, cheese, and onion. Transfer to an ungreased 2-quart rectangular baking dish.

2 Bake, covered, in a 350°F oven about 45 minutes or until heated through.

Nutrition Facts per serving: 408 cal., 27 g total fat (11 g sat. fat), 69 mg chol., 747 mg sodium, 23 g carbo., 3 g fiber, 18 g pro.

Just a couple decades ago, there were only a few brands of marinara sauce available. These days, there are dozens to please all tastes. Choose your favorite for this bold take on stuffed peppers.

STUFFED PIZZA PEPPERS

4	medium red and/or yellow sweet peppers (6 to 8 ounces each)
8	ounces bulk Italian sausage or sweet Italian sausage
1	cup chopped fresh mushrooms
1	cup purchased marinara sauce
1/3	cup sliced pitted ripe or kalamata olives
1/4	teaspoon black pepper
1	cup soft bread crumbs*
1/4	cup shredded mozzarella cheese (1 ounce)
1/4	cup shredded Parmesan cheese (1 ounce)
3	tablespoons pine nuts

PREP:
40 minutes
BAKE:
45 minutes
OVEN:
350°F
MAKES:
4 to 6 servings

1 Cut tops from sweet peppers; chop tops and set aside. Halve peppers lengthwise. Remove seeds. Set the pepper halves, cut sides up, into a greased 3-quart rectangular baking dish.

2 In a large skillet cook sausage until brown. Drain off fat. Stir in chopped sweet pepper and mushrooms; cook and stir until vegetables are tender. Stir in marinara sauce, olives, and black pepper; heat through. Remove from heat. Stir in bread crumbs. Spoon about 1/3 cup of the sausage mixture into each pepper half.

3 Bake stuffed peppers, covered, in a 350°F oven for 40 to 45 minutes or until peppers are tender. Uncover and sprinkle with mozzarella cheese, Parmesan cheese, and pine nuts. Bake, uncovered, about 5 minutes more or until cheese is melted.

*NOTE: Use a blender or food processor to make fluffy soft bread crumbs. One slice yields 3/4 cup crumbs.**

Nutrition Facts per serving: 365 cal., 23 g total fat (8 g sat. fat), 49 mg chol., 837 mg sodium, 22 g carbo., 4 g fiber, 18 g pro.

This pie will be a hit at any potluck with kids present! Cooked spaghetti makes up the crust. The topping is loaded with cheese, tomato sauce, and ground pork.

SOUTHWEST SPAGHETTI PIE

PREP:

40 minutes

BAKE:

10 minutes

STAND:

5 minutes

OVEN:

425°F

MAKES:

8 servings

8	ounces dried spaghetti
½	cup milk
1	egg
1	pound ground pork
1	cup chopped onion (1 large)
¾	cup chopped green sweet pepper (1 medium)
1	clove garlic, minced
1	tablespoon chili powder
½	teaspoon salt
½	teaspoon ground cumin
½	teaspoon dried oregano, crushed
¼	teaspoon black pepper
1	15-ounce can tomato sauce
1	cup shredded Monterey Jack cheese with jalapeño peppers (4 ounces)
1	cup shredded cheddar cheese (4 ounces)

1 Cook spaghetti according to package directions; drain. Return to pan. Whisk together milk and egg; stir into hot pasta. Transfer to a buttered 3-quart rectangular baking dish.

2 Meanwhile, in a large skillet cook pork, onion, sweet pepper, and garlic over medium heat until meat is brown; drain. Stir in chili powder, salt, cumin, oregano, and black pepper. Cook and stir for 2 minutes. Stir in tomato sauce. Bring to boiling; reduce heat. Simmer, uncovered, for 2 minutes more. Spoon over spaghetti in baking dish. Sprinkle with cheeses.

3 Bake, uncovered, in a 425°F oven about 10 minutes or until bubbly around edges. Let stand for 5 minutes before serving.

Nutrition Facts per serving: 330 cal., 15 g total fat (8 g sat. fat), 84 mg chol., 621 mg sodium, 29 g carbo., 2 g fiber, 20 g pro.

Pork sausage and spices from Mexican-style stewed tomatoes give this casserole its flavorful punch. For more heat, use shredded Monterey Jack cheese with jalapeños instead of cheddar.

MEXICAN RICE & BLACK BEAN CASSEROLE

1   pound bulk pork sausage

2   14½-ounce cans Mexican-style stewed tomatoes, undrained

2   cups cooked white rice

1   15-ounce can black beans, rinsed and drained

¾   cup coarsely chopped green sweet pepper (1 medium)

½   cup shredded cheddar cheese (2 ounces)

    Dairy sour cream (optional)

1 In a large skillet cook sausage over medium heat until brown; drain. Stir in undrained tomatoes, rice, beans, and sweet pepper. Transfer to an ungreased 3-quart rectangular baking dish.

2 Bake, covered, in a 350°F oven for 40 to 45 minutes or until heated through. Sprinkle with cheese. Let stand for 5 minutes before serving. If desired, serve with sour cream.

Nutrition Facts per serving: 343 cal., 19 g total fat (8 g sat. fat), 40 mg chol., 811 mg sodium, 27 g carbo., 3 g fiber, 14 g pro.

PREP:
20 minutes

BAKE:
40 minutes

STAND:
5 minutes

OVEN:
350°F

MAKES:
8 servings

A stuffing mixture creates a bottom layer and topper for this tasty dish. Baking this robust one-dish meal is a great way to use your summer crop of zucchini.

ZUCCHINI-SAUSAGE CASSEROLE

PREP:

25 minutes

BAKE:

30 minutes

OVEN:

350°F

MAKES:

8 to 10 servings

1   pound bulk pork sausage

4   medium zucchini

1   $10^{3}/_{4}$-ounce can condensed cream of chicken soup

1   8-ounce carton dairy sour cream

4   cups chicken-flavored stuffing mix

$^{1}/_{3}$ cup butter, melted

1 In a large skillet cook sausage over medium heat until brown; drain. Return sausage to skillet. Meanwhile, quarter zucchini lengthwise; cut each quarter crosswise into $^{1}/_{2}$-inch slices. Add zucchini to sausage in skillet. In a small bowl combine soup and sour cream; stir into skillet. Set aside.

2 In a large bowl combine stuffing mix and melted butter. Spoon half of the stuffing mixture into a lightly greased 3-quart rectangular baking dish. Spread sausage mixture over stuffing. Spoon remaining stuffing mixture evenly over top.

3 Bake, covered, in a 350°F oven about 30 minutes or until heated through.

Nutrition Facts per serving: 487 cal., 34 g total fat (16 g sat. fat), 70 mg chol., 1,128 mg sodium, 28 g carbo., 2 g fiber, 14 g pro.

Potatoes substitute deliciously for noodles in this contemporary take on traditional lasagna.

SAUSAGE & POTATO LASAGNA

1	pound bulk Italian sausage or bulk pork sausage
2	cups thinly sliced fresh mushrooms
½	cup chopped onion (1 medium)
2	cloves garlic, minced
1	tablespoon all-purpose flour
½	teaspoon salt
¼	teaspoon ground white pepper
¼	teaspoon ground nutmeg
1	cup milk
1	15-ounce carton ricotta cheese
1	10-ounce package frozen chopped spinach, thawed and drained well
½	cup grated Parmesan cheese
1	slightly beaten egg
1	20-ounce package (4 cups) refrigerated sliced potatoes*
2	cups shredded mozzarella cheese (8 ounces)

PREP:
25 minutes
BAKE:
35 minutes
STAND:
10 minutes
OVEN:
350°F
MAKES:
8 servings

1 In a large skillet, cook sausage, mushrooms, onion, and garlic over medium heat until sausage is brown; drain. Stir in flour, salt, pepper, and nutmeg. Add milk all at once. Cook and stir until thickened and bubbly; set aside.

2 In a medium bowl combine ricotta cheese, spinach, Parmesan cheese, and egg.

3 Spread half of the potatoes into a greased 3-quart rectangular baking dish. Layer half of the spinach mixture and half of the sausage mixture on top. Sprinkle with 1 cup of the mozzarella cheese. Repeat with remaining potatoes, spinach mixture, and sausage mixture.

4 Bake, covered, in a 350°F oven for 25 minutes. Sprinkle with remaining 1 cup mozzarella cheese. Bake, uncovered, about 10 minutes more or until cheese is melted and mixture is bubbly around edges. Let stand for 10 minutes before serving.

*NOTE: If you prefer to use fresh potatoes, cook 4 cups sliced potatoes in a small amount of boiling lightly salted water for 5 minutes. Drain well. Continue as directed.

Nutrition Facts per serving: 462 cal., 27 g total fat (14 g sat. fat), 116 mg chol., 888 mg sodium, 22 g carbo., 2 g fiber, 28.0 g pro.

Here's a recipe for cabbage lovers. Sour cream and American cheese create a creamy sauce, while the pork sausage adds flavor and spiciness.

CREAMY CABBAGE & SAUSAGE

PREP:

35 minutes

BAKE:

20 minutes

OVEN:

375°F

MAKES:

8 to 10 servings

1½   pounds bulk pork sausage

¾   cup chopped onions (1½ medium)

10   cups coarsely chopped cabbage (1 medium)

1½   cups dairy sour cream

1½   cups shredded American cheese (6 ounces)

¼   teaspoon salt

¼   teaspoon black pepper

1½   cups soft bread crumbs*

2   tablespoons butter, melted

1 In a Dutch oven cook sausage and onions over medium-high heat until sausage is brown; drain. Stir in cabbage. Cook, covered, over medium heat about 10 minutes or until cabbage is crisp-tender, stirring occasionally. Drain any excess liquid. Stir in sour cream, cheese, salt, and pepper. Transfer to an ungreased 3-quart rectangular baking dish.

2 In a small bowl combine bread crumbs and melted butter; sprinkle over sausage mixture. Bake, uncovered, in a 375°F oven for 20 minutes or until topping is golden.

*NOTE: Use a blender or food processor to make fluffy soft bread crumbs. One slice yields ¾ cup crumbs.

Nutrition Facts per serving: 520 cal., 42 g total fat (21 g sat. fat), 93 mg chol., 902 mg sodium, 12 g carbo., 2 g fiber, 18 g pro.

If you relish German-flavored dishes, you'll be in heaven with this casserole filled with sausage, cabbage, Swiss cheese, and seasonings.

GERMAN SAUSAGE CASSEROLE

1	pound red potatoes, thinly sliced
2	teaspoons anise seeds
1	teaspoon coriander seeds
1	teaspoon caraway seeds
⅔	cup beer
3	tablespoons spicy brown mustard
1	tablespoon cornstarch
1	tablespoon sugar
¼	teaspoon black pepper
3	cups shredded cabbage
1	cup chopped onion (1 large)
1	cup sliced celery (2 stalks)
1	tablespoon olive oil
1	pound cooked Polish sausage, cut into ½-inch slices
1	cup shredded Swiss cheese (4 ounces)

PREP:
35 minutes
BAKE:
35 minutes
STAND:
10 minutes
OVEN:
375°F
MAKES:
6 servings

1 In a large saucepan cook potatoes in boiling lightly salted water for 10 minutes or just until tender; drain. Set aside. Using a mortar and pestle, coarsely crush the anise, coriander, and caraway seeds, or use a spice grinder to pulse seeds with several short on/off turns. In a small bowl combine seeds, beer, mustard, cornstarch, sugar, and pepper; set aside.

2 In a large skillet cook cabbage, onion, and celery in hot oil over medium-high heat for 3 to 4 minutes or until crisp-tender.

3 In an ungreased 2-quart rectangular baking dish combine cabbage mixture, potatoes, sausage, and ½ cup of the cheese. Stir seeds mixture; drizzle evenly over sausage mixture in dish.

4 Bake, uncovered, in a 375°F oven about 35 minutes or until bubbly. Top with remaining ½ cup cheese. Let stand for 10 minutes before serving.

Nutrition Facts per serving: 435 cal., 30 g total fat (11 g sat. fat), 73 mg chol., 829 mg sodium, 22 g carbo., 3 g fiber, 19 g pro.

While this dish makes a perfect main course, also try serving it as a side dish.
It easily makes 6 to 8 side-size portions.

HEARTY TUSCAN BEAN CASSEROLE

PREP:

25 minutes

BAKE:

30 minutes

OVEN:

350°F

MAKES:

4 servings

3	cups shredded fresh kale (thick stems removed)
½	cup chopped onion (1 medium)
½	cup chopped celery (1 stalk)
2	tablespoons olive oil
2	19-ounce cans cannellini beans, rinsed and drained
1	14½-ounce can diced tomatoes, undrained
4	ounces sliced prosciutto, cut into strips, or cooked ham, cut into bite-size strips
4	tablespoons fine dry bread crumbs
1	clove garlic, minced
½	teaspoon dried sage, crushed
¼	teaspoon black pepper

1 Wash kale thoroughly in cold water; drain well. Cook in a small amount of boiling water for 8 to 10 minutes or until tender. Drain well in a colander.

2 In a small skillet cook onion and celery in 1 tablespoon of the olive oil over medium heat until tender. In a large bowl combine onion mixture, drained kale, beans, undrained tomatoes, the prosciutto, 2 tablespoons of the bread crumbs, the garlic, sage, and pepper. Transfer to an ungreased 2-quart casserole. Combine remaining 2 tablespoons bread crumbs and remaining 1 tablespoon oil; sprinkle over bean mixture.

3 Bake, covered, in a 350°F oven for 20 minutes. Uncover. Bake for 10 minutes more or until heated through.

Nutrition Facts per serving: 353 cal., 11 g total fat (2 g sat. fat), 20 mg chol., 1,560 mg sodium, 53 g carbo., 14 g fiber, 26 g pro.

No crust required. Just spoon this pasta mixture, boasting all the typical pizza toppers, into a casserole.

PIZZA IN A BOWL

2	cups dried rotini pasta (5 ounces)
1	3½-ounce package thinly sliced pepperoni
1	pound lean ground beef
⅓	cup finely chopped onion (1 small)
1	15-ounce can pizza sauce
1	8-ounce can tomato sauce
1	6-ounce can tomato paste
½	teaspoon sugar
¼	teaspoon garlic salt or onion salt
⅛	teaspoon black pepper
2	cups shredded mozzarella cheese (8 ounces)
2	tablespoons grated Parmesan cheese

1 Cook pasta according to package directions; drain. Meanwhile, cut half of the pepperoni slices into quarters; set aside.

2 In a large skillet cook ground beef and onion over medium heat until meat is brown and onion is tender; drain. Stir in pizza sauce, tomato sauce, tomato paste, sugar, garlic salt, and pepper. Stir in the cooked rotini and pepperoni quarters.

3 Spoon half of the rotini mixture into an ungreased 2-quart casserole; sprinkle with 1 cup of the mozzarella cheese. Repeat layers. Top with Parmesan cheese and remaining pepperoni slices. Bake, uncovered, in a 350°F oven for 35 to 40 minutes or until heated through.

Nutrition Facts per serving: 521 cal., 21 g total fat (10 g sat. fat), 84 mg chol., 1,184 mg sodium, 45 g carbo., 3 g fiber, 35 g pro.

PREP:

30 minutes

BAKE:

35 minutes

OVEN:

350°F

MAKES:

6 servings

Tailor this recipe to your heat tolerance. If spicy food is your style, use more hot Italian sausage and less sweet. Or use all of one or the other.

SAUSAGE-RICE CASSEROLE

PREP:

25 minutes

BAKE:

50 minutes

OVEN:

350°F

MAKES:

6 servings

1	pound uncooked sweet (mild) and/or hot Italian sausage links
½	cup chopped onion (1 medium)
2½	cups cooked white rice
1	4-ounce can chopped green chile peppers, drained
1	4-ounce can (drained weight) mushroom stems and pieces, drained
1	10¾-ounce can condensed cream of chicken soup
1	cup milk
¾	cup shredded cheddar cheese (3 ounces)

1 Remove casings from sausage, if present. In a large skillet cook sausage and onion over medium heat until sausage is brown and onion is tender; drain.

2 Meanwhile, in a large bowl combine rice, chile peppers, and mushrooms. Stir in soup, milk, and cheese. Stir in sausage mixture. Transfer to an ungreased 2-quart rectangular baking dish. Bake, covered, in a 350°F oven about 50 minutes or until heated through.

Nutrition Facts per serving: 442 cal., 26 g total fat (11 g sat. fat), 73 mg chol., 1,056 mg sodium, 28 g carbo., 1 g fiber, 20 g pro.

Pair this main-dish casserole with an Italian dressing-tossed green salad and buttered garlic bread for a complete Italian meal. Don't forget to pass the Parmesan cheese at the table.

ITALIAN SAUSAGE & SPINACH PIE

1	pound bulk Italian sausage
½	cup chopped onion
5	eggs
1	egg white
1	10-ounce package frozen chopped spinach, thawed and drained well
2	cups shredded mozzarella cheese (8 ounces)
½	of a 15-ounce carton part-skim ricotta cheese (about 1 cup)
½	teaspoon garlic powder
	Pastry for a double-crust 9- or 10-inch pie
1	egg yolk
1	tablespoon water

PREP:
45 minutes
BAKE:
50 minutes
STAND:
10 minutes
OVEN:
375°F
MAKES:
10 servings

1 In a large skillet cook sausage and onion over medium heat until sausage is brown and onion is tender; drain. Set aside.

2 In a large bowl whisk together whole eggs and egg white. Stir in spinach, mozzarella cheese, ricotta cheese, garlic powder, and sausage mixture.

3 Divide pastry in half. Roll each half to a circle 12 inches in diameter. Line an ungreased 9- or 10-inch pie plate with 1 pastry circle. Transfer sausage mixture to the pastry-lined pie plate. Trim pastry to edge of pie plate. Cut slits in remaining pastry circle. Place on filling. Trim to ½ inch beyond edge of plate. Fold top pastry under bottom pastry. Crimp edge as desired. In a small bowl whisk together egg yolk and the water. Brush top of pastry with egg yolk mixture.

4 Bake in a 375°F oven for 50 to 55 minutes or until top is golden. Cover edge with foil, if necessary, to prevent overbrowning. Let stand for 10 minutes before serving. Cut into wedges to serve.

Nutrition Facts per serving: 459 cal., 32 g total fat (11 g sat. fat), 178 mg chol., 578 mg sodium, 22 g carbo., 1 g fiber, 20 g pro.

Don't think of bread pudding just as a well-loved dessert. This version is a marvelous main dish. Basil pesto gives it terrific flavor.

SAUSAGE BREAD PUDDING

PREP:

40 minutes

BAKE:

40 minutes

STAND:

10 minutes

OVEN:

350°F

MAKES:

8 servings

1	pound sweet Italian sausage
½	cup chopped onion (1 medium)
2	cloves garlic, minced
⅓	cup purchased basil pesto
9	slices white or wheat bread, cut into ½-inch cubes and dried*
1	cup shredded provolone or cheddar cheese (4 ounces)
2½	cups milk
1	10¾-ounce can condensed cream of mushroom soup
4	eggs
¼	teaspoon salt
⅛	teaspoon black pepper

1 Remove casings from sausage, if present. In a large skillet cook sausage, onion, and garlic over medium heat until sausage is brown and onion is tender; drain. Stir in pesto; set aside.

2 Spread half of the bread cubes into the bottom of a lightly greased 3-quart rectangular baking dish. Top evenly with sausage mixture and cheese. Top with remaining bread cubes.

3 In a large bowl whisk together milk, soup, eggs, salt, and pepper. Pour soup mixture evenly over bread cubes in dish, pressing lightly to thoroughly moisten the bread.

4 Bake, uncovered, in a 350°F oven for 40 to 45 minutes or until a knife inserted near the center comes out clean. Let stand for 10 minutes before serving.

***NOTE:** To dry bread cubes, spread cubes into a 15×10×1-inch baking pan. Bake in a 300°F oven for 10 to 15 minutes or until dry, stirring once; cool. (Bread cubes will continue to dry and crisp as they cool.) Or let bread cubes stand, loosely covered, at room temperature for 8 to 12 hours.

Nutrition Facts per serving: 501 cal., 35 g total fat (11 g sat. fat), 167 mg chol., 1,174 mg sodium, 24 g carbo., 2 g fiber, 22 g pro.

Stock up on frozen meatballs. For something off the beaten path, try them in this sumptuously saucy and easy presentation.

MEATBALL & POLENTA CASSEROLE

1	16-ounce package refrigerated polenta
2	16-ounce packages frozen cooked Italian meatballs
1	10¾-ounce can condensed golden mushroom soup
¾	cup water
1	4½-ounce jar (drained weight) sliced mushrooms, drained
1	teaspoon dried Italian seasoning, crushed
¼	teaspoon garlic powder
⅛	teaspoon black pepper
½	cup shredded Parmesan cheese (2 ounces)

PREP:
20 minutes
BAKE:
45 minutes
STAND:
5 minutes
OVEN:
350°F
MAKES:
8 servings

1 Cut polenta into 12 slices (about ½ inch thick). Line the bottom of a greased 3-quart rectangular baking dish with polenta. Place frozen meatballs on polenta. In a medium bowl combine soup, the water, mushrooms, Italian seasoning, garlic powder, and pepper. Pour over meatballs.

2 Bake, uncovered, in a 350°F oven about 45 minutes or until heated through. Sprinkle with Parmesan cheese. Let stand for 5 minutes before serving.

Nutrition Facts per serving: 551 cal., 35 g total fat (18 g sat. fat), 98 mg chol., 1,963 mg sodium, 22 g carbo., 6 g fiber, 34 g pro.

Lasagna—ready for the oven in 20 minutes? Yes, thanks to no-boil lasagna noodles, a jar of pasta sauce, and smoked sausage, which doesn't require precooking.

SMOKED SAUSAGE LASAGNA

PREP:

20 minutes

BAKE:

50 minutes

STAND:

10 minutes

OVEN:

350°F

MAKES:

6 servings

2   cups tomato-basil pasta sauce

½   cup pitted kalamata olives, halved

6   no-boil lasagna noodles

½   of a 15-ounce container ricotta cheese (about 1 cup)

1½ cups shredded Monterey Jack cheese with jalapeño peppers (6 ounces)

¼   cup shredded Parmesan cheese (1 ounce)

8   ounces smoked sausage or smoked chicken sausage with apple, halved lengthwise and sliced

1   medium fennel bulb, trimmed, halved lengthwise, and thinly sliced

1 In a medium bowl combine pasta sauce and olives. Spread ⅓ cup of the sauce mixture into a greased 2-quart square baking dish. Top with 2 lasagna noodles.

2 In a small bowl combine ricotta cheese and 1 cup of the Monterey Jack cheese. Spoon half of the cheese mixture over noodles in dish. Sprinkle with 2 tablespoons of the Parmesan cheese. Top with half of the sausage and half of the fennel. Spoon half of the remaining sauce mixture on top.

3 Top with 2 more noodles and the remaining cheese mixture, sausage, and fennel. Layer remaining noodles and the remaining sauce mixture on top. Sprinkle with remaining ½ cup Monterey Jack cheese and 2 tablespoons Parmesan cheese.

4 Bake, covered, in a 350°F oven for 50 minutes. Let stand, covered, for 10 minutes before serving.

Nutrition Facts per serving: 451 cal., 29 g total fat (14 g sat. fat), 75 mg chol., 1,229 mg sodium, 21 g carbo., 2 g fiber, 25 g pro.

This homey casserole contains all the classically great pasta dish mainstays—marinara sauce, mushrooms, onion, green sweet peppers, pepperoni, and lots of cheese.

ITALIAN PENNE BAKE

6	ounces dried penne pasta (6 ounces)
2	medium green or red sweet peppers, cut into thin, bite-size strips
1	cup sliced fresh mushrooms
1	medium onion, quartered and thinly sliced
6	ounces sliced pepperoni or Canadian-style bacon, cut up
6	cloves garlic, minced
1	tablespoon olive oil or cooking oil
1	26- to 29-ounce jar marinara sauce
1¼	cups shredded Italian-style cheese blend (5 ounces)

PREP:
25 minutes
BAKE:
30 minutes
OVEN:
350°F
MAKES:
8 servings

1 Cook pasta according to package directions; drain. Place pasta in a large bowl. Meanwhile, in a large skillet cook sweet peppers, mushrooms, onion, pepperoni, and garlic in hot oil over medium heat for 3 minutes. Add vegetable mixture and marinara sauce to pasta in bowl; toss to coat. Spread pasta mixture evenly into a lightly greased 3-quart rectangular baking dish.

2 Bake, covered, in a 350°F oven about 25 minutes or until heated through. Sprinkle with cheese. Bake, uncovered, about 5 minutes more or until cheese is melted.

Nutrition Facts per serving: 373 cal., 17 g total fat (6 g sat. fat), 27 mg chol., 905 mg sodium, 40 g carbo., 3 g fiber, 16 g pro.

This sensational stew is super quick and easy to prepare, thanks to condensed soup, refrigerated biscuits, and frozen Italian-style meatballs.

BISCUIT-TOPPED OVEN MEATBALL STEW

PREP:

15 minutes

BAKE:

40 minutes

OVEN:

400°F

MAKES:

6 servings

2 10¾-ounce cans condensed cream of onion soup

¾ cup water

1 tablespoon bottled steak sauce

1 teaspoon dried basil, crushed

1 16- or 18-ounce package frozen Italian-style meatballs

1 16-ounce package frozen California vegetable blend (broccoli, cauliflower, and carrots), thawed

1 7½-ounce package (10) refrigerated biscuits

1 tablespoon butter, melted

2 tablespoons grated Parmesan cheese

1 In an ungreased 2½-quart casserole combine soup, the water, steak sauce, and basil. Stir in frozen meatballs and vegetables. Bake, covered, in a 400°F oven for 40 to 45 minutes or until heated through, stirring once.

2 Meanwhile, place biscuits on an ungreased baking sheet. Brush tops with melted butter; sprinkle with Parmesan cheese. If space allows, bake during the last 8 to 10 minutes of stew baking time. If there is not enough room in the oven, let stew stand, covered, while biscuits bake. Serve biscuits on top of stew.

Nutrition Facts per serving: 474 cal., 29 g total fat (12 g sat. fat), 68 mg chol., 1,837 mg sodium, 36 g carbo., 6 g fiber, 19 g pro.

Busy day tomorrow? Assemble this casserole tonight, then store it in the refrigerator. Tomorrow night when you get home, pop it in the oven to heat through. Then relax and savor the hearty Italian aromas that soon will fill the house.

WHITE BEAN & SAUSAGE RIGATONI

8   ounces dried rigatoni (5 cups)

8   ounces cooked kielbasa

½   of a 6-ounce can Italian-style tomato paste (⅓ cup)

¼   cup dry red wine or reduced-sodium chicken broth

1   10-ounce package frozen chopped spinach, thawed and drained well

2   14½-ounce cans diced tomatoes with basil, oregano, and garlic, undrained

1   15-ounce can Great Northern beans, rinsed and drained

⅓   cup shredded or grated Parmesan cheese (1½ ounces)

1 Cook pasta according to package directions; drain. Return to saucepan. Cut kielbasa in half lengthwise and then into bias slices. In a small bowl combine tomato paste and wine.

2 Add kielbasa, spinach, undrained tomatoes, beans, and tomato paste mixture to the cooked pasta; mix well. Transfer to an ungreased 3-quart rectangular baking dish.

3 Bake, covered, in a 375°F oven about 25 minutes or until heated through. Sprinkle with Parmesan cheese. Bake, uncovered, for 5 minutes more or until cheese is melted.

Nutrition Facts per serving: 564 cal., 20 g total fat (11 g sat. fat), 48 mg chol., 1,706 mg sodium, 62 g carbo., 7 g fiber, 30 g pro.

PREP:
25 minutes
BAKE:
30 minutes
OVEN:
375°F
MAKES:
6 servings

Go hot or mild with the Italian sausage in this dish and control the heat the pie will pack.

ITALIAN SAUSAGE PIE

PREP:

40 minutes

BAKE:

40 minutes

STAND:

20 minutes

OVEN:

350°F

MAKES:

10 servings

1½	pounds bulk sweet or hot Italian sausage
1	cup chopped red sweet pepper (1 large)
½	cup chopped onion (1 medium)
2	cloves garlic, minced
1	16-ounce package hot roll mix
5	eggs
3	cups shredded mozzarella or provolone cheese (12 ounces)
½	of a 15-ounce carton ricotta cheese (about 1 cup)
½	of a 10-ounce package frozen chopped spinach, thawed and drained well
2	4-ounce cans (drained weight) sliced mushrooms, drained
1	slightly beaten egg
1	tablespoon water
1	tablespoon shredded Parmesan cheese

1 In a large skillet cook sausage, sweet pepper, onion, and garlic over medium heat until sausage is brown; drain.

2 Prepare hot roll mix according to package directions through kneading step. Cover; let dough rest for 5 minutes.

3 In large bowl beat the 5 eggs. Stir in 1 cup of the mozzarella cheese, the ricotta cheese, and spinach. Stir in sausage mixture and mushrooms.

4 On a lightly floured surface roll three-fourths of the hot roll dough into a 15-inch circle. Fit into the bottom and press up side of a greased 9-inch springform pan. Sprinkle bottom of dough with ½ cup of the mozzarella cheese. Spoon sausage mixture over cheese. Sprinkle with remaining 1½ cups cheese; press lightly into sausage mixture.

5 Roll remaining dough into a 9-inch circle; place on sausage-cheese mixture. Fold edge of bottom dough over top dough; pinch to seal.

6 In small bowl combine the 1 egg and the water. Brush on top of pie; allow to dry for 5 minutes. Using a sharp knife, score top of pie in a diamond pattern, being careful not to cut all the way through dough. Sprinkle with Parmesan cheese.

7 Bake, uncovered, in a 350°F oven for 40 to 45 minutes or until golden. Let stand in pan on a wire rack for 20 minutes. Using a small spatula, loosen pie from side of pan; remove side of pan. Cut pie into wedges.

Nutrition Facts per serving: 625 cal., 37 g total fat (14 g sat. fat), 233 mg chol., 1,234 mg sodium, 40 g carbo., 1 g fiber, 33 g pro.

The Italian influence is evident in the hearty nature of this bake. It includes mozzarella cheese, sliced tomato, Italian sausage, and kalamata olives.

TUSCAN MAC 'N' CHEESE

8	ounces dried gemelli pasta or elbow macaroni (2 cups)
8	ounces bulk sweet or hot Italian sausage
1	8-ounce package cream cheese, cut into cubes and softened
4	ounces crusty Italian bread, cut into 1-inch cubes (about 2 cups)
1	cup pitted kalamata olives, halved
1	cup shredded mozzarella cheese (4 ounces)
1	tablespoon butter
1	tablespoon all-purpose flour
1	teaspoon dried sage, crushed
½	teaspoon salt
¼	teaspoon dried thyme, crushed
⅛	teaspoon cayenne pepper
1½	cups milk
1	medium tomato, sliced
½	cup shredded Asiago, Parmesan, or Romano cheese (2 ounces)
	Fresh thyme (optional)

PREP:
45 minutes
BAKE:
50 minutes
STAND:
15 minutes
OVEN:
350°F
MAKES:
6 to 8 servings

1 Cook pasta according to package directions; drain. Meanwhile, in a large skillet cook sausage over medium heat until brown; drain. In a very large bowl combine sausage, cooked pasta, cream cheese, bread cubes, olives, and mozzarella cheese. Set aside.

2 In a medium saucepan melt butter over medium heat. Stir in flour, sage, salt, dried thyme, and cayenne pepper. Add milk all at once. Cook and stir until slightly thickened and bubbly. Pour over pasta mixture in bowl; stir gently. Transfer to an ungreased 2-quart casserole.

3 Bake, covered, in a 350°F oven for 35 minutes. Top with tomato slices and Asiago cheese. Bake, uncovered, about 15 minutes more or until heated through. Let stand for 15 minutes before serving. If desired, sprinkle with fresh thyme.

Nutrition Facts per serving: 637 cal., 39 g total fat (19 g sat. fat), 101 mg chol., 1,187 mg sodium, 46 g carbo., 3 g fiber, 24 g pro.

You can't beat this tried-and-true Italian mainstay.

LASAGNA

PREP:
45 minutes

BAKE:
30 minutes

STAND:
10 minutes

OVEN:
375°F

MAKES:
8 servings

12	ounces bulk Italian or pork sausage, or ground beef
1	cup chopped onion (1 large)
2	cloves garlic, minced
1	14½-ounce can diced tomatoes, undrained
1	8-ounce can tomato sauce
1	tablespoon dried Italian seasoning, crushed
1	teaspoon fennel seeds, crushed (optional)
¼	teaspoon black pepper
6	dried lasagna noodles (6 ounces)
1	15-ounce container ricotta cheese or 2 cups cream-style cottage cheese, drained
1	beaten egg
¼	cup grated Parmesan cheese
1½	cups shredded mozzarella cheese (6 ounces)
	Grated Parmesan cheese (optional)

1 For sauce, in a large saucepan cook sausage, onion, and garlic over medium heat until sausage is brown and onion is tender; drain. Stir in undrained tomatoes, the tomato sauce, Italian seasoning, fennel seeds (if desired), and pepper. Bring to boiling; reduce heat. Simmer, covered, for 15 minutes, stirring occasionally.

2 Meanwhile, cook noodles according to package directions until tender but still firm; drain. Rinse with cold water; drain well. Set aside. In a bowl combine ricotta cheese, egg, and the ¼ cup Parmesan cheese. Set aside.

3 Spread about ½ cup of the sausage mixture over the bottom of an ungreased 2-quart rectangular baking dish. Place 3 of the noodles on sausage mixture in dish, overlapping as necessary to fit. Spread with half of the ricotta cheese mixture. Top with half of the remaining sausage mixture and ¾ cup of the mozzarella cheese. Repeat layers. If desired, sprinkle additional Parmesan cheese over top.

4 Place baking dish on a baking sheet. Bake, uncovered, in a 375°F oven for 30 to 35 minutes or until heated through. Let stand for 10 minutes before serving.

Nutrition Facts per serving: 441 cal., 22 g total fat (11 g sat. fat), 97 mg chol., 658 mg sodium, 33 g carbo., 2 g fiber, 24 g pro.

There's no need to head to an Italian restaurant when you can enjoy this easy baked pasta at home.

BAKED CAVATELLI

7	ounces dried cavatelli or wagon wheel pasta (2½ cups)
10	ounces uncooked Italian sausage links, sliced ½ inch thick
¾	cup chopped onions (½ medium)
2	cloves garlic, minced
1	26- to 28-ounce jar spaghetti sauce
¼	teaspoon black pepper
1	cup mozzarella cheese, shredded (4 ounces)

1 Cook pasta according to package directions; drain. Place pasta in a large bowl; set aside.

2 Meanwhile, in a large skillet cook sausage, onions, and garlic over medium heat until sausage is brown and onions are tender; drain. Stir in spaghetti sauce and pepper. Add to pasta in bowl along with ½ cup of the cheese. Stir gently to combine. Transfer to an ungreased 2-quart casserole.

3 Bake, covered, in a 375°F oven for 25 to 30 minutes or until heated through. Sprinkle with the remaining ½ cup cheese. Bake, uncovered, about 5 minutes more or until cheese is melted.

Nutrition Facts per serving: 350 cal., 15 g total fat (6 g sat. fat), 43 mg chol., 643 mg sodium, 36 g carbo., 3 g fiber, 17 g pro.

PREP:
35 minutes
BAKE:
30 minutes
OVEN:
375°F
MAKES:
6 servings

Just before serving, be sure to give the casserole a good stir to mix the chunks of ham, bits of spinach, and pasta with the rich, creamy sauce.

HAM, SPINACH & MOSTACCIOLI CASSEROLE

PREP:

20 minutes

BAKE:

30 minutes

STAND:

5 minutes

OVEN:

350°F

MAKES:

6 servings

8	ounces dried mostaccioli, cut ziti, or elbow macaroni
2	medium onions, cut into thin wedges, or 5 medium leeks, sliced
2	cloves garlic, minced
3	tablespoons butter
¼	cup all-purpose flour
½	teaspoon dried thyme, crushed
⅛	teaspoon black pepper
1	14-ounce can chicken broth (1¾ cups)
1½	cups reduced-fat milk
1½	cups cubed cooked ham (about 1 pound)
1	10-ounce package frozen chopped spinach, thawed and drained well

1 Cook pasta according to package directions; drain. Rinse with cold water; drain well. Set aside.

2 In a large saucepan cook onions and garlic in hot butter over medium heat until tender. Stir in flour, thyme, and pepper. Add broth and milk all at once. Cook and stir until thickened and bubbly. Cook and stir for 2 minutes more. Stir in cooked pasta, ham, and spinach. Transfer to an ungreased 2-quart casserole.

3 Bake, covered, in a 350°F oven for 30 to 35 minutes or until heated through. Let stand for 5 minutes. Stir gently before serving.

Nutrition Facts per serving: 340 cal., 12 g total fat (6 g sat. fat), 42 mg chol., 863 mg sodium, 40 g carbo., 3 g fiber, 18 g pro.

This luscious white version of lasagna is layered with spinach, ham, cheese, and a lightened "cream" sauce. Ham adds a tasty smoky flavor.

SPINACH & HAM LASAGNA

6	dried lasagna noodles (6 ounces)
2	cups milk
¼	cup chopped onion
3	tablespoons cornstarch
¼	teaspoon salt
1½	cups diced low-fat, reduced-sodium cooked ham (about 8 ounces)
½	teaspoon dried Italian seasoning, crushed
1	10-ounce package frozen chopped spinach, thawed and drained well
1	cup cottage cheese
1	cup shredded mozzarella cheese (4 ounces)

PREP:
40 minutes
BAKE:
30 minutes
STAND:
10 minutes
OVEN:
375°F
MAKES:
6 servings

1 Cook lasagna noodles according to package directions; drain. Rinse with cold water; drain well.

2 Meanwhile, for sauce, in a medium saucepan combine milk, onion, cornstarch, and salt. Cook and stir over medium heat until thickened and bubbly. Cook and stir for 2 minutes more. Spread 2 tablespoons of the sauce evenly into the bottom of an ungreased 2-quart rectangular baking dish. Stir ham and Italian seasoning into remaining sauce.

3 Arrange 3 of the lasagna noodles over sauce in baking dish. Spread with one-third of the remaining sauce. Top with spinach. Layer another one-third of the sauce, the cottage cheese, and ½ cup of the mozzarella cheese over the spinach. Place remaining noodles on top. Top with remaining sauce and remaining ½ cup mozzarella cheese.

4 Bake, uncovered, in a 375°F oven for 30 to 35 minutes or until heated through. Let stand for 10 minutes before serving.

Nutrition Facts per serving: 305 cal., 9 g total fat (5 g sat. fat), 43 mg chol., 874 mg sodium, 32 g carbo., 2 g fiber, 23 g pro.

The broccoli florets add color contrast and smart nutrition to this family-friendly dish.

BAKED RIGATONI WITH SAUSAGE

PREP:

30 minutes

BAKE:

20 minutes

OVEN:

375°F

MAKES:

6 servings

12 ounces dried rigatoni pasta (4½ cups)

 4 cups broccoli florets

12 ounces bulk hot Italian sausage

½ cup finely chopped onion (1 medium)

 1 26- to 32-ounce jar marinara sauce

 1 8-ounce package shredded part-skim mozzarella cheese

 2 tablespoons grated Parmesan cheese

1 Cook pasta according to package directions, adding broccoli during the last 2 minutes of cooking; drain. Return to pan.

2 Meanwhile, in a large skillet cook sausage and onion over medium heat until meat is brown and onion is tender; drain. Stir in marinara sauce; heat through. Stir meat sauce and cheeses into the cooked pasta. Transfer to a lightly greased 3-quart rectangular baking dish.

3 Bake, covered, in a 375°F oven for 20 to 25 minutes or until mixture is heated through.

Nutrition Facts per serving: 581 cal., 24 g total fat (10 g sat. fat), 64 mg chol., 1,134 mg sodium, 58 g carbo., 5 g fiber, 29 g pro.

A traditional lasagna in most respects—except for the colorful addition of spinach—this classic Italian casserole will taste great with a salad of chilled, cooked green beans tossed with a vinaigrette.

FLORENTINE LASAGNA

12	ounces Italian sausage or uncooked turkey Italian sausage
½	cup chopped onion (1 medium)
1	8-ounce can tomato sauce
1	7½-ounce can tomatoes, undrained and cut up
2	teaspoons dried Italian seasoning, crushed
6	dried lasagna noodles (6 ounces)
1	slightly beaten egg
1	15-ounce container ricotta cheese or 2 cups cream-style cottage cheese, drained
⅓	cup grated Parmesan cheese
¼	teaspoon coarsely ground black pepper
½	of a 10-ounce package frozen chopped spinach, thawed and drained well
8	ounces sliced mozzarella cheese

PREP:
30 minutes
BAKE:
30 minutes
STAND:
10 minutes
OVEN:
375°F
MAKES:
8 servings

1 Remove casings from sausage, if present. For meat sauce, in a medium saucepan cook sausage and onion over medium heat until meat is brown and onion is tender; drain. Stir in tomato sauce, undrained tomatoes, and Italian seasoning. Bring to boiling; reduce heat. Simmer, uncovered, for 15 to 20 minutes or until desired consistency.

2 Meanwhile, cook lasagna noodles according to package directions until tender but still firm; drain. Rinse with cold water; drain well. For filling, in a medium bowl combine egg, ricotta cheese, ¼ cup of the Parmesan cheese, and the pepper. Fold in spinach.

3 Place 3 noodles in the bottom of an ungreased 2-quart rectangular baking dish. Spread half of the filling over noodles. Top with half of the meat sauce and half of the mozzarella cheese. Repeat layers. Sprinkle with remaining Parmesan cheese.

4 Bake, uncovered, in a 375°F oven about 30 minutes or until heated through. Let stand for 10 minutes before serving.

MAKE-AHEAD DIRECTIONS: Assemble as directed. Cover and chill unbaked casserole up to 24 hours. Bake, covered, in a 375°F oven for 40 minutes. Uncover. Bake about 20 minutes more or until heated through.

Nutrition Facts per serving: 343 cal., 19 g total fat (9 g sat. fat), 87 mg chol., 796 mg sodium, 19 g carbo., 2 g fiber, 24 g pro.

This zesty dish is infused with vermicelli, which is thinner than spaghetti but thicker than angel hair pasta. Here, it creates the crust to hold together a spicy sausage bake.

SPICY PASTA PIE

PREP:
25 minutes

BAKE:
25 minutes

STAND:
10 minutes

OVEN:
350°F

MAKES:
6 servings

4	ounces dried vermicelli, broken
1	beaten egg white
1	cup shredded mozzarella cheese (4 ounces)
1	pound bulk Italian or pork sausage
1	cup sliced fresh mushrooms
½	cup chopped onion (1 medium)
1	clove garlic, minced
1	14½-ounce can diced tomatoes, undrained
½	of a 6-ounce can (⅓ cup) tomato paste
1	teaspoon dried Italian seasoning, crushed
⅛	teaspoon crushed red pepper
2	tablespoons grated Parmesan or Romano cheese

1 Cook vermicelli according to package directions; drain. Toss with egg white. Press vermicelli mixture over the bottom and up side of a greased 10-inch quiche dish or 9-inch deep-dish pie plate. Sprinkle with mozzarella cheese. Set aside.

2 Meanwhile, in a large skillet cook sausage, mushrooms, onion, and garlic over medium heat until sausage is brown and onion is tender; drain. Stir in undrained tomatoes, the tomato paste, Italian seasoning, and crushed red pepper. Pour sausage mixture over cheese in dish. Cover loosely with foil.

3 Bake in a 350°F oven for 25 to 30 minutes or until heated through. Sprinkle with Parmesan cheese. Let stand for 10 minutes before serving.

Nutrition Facts per serving: 388 cal., 21 g total fat (9 g sat. fat), 65 mg chol., 824 mg sodium, 23 g carbo., 1 g fiber, 21 g pro.

Polenta is a northern Italian staple made of cornmeal that can be served soft, like mashed potatoes, or chilled and shaped, as it is here. It's easy enough to prepare your own homemade polenta, but if you're short on time, use the recipe variation that calls for prepared refrigerated polenta.

LAYERED POLENTA CASSEROLE

2¾ cups water
1 cup yellow cornmeal
1 cup cold water
¾ teaspoon dried basil, crushed
½ teaspoon salt
½ cup shredded Parmesan cheese (2 ounces)
8 ounces Italian sausage or uncooked turkey Italian sausage
½ cup chopped carrot (1 medium)
1⅓ cups tomato and herb pasta sauce
1 cup shredded provolone or mozzarella cheese (4 ounces)

PREP:
35 minutes
CHILL:
2 hours or overnight
BAKE:
30 minutes
STAND:
10 minutes
OVEN:
400°F
MAKES:
6 servings

1 For polenta, in a saucepan bring the 2¾ cups water to boiling. Meanwhile, in a medium bowl combine cornmeal, the 1 cup cold water, the basil, and salt. Slowly add the cornmeal mixture to the boiling water, stirring constantly. Cook and stir until mixture returns to boiling. Reduce heat to low. Cook, uncovered, for 10 to 15 minutes or until mixture is very thick, stirring constantly. Stir in ¼ cup of the Parmesan cheese until melted. Spread polenta into a greased 2-quart rectangular baking dish. Cover and chill for 2 hours or overnight.

2 Remove casings from sausage, if present. In a medium saucepan cook sausage and carrot over medium heat until sausage is brown; drain. Reserve ¾ cup of the pasta sauce; cover and chill. Stir remaining pasta sauce into sausage mixture. Cool slightly; cover and chill.

3 When ready to assemble, remove polenta from baking dish; cut into 24 triangles or squares. Spread reserved ¾ cup sauce into the same baking dish. Arrange polenta on top of sauce. Spoon sausage mixture over polenta. Sprinkle with provolone cheese. Cover with foil.

4 Bake in a 400°F oven for 25 minutes. Sprinkle remaining ¼ cup Parmesan cheese on top. Bake, uncovered, for 5 to 10 minutes more or until cheese is bubbly. Let stand for 10 minutes before serving.

Nutrition Facts per serving: 340 cal., 16 g total fat (6 g sat. fat), 42 mg chol., 932 mg sodium, 31 g carbo., 2 g fiber, 17 g pro.

EASY LAYERED POLENTA CASSEROLE: Substitute one and one-half 16-ounce tubes refrigerated herb-flavored or plain cooked polenta for all of the water, cornmeal, basil, and salt. Cut polenta into ½-inch slices; arrange on the ¾ cup sauce spread in baking dish. Continue as directed.

Nutrition Facts per serving: 351 cal., 20 g total fat (9 g sat. fat), 48 mg chol., 1,103 mg sodium, 25 g carbo., 2 g fiber, 17 g pro.

Macaroni and cheese with a twist—ham and broccoli. A little red sweet pepper also adds flavor.

HAM & CHEESE MACARONI

PREP:

30 minutes

BAKE:

45 minutes

OVEN:

350°F

MAKES:

6 servings

6	ounces dried elbow macaroni (1½ cups)
3	cups broccoli florets
1½	cups coarsely chopped red sweet pepper (2 medium)
1½	cups cubed cooked ham (8 ounces)
1½	cups milk
4½	teaspoons cornstarch
¼	teaspoon black pepper
1½	cups cubed American cheese (6 ounces)
1	cup soft bread crumbs*
1	tablespoon butter, melted

1 Cook macaroni according to package directions, adding broccoli and sweet pepper during the last 2 minutes of cooking; drain. In an ungreased 3-quart casserole combine macaroni mixture and ham; set aside.

2 For sauce, in a small saucepan combine milk, cornstarch, and black pepper. Cook and stir over medium heat until thickened and bubbly. Add cheese; stir until melted. Stir sauce into macaroni mixture in casserole. Combine bread crumbs and butter; sprinkle over top.

3 Bake, uncovered, in a 350°F oven about 45 minutes or until bubbly and bread crumbs are golden.

*NOTE: Use a blender or food processor to make fluffy soft bread crumbs. One slice yields ¾ cup crumbs.

Nutrition Facts per serving: 373 cal., 16 g total fat (9 g sat. fat), 58 mg chol., 1,036 mg sodium, 35 g carbo., 3 g fiber, 22 g pro.

Shorten your preparation time at mealtime by cutting up the vegetables and ham in advance. Or simply purchase stir-fry veggies and chopped ham from the grocery store.

SAVORY HAM & RICE

1	cup chopped carrots (2 medium)
½	cup chopped onion (1 medium)
½	cup chopped green or red sweet pepper (1 small)
½	cup water
1	10¾-ounce can condensed cream of celery soup
¾	cup uncooked quick-cooking rice
8	ounces cooked ham, cut into bite-size pieces (1½ cups)
¼	teaspoon ground sage
⅛	teaspoon black pepper
	Paprika (optional)

PREP:
20 minutes

BAKE:
30 minutes

OVEN:
350°F

MAKES:
4 servings

1 In a medium saucepan combine carrots, onion, sweet pepper, and the water. Bring to boiling; reduce heat. Cover and simmer for 4 to 5 minutes or until crisp-tender. Do not drain.

2 Stir in soup, rice, ham, sage, and black pepper. Transfer to an ungreased 1-quart casserole. If desired, sprinkle with paprika.

3 Bake, covered, in a 350°F oven for 30 to 35 minutes or until rice is tender and mixture is heated through.

Nutrition Facts per serving: 246 cal., 9 g total fat (3 g sat. fat), 34 mg chol., 1,316 mg sodium, 28 g carbo., 3 g fiber, 13 g pro.

This casserole dresses up ordinary mac 'n' cheese with ham, sour cream, and cottage cheese for a cheesy dish your kids will love.

CREAMY MACARONI & CHEESE HAM BAKE

PREP:

25 minutes

BAKE:

30 minutes

OVEN:

375°F

MAKES:

4 servings

1	7¼-ounce package macaroni and cheese dinner mix
1½	cups cubed cooked ham or chopped cooked chicken (about 8 ounces)
1	cup cream-style cottage cheese
½	cup dairy sour cream
1	teaspoon dried minced onion
¼	teaspoon black pepper
¼	cup fine dry bread crumbs
1	tablespoon butter, melted
1	teaspoon dried parsley flakes, crushed (optional)

1 Prepare macaroni and cheese mix according to package directions, except do not add salt to water. Stir in ham, cottage cheese, sour cream, dried onion, and pepper. Transfer to an ungreased 1½-quart casserole.

2 In a small bowl combine bread crumbs, melted butter, and, if desired, parsley flakes. Sprinkle over macaroni mixture.

3 Bake, uncovered, in a 375°F oven about 30 minutes or until mixture is heated through.

Nutrition Facts per serving: 434 cal., 18 g total fat (9 g sat. fat), 63 mg chol., 1,462 mg sodium, 43 g carbo., 1 g fiber, 25 g pro.

A host of fresh veggies, a bevy of flavorful seasonings, and two kinds of delectable cheeses drive this one-dish dinner to the winner's circle.

HERBED CHEESE, VEGETABLE & HAM BAKE

1	cup sliced zucchini and/or yellow summer squash (1 small)
1	cup chopped onion (1 large)
½	cup chopped red sweet pepper (1 small)
1	tablespoon butter
1	tablespoon dried parsley flakes, crushed
1	teaspoon dried basil, crushed
¼	teaspoon dried oregano, crushed
¼	teaspoon garlic powder
⅛	teaspoon black pepper
2	beaten eggs
1	cup diced cooked ham (5 ounces)
1	cup shredded mozzarella cheese (4 ounces)
½	cup shredded fontina or provolone cheese (2 ounces)
1	4½-ounce can (drained weight) sliced mushrooms, drained
2	10.2-ounce packages (5 each) refrigerated large flaky biscuits or two 7.5 oz. packages (10 each) regular refrigerated biscuits

PREP:
30 minutes

BAKE:
30 minutes

STAND:
15 minutes

OVEN:
375°F

MAKES:
6 servings

1 For filling, in a large skillet cook zucchini, onion, and sweet pepper in hot butter over medium heat about 6 minutes or until tender. Remove from heat. Stir in parsley, basil, oregano, garlic powder, and black pepper. Stir in eggs, ham, mozzarella cheese, fontina cheese, and mushrooms; set aside.

2 For crust, arrange 7 slightly flattened biscuits around edge of a lightly greased 10-inch tart pan with removable bottom or a 10-inch quiche dish, allowing dough to extend over side. Place the remaining 3 biscuits in bottom of dish.* Pinch edges to seal securely. Flatten slightly to form an even crust. Spread filling evenly into crust. (If using tart pan, place pan in a shallow baking pan.)

3 Bake, uncovered, in a 375°F oven about 30 minutes or until a knife inserted near the center comes out clean; cover edge with foil the last 10 minutes of baking to prevent overbrowning. Let stand for 15 minutes before cutting into wedges.

*NOTE: **If using regular-size biscuits, arrange 14 around the edges and 6 in the center.**

Nutrition Facts per serving: 496 cal., 27 g total fat (10 g sat. fat), 114 mg chol., 1,486 mg sodium, 45 g carbo., 3 g fiber, 20 g pro.

Yukon gold potatoes are known for their buttery flavor and hold their shape well when baked in this simply yummy casserole.

DENVER POTATO CASSEROLE

PREP:

20 minutes

BAKE:

1 hour 5 minutes

OVEN:

350°F

MAKES:

4 servings

4   medium (1⅓ pounds) Yukon gold potatoes, thinly sliced

1½   cups cubed cooked ham (about 8 ounces)

¾   cup chopped green or red sweet pepper (1 medium)

⅓   cup chopped sweet yellow onion (1 small)

1   cup shredded Colby-Monterey Jack cheese (4 ounces)

1 In a greased 2-quart square baking dish layer half of the potatoes, half of the ham, half of the sweet pepper, half of the onion, and half of the cheese. Repeat with the remaining ham, sweet pepper, and onion. Top with the remaining potatoes.

2 Bake, covered, in a 350°F oven for 45 minutes. Uncover. Bake about 15 minutes more or until potatoes are tender. Sprinkle with remaining ½ cup cheese and bake about 5 minutes more or until cheese is melted.

Nutrition Facts per serving: 315 cal., 12 g total fat (6 g sat. fat), 56 mg chol., 1,010 mg sodium, 27 g carbo., 3 g fiber, 24 g pro.

Refrigerated hash brown potatoes simplify the preparation of this family-favorite dish.

HAM & POTATO AU GRATIN

3	tablespoons butter
3	tablespoons all-purpose flour
1¾	cups milk
2	slightly beaten eggs
1½	cups shredded cheddar cheese (6 ounces)
1	tablespoon Dijon-style mustard
¼	teaspoon black pepper
2	small onions, thinly sliced
2	tablespoons olive oil or cooking oil
1	10-ounce package frozen chopped spinach, thawed and drained well
12	ounces cooked ham, cut into thin bite-size strips
1	20-ounce package refrigerated shredded hash brown potatoes
¼	cup grated Parmesan cheese

PREP:
30 minutes
BAKE:
30 minutes
STAND:
10 minutes
OVEN:
350°F
MAKES:
8 servings

1 In a medium saucepan melt butter over medium heat; stir in flour. Add milk all at once. Cook and stir until thickened and bubbly. Cook and stir for 1 minute more. Remove from heat. Stir 1 cup of the hot mixture into eggs; return egg mixture to saucepan. Stir in cheddar cheese, mustard, and pepper until cheese melts. Set aside.

2 In a large skillet cook onions in hot oil over medium heat until tender. Stir in spinach; set aside.

3 Spread half of the ham into an ungreased 3-quart rectangular baking dish. Sprinkle half of the hash browns over ham. Spoon half of the cheese mixture over hash browns. Spoon the spinach mixture over cheese mixture in dish. Repeat layers with remaining ham, hash browns, and cheese mixture. Sprinkle with Parmesan cheese.

4 Bake, uncovered, in a 350°F oven about 30 minutes or until heated through. Let stand for 10 minutes before serving.

Nutrition Facts per serving: 371 cal., 22 g total fat (10 g sat. fat), 118 mg chol., 940 mg sodium, 24 g carbo., 3 g fiber, 20 g pro.

These rich, creamy scalloped potatoes have two surefire points in their favor: the perfect recipe and the right potatoes. Russets make this dish thicken properly.

ULTIMATE SCALLOPED POTATOES & HAM

PREP:

25 minutes

BAKE:

1 hour

STAND:

10 minutes

OVEN:

350°F

MAKES:

6 to 8 servings

1	cup whipping cream
⅓	cup milk
1	clove garlic, minced
½	teaspoon salt
⅛	teaspoon black pepper
2	pounds russet potatoes (peeled if desired), sliced ⅛ inch thick
1	cup coarsely chopped cooked ham (8 ounces)
1	cup coarsely shredded Gruyère cheese (4 ounces)
¼	cup shredded Parmesan cheese (1 ounce)

1 In a small bowl combine cream, milk, garlic, salt, and pepper.

2 Arrange half of the potatoes in a greased 2-quart square baking dish, overlapping as necessary to fit. Sprinkle with ham. Pour half the cream mixture over ham; sprinkle with half of the Gruyère cheese and half of the Parmesan cheese. Layer remaining potatoes over cheese; add remaining cream mixture, remaining Gruyère cheese, and remaining Parmesan cheese.

3 Bake, uncovered, in a 350°F oven for 60 to 70 minutes or until top is golden brown and potatoes are tender. Let stand for 10 minutes before serving.

Nutrition Facts per serving: 488 cal., 31 g total fat (18 g sat. fat), 114 mg chol., 1,158 mg sodium, 29 g carbo., 3 g fiber, 25 g pro.

If you like "ham-and-Swiss on rye" at the deli, bring the idea home and make it even better by baking it up into a creamy, warming casserole.

HAM-SAUERKRAUT CASSEROLE

2	cups diced cooked ham (10 ounces)
1	14-ounce can Bavarian-style sauerkraut, rinsed, drained, and snipped*
1	10¾-ounce can condensed cream of potato soup
1	cup shredded Swiss cheese (4 ounces)
½	cup milk
1	tablespoon yellow mustard
¾	cup soft rye bread crumbs**
1	tablespoon butter, melted

PREP:

15 minutes

BAKE:

25 minutes

OVEN:

375°F

MAKES:

6 servings

1 In a large bowl combine ham, sauerkraut, soup, cheese, milk, and mustard. Transfer to an ungreased 1½-quart casserole. In a small bowl combine bread crumbs and melted butter; sprinkle over ham mixture.

2 Bake, uncovered, in a 375°F oven about 25 minutes or until mixture is heated through.

*NOTE: If Bavarian-style sauerkraut is not available, substitute one 14½-ounce can sauerkraut plus 2 tablespoons brown sugar and ½ teaspoon caraway seeds.

**NOTE: Use a blender or food processor to make fluffy soft bread crumbs. One slice yields ¾ cup.

Nutrition Facts per serving: 236 cal., 13 g total fat (7 g sat. fat), 53 mg chol., 1,611 mg sodium, 13 g carbo., 2 g fiber, 17 g pro.

Lots of good-old American casseroles started with a sauté of ground beef, onions, and celery.
For a tasty update, this one starts with lamb and fennel. It's decidedly different, but so easy.

LAMB & POLENTA BAKE

PREP:

30 minutes

BAKE:

35 minutes

STAND:

10 minutes

OVEN:

375°F

MAKES:

4 servings

¾   pound ground lamb

½   cup chopped onion (1 medium)

1   cup chopped fennel bulb (1 small)

3   cloves garlic, minced

1   14½-ounce can whole Italian-style tomatoes, undrained and cut up

1   teaspoon dried oregano, crushed

¼   teaspoon coarsely ground black pepper

1   16-ounce tube refrigerated cooked polenta

½   cup crumbled feta or garlic-and-herb feta cheese (2 ounces)

1   cup purchased pasta sauce

1 In a large skillet cook lamb, onion, fennel, and garlic over medium heat until meat is brown and onion is tender; drain. Add undrained tomatoes, the oregano, and pepper. Bring to boiling; reduce heat. Simmer, uncovered, for 10 to 15 minutes or until most of the liquid is evaporated, stirring occasionally.

2 Slice polenta tube in half lengthwise. Slice each half into ¼-inch slices. Press half of the slices over the bottom of a lightly greased 1½-quart casserole, overlapping as necessary.

3 Spoon lamb mixture over polenta. Sprinkle ¼ cup of the cheese over the lamb mixture. Layer the remaining polenta slices over the cheese, overlapping as necessary.

4 Bake, covered, in a 375°F oven for 25 minutes. Uncover. Bake for 10 to 15 minutes more or until heated through. Sprinkle the remaining ¼ cup cheese on top. Let stand for 10 minutes before serving.

5 Meanwhile, in a small saucepan heat the pasta sauce just to boiling. To serve, drizzle heated sauce over casserole.

Nutrition Facts per serving: 405 cal., 20 g total fat (10 g sat. fat), 75 mg chol., 1,165 mg sodium, 34 g carbo., 10 g fiber, 21 g pro.

Some call pastitsio (pronounced pah-STEET-see-o) "the Greek lasagna."

SPICE MARKET PASTITSIO

8	ounces dried elbow macaroni (2 cups)
8	ounces ground lamb or lean ground beef
1	14-ounce jar (1⅔ cups) spaghetti sauce with onion and garlic
1	teaspoon ground cinnamon
¼	teaspoon fennel seeds, crushed
1	cup milk
1	1.8-ounce envelope white sauce mix
2	slightly beaten eggs
¼	cup crumbled feta cheese (1 ounce)
½	teaspoon ground nutmeg
¼	cup shredded Parmesan or kasseri cheese (1 ounce)
	Greek or ripe olives or chopped tomatoes (optional)

1 Cook pasta according to package directions; drain. In a medium skillet cook lamb over medium heat until meat is brown; drain. Stir in spaghetti sauce, cinnamon, and fennel seeds; set aside.

2 In a medium saucepan combine milk and white sauce mix. Cook and stir over medium heat until thickened and bubbly. Remove from heat. Gradually stir half of the sauce into eggs; return egg mixture to saucepan. Stir in feta cheese and nutmeg.

3 To assemble, place half of the pasta in a lightly greased 2-quart square baking dish. Spread meat mixture over pasta; top with remaining pasta. Pour the white sauce mixture evenly over all. Sprinkle with Parmesan cheese.

4 Bake, uncovered, in a 350°F oven about 35 minutes or until set. Let stand for 10 minutes before serving. If desired, garnish with olives or tomatoes.

Nutrition Facts per serving: 355 cal., 12 g total fat (5 g sat. fat), 106 mg chol., 761 mg sodium, 43 g carbo., 2 g fiber, 17 g pro.

PREP:
30 minutes
BAKE:
35 minutes
STAND:
10 minutes
OVEN:
350°F
MAKES:
6 servings

Root vegetables star in this one-dish dinner—potatoes, fennel bulbs, and parsnips all make a tasty aboveground appearance.

LAMB & ROOT VEGETABLE GRATIN

PREP:

40 minutes

BAKE:

1 hour

OVEN:

350°F

MAKES:

6 servings

1	pound ground lamb
½	cup chopped onion (1 medium)
3	tablespoons butter
¼	cup all-purpose flour
½	teaspoon salt
¼	teaspoon black pepper
2	cups milk
½	cup shredded Parmesan cheese (2 ounces)
2	large potatoes (1 pound), peeled and thinly sliced
1	large fennel bulb (1 pound), trimmed* and very thinly sliced
2	parsnips (8 ounces), peeled and thinly sliced
3	cups fresh bread cubes
¼	cup butter, melted
	Snipped fennel tops (optional)

1 In a large skillet cook lamb over medium heat until brown; drain. Set aside.

2 For sauce, in a medium saucepan cook onion in the 3 tablespoons butter over medium heat until tender. Stir in flour, salt, and pepper. Add milk all at once. Cook and stir until thickened and bubbly. Remove from heat. Stir in cheese until melted.

3 In a large bowl combine lamb, sauce, potatoes, fennel, and parsnips; toss to coat. Transfer to a lightly greased 2-quart oval or rectangular au gratin or baking dish. Bake, covered, in a 350°F oven for 45 minutes.

4 Meanwhile, in a medium bowl combine bread cubes and the melted butter. Sprinkle over partially baked casserole. Bake, uncovered, for 15 to 20 minutes more or until vegetables are tender and bread cubes are browned. If desired, garnish with snipped fennel tops.

*NOTE: To trim fennel, remove green leafy tops from fennel; snip some of the tops for a garnish, if desired. Set aside. Cut off and discard upper stalks. Remove any wilted outer layers, cut in half lengthwise, and core.

Nutrition Facts per serving: 503 cal., 29 g total fat (13 g sat. fat), 100 mg chol., 607 mg sodium, 39 g carbo., 4 g fiber, 22 g pro.

The combination of lamb and eggplant is outstanding in almost any dish—especially Greek-influenced ones like this. It features a kaleidoscope of wonderful flavors and seasonings, including onion, garlic, oregano, red wine, cinnamon, and Parmesan cheese.

MOUSSAKA

1	eggplant (1 pound), peeled and cut into ½-inch slices
2	tablespoons cooking oil
1	pound ground lamb or ground beef
½	cup chopped onion (1 medium)
1	clove garlic, minced
1	8-ounce can tomato sauce
¼	cup dry red wine or beef broth
½	teaspoon salt
¼	teaspoon dried oregano, crushed
⅛	teaspoon ground cinnamon
1	beaten egg
2	tablespoons butter
2	tablespoons all-purpose flour
	Dash black pepper
1	cup milk
1	beaten egg
¼	cup shredded Parmesan cheese (1 ounce)

PREP:
50 minutes
BAKE:
35 minutes
STAND:
10 minutes
OVEN:
325°F
MAKES:
4 to 6 servings

1 In a large skillet brown half of the eggplant slices in hot oil over medium-high heat about 2 minutes per side. Drain; set aside. Repeat with remaining eggplant slices, adding more oil if necessary.

2 In the same skillet cook lamb, onion, and garlic over medium heat until meat is brown; drain. Stir in the tomato sauce, wine, ¼ teaspoon of the salt, the oregano, and cinnamon. Bring to boiling; reduce heat. Simmer, uncovered, about 10 minutes or until most of the liquid is absorbed. Cool mixture slightly. Stir ½ cup of the meat mixture into 1 beaten egg. Return to meat mixture in skillet.

3 Meanwhile, for sauce, in a medium saucepan melt butter over medium heat. Stir in flour, remaining ¼ teaspoon salt, and the pepper. Add milk all at once. Cook and stir until thickened and bubbly. Gradually stir thickened milk mixture into 1 beaten egg.

4 Arrange half of the eggplant slices in an ungreased 2-quart rectangular baking dish. Spread meat mixture over eggplant and top with remaining eggplant. Pour the sauce on top. Sprinkle with Parmesan cheese.

5 Bake, uncovered, in a 325°F oven for 35 to 40 minutes or until edges are bubbly. Let stand for 10 minutes before serving.

Nutrition Facts per serving: 499 cal., 34 g total fat (13 g sat. fat), 207 mg chol., 801 mg sodium, 18 g carbo., 5 g fiber, 29 g pro.

Chutney complements this Asian dish perfectly. Chutney is a spicy condiment that traditionally contains fruit, vinegar, sugar, and spices. It ranges in degrees of spiciness from mild to hot.

INDIAN-STYLE LAMB CURRY

PREP:

30 minutes

BAKE:

25 minutes

OVEN:

350°F

MAKES:

8 servings

1½	pounds ground lamb
1	large red onion, halved lengthwise and thinly sliced
2	cloves garlic, minced
2	medium potatoes (12 ounces), cut into ½-inch chunks
2	cups cauliflower florets
1	cup apple juice
½	cup sliced carrot (1 medium)
1	tablespoon curry powder
1	teaspoon salt
¼	teaspoon ground ginger
¼	cup cold water
2	tablespoons cornstarch
1	medium zucchini, halved lengthwise and sliced
1	cup frozen peas
⅓	cup golden raisins
3	cups hot cooked white rice
	Purchased chutney (optional)

1 In a very large skillet or Dutch oven cook lamb, onion, and garlic over medium heat until meat is brown and onion is tender; drain. Carefully add potatoes, cauliflower, apple juice, carrot, curry powder, salt, and ginger. Bring to boiling; reduce heat. Cover and simmer for 10 minutes.

2 Combine the cold water and cornstarch; add to skillet. Cook and stir just until mixture comes to boiling. Stir zucchini, peas, and raisins into lamb mixture. Transfer to a greased 3-quart casserole.

3 Bake, covered, in a 350°F oven for 25 to 30 minutes or until cauliflower and potatoes are tender. Serve over hot cooked rice. If desired, serve with chutney.

Nutrition Facts per serving: 337 cal., 12 g total fat (5 g sat. fat), 57 mg chol., 378 mg sodium, 39 g carbo., 3 g fiber, 19 g pro.

This classic dish is a welcome addition to any potluck gathering. To speed up preparation, use leftover or purchased refrigerated or frozen mashed potatoes.

SHEPHERD'S PIE

¼	cup butter
¼	cup all-purpose flour
1	teaspoon dried thyme, crushed
¼	teaspoon black pepper
1	cup beef broth
⅔	cup milk
4	cups cubed cooked lamb or beef (12 ounces)
1	16-ounce package frozen mixed vegetables, thawed and drained
1½	cups frozen small whole onions, thawed and drained
3½	cups prepared mashed potatoes
¾	cup shredded cheddar cheese (3 ounces)

PREP:
30 minutes
BAKE:
40 minutes
STAND:
10 minutes
OVEN:
400°F
MAKES:
8 servings

1 In a 4-quart Dutch oven melt butter over medium heat. Stir in flour, thyme, and pepper. Add broth and milk all at once. Cook and stir until thickened and bubbly. Remove from heat. Stir in lamb, vegetables, and onions. Transfer to an ungreased 3-quart casserole. Spoon mashed potatoes around the edge.

2 Bake, uncovered, in a 400°F oven for 35 minutes. Sprinkle with cheddar cheese. Bake about 5 minutes more or until bubbly and potatoes are brown. Let stand for 10 minutes before serving.

Nutrition Facts per serving: 377 cal., 16 g total fat (9 g sat. fat), 94 mg chol., 578 mg sodium, 31 g carbo., 5 g fiber, 28 g pro.

Make this delightful dish meaty or meatless by adding or subtracting the Italian sausage.
It's perfect for a twist on the old favorite lasagna.

RED PEPPER LASAGNA

PREP:

50 minutes

BAKE:

35 minutes

STAND:

20 minutes

OVEN:

350°F

MAKES:

8 servings

2	7-ounce jars roasted red sweet peppers, drained
1	tablespoon olive oil
1	28-ounce can crushed tomatoes, undrained
2	tablespoons dried basil, crushed
4	cloves garlic, minced
³⁄₄	teaspoon black pepper
1	teaspoon salt
8	ounces bulk sweet or hot Italian sausage, cooked until brown and drained (optional)
¹⁄₃	cup butter
¹⁄₃	cup all-purpose flour
¹⁄₂	teaspoon ground nutmeg
3	cups milk
12	no-boil lasagna noodles
1¹⁄₄	cups shredded Parmesan cheese (5 ounces)

1 Cut roasted red sweet peppers into thin strips. In a large saucepan cook sweet peppers in hot oil over medium heat for 1 minute. Stir in undrained tomatoes, the basil, garlic, black pepper, and ¹⁄₂ teaspoon of the salt. Bring to boiling; reduce heat. Simmer, uncovered, for 20 minutes, stirring often. Set aside to cool. Stir in sausage, if desired.

2 For béchamel sauce, in a medium saucepan melt butter over medium heat. Stir in flour, nutmeg, and the remaining ¹⁄₂ teaspoon salt. Add milk all at once. Cook and stir until thickened and bubbly. Set aside to cool.

3 To assemble, place 3 lasagna noodles in the bottom of a greased 3-quart rectangular baking dish. Spread about 1 cup of the red pepper mixture over the noodles. Top with ³⁄₄ cup of the béchamel sauce, spreading evenly; sprinkle with ¹⁄₄ cup of the Parmesan cheese. Repeat three more times with the remaining noodles, red pepper mixture, and béchamel sauce. Be sure the top layer of noodles is completely covered in sauce. Sprinkle with the remaining ¹⁄₄ cup Parmesan cheese.

4 Bake, uncovered, in a 350°F oven for 35 to 40 minutes or until top is golden and edges are bubbly. Let stand for 20 minutes before serving.

MAKE-AHEAD DIRECTIONS: Assemble as directed. Cover unbaked casserole with plastic wrap; refrigerate up to 24 hours. Remove plastic wrap and cover with foil. Bake in a 350°F oven for 30 minutes. Remove foil. Bake for 15 to 25 minutes more or until bubbly.

Nutrition Facts per serving: 753 cal., 44 g total fat (23 g sat. fat), 110 mg chol., 2,145 mg sodium, 44 g carbo., 3 g fiber, 46 g pro.

MEATLESS

6

This meatless casserole delivers the heartiness and warmth you seek in the winter while providing a nice break from the usual. Serve it with a green salad topped with citrus slices and Asiago cheese.

CREAMY PENNE WITH VEGETABLES

PREP:
25 minutes

BAKE:
30 minutes

OVEN:
350°F

MAKES:
4 servings

8	ounces dried penne pasta
¾	cup chopped red sweet pepper (1 medium)
½	cup chopped celery (1 stalk)
½	cup chopped onion (1 medium)
½	teaspoon dried thyme, crushed
1	clove garlic, minced
1	tablespoon butter
1	10¾-ounce can condensed golden mushroom soup
½	cup dairy sour cream
½	cup milk

1 Cook penne according to package directions; drain. Meanwhile, in a large saucepan cook sweet pepper, celery, onion, thyme, and garlic in hot butter over medium heat until tender. Remove from heat. Stir in soup, sour cream, and milk. Stir in cooked penne.

2 Transfer pasta mixture to an ungreased 1½-quart casserole. Bake, covered, in a 350°F oven about 30 minutes or until heated through.

Nutrition Facts per serving: 376 cal., 12 g total fat (6 g sat. fat), 24 mg chol., 663 mg sodium, 56 g carbo., 3 g fiber, 11 g pro.

Keeping these five ingredients on hand is easy to do—then you'll always have the option of whipping up this quick and tasty dish.

CHIPOTLE BEAN ENCHILADAS

10	6-inch corn tortillas
1	15-ounce can pinto beans or black beans, rinsed and drained
1	tablespoon chopped chipotle pepper in adobo sauce*
2	cups shredded 4-cheese Mexican blend (8 ounces)
2	10-ounce cans enchilada sauce

1 Grease a 2-quart rectangular baking dish; set aside. Stack the tortillas and wrap tightly in foil. Bake in a 350°F oven for about 10 minutes or until warm.

2 Meanwhile, for filling, in a medium bowl combine beans, chipotle pepper, 1 cup of the cheese, and ½ cup of the enchilada sauce. Spoon about ¼ cup of the filling onto 1 edge of each tortilla. Starting at the edge with the filling, roll up each tortilla.

3 Arrange tortillas, seam sides down, in a prepared baking dish. Top with remaining enchilada sauce. Cover with foil.

4 Bake in the 350°F oven about 25 minutes or until heated through. Remove foil. Sprinkle with remaining 1 cup cheese. Bake, uncovered, about 5 minutes or until cheese melts.

*NOTE: **Because hot chile peppers contain volatile oils that can burn your skin and eyes, avoid direct contact with chiles as much as possible. When working with chile peppers, wear plastic or rubber gloves. If your bare hands do touch the chile peppers, wash your hands well with soap and water.**

Nutrition Facts per serving: 487 cal., 19 g total fat (8 g sat. fat), 40 mg chol., 1,091 mg sodium, 63 g carbo., 14 g fiber, 23 g pro.

PREP:
25 minutes
BAKE:
30 minutes
OVEN:
350°F
MAKES:
5 servings

Pair this rich dish with a garlicky mixed green salad and refreshing ice cream or sorbet for dessert.

BAKED CHILE RICE

PREP:
30 minutes

BAKE:
30 minutes

OVEN:
325°F

MAKES:
6 servings

1	cup chopped onion (1 large)
2	cloves garlic, minced
2	tablespoons butter
1	10-ounce package frozen whole kernel corn
1	cup uncooked long grain rice
2	cups chicken broth
1	4-ounce can chopped green chile peppers, drained
1½	cups dairy sour cream
1	medium tomato, halved and sliced
½	cup shredded mild cheddar cheese or grated Chihuahua cheese (2 ounces)

1 In a large saucepan cook onion and garlic in butter over medium heat until onion is tender. Stir in corn, uncooked rice, broth, and chile peppers. Bring to boiling; reduce heat. Simmer, covered, for 15 to 20 minutes or until rice is tender. Stir in sour cream.

2 Transfer rice mixture to an ungreased 2-quart square baking dish. Bake, uncovered, in a 325°F oven for 25 to 30 minutes or until heated through. Top with tomato slices and sprinkle with cheese. Bake, uncovered, about 5 minutes more or until cheese is melted.

Nutrition Facts per serving: 356 cal., 18 g total fat (10 g sat. fat), 43 mg chol., 497 mg sodium, 41 g carbo., 2 g fiber, 9 g pro.

A cousin of the shepherd's pie, this dish has only five ingredients and makes an easy midweek meal.

GARDENER'S PIE

1	16-ounce package frozen loose-pack vegetable blend, thawed
1	11-ounce can condensed cheddar cheese soup
½	teaspoon dried thyme, crushed
1	20-ounce package refrigerated mashed potatoes
1	cup shredded smoked cheddar cheese (4 ounces)

1 In an ungreased 1½-quart casserole combine vegetables, soup, and thyme. Stir mashed potatoes to soften. Spread mashed potatoes carefully over vegetable mixture to cover surface.

2 Bake, covered, in a 350°F oven for 30 minutes. Uncover and bake about 15 minutes more or until heated through, topping with cheese the last 5 minutes of baking. Serve in shallow bowls.

Nutrition Facts per serving: 349 cal., 17 g total fat (8 g sat. fat), 39 mg chol., 1,031 mg sodium, 40 g carbo., 4 g fiber, 15 g pro.

PREP:
15 minutes
BAKE:
45 minutes
OVEN:
350°F
MAKES:
4 servings

This mac 'n' cheesy update showcases veggies and an oregano-seasoned cream sauce.

VEGETABLE PRIMAVERA CASSEROLE

PREP:
30 minutes
BAKE:
30 minutes
STAND:
5 minutes
OVEN:
375°F
MAKES:
8 servings

1½ cups dried elbow macaroni (6 ounces)

1 16-ounce bag frozen loose-pack vegetable blend

2 medium zucchini, halved lengthwise and sliced

½ cup chopped red sweet pepper

2 12-ounce cans (3 cups) evaporated milk

1 cup vegetable broth or chicken broth

⅓ cup all-purpose flour

1 teaspoon dried oregano, crushed

½ teaspoon garlic powder

½ teaspoon salt

½ teaspoon black pepper

¾ cup grated Parmesan cheese or Romano cheese

1 medium tomato, halved and sliced

1 In a 4- to 5-quart Dutch oven cook macaroni in boiling lightly salted water for 8 minutes, adding the frozen vegetables, zucchini, and sweet pepper during the last 3 minutes of cooking; drain. Return macaroni mixture to the pan.

2 Meanwhile, in a medium saucepan whisk together evaporated milk, broth, flour, oregano, garlic powder, salt, and black pepper. Cook and stir over medium heat until thickened and bubbly. Add to macaroni mixture; toss to coat. Stir in ½ cup of the Parmesan cheese. Transfer macaroni mixture to a lightly greased 3-quart rectangular baking dish.

3 Bake, uncovered, in a 375°F oven for 25 minutes. Top with tomato slices and remaining ¼ cup Parmesan cheese. Bake, uncovered, about 5 minutes more or until heated through. Let stand for 5 minutes.

Nutrition Facts per serving: 280 cal., 9 g total fat (5 g sat. fat), 31 mg chol., 499 mg sodium, 35 g carbo., 3 g fiber, 13 g pro.

Creamy and rich, this pasta dish boasts the perfect combination of tangy Gorgonzola, nutty fontina, and sharp Parmesan cheeses.

BAKED ZITI WITH THREE CHEESES

12	ounces dried ziti or penne pasta (4 cups)
1	14½-ounce can fire-roasted crushed tomatoes or one 14½-ounce can diced tomatoes, undrained
1	cup chopped onion (1 large)
12	cloves garlic, minced
2	tablespoons olive oil
½	cup dry white wine
2	cups whipping cream
1	cup shredded Parmesan cheese (4 ounces)
¾	cup crumbled Gorgonzola or other blue cheese (3 ounces)
½	cup shredded fontina cheese (2 ounces)
¾	teaspoon salt
¼	teaspoon black pepper
	Snipped fresh Italian (flat-leaf) parsley (optional)

PREP:
30 minutes

BAKE:
30 minutes

OVEN:
425°F

MAKES:
6 servings

1 Cook pasta according to package directions; drain. Place in an ungreased 3-quart rectangular baking dish; stir in undrained tomatoes. Set aside.

2 Meanwhile, in a large saucepan cook onion and garlic in hot oil over medium heat just until tender. Carefully stir in wine and cook about 3 minutes or until liquid is reduced by half. Add cream; heat to boiling. Boil gently, uncovered, about 5 minutes or until mixture thickens slightly, stirring frequently. Remove from heat. Stir in cheeses, salt, and pepper.

3 Pour cheese mixture over pasta. Bake, covered, in a 425°F oven for 30 to 35 minutes or until sauce is bubbly. Stir pasta to coat. If desired, sprinkle with parsley.

Nutrition Facts per serving: 748 cal., 47 g total fat (27 g sat. fat), 145 mg chol., 1,088 mg sodium, 55 g carbo., 3 g fiber, 23 g pro.

Want a main dish infused with a variety of veggies? This meatless one-dish wonder is filled with artichokes, asparagus, carrots, mushrooms, zucchini, and peas.

VEGETARIAN LASAGNA

PREP:
50 minutes

BAKE:
30 minutes

STAND:
10 minutes

OVEN:
350°F

MAKES:
8 to 10 servings

9	dried lasagna noodles (8 ounces)
1	9-ounce package frozen artichokes, thawed
3	tablespoons olive oil
2	tablespoons dry white wine
1½	pound asparagus, trimmed and cut into bite-size pieces
1	cup chopped carrots (2 medium)
½	cup finely chopped shallots (4)
3	cloves garlic, minced
3	cups quartered fresh mushrooms (such as button or cremini)
1	cup chopped zucchini (1 medium)
½	frozen peas, thawed
6	tablespoons butter
½	cup all-purpose flour
4	cups milk
2	tablespoons dried basil, crushed
2	tablespoons dried parsley flakes, crushed
2	small bay leaves
1	cup shredded Parmesan cheese (4 ounces)

1 Cook lasagna according to package directions; drain. Rinse with cold water; drain again. Quarter artichokes lengthwise; drain well. In a large skillet cook and stir artichokes in 1 tablespoon of the oil over medium heat for 5 minutes. Carefully add wine; cook and stir for 1 minute. Transfer to a medium bowl. Set aside. In a saucepan cook asparagus and carrots in boiling water for 2 minutes; drain. Set aside.

2 In the large skillet cook shallots and garlic in remaining 2 tablespoons oil over medium heat until tender. Add asparagus, carrots, mushrooms, zucchini, and peas; cook and stir about 5 minutes or until vegetables are tender. In the large saucepan melt butter over medium heat; stir in flour until smooth. Cook and stir for 2 minutes more or until mixture begins to brown. Stir in milk. Add basil, parsley, and bay leaves. Cook and stir until thickened and bubbly. Remove and discard bay leaves. Stir in vegetable mixture, artichokes, ¾ teaspoon *salt,* and ½ teaspoon *black pepper.*

3 Arrange 3 of the noodles in a greased 3-quart rectangular baking dish. Spoon one-third of the vegetable mixture over noodles; sprinkle with ⅓ cup of the cheese. Repeat the layers twice. Bake, uncovered, in a 350°F oven about 30 minutes or until golden. Let stand for 10 minutes.

Nutrition Facts per serving: 456 cal., 24 g total fat (12 g sat. fat), 54 mg chol., 562 mg sodium, 44 g carbo., 5 g fiber, 18 g pro.

This veggie-filled lasagna is a treat after those summer trips to the farmer's market, where you can get all the fresh ingredients straight from the farmer.

LIGHT VEGETABLE LASAGNA

9	dried lasagna noodles (8 ounces)
6	cups broccoli florets
1	large red sweet pepper, cut into bite-size strips
1¼	cups sliced zucchini (1 medium)
1¼	cups sliced yellow summer squash (1 medium)
2	beaten eggs
1	16-ounce container low-fat cottage cheese (2 cups)
1	15-ounce container light ricotta cheese (2 cups)
2½	tablespoons dried basil, crushed
2	teaspoons dried thyme, crushed
3	cloves garlic, minced
½	teaspoon salt
¼	teaspoon black pepper
¼	teaspoon bottled hot pepper sauce
3	cups shredded mozzarella cheese (12 ounces)

PREP:
45 minutes
BAKE:
45 minutes
STAND:
10 minutes
OVEN:
375°F
MAKES:
8 to 10 servings

1 Cook lasagna noodles according to package directions; drain. Rinse with cold water; drain well. Set aside.

2 Meanwhile, place a steamer basket in a Dutch oven. Add water to just below the bottom of the steamer basket. Bring to boiling. Add broccoli, sweet pepper, zucchini, and yellow squash. Reduce heat; cover and steam for 6 to 8 minutes or until vegetables are crisp-tender. Remove from heat.

3 In a medium bowl combine eggs, cottage cheese, ricotta cheese, basil, thyme, garlic, salt, black pepper, and hot pepper sauce.

4 To assemble, arrange 3 of the cooked noodles in a greased 3-quart rectangular baking dish. Spread with one-third of the ricotta cheese mixture. Top with one-third of the vegetable mixture and 1 cup of the mozzarella cheese. Repeat the layers twice more.

5 Bake, covered, in a 375°F oven for 45 to 50 minutes or until heated through. Uncover; let stand for 10 minutes before serving.

MAKE-AHEAD DIRECTIONS: After assembling the dish in step 4, cover with foil and chill for up to 24 hours. Bake, covered, in a 375°F oven for 55 to 65 minutes or until heated through. Uncover; let stand for 10 minutes.

Nutrition Facts per serving: 388 cal., 15 g total fat (8 g sat. fat), 101 mg chol., 683 mg sodium, 32 g carbo., 4 g fiber, 32 g pro.

Use leftovers of this bean-packed cassoulet on toasted baguette-style French bread slices to create a delightfully hearty bruschetta.

VEGETARIAN CASSOULET

PREP:

45 minutes

STAND:

1 hour

COOK:

1 hour + 30 minutes

BAKE:

15 minutes

OVEN:

350°F

MAKES:

6 to 8 servings

1½ cups dry Great Northern beans

1½ cups dry pinto beans

1 cup dry garbanzo beans (chickpeas)

1 cup chopped celery (2 stalks)

1 cup chopped onion (1 large)

1 cup chopped carrots (2 medium)

2 tablespoons olive oil

4 14-ounce cans vegetable broth

1 0.75-ounce package dried porcini mushrooms (about 1 cup)

½ cup bottled roasted red sweet peppers, chopped

½ cup oil-packed dried tomatoes, drained and snipped

¼ cup roasted garlic puree

½ teaspoon dried oregano, crushed

½ teaspoon dried thyme, crushed

1 bay leaf

2 cups soft sourdough bread crumbs

2 tablespoons butter, melted

1 clove garlic, minced

1 In 6-quart Dutch oven mix beans and 12 cups *water.* Bring to boiling; reduce heat. Simmer 2 minutes. Remove from heat. Let stand 1 hour. Drain beans. Rinse in a colander; drain again. In the same pan cook celery, onion, and carrots in hot oil over medium heat for 5 minutes. Add beans, broth, and mushrooms. Bring to boiling; reduce heat. Simmer, covered, for 1 hour.

2 Add roasted red sweet peppers, dried tomatoes, garlic puree, oregano, thyme, bay leaf, ½ teaspoon *salt,* and ½ teaspoon *black pepper.* Return to boiling; reduce heat. Simmer, covered, about 30 minutes more or until beans are tender and most of the liquid is absorbed. Remove bay leaf.

3 Remove 5 cups of bean mixture. Place in an airtight freezer container or a self-sealing freezer bag. Seal and freeze up to 3 months to use in a future batch of cassoulet. Transfer remaining bean mixture to an ungreased 2-quart casserole. In a small bowl combine bread crumbs, melted butter, and garlic. Sprinkle bread crumb mixture over bean mixture in casserole. Bake, uncovered, in a 350°F oven for 15 to 20 minutes or until bread crumbs are lightly toasted.

Nutrition Facts per serving: 394 cal., 11 g total fat (3 g sat. fat), 7 mg chol., 600 mg sodium, 61 g carbo., 18 g fiber, 18 g pro.

If you want to cut down on meat, try this two-bean casserole featuring garbanzo and red beans.

LAYERED BEAN & POTATO PIE

1	cup chopped onion (1 large)
1	cup chopped green sweet pepper (1 large)
1	cup sliced celery (2 stalks)
4	cloves garlic, minced
¼	teaspoon black pepper
1	tablespoon cooking oil
1	15-ounce can garbanzo beans, rinsed and drained
1	15-ounce can small red beans, rinsed and drained
1	10¾-ounce can condensed cream of potato soup
1	cup frozen peas
¼	cup milk
½	teaspoon ground cumin
½	teaspoon ground coriander
1	pound small red potatoes, thinly sliced
½	cup shredded Monterey Jack cheese or Monterey Jack cheese with jalapeño peppers (2 ounces)

PREP:

25 minutes

BAKE:

55 minutes

OVEN:

350°F

MAKES:

5 servings

1 In a large saucepan cook onion, sweet pepper, celery, garlic, and black pepper in hot oil over medium heat for 5 minutes or until vegetables are tender. Mash ½ cup of the garbanzo beans; add to vegetable mixture along with the remaining whole garbanzo beans, the red beans, soup, peas, milk, cumin, and coriander. Stir gently to combine.

2 Spread half of the potato slices into a greased 2-quart square baking dish. Spoon bean mixture over potatoes and top with remaining potato slices, overlapping as necessary.

3 Bake, covered, in a 350°F oven for 45 minutes. Uncover and sprinkle with cheese. Bake, uncovered, about 10 minutes more or until cheese melts and potatoes are tender.

Nutrition Facts per serving: 360 cal., 9 g total fat (3 g sat. fat), 16 mg chol., 963 mg sodium, 56 g carbo., 13 g fiber, 18 g pro.

Canned beans make this dish a snap to prepare. You can use any combination of beans that you like, so go ahead and raid your pantry!

BEAN ENCHILADA CASSEROLE

PREP:
25 minutes

BAKE:
40 minutes

STAND:
5 minutes

OVEN:
350°F

MAKES:
4 to 6 servings

1　15-ounce can red kidney beans, pinto beans, or black beans, rinsed and drained

1　15-ounce can garbanzo beans (chickpeas), navy beans, and/or Great Northern beans, rinsed and drained

1　10¾-ounce can condensed cheddar cheese soup or one 11-ounce can condensed nacho cheese soup

1　10-ounce can enchilada sauce

1　8-ounce can tomato sauce

2　cups corn chips or tortilla chips, broken

¾　cup shredded Monterey Jack cheese with jalapeño peppers or Monterey Jack cheese (3 ounces)

Toppers: sliced pitted ripe olives, sliced green onions, chopped tomatoes, chopped green sweet pepper, and/or shredded lettuce (optional)

1 For filling, in a large bowl combine kidney beans, garbanzo beans, and soup. In a medium bowl combine enchilada sauce and tomato sauce. Spoon bean mixture into a greased 2-quart rectangular baking dish; pour sauce mixture over bean mixture. Top with chips.

2 Cover with lightly greased foil. Bake in a 350°F oven about 40 minutes or until heated through. Remove foil; sprinkle with cheese. Let stand about 5 minutes or until cheese melts. If desired, sprinkle with desired toppers.

Nutrition Facts per serving: 426 cal., 18 g total fat (7 g sat. fat), 28 mg chol., 2,037 mg sodium, 54 g carbo., 13 g fiber, 23 g pro.

Serve bowls of sour cream, salsa, and guacamole alongside this casserole—these extras will make it all the more enticing.

BLACK BEAN TORTILLA CASSEROLE

10	6-inch corn tortillas
1	14½-ounce can diced tomatoes, undrained
1½	cups chopped green or red sweet peppers (2 medium)
1	cup chopped onion (1 large)
¾	cup purchased chunky salsa or picante sauce
1	teaspoon ground cumin
1	15-ounce can black beans, rinsed and drained
1	11-ounce can condensed black bean soup
2	cups shredded Mexican-style cheese blend or Monterey Jack cheese (8 ounces)
	Dairy sour cream (optional)
	Purchased salsa (optional)
	Guacamole (optional)

PREP:
20 minutes

BAKE:
25 minutes

STAND:
10 minutes

OVEN:
350°F

MAKES:
6 to 8 servings

1 Place tortillas in a single layer on 2 baking sheets. Bake in a 350°F oven about 10 minutes or until crisp, turning once.

2 Meanwhile, in a large skillet combine undrained tomatoes, sweet peppers, onion, the ¾ cup salsa, and the cumin. Bring to boiling; reduce heat. Simmer, uncovered, for 10 minutes. Stir in black beans and soup.

3 Spread one-third of the bean mixture over the bottom of a lightly greased 2-quart rectangular baking dish. Top with half of the tortillas, overlapping as necessary, and 1 cup of the cheese. Add another one-third of the bean mixture. Layer remaining tortillas and remaining bean mixture on top.

4 Bake, covered, in the 350°F oven for 25 to 30 minutes or until heated through. Sprinkle with remaining 1 cup cheese. Let stand for 10 minutes. To serve, cut casserole into squares. If desired, serve with sour cream, additional salsa, and guacamole.

Nutrition Facts per serving: 399 cal., 14 g total fat (7 g sat. fat), 33 mg chol., 1,190 mg sodium, 52 g carbo., 10 g fiber, 19 g pro.

Bottled minced garlic is a step-saving ingredient you can store in the refrigerator. Use ¹/₂ teaspoon bottled minced garlic for each clove of garlic.

BROWN RICE & BEAN BAKE

PREP:

20 minutes

BAKE:

40 minutes

STAND:

5 minutes

OVEN:

350°F

MAKES:

4 servings

¹/₂	cup chopped onion (1 medium)
2	cloves garlic, minced
1	tablespoon olive oil or cooking oil
2	teaspoons chili powder
1	teaspoon ground cumin
¹/₄	teaspoon salt
1	15-ounce can pinto beans, rinsed and drained
1¹/₂	cups cooked brown rice
1	10¹/₂-ounce can condensed vegetarian vegetable soup
1	cup shredded cheddar cheese or Monterey Jack cheese (4 ounces)
2	slightly beaten eggs
¹/₂	cup crushed tortilla chips
	Purchased salsa (optional)

1 In a medium saucepan cook onion and garlic in hot oil over medium heat until tender. Stir in chili powder, cumin, and salt. Cook for 1 minute more. Remove from heat.

2 Stir in beans, cooked rice, soup, ¹/₂ cup of the cheese, and the eggs. Spoon mixture into a lightly greased 9-inch pie plate or quiche dish.

3 Bake, uncovered, in a 350°F oven for 35 minutes. Top with tortilla chips and remaining ¹/₂ cup cheese. Bake about 5 minutes more or until set. Let stand for 5 minutes before serving. If desired, serve with salsa.

Nutrition Facts per serving: 455 cal., 20 g total fat (8 g sat. fat), 136 mg chol., 1,180 mg sodium, 51 g carbo., 9 g fiber, 20 g pro.

Cheesy and rich tasting, this Mexican-style vegetarian casserole is so satisfying.

BLACK BEAN LASAGNA

9   dried lasagna noodles (8 ounces)

2   15-ounce cans black beans, rinsed and drained

1   beaten egg

1   12-ounce container cottage cheese (1½ cups)

1   8-ounce package cream cheese, cut into cubes and softened

1½   cups shredded Monterey Jack cheese (6 ounces)

1   cup chopped onion (1 large)

¾   cup chopped green sweet pepper (1 medium)

2   cloves garlic, minced

1   tablespoon cooking oil

1   15-ounce can Italian-style tomato sauce

4   teaspoons dried cilantro, crushed

1   teaspoon ground cumin

    Coarsely chopped tomato

PREP:
45 minutes
BAKE:
35 minutes
STAND:
10 minutes
OVEN:
350°F
MAKES:
8 servings

1 Cook lasagna noodles according to package directions; drain. Rinse with cold water; drain well. Set aside. In a small bowl mash one can of the beans with a potato masher; set aside. In a medium bowl combine egg, cottage cheese, cream cheese, and 1 cup of the Monterey Jack cheese; set aside.

2 In a large skillet cook onion, sweet pepper, and garlic in hot oil over medium-high heat until tender. Stir in mashed beans, remaining can of whole beans, tomato sauce, cilantro, and cumin; heat through.

3 Arrange 3 of the noodles in a lightly greased 3-quart rectangular baking dish. Top with one-third (about 1⅓ cups) of the bean mixture. Spoon half (about 1 cup) of the cheese mixture over bean mixture. Repeat layers. Top with remaining noodles and bean mixture.

4 Bake, covered, in a 350°F oven for 35 to 40 minutes or until heated through. Sprinkle with remaining ½ cup Monterey Jack cheese. Let stand for 10 minutes before serving. Garnish with chopped tomato.

Nutrition Facts per serving: 456 cal., 22 g total fat (12 g sat. fat), 83 mg chol., 857 mg sodium, 46 g carbo., 8 g fiber, 25 g pro.

If you're cooking for people who love or hate spiciness, no problem. You can adjust the kick in this layered casserole by choosing mild, medium, or hot salsa.

TORTILLA BEAN & RICE BAKE

PREP:

30 minutes

BAKE:

35 minutes

OVEN:

350°F

MAKES:

6 servings

1½   cups water

⅔   cup uncooked long grain rice

¼   teaspoon salt

6   6-inch corn tortillas

1   14½-ounce can Mexican-style stewed tomatoes, undrained and cut up

1   cup purchased salsa

1   15-ounce can kidney beans or small red beans, rinsed and drained

1   cup shredded Monterey Jack cheese with jalapeño peppers or regular Monterey Jack cheese (4 ounces)

Fresh jalapeño chile peppers, sliced* (optional)

Dairy sour cream (optional)

1 In a medium saucepan combine the water, rice, and salt. Bring to boiling; reduce heat. Cover and simmer about 20 minutes or until rice is tender and water is absorbed. Meanwhile, stack tortillas and wrap in foil. Heat in a 350°F oven for 10 minutes to soften.

2 In a medium bowl combine undrained tomatoes and salsa. Stir beans into cooked rice. Cut softened tortillas into quarters and arrange half of them in the bottom of a lightly greased 2-quart square baking dish. Layer half of the rice mixture over tortillas. Top with half of the tomato mixture and ½ cup of the cheese. Repeat layers.

3 Bake, covered, in a 350°F oven for 35 to 40 minutes or until heated through. If desired, garnish with jalapeño slices and sour cream.

*NOTE: Because hot chile peppers contain volatile oils that can burn your skin and eyes, avoid direct contact with chiles as much as possible. When working with chile peppers, wear plastic or rubber gloves. If your bare hands do touch the chile peppers, wash your hands well with soap and water.

Nutrition Facts per serving: 296 cal., 7 g total fat (4 g sat. fat), 17 mg chol., 644 mg sodium, 49 g carbo., 6 g fiber, 14 g pro.

Top this main-dish casserole with salsa and a spoonful of sour cream.

TWO-BEAN TAMALE PIE

1	cup chopped green sweet pepper (1 large)
½	cup chopped onion (1 medium)
2	cloves garlic, minced
1	tablespoon cooking oil
1	15-ounce can kidney beans, rinsed, drained, and slightly mashed
1	15-ounce can pinto beans, rinsed, drained, and slightly mashed
1	6-ounce can (⅔ cup) vegetable juice
1	4-ounce can diced green chile peppers, undrained
1	teaspoon chili powder
½	teaspoon ground cumin
1	8½-ounce package corn muffin mix
½	cup shredded cheddar cheese (2 ounces)
4	teaspoons dried cilantro or parsley flakes, crushed
	Purchased salsa (optional)
	Dairy sour cream (optional)

PREP:
25 minutes
BAKE:
25 minutes
OVEN:
400°F
MAKES:
6 servings

1 In a medium skillet cook sweet pepper, onion, and garlic in hot oil over medium heat until tender. Stir in kidney beans, pinto beans, vegetable juice, undrained chile peppers, chili powder, and cumin; heat through. Spoon bean mixture into a greased 2-quart square baking dish.

2 Prepare corn muffin mix according to package directions (do not bake). Add cheese and cilantro to muffin mix, stirring just until combined. Spoon corn bread mixture evenly on top of bean mixture.

3 Bake, uncovered, in a 400°F oven about 25 minutes or until golden. If desired, serve with salsa and sour cream.

Nutrition Facts per serving: 387 cal., 13 g total fat (2 g sat. fat), 37 mg chol., 858 mg sodium, 58 g carbo., 9 g fiber, 17 g pro.

Cooks from countries bordering the Mediterranean know how to stretch meat—or leave it out entirely —and still serve satisfying, full-flavored meals. This lively Greek-inspired casserole is proof positive!

GREEK PASTA CASSEROLE

PREP:

25 minutes

BAKE:

20 minutes

STAND:

10 minutes

OVEN:

375°F

MAKES:

6 servings

12	ounces dried rotini pasta (3½ cups)
1	15-ounce can tomato sauce
1	10¾-ounce can condensed tomato soup
1	15-ounce can white kidney beans (cannellini beans) or garbanzo beans (chickpeas), rinsed and drained
2	cups crumbled feta cheese (8 ounces)
1	cup coarsely chopped pitted Greek black olives
½	cup seasoned fine dry bread crumbs
2	tablespoons butter, melted
2	tablespoons grated Parmesan cheese

1 Cook rotini according to package directions; drain. In a very large bowl combine cooked rotini, tomato sauce, and soup; toss to coat. Stir in beans, feta cheese, and olives.

2 Spoon rotini mixture into a lightly greased 3-quart rectangular baking dish. In a small bowl combine bread crumbs, melted butter, and Parmesan cheese; sprinkle over pasta mixture.

3 Bake, uncovered, in a 375°F oven for 20 to 25 minutes or until heated through and top is light brown. Let stand for 10 minutes before serving.

Nutrition Facts per serving: 553 cal., 19 g total fat (10 g sat. fat), 52 mg chol., 1,890 mg sodium, 74 g carbo., 7 g fiber, 24 g pro.

Sweet honeydew melon or cantaloupe wedges would provide a cool complement to this peppy dish.

HUEVOS CON FRIJOLES

4	eggs
1	15-ounce can red kidney beans, rinsed and drained
1	10¾-ounce can condensed cream of celery soup
1	4-ounce can diced green chile peppers, drained
¼	cup sliced green onions (2)
2	teaspoons dried parsley flakes, crushed
⅛	teaspoon black pepper
	Several dashes bottled hot pepper sauce
1½	cups shredded cheddar cheese (6 ounces)
	Purchased salsa (optional)
	Dairy sour cream (optional)

1 In a large bowl whisk eggs. Stir in kidney beans, soup, chile peppers, green onions, parsley, black pepper, and hot pepper sauce. Add cheese; mix well. Pour mixture into a greased 2-quart square baking dish.

2 Bake, uncovered, in a 350°F oven for 30 to 35 minutes or until set in center. Let stand for 5 minutes before serving. If desired, serve with salsa and sour cream.

Nutrition Facts per serving: 408 cal., 24 g total fat (12 g sat. fat), 259 mg chol., 1,154 mg sodium, 26 g carbo., 7 g fiber, 26 g pro.

PREP:
20 minutes
BAKE:
30 minutes
STAND:
5 minutes
OVEN:
350°F
MAKES:
4 servings

It's fun to go meatless now and then—especially with varied, flavor-packed recipes like this one. Hint: Six ounces may look like a lot of spinach at first, but it wilts as you stir it in to end up with just the right amount.

ROASTED VEGETABLES & SPINACH

PREP:
30 minutes

BAKE:
40 minutes

OVEN:
400°F

MAKES:
6 servings

1	eggplant (about 1 pound), peeled and cut into 1-inch cubes (about 6 cups)
1	large red onion, cut into thin wedges
1½	cups coarsely chopped yellow and/or green sweet peppers (2 medium)
1	tablespoon olive oil
½	teaspoon salt
1	teaspoon olive oil
2	cloves garlic, minced
½	teaspoon dried thyme, crushed
¼	teaspoon crushed red pepper
¼	teaspoon fennel seeds, crushed
¼	teaspoon black pepper
1	18.7-ounce can ready-to-serve tomato soup
12	ounces dried ziti or rotini pasta (4 cups)
1	6-ounce bag prewashed baby spinach (about 8 cups)
1	cup shredded mozzarella cheese (4 ounces)

1 In a shallow roasting pan combine eggplant, onion, sweet peppers, and the 1 tablespoon oil. Sprinkle with salt. Bake in a 400°F oven for 30 to 35 minutes or until vegetables begin to brown, stirring twice.

2 Meanwhile, in a small saucepan heat the 1 teaspoon oil over medium heat. Add garlic, thyme, crushed red pepper, fennel seeds, and black pepper. Cook and stir for 2 minutes. Stir in soup. Bring to boiling; reduce heat. Simmer, uncovered, for 5 minutes, stirring occasionally.

3 Meanwhile, cook pasta according to package directions; drain. Transfer to a very large bowl. Add soup mixture and roasted vegetables; toss to coat. Stir in spinach.

4 Spoon pasta mixture into a greased 3-quart rectangular baking dish. Sprinkle with cheese. Bake, uncovered, for 10 to 15 minutes or until heated through and cheese is melted.

Nutrition Facts per serving: 375 cal., 7 g total fat (2 g sat. fat), 12 mg chol., 617 mg sodium, 63 g carbo., 7 g fiber, 15 g pro.

The vegetarians in your crowd will cheer when you serve this meatless ever-favorite casserole.

TOFU MANICOTTI

8   dried manicotti shells
    Nonstick cooking spray
1   cup chopped fresh mushrooms
½   cup chopped green onions (4)
1   teaspoon dried Italian seasoning, crushed
1   12- to 16-ounce package soft tofu (fresh bean curd), drained
1   slightly beaten egg
¼   cup shredded Parmesan cheese (1 ounce)
1   14½-ounce can diced tomatoes with basil, oregano, and garlic, undrained
1   11-ounce can condensed tomato bisque soup
⅛   teaspoon black pepper
¾   cup shredded Italian-style cheese blend (3 ounces)

PREP:
40 minutes
BAKE:
32 minutes
STAND:
10 minutes
OVEN:
350°F
MAKES:
4 servings

1 Cook manicotti shells according to package directions; drain. Rinse with cold water; drain well.

2 Coat an unheated medium skillet with nonstick cooking spray. Heat skillet over medium heat. Add mushrooms and green onions; cook until tender. Stir in Italian seasoning; set aside.

3 In a medium bowl mash tofu. Stir in mushroom mixture, egg, and Parmesan cheese. Gently spoon about ¼ cup of the tofu mixture into each manicotti shell. Arrange stuffed shells in a single layer in an ungreased 3-quart rectangular baking dish.

4 In a medium bowl combine undrained tomatoes, soup, and pepper. Pour soup mixture over stuffed manicotti.

5 Bake, uncovered, in a 350°F oven about 30 minutes or until heated through. Sprinkle with Italian-style cheese. Bake, uncovered, about 2 minutes more or until cheese is melted. Let stand for 10 minutes before serving.

Nutrition Facts per serving: 411 cal., 13 g total fat (6 g sat. fat), 74 mg chol., 1,383 mg sodium, 53 g carbo., 4 g fiber, 21 g pro.

Meatless, yes—but by no means wimpy! With barley, bulgur, black beans, and a lentil soup base, this meatless bake might paradoxically be described as ... meaty!

VEGETABLE TWO-GRAIN CASSEROLE

PREP:

15 minutes

BAKE:

1 hour 15 minutes

STAND:

5 minutes

OVEN:

350°F

MAKES:

4 servings

1	18.8-ounce can ready-to-serve lentil soup
1	15-ounce can black beans, rinsed and drained
1	cup small fresh mushrooms, quartered
1	cup sliced carrots (2 medium)
1	cup frozen whole kernel corn
½	cup pearl barley
⅓	cup bulgur
¼	cup chopped onion
½	teaspoon black pepper
¼	teaspoon salt
½	cup water
½	cup shredded cheddar cheese (2 ounces)

1 In an ungreased 2-quart casserole combine soup, beans, mushrooms, carrots, corn, barley, bulgur, onion, pepper, and salt; stir in the water.

2 Bake, covered, in a 350°F oven about 1 hour 15 minutes or until barley and bulgur are tender, stirring twice. Stir again; sprinkle with cheese. Cover and let stand about 5 minutes or until cheese is melted.

Nutrition Facts per serving: 384 cal., 8 g total fat (3 g sat. fat), 15 mg chol., 929 mg sodium, 66 g carbo., 17 g fiber, 22 g pro.

We trimmed the time needed to prepare this luscious lasagna by using purchased pasta sauce and no-boil lasagna noodles. The zucchini and walnuts add crunch and contrast.

LASAGNA WITH ZUCCHINI & WALNUTS

2	medium zucchini
4	teaspoons olive oil
2	cups finely chopped onions (2 large)
1½	cups finely chopped carrots (2 large)
4	cloves garlic, minced
1	25- to 26-ounce jar chunky tomato pasta sauce (about 2½ cups)
1	teaspoon dried basil, crushed
⅛	teaspoon black pepper
1	cup shredded mozzarella cheese (4 ounces)
⅓	cup shredded Parmesan cheese (1½ ounces)
6	no-boil lasagna noodles
¼	cup chopped walnuts

PREP:
35 minutes
BAKE:
40 minutes
STAND:
15 minutes
OVEN:
350°F
MAKES:
6 servings

1 Trim ends off zucchini. Thinly slice zucchini lengthwise. (You should have a total of 9 long slices, each about ⅛ inch thick.) Place zucchini slices in a single layer on a lightly greased baking sheet; brush lightly with 1 teaspoon of the oil. Broil 3 to 4 inches from heat about 5 minutes or until crisp-tender, turning once. Let cool.

2 Heat the remaining 3 teaspoons oil in a large saucepan over medium-high heat. Add onions, carrots, and garlic; cook and stir about 5 minutes or until tender. Add pasta sauce, basil, and pepper. Bring to boiling; reduce heat. Cover and simmer for 10 minutes, stirring occasionally. In a small bowl combine mozzarella and Parmesan cheeses; set aside.

3 Arrange 2 of the lasagna noodles in a greased 2-quart square baking dish. Spread one-third of the sauce over noodles. Sprinkle with one-third of the nuts. Top with 3 slices of zucchini; sprinkle with one-third of the cheese mixture. Repeat layers twice, alternating the direction of the zucchini slices in each layer and finishing with the zucchini; set remaining cheese mixture aside.

4 Bake, covered, in a 350°F oven for 20 minutes. Uncover and sprinkle with remaining cheese mixture. Bake, uncovered, about 20 minutes more or until heated through. Let stand for 15 minutes before serving.

Nutrition Facts per serving: 272 cal., 12 g total fat (4 g sat. fat), 16 mg chol., 470 mg sodium, 33 g carbo., 3 g fiber, 13 g pro.

This big casserole is ideal for a potluck—just cut it into 16 servings and leave the spatula for self-service. For dinner at home, slice into large wedges.

THREE-CHEESE SPINACH PIE

PREP:

25 minutes

BAKE:

45 minutes

STAND:

15 minutes

OVEN:

375°F

MAKES:

8 side-dish servings

1   15-ounce package rolled refrigerated unbaked piecrust (2 crusts)

4   eggs

1   15-ounce carton ricotta cheese

1   cup shredded Asiago cheese (4 ounces)

¼   cup grated Parmesan cheese

1   teaspoon dried basil, crushed

¾   teaspoon coarsely ground black pepper

1   10-ounce package frozen chopped spinach, thawed and drained well

¼   cup seasoned fine dry bread crumbs

¼   cup oil-packed dried tomatoes, drained and coarsely chopped

1 Let piecrusts stand at room temperature according to package directions. Meanwhile, lightly beat 1 of the eggs; set aside. In a large bowl lightly beat remaining 3 eggs with a fork. Add cheeses, basil, and pepper; stir well. Stir in spinach, bread crumbs, and tomatoes.

2 Line an ungreased 9-inch pie plate with one crust; brush generously with some of the reserved beaten egg. Spread cheese mixture evenly in crust. Top with second crust. Fold edges under to seal. Flute edges. Brush top crust with remaining reserved egg. Cut slits in top crust.

3 Bake in a 375°F oven for 45 minutes. If necessary, cover edges with foil during the last 20 minutes of baking to prevent overbrowning. Let stand on a wire rack for 15 minutes before serving.

Nutrition Facts per serving: 240 cal., 15 g total fat (7 g sat. fat), 80 mg chol., 323 mg sodium, 16 g carbo., 1 g fiber, 8 g pro.

This vegetarian version offers classic rich tetrazzini flavors—minus the chicken.

BROCCOLI-CAULIFLOWER TETRAZZINI

8	ounces dried fettuccine or spaghetti, broken
1	16-ounce package frozen loose-pack broccoli, carrots, and cauliflower
2	tablespoons butter
3	tablespoons all-purpose flour
2½	cups reduced-fat milk
½	cup grated Parmesan cheese
¼	teaspoon salt
¼	teaspoon black pepper
1	4½-ounce jar (drained weight) sliced mushrooms, drained
2	tablespoons grated Parmesan cheese

PREP:
35 minutes
BAKE:
15 minutes
OVEN:
400°F
MAKES:
4 servings

1 Cook pasta according to package directions; drain. Cook vegetables according to package directions; drain. Set aside.

2 Meanwhile, for cheese sauce, in a saucepan melt butter over medium heat. Stir in flour. Add milk all at once. Cook and stir until slightly thickened and bubbly. Cook and stir for 1 minute more. Remove from heat. Stir in the ½ cup Parmesan cheese, the salt, and pepper.

3 In a large bowl toss pasta with ½ cup of the cheese sauce. Spread pasta evenly into a lightly greased 3-quart rectangular baking dish. Top with vegetables and mushrooms. Pour remaining cheese sauce over all. Sprinkle with the 2 tablespoons Parmesan cheese.

4 Bake, uncovered, in a 400°F oven about 15 minutes or until mixture is heated through.

MAKE-AHEAD DIRECTIONS: Assemble as directed. Cover and chill unbaked casserole up to 24 hours. Bake, covered, in a 400°F oven for 15 minutes. Uncover and bake for 10 to 15 minutes more.

Nutrition Facts per serving: 455 cal., 14 g total fat (7 g sat. fat), 39 mg chol., 727 mg sodium, 61 g carbo., 6 g fiber, 21 g pro.

This robust baked pasta bursting with eggplant, zucchini, mushrooms, and onion makes a super satisfying meatless main dish.

RIGATONI WITH VEGETABLES

PREP:

30 minutes

ROAST:

30 minutes

BAKE:

20 minutes

OVEN:

450°F/400°F

MAKES:

4 to 6 servings

Nonstick cooking spray

1   eggplant (about 1 pound), peeled and cut into 1-inch cubes

3   medium zucchini, cut into 1-inch cubes

3   cups coarsely chopped fresh mushrooms (8 ounces)

1   medium onion, cut into thin wedges

2   tablespoons garlic-flavored olive oil or olive oil

½   teaspoon salt

¼   teaspoon black pepper

8   ounces dried rigatoni pasta (2½ cups)

2   cups purchased marinara sauce

¼   cup shredded Parmesan cheese (1 ounce)

1   cup shredded mozzarella cheese (4 ounces)

1 Lightly coat two 15×10×1-inch baking pans* with nonstick cooking spray. Divide eggplant, zucchini, mushrooms, and onion evenly between prepared pans. Drizzle oil over vegetables. Sprinkle with salt and pepper. Toss vegetables to coat; spread into an even layer. Roast, uncovered, on 2 separate oven racks in a 450°F oven for 30 minutes or until vegetables are tender, stirring once during roasting. (Move baking pan on top oven rack to bottom rack and pan on bottom rack to top rack halfway through roasting.) Meanwhile, cook rigatoni according to package directions; drain and return to saucepan.

2 Reduce oven temperature to 400°F. Add vegetables, marinara sauce, and Parmesan cheese to pasta; toss to combine. Transfer to an ungreased 2-quart rectangular baking dish. Sprinkle with mozzarella cheese. Bake, uncovered, for 20 to 25 minutes or until bubbly and cheese browns.

*NOTE: If you don't have two 15×10×1-inch baking pans, use 1 large shallow roasting pan. Drain off any liquid that remains after roasting.

Nutrition Facts per serving: 668 cal., 27 g total fat (10 g sat. fat), 42 mg chol., 1,480 mg sodium, 78 g carbo., 9 g fiber, 33 g pro.

Filled with meaty mushrooms, vibrant chard, and plenty of rich, luscious cheese, this pasta pleases all guests—vegetarians and meat eaters alike.

BAKED PASTA WITH MUSHROOMS & CHARD

12	ounces dried ziti or penne pasta (about 3½ cups)
1	15-ounce carton whole-milk ricotta cheese
1	cup half-and-half or light cream
1	egg
1	teaspoon sugar
½	teaspoon salt
¼	teaspoon freshly ground black pepper
⅛	teaspoon ground nutmeg
¼	cup snipped fresh thyme, parsley, basil, and/or rosemary
¼	cup cooking oil
1	pound cremini mushrooms, sliced (about 6 cups)
12	ounces shiitake mushrooms, sliced (about 4½ cups)
¼	cup finely chopped shallots
2	cloves garlic, minced
4	cups chopped Swiss chard or spinach*
2	cups shredded Gruyère cheese (8 ounces)
½	cup shredded Parmigiano-Reggiano cheese

PREP:
45 minutes
BAKE:
30 minutes
OVEN:
350°F
MAKES:
8 servings

1 Cook pasta according to package directions; drain. Meanwhile, place the ricotta cheese in a food processor; cover and process until smooth. Add half-and-half, egg, sugar, salt, pepper, and nutmeg; process until well blended. Stir in thyme. Stir into cooked pasta; set aside.

2 In a large skillet heat oil over medium-high heat. Add cremini mushrooms; cook and stir until tender and liquid is reduced. Remove mushrooms from skillet. Add shiitake mushrooms, shallots, and garlic to skillet. Cook and stir until tender and liquid is reduced. Return cremini mushrooms to skillet. Add Swiss chard. Cook and stir for 2 to 3 minutes or until chard is wilted. Drain mixture well in a colander or sieve. Stir into pasta mixture; stir in half of the Gruyère cheese. Transfer to a 3-quart rectangular baking dish.

3 Bake, covered, in 350°F oven for 20 minutes. Sprinkle with remaining Gruyère cheese and the Parmigiano-Reggiano cheese. Bake, uncovered, for 10 to 15 minutes more or until heated through and the top begins to brown.

*NOTE: For best results, if using Swiss chard, use green chard, not red, as red will color the pasta a pinkish hue. If green chard is not available, use spinach.

Nutrition Facts per serving: 554 cal., 31 g total fat (15 g sat. fat), 101 mg chol., 468 mg sodium, 45 g carbo., 3 g fiber, 27 g pro.

With prepared piecrust and frozen spinach, this dish comes together easily.
The quiche-like bake is a hit for breakfast too.

THREE-CHEESE SPINACH EGG BAKE

PREP:

35 minutes

BAKE:

45 minutes

STAND:

10 minutes

OVEN:

325°F

MAKES:

6 to 8 servings

½	of a 15-ounce package rolled refrigerated unbaked piecrust (1 crust)
⅓	cup thinly sliced green onions (3)
2	tablespoons olive oil
½	cup oil-packed dried tomatoes, drained and finely snipped
3	tablespoons all-purpose flour
¾	cup milk
4	beaten eggs
1¼	cups ricotta cheese
1	10-ounce package frozen chopped spinach, thawed and drained well
¾	cup crumbled feta cheese (3 ounces)
⅓	cup fine dry bread crumbs
⅓	cup shredded Parmesan cheese (1½ ounces)

1 Let piecrust stand at room temperature according to package directions. Unroll piecrust and ease into an ungreased 9-inch pie plate, being careful not to stretch crust. Crimp edge as desired. Bake according to package directions for a baked pie shell; set aside.

2 In a small saucepan cook green onions in hot oil over medium heat for 1 minute. Stir in dried tomatoes and flour. Add milk all at once. Cook and stir until mixture is thickened and bubbly (mixture will be very thick). Gradually whisk the hot mixture into eggs. Stir in ricotta cheese, spinach, and ½ cup of the feta cheese. Pour into prepared piecrust. Combine bread crumbs and Parmesan cheese. Sprinkle spinach mixture with remaining ¼ cup feta cheese and the Parmesan cheese mixture.

3 Bake, uncovered, in 325°F oven for 45 to 50 minutes or until set and golden brown. Let stand for 10 minutes before serving. Serve warm.

Nutrition Facts per serving: 559 cal., 34 g total fat (16 g sat. fat), 199 mg chol., 1,159 mg sodium, 34 g carbo., 2 g fiber, 28 g pro.

Fennel takes center stage in this casserole. The bulbous plant looks like a feather-topped, potbellied cousin to celery, but its flavor is a mild, deliciously different licorice.

FENNEL-LEEK MOUSSAKA

1	10-ounce package frozen chopped spinach, thawed and drained well
2	medium fennel bulbs
1	cup thinly sliced leeks (2 large)
½	teaspoon salt
¼	teaspoon black pepper
2	tablespoons olive oil
1	cup crumbled feta cheese (4 ounces)
3	tablespoons butter
3	tablespoons all-purpose flour
½	teaspoon salt
½	teaspoon fennel seeds, crushed
⅛	teaspoon ground nutmeg
⅛	teaspoon black pepper
1¾	cups milk
2	beaten eggs
2	roma tomatoes, coarsely chopped

PREP:

20 minutes

BAKE:

30 minutes

STAND:

5 minutes

OVEN:

350°F

MAKES:

*6 main-dish or
8 to 10 side-dish servings*

1 Spread spinach in a greased 2-quart square baking dish; set aside. Reserve the leafy tops from the fennel. Slice remaining fennel (you should have about 4 cups). In a medium skillet cook fennel, leeks, ½ teaspoon salt, and the ¼ teaspoon pepper in hot oil over medium-high heat until tender. Spoon fennel mixture over spinach in dish. Sprinkle feta cheese over fennel mixture.

2 In a medium saucepan melt butter over medium heat. Stir in flour, ½ teaspoon salt, fennel seeds, nutmeg, and the ⅛ teaspoon pepper. Add milk all at once. Cook and stir until thickened and bubbly. Stir half of the hot mixture into eggs; return all to saucepan. Pour hot sauce over feta cheese.

3 Bake, uncovered, in a 350°F oven for 30 to 35 minutes or until set. Finely snip 1 tablespoon of the reserved fennel tops. Sprinkle tomatoes and snipped fennel tops over moussaka. Let stand for 5 minutes before serving.

Nutrition Facts per main-dish serving: 252 cal., 18 g total fat (8 g sat. fat), 109 mg chol., 781 mg sodium, 14 g carbo., 9 g fiber, 10 g pro.

After tasting this comforting pasta that's been kicked up a notch with three types of gourmet cheese, you'll never go back to your old recipe.

MODERN MACARONI & CHEESE

PREP:
25 minutes
BAKE:
20 minutes
OVEN:
350°F
MAKES:
4 to 6 servings

7   ounces dried elbow macaroni (about 2 cups)

3   tablespoons butter

2   tablespoons finely chopped shallot (1 medium)

2   cloves garlic, minced

1⅓ cups milk

1   cup shredded Gruyère cheese (4 ounces)

1   cup shredded fontina cheese (4 ounces)

1   cup shredded Emmentaler cheese (4 ounces)

1   tablespoon cornstarch

1   tablespoon Dijon-style mustard

¼   teaspoon black pepper

⅛   teaspoon ground nutmeg (optional)

¼   cup seasoned fine dry bread crumbs or fine cracker crumbs

1 Cook macaroni according to package directions until tender but still firm; drain. Set aside.

2 Meanwhile, in a large saucepan melt 2 tablespoons of the butter over medium heat. Add shallot and garlic; cook about 3 minutes or until tender. Carefully stir in milk; heat through.

3 In a small bowl toss together shredded cheeses and cornstarch until evenly coated. Reduce heat under saucepan to medium-low. Add cheese mixture to saucepan, about one-fourth at a time, stirring after each addition until cheeses are melted. Cook and stir until thickened and bubbly. (Mixture may appear to curdle at first but should become smooth with continued cooking and stirring.) Add mustard, pepper, and nutmeg, if using. Stir in cooked macaroni.

4 Transfer macaroni mixture to an ungreased 1½-quart casserole. Melt the remaining 1 tablespoon butter and combine with bread crumbs; sprinkle over macaroni mixture in casserole. Bake, uncovered, in a 350°F oven for 20 to 25 minutes or until heated through and bubbly.

Nutrition Facts per serving: 682 cal., 37 g total fat (21 g sat. fat), 120 mg chol., 774 mg sodium, 52 g carbo., 1 g fiber, 35 g pro.

While the preparation time on this cheesy dish is short, the longer baking time allows the flavors to mingle into a mouthwatering treat.

TWO-CHEESE MACARONI BAKE

2	cups dried elbow macaroni (8 ounces)
2½	cups milk
2	cups crumbled feta cheese with basil and tomato or plain feta cheese (8 ounces)
4	slightly beaten eggs
¾	cup cream-style cottage cheese
½	teaspoon salt

1 Cook macaroni according to package directions; drain.

2 Place macaroni in a greased 2-quart square baking dish. In a medium bowl combine milk, feta cheese, eggs, cottage cheese, and salt. Pour over macaroni in dish.

3 Bake, uncovered, in a 375°F oven about 45 minutes or until heated through and bubbly. Let stand for 10 minutes before serving.

Nutrition Facts per serving: 266 cal., 11 g total fat (6 g sat. fat), 140 mg chol., 609 mg sodium, 25 g carbo., 1 g fiber, 15 g pro.

PREP:
20 minutes
BAKE:
45 minutes
STAND:
10 minutes
OVEN:
375°F
MAKES:
8 servings

This yummy favorite gets its flavor from the smoke-kissed cheese. The chopped apple on top adds just the right note of sweetness.

SMOKY MACARONI & CHEESE

PREP:

20 minutes

BAKE:

20 minutes

STAND:

5 minutes

OVEN:

350°F

MAKES:

4 servings

8   ounces dried large elbow macaroni

3   ounces smoked cheddar cheese or smoked Gouda cheese

½   cup chopped onion (1 medium)

1   cup vegetable broth or chicken broth

¾   cup fat-free half-and-half

1   tablespoon all-purpose flour

½   teaspoon dry mustard

¼   teaspoon black pepper

⅔   cup coarsely chopped tart apple (1 medium)

1   tablespoon shredded Parmesan cheese

1 Cook macaroni according to package directions; drain. Place macaroni into an ungreased 1½-quart casserole; set aside. If desired, use a vegetable peeler to remove any darker outer layer from smoked cheddar cheese. Shred cheese (you should have about ¾ cup); set aside.

2 For cheese sauce, in a covered saucepan cook onion in broth over medium-high heat about 5 minutes or until tender. In a screw-top jar combine half-and-half, flour, dry mustard, and pepper; shake well and add to saucepan. Cook and stir over medium heat just until bubbly. Remove from heat; add cheddar cheese, stirring until most of the cheese is melted. Pour sauce over pasta in casserole, stirring until combined.

3 Bake, covered, in a 350°F oven for 10 minutes. Uncover. Bake about 10 minutes more or until heated through and bubbly. Let stand for 5 minutes. Top with apple and Parmesan cheese.

Nutrition Facts per serving: 371 cal., 9 g total fat (5 g sat. fat), 23 mg chol., 444 mg sodium, 56 g carbo., 3 g fiber, 15 g pro.

Macaroni and cheese, grown-up style! With a sophisticated medley of cheeses, a selection of colorful vegetables, and even a little cayenne pepper kick, this casserole transcends memories of school cafeteria fare and gives the baked classic back its good name.

SPICY TOMATO & CHEESE MACARONI

1½	cups dried elbow macaroni
2	cups broccoli florets
⅓	cup dried tomatoes (not oil pack)
⅓	cup sliced green onions (3)
2	tablespoons butter
2	tablespoons all-purpose flour
1½	teaspoons dried basil, crushed
¼	teaspoon cayenne pepper
⅛	teaspoon salt
1¾	cups milk
¾	cup shredded sharp cheddar cheese (3 ounces)
¾	cup shredded Gruyère cheese (3 ounces)
¾	cup shredded Gouda cheese (3 ounces)

PREP:
30 minutes
BAKE:
30 minutes
STAND:
10 minutes
OVEN:
350°F
MAKES:
5 servings

1 Cook macaroni according to package directions until tender but still firm. Add broccoli; drain. Set aside. Meanwhile, snip dried tomatoes. Place tomatoes in a small bowl; add enough warm water to cover. Let stand for 10 minutes or until softened; drain well. Set aside.

2 In a medium saucepan cook green onions in hot butter over medium heat until tender. Stir in flour, basil, cayenne pepper, and salt. Add milk all at once. Cook and stir until slightly thickened and bubbly. Add cheeses, a little at a time, stirring constantly after each addition until melted. Stir in macaroni-broccoli mixture and softened tomatoes. Transfer to an ungreased 1½-quart casserole.

3 Bake, uncovered, in a 350°F oven about 30 minutes or until hot and bubbly. Let stand for 10 minutes before serving.

Nutrition Facts per serving: 447 cal., 23 g total fat (13 g sat. fat), 76 mg chol., 526 mg sodium, 37 g carbo., 3 g fiber, 23 g pro.

This Italian mainstay packs no surprises—tender, crispy eggplant slices are covered with spaghetti sauce and cheese. Serve it with your favorite pasta.

EGGPLANT PARMIGIANA

PREP:

25 minutes

BAKE:

10 minutes

OVEN:

400°F

MAKES:

4 servings

1	small eggplant (12 ounces)
1	beaten egg
1	tablespoon water
¼	cup all-purpose flour
2	tablespoons cooking oil
⅓	cup grated Parmesan cheese
1	cup spaghetti sauce
¾	cup shredded mozzarella cheese (3 ounces)

1 Wash and peel eggplant; cut crosswise into ½-inch slices. Combine egg and the water; dip eggplant slices into egg mixture, then into flour, turning to coat both sides. In a large skillet cook eggplant slices, half at a time, in hot oil over medium-high heat for 4 to 6 minutes or until golden, turning once. (If necessary, add additional oil.) Drain on paper towels.

2 Place eggplant slices in a single layer into an ungreased 2-quart rectangular baking dish, cutting slices to fit. Sprinkle with Parmesan cheese. Top with spaghetti sauce and mozzarella cheese.

3 Bake, uncovered, in a 400°F oven for 10 to 12 minutes or until mixture is heated through.

Nutrition Facts per serving: 269 cal., 18 g total fat (6 g sat. fat), 76 mg chol., 660 mg sodium, 17 g carbo., 3 g fiber, 12 g pro.

If you love hearty foods but want to cut out some of the meat from your diet, add this eggplant medley to your repertoire. It's one of the most robust and filling vegetarian dishes around.

EGGPLANT PARMESAN CASSEROLE

1	egg
½	cup milk
¾	cup all-purpose flour
¼	teaspoon salt
¼	teaspoon black pepper
1	large eggplant (1¼ to 1½ pounds), peeled (if desired) and sliced ½ inch thick
2	tablespoons cooking oil
1	14½-ounce can diced tomatoes with green pepper and onion, undrained
1	10¾-ounce can condensed tomato soup
1	teaspoon dried Italian seasoning, crushed
¼	teaspoon black pepper
1	cup shredded mozzarella cheese (4 ounces)
¼	cup shredded Parmesan cheese (1 ounce)

PREP:
30 minutes
BAKE:
20 minutes
STAND:
10 minutes
OVEN:
350°F
MAKES:
6 servings

1 In a shallow dish whisk together egg and milk. In another shallow dish combine flour, salt, and ¼ teaspoon pepper. Dip eggplant slices into egg mixture, then into flour mixture, turning to coat both sides. In a large nonstick skillet cook eggplant slices, a few at a time, in hot oil over medium-high heat for 4 to 6 minutes or until golden, turning once. (If necessary, add additional oil.) Drain eggplant slices on paper towels.

2 In a medium saucepan combine undrained tomatoes, soup, Italian seasoning, and ¼ teaspoon pepper. Bring to boiling over medium heat, stirring occasionally.

3 Layer half of the eggplant slices in a greased 2-quart rectangular baking dish, cutting slices to fit. Top with half of the tomato mixture; sprinkle with ½ cup of the mozzarella cheese. Repeat layers. Sprinkle with Parmesan cheese.

4 Bake, uncovered, in a 350°F oven about 20 minutes or until heated through. Let stand for 10 minutes before serving.

Nutrition Facts per serving: 342 cal., 17 g total fat (8 g sat. fat), 68 mg chol., 1,110 mg sodium, 31 g carbo., 4 g fiber, 18 g pro.

This meat-free version of the classic Greek casserole makes a family-pleasing entrée.

VEGETABLE PASTITSIO

PREP:

35 minutes

BAKE:

30 minutes

STAND:

5 minutes

OVEN:

350°F

MAKES:

6 servings

8	ounces dried elbow macaroni
2	beaten eggs
¼	teaspoon salt
3	cups fresh spinach leaves, torn
½	cup chopped onion (1 medium)
1	clove garlic, minced
3	tablespoons butter
1	8-ounce can tomato sauce
1	cup frozen whole kernel corn
1	cup cubed, cooked potatoes
¾	teaspoon dried mint, crushed
½	teaspoon dried oregano, crushed
¼	teaspoon salt
¼	teaspoon ground cinnamon
¼	teaspoon black pepper
¼	cup all-purpose flour
¼	teaspoon ground nutmeg
2	cups milk

1 Cook pasta according to package directions; drain. Rinse with cold water; drain well. In a large bowl combine cooked pasta, eggs, and ¼ teaspoon salt. Spread mixture evenly into a lightly greased 3-quart rectangular baking dish. Arrange spinach over pasta mixture.

2 In a large skillet cook onion and garlic in 1 tablespoon of the butter over medium heat about 3 minutes or until onion is tender. Add tomato sauce, corn, potatoes, mint, oregano, ¼ teaspoon salt, the cinnamon, and pepper; cook and stir until heated through. Spread mixture over spinach.

3 In a medium saucepan melt remaining 2 tablespoons butter over medium heat. Stir in flour and nutmeg. Add milk all at once. Cook and stir until thickened and bubbly. Pour over vegetable mixture.

4 Bake, uncovered, in a 350°F oven about 30 minutes or until heated through. Let stand for 5 minutes before serving.

Nutrition Facts per serving: 343 cal., 10 g total fat (5 g sat. fat), 93 mg chol., 488 mg sodium, 51 g carbo., 3 g fiber, 12 g pro.

Orzo is among the tiniest of pastas, resembling grains of rice. Here it provides a nifty crust for the spinach-and-ricotta filling.

SPINACH & ORZO PIE

1½   cups dried orzo pasta (about 9 ounces)

2   lightly beaten eggs

2   cups spaghetti sauce

⅓   cup grated Parmesan cheese

1   10-ounce package frozen chopped spinach, thawed and drained well

½   cup ricotta cheese

¼   teaspoon ground nutmeg

½   cup shredded fontina cheese or mozzarella cheese (2 ounces)

1 Cook orzo according to package directions; drain. Rinse with cold water; drain well. Set aside.

2 In a large bowl combine eggs, ½ cup of the spaghetti sauce, and the Parmesan cheese. Add orzo; toss to coat. Spread orzo mixture in a lightly greased 9-inch pie plate, lightly pressing the mixture on the bottom and up the side to form an even shell; set aside.

3 In a medium bowl combine spinach, ricotta cheese, and nutmeg. Spoon into the orzo-lined pie plate. Pour remaining 1½ cups spaghetti sauce over the spinach mixture. Cover edge of pie with foil.

4 Bake, uncovered, in a 350°F oven for 30 minutes. Sprinkle with fontina cheese. Bake about 5 minutes more or until cheese melts. Let stand for 10 minutes before serving.

Nutrition Facts per serving: 352 cal., 12 g total fat (6 g sat. fat), 97 mg chol., 665 mg sodium, 42 g carbo., 4 g fiber, 17 g pro.

PREP:
30 minutes
BAKE:
35 minutes
STAND:
10 minutes
OVEN:
350°F
MAKES:
6 to 8 servings

A golden mashed-potato crust gives way to a creamy vegetable-filled layer in this savory pie. If you're short on prep time, just stir the thyme, milk, and cheese into refrigerated mashed potatoes (which already contain butter and salt) rather than making the potatoes from scratch.

VEGETARIAN SHEPHERD'S PIE

PREP:

50 minutes

CHILL:

overnight

BAKE:

50 minutes

OVEN:

350°F

MAKES:

6 servings

1	14-ounce can vegetable broth or chicken broth
1	cup dry lentils, rinsed and drained
¾	cup water
3	cloves garlic, minced
1½	pounds parsnips, peeled and cut into ½-inch slices (about 3½ cups)
6	purple boiling onions (8 ounces), halved, or 1 medium red onion, cut into wedges
1	14½-ounce can diced tomatoes with Italian herbs, undrained
2	tablespoons tomato paste
4	medium potatoes, peeled and cut up
3	tablespoons butter or margarine
½	teaspoon dried thyme, crushed
½	teaspoon salt
¼	to ⅓ cup milk
1½	cups shredded Colby and Monterey Jack or cheddar cheese (6 ounces)

1 In a large saucepan combine broth, lentils, water, and garlic. Bring to boiling; reduce heat. Cover and simmer for 20 minutes. Add parsnips and onions. Return to boiling; reduce heat. Cover and simmer for 10 to 15 minutes more or until vegetables and lentils are just tender. Remove from heat. Stir in undrained tomatoes and tomato paste.

2 Meanwhile, in a 2-quart saucepan cook potatoes in boiling lightly salted water for 20 to 25 minutes or until tender; drain. Mash potatoes with a potato masher or beat with an electric mixer on low speed. Add butter, thyme, and salt. Gradually beat in enough milk to make potatoes light and fluffy. Stir in 1 cup of the cheese until melted.

3 Divide lentil mixture among six 12- to 15-ounce au gratin dishes. Spoon potato mixture evenly over lentil mixture. Cover each dish with plastic wrap; chill overnight.

4 Remove plastic wrap; cover each dish with foil. Bake in a 350°F oven for 45 to 50 minutes or until heated through. Uncover. Sprinkle potatoes evenly with remaining ½ cup cheese. Bake about 5 minutes more or until cheese melts.

Nutrition Facts per serving: 449 cal., 16 g total fat (10 g sat. fat), 42 mg chol., 1,122 mg sodium, 58 g carbo., 17 g fiber, 20 g pro.

This homemade polenta, layered between a tangy tomato sauce and a creamy white sauce, is seasoned with Asiago cheese and baked until bubbly.

POLENTA WITH TWO SAUCES

3	cups water
1	cup yellow cornmeal
1	cup cold water
½	teaspoon salt
¾	cup shredded Asiago cheese or Parmesan cheese (3 ounces)
1	15-ounce can Italian-style tomato sauce
2	tablespoons all-purpose flour
½	teaspoon dried basil, crushed
¼	teaspoon salt
⅛	teaspoon black pepper
	Dash ground nutmeg
1¼	cups milk

PREP:
45 minutes

CHILL:
2 hours or overnight

BAKE:
12 minutes

OVEN:
450°F

MAKES:
4 servings

1 For polenta, in a medium saucepan bring the 3 cups water to boiling. In a small bowl combine cornmeal, the 1 cup cold water, and the ½ teaspoon salt. Slowly add the cornmeal mixture to the boiling water, stirring constantly. Cook and stir until mixture returns to boiling. Reduce heat to low. Cook, uncovered, for 10 to 15 minutes or until thick, stirring frequently. Stir in ¼ cup of the cheese until melted.

2 Spread hot polenta evenly into a lightly greased 2-quart square baking dish; cool slightly. Cover; chill 2 hours or overnight. Cut polenta into 1-inch squares; set aside.

3 For red sauce, in a medium saucepan bring tomato sauce to boiling; reduce heat. Simmer, uncovered, about 10 minutes or until slightly thickened and reduced to 1⅓ cups.

4 For white sauce, in another medium saucepan combine flour, basil, the ¼ teaspoon salt, pepper, and nutmeg. Gradually stir in milk. Cook and stir over medium heat until thickened and bubbly. Cook and stir 1 minute more. Remove from heat; stir in ¼ cup of the cheese until melted.

5 To assemble, divide red sauce among 4 shallow casseroles or au gratin dishes (about ⅓ cup each). Divide polenta cubes among casseroles. Spoon white sauce over cubes; sprinkle each serving with 1 tablespoon of the remaining cheese.

6 Bake, uncovered, in a 450°F oven for 12 to 15 minutes or until sauce is bubbly around edges and cheese begins to brown. Serve immediately.

Nutrition Facts per serving: 318 cal., 11 g total fat (6 g sat. fat), 29 mg chol., 1,133 mg sodium, 42 g carbo., 5 g fiber, 13 g pro.

Serve this Mexican-style bean-and-rice main dish with warm tortillas and a simple green salad. Garlic, onion, chili powder, and cumin pack the punch here.

SOUTH-OF-THE-BORDER PIE

PREP:

20 minutes

BAKE:

25 minutes

STAND:

10 minutes

OVEN:

350°F

MAKES:

4 servings

½	cup chopped onion (1 medium)
2	cloves garlic, minced
1	tablespoon olive oil or cooking oil
2	teaspoons chili powder
1	teaspoon ground cumin
¼	teaspoon salt
1	15-ounce can red kidney beans, rinsed and drained
1½	cups cooked brown rice
1	cup shredded cheddar cheese (4 ounces)
¾	cup milk
2	beaten eggs
	Chopped green sweet pepper (optional)
	Purchased salsa (optional)

1 In a medium saucepan cook onion and garlic in hot oil over medium heat until tender. Stir in chili powder, cumin, and salt. Cook for 1 minute more. Cool. Stir in beans, cooked rice, cheese, milk, and eggs.

2 Spoon rice mixture into a lightly greased 10-inch pie plate or quiche dish. Bake, uncovered, in a 350°F oven about 25 minutes or until the center is set. Let stand for 10 minutes. If desired, sprinkle with sweet pepper and serve with salsa.

Nutrition Facts per serving: 383 cal., 17 g total fat (8 g sat. fat), 139 mg chol., 570 mg sodium, 40 g carbo., 8 g fiber, 22 g pro.

Delve into this Southwestern-style casserole and you'll find layers of corn tortillas, Monterey Jack cheese, and vegetables, all baked in a savory custard.

DOUBLE CORN TORTILLA CASSEROLE

6	6-inch corn tortillas
1	cup shredded Monterey Jack cheese or cheddar cheese (4 ounces)
1½	cups frozen whole kernel corn, thawed
½	cup sliced green onions (4)
1	4-ounce can diced green chile peppers, drained
¼	cup finely chopped red sweet pepper
1	cup buttermilk or sour milk*
2	eggs
½	teaspoon garlic salt
⅓	cup purchased salsa

PREP:
25 minutes
BAKE:
35 minutes
STAND:
5 minutes
OVEN:
325°F
MAKES:
4 servings

1 Tear tortillas into bite-size pieces. Arrange half of the tortillas in a lightly greased 2-quart square baking dish. Top with half of the cheese, half of the corn, half of the green onions, half of the chile peppers, and half of the sweet pepper. Repeat the layers.

2 In a medium mixing bowl whisk together buttermilk, eggs, and garlic salt. Pour over tortilla mixture.

3 Bake, uncovered, in a 325°F oven about 35 minutes or until a knife inserted near the center comes out clean. Let stand for 5 minutes before serving. Serve with salsa.

*NOTE: **To make 1 cup sour milk, place 1 tablespoon lemon juice or vinegar in a glass measuring cup. Add enough milk to make 1 cup liquid; stir. Let the mixture stand for 5 minutes before using.**

Nutrition Facts per serving: 322 cal., 14 g total fat (7 g sat. fat), 133 mg chol., 561 mg sodium, 37 g carbo., 4 g fiber, 17 g pro.

A simple pasta sauce is easily transformed into a Mediterranean-style sauce by adding roasted sweet peppers, kalamata olives, and a splash of balsamic vinegar.

BAKED MEDITERRANEAN POLENTA

PREP:

20 minutes

BAKE:

20 minutes

OVEN:

350°F

MAKES:

8 side-dish servings

1	16-ounce jar tomato-based pasta sauce
¾	cup chopped bottled roasted red sweet peppers
⅓	cup chopped pitted kalamata olives
1	tablespoon balsamic vinegar
4	cups water
1	cup quick-cooking polenta mix
½	teaspoon salt
1	cup shredded fontina cheese (4 ounces)

1 In a large bowl combine pasta sauce, sweet peppers, olives, and vinegar. Transfer half of the sauce to an ungreased 2-quart casserole. Set aside.

2 In a large saucepan bring 3 cups of the water to boiling. In a small bowl combine remaining 1 cup water, the polenta mix, and salt. Stir polenta mixture into boiling water. Reduce heat and simmer about 5 minutes or until thick, stirring occasionally. (Watch carefully, as mixture may plop.) Spoon polenta over sauce in casserole. Pour remaining sauce over polenta. Sprinkle with cheese.

3 Bake, uncovered, in a 350°F oven about 20 minutes or until mixture is heated through.

Nutrition Facts per serving: 182 cal., 7 g total fat (3 g sat. fat), 18 mg chol., 749 mg sodium, 23 g carbo., 3 g fiber, 7 g pro.

Named for a town outside Milan where it was originally made, Gorgonzola is one of Italy's great cheeses. Accompany these roll-ups with complementary fresh fruits—pears, apples, and peaches—as well as some hearty red wine for a splendid summer meal.

NUTTY GORGONZOLA ROLL-UPS

8	dried lasagna noodles (about 8 ounces)
1½	8-ounce packages cream cheese, softened
2	cups shredded Italian-style cheese blend (8 ounces)
1	cup crumbled Gorgonzola or blue cheese (4 ounces)
1	cup chopped walnuts, toasted
2	teaspoons dried basil, crushed
1	26-ounce jar tomato-basil pasta sauce
6	cups shredded fresh spinach

PREP:
45 minutes
BAKE:
40 minutes
OVEN:
375°F
MAKES:
8 servings

1 Cook lasagna noodles according to package directions; drain. Rinse with cold water; drain well.

2 In a large bowl combine cheeses, ¾ cup of the walnuts, and the basil. Spread some of the cheese mixture on 1 side of each lasagna noodle. Roll up noodles and place, seam sides down, into an ungreased 2-quart rectangular baking dish. Pour sauce over rolls.

3 Bake, covered, in a 375°F oven about 40 minutes or until rolls are heated through.

4 Divide spinach evenly among 8 plates. Add a hot lasagna roll to each plate. Spoon sauce in dish evenly over rolls. Sprinkle with remaining ¼ cup walnuts.

Nutrition Facts per serving: 513 cal., 37 g total fat (17 g sat. fat), 77 mg chol., 813 mg sodium, 28 g carbo., 4 g fiber, 21 g pro.

Walnuts add crunch to these mozzarella and Parmesan cheese-filled pasta shells.

CHEESE & NUT STUFFED SHELLS

PREP:

45 minutes

BAKE:

45 minutes

OVEN:

350°F

MAKES:

6 servings

24	dried jumbo shell macaroni*
2	slightly beaten eggs
1	15-ounce carton ricotta cheese
1½	cups shredded mozzarella cheese (6 ounces)
1	cup shredded Parmesan cheese (4 ounces)
1	cup chopped walnuts
1	teaspoon dried parsley flakes, crushed
½	teaspoon salt
¼	teaspoon black pepper
⅛	teaspoon ground nutmeg
1	26-ounce jar thick and chunky pasta sauce (2¾ cups)

1 Cook pasta shells according to package directions; drain. Rinse with cold water; drain well. Set shells aside.

2 Meanwhile, for filling, in a large bowl combine eggs, ricotta cheese, 1 cup of the mozzarella cheese, ¾ cup of the Parmesan cheese, the walnuts, parsley, salt, pepper, and nutmeg.

3 Spread 1 cup of the pasta sauce into the bottom of an ungreased 3-quart rectangular baking dish. Carefully spoon a heaping tablespoon of filling into each cooked shell. Arrange filled shells in the baking dish. Pour remaining 1¾ cup sauce over shells. Sprinkle with the remaining ½ cup mozzarella cheese and the remaining ¼ cup Parmesan cheese.

4 Bake, covered, in a 350°F oven about 45 minutes or until shells are heated through.

*NOTE: Cook a few extra shells to replace any that may tear during cooking.

Nutrition Facts per serving: 549 cal., 32 g total fat (12 g sat. fat), 132 mg chol., 1,072 mg sodium, 36 g carbo., 4 g fiber, 30 g pro.

Turn this terrific vegetarian main dish into a family-favorite chicken dish by adding some shredded cooked chicken just before serving.

OVEN-ROASTED VEGETABLE PENNE

9	medium roma tomatoes, sliced ¼ inch thick
2	medium zucchini, halved lengthwise and sliced ½ inch thick
2	tablespoons olive oil
4	cloves garlic, minced
½	teaspoon salt
¼	teaspoon black pepper
6	ounces dried penne or rotini pasta
3	tablespoons Italian-style tomato paste
½	cup shredded Parmesan cheese (2 ounces)
¼	cup slivered fresh basil (optional)

PREP:
15 minutes
BAKE:
30 minutes
OVEN:
400°F
MAKES:
4 servings

1 Arrange tomatoes and zucchini in an ungreased 3-quart rectangular baking dish. In a small bowl combine oil, garlic, salt, and pepper; drizzle over tomato mixture. Roast vegetables, uncovered, in a 400°F oven for 20 minutes, stirring once.

2 Meanwhile, cook pasta according to package directions; drain. Stir pasta into the roasted vegetable mixture along with the tomato paste. Bake, uncovered, for 10 minutes more.

3 To serve, stir pasta and vegetable mixture. Divide mixture evenly among 4 dinner plates. Sprinkle each with Parmesan cheese and, if desired, basil.

Nutrition Facts per serving: 333 cal., 12 g total fat (4 g sat. fat), 10 mg chol., 647 mg sodium, 44 g carbo., 4 g fiber, 14 g pro.

Four different cheeses—Swiss, ricotta, Parmesan, and feta—plus spinach are the main ingredients in this appetizing meatless main dish.

SPINACH MANICOTTI

PREP:

40 minutes

BAKE:

35 minutes

OVEN:

350°F

MAKES:

4 servings

8	dried manicotti shells
¼	cup sliced green onions (2)
1	clove garlic, minced
2	tablespoons butter
2	tablespoons all-purpose flour
1⅓	cups milk
1	cup shredded process Swiss cheese (4 ounces)
¼	cup dry white wine
1	beaten egg
1	10-ounce package frozen chopped spinach, thawed and drained well
½	cup ricotta cheese
½	cup grated Parmesan cheese
½	cup crumbled feta cheese (2 ounces)
¼	teaspoon finely shredded lemon peel
⅛	teaspoon ground nutmeg

1 Cook manicotti according to package directions until tender but still firm; drain. Cool manicotti in a single layer on a piece of greased foil.

2 Meanwhile, for sauce, in a medium saucepan cook green onions and garlic in butter over medium heat until tender. Stir in flour. Add milk all at once. Cook and stir until thickened and bubbly. Add Swiss cheese and wine, stirring until cheese melts. Set aside.

3 For filling, in a medium bowl combine egg, spinach, ricotta cheese, Parmesan cheese, feta cheese, lemon peel, and nutmeg. Carefully spoon filling evenly into manicotti shells. Arrange filled shells in an ungreased 2-quart rectangular baking dish. Pour sauce over filled shells.

4 Bake, covered, in a 350°F oven for 35 to 40 minutes or until manicotti are heated through.

Nutrition Facts per serving: 383 cal., 11 g total fat (6 g sat. fat), 44 mg chol., 672 mg sodium, 37 g carbo., 3 g fiber, 29 g pro.

This airy baked casserole resembles a soufflé but without all the fuss.

EASY COTTAGE CHEESE SOUFFLÉ

2   cups cottage cheese

¾   cup soft whole wheat bread crumbs*

½   cup all-purpose flour

⅓   cup finely chopped green onions

2   tablespoons dried parsley flakes, crushed

2   tablespoons butter, melted

¼   teaspoon salt

4   eggs

1 In a large bowl combine cottage cheese, bread crumbs, flour, green onions, parsley, melted butter, and salt. Set aside.

2 In a large mixing bowl beat eggs with an electric mixer on high speed about 5 minutes or until thick and lemon colored. Gradually fold beaten eggs into the cottage cheese mixture. Pour the egg mixture into an ungreased 5- or 6-cup soufflé dish or casserole.

3 Bake, uncovered, in a 350°F oven about 1 hour or until mixture is set. Serve immediately.

*NOTE: Use a blender or food processor to make fluffy soft bread crumbs. One slice yields ¾ cup crumbs.

Nutrition Facts per serving: 258 cal., 13 g total fat (6 g sat. fat), 195 mg chol., 610 mg sodium, 16 g carbo., 1 g fiber, 18 g pro.

PREP:
25 minutes

BAKE:
1 hour

OVEN:
350°F

MAKES:
5 servings

This easy-on-the-cook main dish is layered with sliced potatoes, a savory leek and mushroom mixture, and Parmesan cheese. Serve it with a salad of mixed greens and vinaigrette dressing.

LAYERED POTATOES & LEEKS

PREP:

35 minutes

BAKE:

35 minutes

STAND:

10 minutes

OVEN:

400°F

MAKES:

*4 main-dish servings or
6 side-dish servings*

1	pound (3 medium) potatoes, sliced ¼ inch thick
⅔	cup thinly sliced leeks (2 medium)
3	cups sliced fresh mushrooms (8 ounces)
2	cloves garlic, minced
½	teaspoon dried rosemary, crushed
1	tablespoon olive oil or cooking oil
½	cup whipping cream
¼	teaspoon salt
¾	cup shredded Parmesan cheese (3 ounces)
1	tablespoon olive oil or cooking oil
	Dairy sour cream (optional)

1 Cook potatoes, covered, in a large amount of boiling lightly salted water for 3 minutes; drain. (Potatoes will not be tender.) Cool slightly. Meanwhile, in a large skillet cook the leeks, mushrooms, garlic, and rosemary in 1 tablespoon hot oil over medium heat until leeks are tender. Add cream and salt to leek mixture. Bring to boiling. Boil gently, uncovered, about 30 seconds or until slightly thickened.

2 Arrange 1 cup of the potato slices in the bottom of a greased 1½-quart soufflé dish or casserole, overlapping if necessary. Spoon one-third of the leek mixture over potatoes. Sprinkle with ¼ cup of the Parmesan cheese. Repeat layers. Top with remaining potatoes and leek mixture. Drizzle with 1 tablespoon oil.

3 Bake, uncovered, in a 400°F oven for 30 minutes. Top with remaining ¼ cup Parmesan cheese. Bake for 5 to 10 minutes more or until potatoes are tender. Cover and let stand for 10 minutes. If desired, serve with sour cream.

Nutrition Facts per main-dish serving: 668 cal., 46 g total fat (25 g sat. fat), 113 mg chol., 1,863 mg sodium, 23 g carbo., 2 g fiber, 42 g pro.

You'll be amazed at the richness just a half cup of mozzarella cheese brings to this spinach-and-tofu-packed bake.

SPINACH-RICE CASSEROLE

1/3	cup chopped onion (1 small)
1	clove garlic, minced
1	tablespoon cooking oil
1	14½-ounce can diced tomatoes with basil, oregano, and garlic, undrained
½	teaspoon dried oregano or basil, crushed
2	cups cooked brown rice
1	10-ounce package frozen chopped spinach, thawed and drained well
½	cup shredded mozzarella cheese or provolone cheese (2 ounces)
½	teaspoon salt
¼	teaspoon black pepper
8	ounces extra-firm tofu (fresh bean curd), drained and cut into ½-inch cubes

PREP:

20 minutes

BAKE:

30 minutes

OVEN:

350°F

MAKES:

4 servings

1 In a large saucepan cook onion and garlic in hot oil over medium heat until tender. Add undrained tomatoes and oregano. Bring to boiling; reduce heat. Simmer, uncovered, for 3 minutes. Stir in cooked rice, spinach, ¼ cup of the mozzarella cheese, the salt, and pepper. Carefully stir in tofu.

2 Transfer mixture to a greased 2-quart rectangular baking dish. Bake, covered, in a 350°F oven about 30 minutes or until mixture is heated through. Sprinkle with remaining ¼ cup mozzarella cheese.

Nutrition Facts per serving: 296 cal., 9 g total fat (2 g sat. fat), 9 mg chol., 1,011 mg sodium, 37 g carbo., 5 g fiber, 15 g pro.

This casserole is plenty spicy for most tastes, but if you like your flavors bold, pass a bottle of hot pepper sauce at the table.

CREAMY VEGETABLE ENCHILADAS

PREP:

30 minutes

BAKE:

23 minutes

OVEN:

350°F

MAKES:

4 servings

8　6- or 7-inch corn or flour tortillas

2　tablespoons olive oil or cooking oil

1　cup thinly sliced carrots (2 medium)

1　medium zucchini or yellow summer squash, quartered lengthwise and sliced (2 cups)

1　teaspoon chili powder or ½ teaspoon ground cumin

1　10¾-ounce can condensed cream of onion soup

1　cup shredded Monterey Jack cheese (4 ounces)

1　10-ounce can enchilada sauce or 1 cup bottled chunky salsa

　Dairy sour cream (optional)

1 Wrap tortillas tightly in foil. Heat in a 350°F oven for 10 minutes to soften.

2 Meanwhile, in a large skillet heat 1 tablespoon of the oil over medium-high heat. Add carrots; cook and stir for 2 minutes. Add zucchini and chili powder; cook and stir for 2 to 3 minutes more or until vegetables are crisp-tender. Remove skillet from heat. Stir in soup and ¾ cup of the cheese.

3 Divide vegetable mixture evenly among warm tortillas; roll up tortillas. Arrange filled tortillas, seam sides down, in a lightly greased 2-quart rectangular baking dish. Lightly brush tops of tortillas with remaining 1 tablespoon oil.

4 Bake, uncovered, in a 350°F oven for 18 to 20 minutes or until enchiladas are heated through. Top with enchilada sauce and remaining ¼ cup cheese. Bake about 5 minutes more or until cheese is melted. If desired, serve with sour cream.

Nutrition Facts per serving: 431 cal., 22 g total fat (7 g sat. fat), 38 mg chol., 974 mg sodium, 47 g carbo., 5 g fiber, 13 g pro.

POTLUCK

7

Add this jalapeño cheese-spiced casserole that uses leftover chicken to your collection of potluck favorites. It's extremely versatile because just about any frozen vegetable will work.

CHEESY CHICKEN & MOSTACCIOLI

PREP:
30 minutes

BAKE:
20 minutes

STAND:
10 minutes

OVEN:
375°F

MAKES:
6 servings

6	ounces dried mostaccioli pasta (2 cups)
2	cups frozen loose-pack cut broccoli or frozen mixed vegetables
½	cup chopped onion (1 medium)
2	tablespoons butter
2	tablespoons all-purpose flour
2	teaspoons instant chicken bouillon granules
2	cups milk
1½	cups shredded Monterey Jack cheese with jalapeño peppers (6 ounces)
1	teaspoon dried cilantro or parsley flakes, crushed
1½	cups chopped cooked chicken (about 8 ounces) or one 9¼-ounce can tuna, drained and broken into chunks
½	cup chopped tomato (1 medium)

1 Cook mostaccioli according to package directions, except add broccoli during the last 5 minutes of cooking; drain. Set aside.

2 Meanwhile, in a large saucepan cook onion in hot butter over medium heat until tender. Stir in flour and bouillon granules. Add milk all at once. Cook and stir until thickened and bubbly. Add cheese and cilantro, stirring until cheese is melted. Remove from heat.

3 Add mostaccioli mixture and chicken to the sauce; toss to coat. Spoon mixture into an ungreased 2-quart square baking dish.

4 Bake, covered, in a 375°F oven for 15 minutes. Uncover and top with tomato. Bake, uncovered, for 5 to 10 minutes more or until heated through. Let stand for 10 minutes before serving.

TO TOTE: **Do not let stand after baking. Cover tightly. Transport in an insulated carrier.**

Nutrition Facts per serving: 381 cal., 17 g total fat (9 g sat. fat), 73 mg chol., 624 mg sodium, 31 g carbo., 2 g fiber, 25 g pro.

Water chestnuts and almonds offer contrasting crunch to this creamy bake.

CREAMY CHICKEN CASSEROLE

3½   ounces dried elbow macaroni (about 1 cup)
¾   cup milk
1   10¾-ounce can condensed cream of chicken soup
2   cups chopped cooked chicken (10 ounces)
1   cup shredded American cheese (4 ounces)
1   8-ounce can sliced water chestnuts, drained
1   4-ounce can (drained weight) sliced mushrooms, drained
¼   cup chopped bottled roasted red sweet pepper
1   teaspoon dried thyme, crushed
3   tablespoons sliced almonds, toasted (optional)

PREP:
25 minutes
BAKE:
45 minutes
STAND:
5 minutes
OVEN:
350°F
MAKES:
6 servings

1 Cook macaroni according to package directions; drain. In a large bowl combine milk and soup. Stir in chicken, ½ cup of the American cheese, the water chestnuts, mushrooms, roasted sweet pepper, thyme, and cooked macaroni. Transfer to an ungreased 2-quart casserole.

2 Bake, covered, in a 350°F oven for 45 to 50 minutes or until heated through. Top with remaining ½ cup American cheese. Let stand about 5 minutes or until cheese is melted. If desired, sprinkle with toasted almonds.

TO TOTE: Do not let stand after baking. Cover tightly. Transport in an insulated carrier. If using toasted almonds, transport separately in a self-sealing plastic bag and sprinkle on casserole just before serving.

Nutrition Facts per serving: 311 cal., 14 g total fat (6 g sat. fat), 66 mg chol., 776 mg sodium, 22 g carbo., 2 g fiber, 23 g pro.

This family favorite travels well to potlucks. For a lower-sodium version use reduced-sodium condensed cream of chicken soup.

CHICKEN CHOW MEIN CASSEROLE

PREP:

25 minutes

BAKE:

50 minutes

OVEN:

350°F

MAKES:

8 servings

4	cups chopped cooked chicken (about 1¼ pounds)
2	cups chopped celery (4 stalks)
1	cup shredded carrots (2 medium)
1	cup chopped green sweet pepper (1 large)
2	4-ounce cans (drained weight) sliced mushrooms, drained
⅔	cup sliced or slivered almonds, toasted
2	tablespoons diced pimiento, drained
2	10¾-ounce cans condensed cream of chicken soup
2	cups chow mein noodles

1 In a very large bowl combine chicken, celery, carrots, sweet pepper, mushrooms, almonds, and pimiento. Add soup to chicken mixture; mix well.

2 Transfer chicken mixture to an ungreased 3-quart rectangular baking dish. Bake, covered, in a 350°F oven for 45 minutes. Uncover and top with chow mein noodles. Bake, uncovered, for 5 to 10 minutes more or until heated through.

TO TOTE: **Cover tightly. Transport in an insulated carrier.**

Nutrition Facts per serving: 366 cal., 19 g total fat (4 g sat. fat), 68 mg chol., 921 mg sodium, 21 g carbo., 4 g fiber, 27 g pro.

This old-fashioned dish is perfect for Sunday dinner. Invite some family and friends over soon.

CHICKEN SUPREME CASSEROLE

8	ounces dried rotini pasta
1	16-ounce package frozen stir-fry vegetables (broccoli, carrots, onions, red sweet peppers, celery, water chestnuts, and mushrooms)
2	10¾-ounce cans condensed cream of chicken soup
2	cups milk
¼	cup mayonnaise or salad dressing
¼	teaspoon black pepper
2	cups chopped cooked chicken (10 ounces)
2	cups cubed French bread
2	tablespoons butter, melted
¼	teaspoon garlic powder

PREP:
25 minutes
BAKE:
30 minutes
STAND:
10 minutes
OVEN:
350°F
MAKES:
6 to 8 servings

1 Cook rotini according to package directions, except add the stir-fry vegetables during the last 5 minutes of cooking; drain.

2 Meanwhile, in a large bowl combine soup, milk, mayonnaise, and pepper. Stir in cooked rotini mixture and chicken. Transfer to an ungreased 3-quart rectangular baking dish. In a medium bowl toss bread cubes with melted butter and garlic powder; sprinkle over pasta mixture.

3 Bake, uncovered, in a 350°F oven for 30 to 35 minutes or until heated through and bread cubes are golden. Let stand for 10 minutes before serving.

TO TOTE: Do not let stand after baking. Cover tightly. Transport in an insulated carrier.

Nutrition Facts per serving: 584 cal., 25 g total fat (8 g sat. fat), 71 mg chol., 1,123 mg sodium, 60 g carbo., 4 g fiber, 28 g pro.

For potluck dinners, let guests serve themselves out of the baking dish. At home, for a special presentation, spoon hot portions of the casserole into steamed fresh sweet pepper halves.

CHICKEN, WILD RICE & VEGETABLE CASSEROLE

PREP:

25 minutes

BAKE:

35 minutes

OVEN:

350°F

MAKES:

8 to 10 servings

1	6-ounce package long grain and wild rice mix
3	cups bite-size pieces cooked chicken (about 1 pound)
1	14½-ounce can French-cut green beans, drained
1	10¾-ounce can condensed cream of celery soup
1	8-ounce can sliced water chestnuts, drained
½	cup mayonnaise or salad dressing
½	cup chopped onion (1 medium)
3	tablespoons sliced almonds
1	2-ounce jar sliced pimiento, drained
1	teaspoon lemon juice
1	cup shredded cheddar cheese (4 ounces)

1 Cook rice mix according to package directions. Meanwhile, in a very large bowl combine chicken, green beans, soup, water chestnuts, mayonnaise, onion, almonds, pimiento, and lemon juice. Stir in cooked rice mixture. Transfer to an ungreased 3-quart rectangular baking dish.

2 Bake, covered, in a 350°F oven for 30 minutes. Sprinkle with cheese. Bake, uncovered, about 5 minutes more or until heated through and cheese is melted.

MAKE-AHEAD DIRECTIONS: Assemble as directed. Cover unbaked casserole; seal cheese in a self-sealing plastic bag. Chill up to 24 hours. Bake, covered, in a 350°F oven for 45 minutes. Uncover; sprinkle with cheese. Bake, uncovered, about 5 minutes more or until heated through and cheese is melted.

TO TOTE: Cover tightly. Transport in an insulated carrier.

Nutrition Facts per serving: 434 cal., 25 g total fat (6 g sat. fat), 75 mg chol., 971 mg sodium, 30 g carbo., 2 g fiber, 24 g pro.

Pesto is made from garlic, basil, nuts, olive oil, and Parmesan cheese and is traditionally a sauce for pasta. Here it's used to add flavor and freshness to the chicken and asparagus.

CHICKEN-ASPARAGUS CASSEROLE

2	10-ounce packages frozen cut asparagus
1	10¾-ounce can condensed cream of chicken soup
⅓	cup grated Parmesan cheese
¼	cup purchased pesto
¼	cup half-and-half, light cream, or milk
2	cups chopped cooked chicken (10 ounces)
2	tablespoons grated Parmesan cheese

1 Cook asparagus according to package directions, except cook for only half of the time suggested; drain. Set aside.

2 In a large bowl combine soup, the ⅓ cup Parmesan cheese, the pesto, and half-and-half. Stir in asparagus and chicken. Transfer to an ungreased 2-quart rectangular baking dish.

3 Bake, uncovered, in a 350°F oven about 25 minutes or until heated through. Sprinkle with the 2 tablespoons Parmesan cheese. Bake for 10 to 15 minutes more or until topping is golden. Let stand for 10 minutes before serving.

TO TOTE: Do not let stand after baking. Cover tightly. Transport in an insulated carrier.

Nutrition Facts per serving: 259 cal., 15 g total fat (5 g sat. fat), 56 mg chol., 613 mg sodium, 10 g carbo., 3 g fiber, 22 g pro.

PREP:
25 minutes
BAKE:
35 minutes
STAND:
10 minutes
OVEN:
350°F
MAKES:
6 servings

Here's a creative take on a much-loved casserole formula—meat, vegetables, pasta, and a creamy sauce. Bacon, spaghetti, and golden mushroom soup make this a dish you'll serve time and again.

CHICKEN-SPAGHETTI CASSEROLE

PREP:

25 minutes

BAKE:

45 minutes

OVEN:

350°F

MAKES:

6 servings

4   ounces dried spaghetti

3   slices bacon, chopped

½   cup chopped onion (1 medium)

1   clove garlic, minced

3   tablespoons all-purpose flour

1   14½-ounce can diced tomatoes, undrained

1   10¾-ounce can condensed golden mushroom soup

½   cup milk

1   cup shredded Swiss cheese (4 ounces)

2   cups cubed cooked chicken (about 10 ounces)

½   of a 16-ounce package frozen loose-pack cauliflower, broccoli, and carrots, thawed

1 Break spaghetti pieces in half. Cook according to package directions; drain. Set aside.

2 Meanwhile, in a large saucepan cook bacon, onion, and garlic over medium heat until bacon is crisp; stir in flour. Add undrained tomatoes, soup, and milk. Cook and stir until thickened and bubbly. Add Swiss cheese; stir until melted. Stir in cooked spaghetti, chicken, and vegetables. Transfer to an ungreased 2½-quart casserole.

3 Bake, uncovered, in a 350°F oven about 45 minutes or until mixture is heated through.

TO TOTE: **Cover tightly. Transport in an insulated carrier.**

Nutrition Facts per serving: 366 cal., 15 g total fat (7 g sat. fat), 68 mg chol., 701 mg sodium, 29 g carbo., 3 g fiber, 26 g pro.

Old-fashioned goodness fills this chicken pie. The topper is made easy with corn muffin mix.

CORN BREAD-TOPPED CHICKEN PIE

1   8½-ounce package corn muffin mix

1   pound skinless, boneless chicken breasts or thighs,
     cut into 1-inch pieces

⅓   cup chopped onion (1 small)

⅓   cup chopped green sweet pepper

1   tablespoon olive oil or cooking oil

1   10¾-ounce can condensed cream of mushroom soup

¼   cup all-purpose flour

1   teaspoon dried sage, crushed

1   cup chicken broth

1   10-ounce package frozen peas and carrots

PREP:

20 minutes

BAKE:

18 minutes

OVEN:

425°F

MAKES:

6 servings

1 Prepare corn muffin mix according to package directions (do not bake); set aside.

2 In a large skillet cook chicken, onion, and sweet pepper in hot oil over medium-high heat until chicken is brown and vegetables are tender. In a medium bowl combine soup, flour, and sage; stir into chicken mixture. Stir in broth and peas and carrots. Cook and stir until thickened and bubbly.

3 Transfer bubbling chicken mixture to an ungreased 2-quart square baking dish. Spoon corn muffin batter over casserole.

4 Bake, uncovered, in a 425°F oven for 18 to 20 minutes or until a wooden toothpick inserted into corn bread comes out clean.

TO TOTE: **Cover tightly. Transport in an insulated carrier.**

Nutrition Facts per serving: 399 cal., 15 g total fat (2 g sat. fat), 71 mg chol., 927 mg sodium, 44 g carbo., 2 g fiber, 25 g pro.

Two cheeses, rice mix, and cream of chicken soup transform ordinary turkey into a rich oven meal.

TURKEY-WILD RICE BAKE

PREP:

35 minutes

BAKE:

15 minutes

OVEN:

350°F

MAKES:

6 servings

1   6-ounce package long grain and wild rice mix

1   cup chopped onion (1 large)

3   cloves garlic, minced

1   tablespoon butter

1   10¾-ounce can condensed cream of chicken soup

1   cup milk

1½   teaspoons dried basil, crushed

2   cups shredded Swiss cheese (8 ounces)

3   cups chopped cooked turkey (about 1 pound)

1   4½-ounce jar (drained weight) sliced mushrooms, drained

½   cup shredded Parmesan cheese (2 ounces)

⅓   cup sliced almonds, toasted

1 Prepare rice mix according to package directions, except discard the seasoning packet. Set aside.

2 In a 12-inch skillet cook onion and garlic in hot butter over medium heat until onion is tender. Stir in soup, milk, and basil; heat through. Slowly add Swiss cheese, stirring until cheese is melted. Stir in cooked rice, turkey, and mushrooms. Transfer to an ungreased 3-quart rectangular baking dish. Sprinkle with Parmesan cheese.

3 Bake, uncovered, in a 350°F oven for 15 to 20 minutes or until heated through. Sprinkle with almonds before serving.

TO TOTE: Do not sprinkle with almonds. Cover casserole tightly. Transport in an insulated carrier. Transport almonds separately in a self-sealing plastic bag. Sprinkle on casserole just before serving.

Nutrition Facts per serving: 700 cal., 36 g total fat (19 g sat. fat), 132 mg chol., 1,400 mg sodium, 37 g carbo., 4 g fiber, 56 g pro.

This creamy rice bake is a delicious way to use up leftover turkey or chicken after the holidays.

ARTICHOKE-TURKEY CASSEROLE

½ cup chopped carrot (1 medium)

½ cup chopped red sweet pepper (1 small)

¼ cup sliced green onions (2)

1 tablespoon butter

1 10¾-ounce can condensed cream of chicken soup

1 8- to 9-ounce package frozen artichoke hearts, thawed and cut up

1½ cups chopped cooked turkey or chicken (about 8 ounces)

1 cup cooked white rice or wild rice

⅔ cup milk

½ cup shredded mozzarella cheese (2 ounces)

2 slices bacon, crisp-cooked, drained, and crumbled

½ teaspoon dried thyme, crushed

3 tablespoons grated Parmesan cheese

PREP:
20 minutes
BAKE:
40 minutes
STAND:
10 minutes
OVEN:
350°F
MAKES:
6 servings

1 In a large skillet cook carrot, sweet pepper, and green onions in hot butter over medium heat until carrot is crisp-tender. Remove from heat and stir in soup, artichoke hearts, turkey, rice, milk, mozzarella cheese, bacon, and thyme. Transfer to an ungreased 2-quart rectangular baking dish. Sprinkle with Parmesan cheese.

2 Bake, covered, in a 350°F oven for 20 minutes. Uncover and bake about 20 minutes more or until bubbly. Let stand for 10 minutes before serving.

MAKE-AHEAD DIRECTIONS: Assemble as directed. Cover unbaked casserole and chill up to 24 hours. Bake, covered, in a 350°F oven for 30 minutes. Uncover and bake about 20 minutes more or until bubbly.

TO TOTE: Do not let stand after baking. Cover tightly. Transport in an insulated carrier.

Nutrition Facts per serving: 248 cal., 11 g total fat (5 g sat. fat), 47 mg chol., 611 mg sodium, 18 g carbo., 3 g fiber, 18 g pro.

How do you improve on Mom's cooking? In this case, you don't. Her tuna casserole tastes as good today as it did 30 years ago.

MOM'S TUNA-NOODLE CASSEROLE

PREP:

20 minutes

BAKE:

30 minutes

OVEN:

375°F

MAKES:

6 servings

4   ounces dried medium noodles (2 cups)

1   cup frozen loose-pack peas or peas and carrots

½   cup finely chopped onion (1 medium)

½   cup finely chopped celery (1 stalk)

2   tablespoons butter

1   10¾-ounce can condensed cream of mushroom or cream of celery soup

¾   cup milk

1   9-ounce can tuna, drained and flaked

¼   cup chopped red sweet pepper

⅛   teaspoon black pepper

¼   cup grated Parmesan cheese

1   Cook noodles according to package directions, except add peas and carrots during the last 3 minutes of cooking; drain. Set aside.

2   Meanwhile, in a medium saucepan cook onion and celery in hot butter over medium heat until tender. Stir in soup and milk. Gently stir in tuna, sweet pepper, and black pepper. Add tuna mixture to noodle mixture; toss gently to coat. Transfer to an ungreased 2-quart casserole. Sprinkle with cheese.

3   Bake, uncovered, in a 375°F oven for 30 to 35 minutes or until heated through.

TO TOTE: **Cover tightly. Transport in an insulated carrier.**

Nutrition Facts per serving: 267 cal., 11 g total fat (5 g sat. fat), 47 mg chol., 652 mg sodium, 24 g carbo., 2 g fiber, 18 g pro.

Many old favorites make top-notch potluck dishes. Here a double dose of cheese adds a flavorful twist to a beloved comfort food.

CHEESY TUNA-NOODLE CASSEROLE

8	ounces dried medium noodles (4 cups)
⅓	cup chopped onion (1 small)
2	tablespoons butter
2	tablespoons all-purpose flour
1	10¾-ounce can condensed cheddar cheese soup
¾	cup milk
1	10-ounce package frozen chopped broccoli
1	9-ounce can tuna, drained and flaked
1	2¼-ounce can sliced pitted ripe olives, drained
½	cup shredded cheddar cheese (2 ounces)

1 Cook noodles according to package directions; drain. Return noodles to saucepan.

2 Meanwhile, in a medium saucepan cook onion in hot butter over medium heat until tender. Stir in flour, then soup. Gradually stir in milk. Cook and stir until thickened and bubbly. Gently stir in broccoli, tuna, and olives. Add tuna mixture to noodles; toss gently to coat. Transfer to an ungreased 2-quart casserole.

3 Bake, covered, in a 375°F oven for 25 minutes. Top with cheese. Bake, uncovered, about 5 minutes more or until cheese is melted and mixture is heated through.

TO TOTE: Cover tightly. Transport in an insulated carrier.

Nutrition Facts per serving: 358 cal., 14 g total fat (7 g sat. fat), 79 mg chol., 769 mg sodium, 38 g carbo., 3 g fiber, 23 g pro.

PREP:
25 minutes

BAKE:
30 minutes

OVEN:
375°F

MAKES:
6 servings

Swiss and cheddar cheeses combine with mushroom soup for this shrimp dish. Using cooked, deveined shrimp helps keep down preparation time.

CHEESY SHRIMP & RICE

PREP:

40 minutes

BAKE:

35 minutes

STAND:

10 minutes

OVEN:

375°F

MAKES:

12 servings

2	6.2-ounce packages quick-cooking long grain and wild rice mix
2	cups chopped red sweet peppers (2 large)
2	cups chopped celery (4 stalks)
2	cups chopped onions (2 large)
1/3	cup butter
2	10¾-ounce cans condensed golden mushroom soup
2	cups shredded Swiss cheese (8 ounces)
2	cups shredded cheddar cheese (8 ounces)
1/2	teaspoon black pepper
2	pounds cooked, peeled, and deveined medium shrimp

1 Prepare rice mix according to package directions. Meanwhile, in a 4-quart Dutch oven cook sweet peppers, celery, and onions in hot butter over medium heat about 5 minutes or just until tender.

2 In a very large bowl combine the cooked rice mixture, cooked vegetable mixture, soup, Swiss cheese, 1 cup of the cheddar cheese, and black pepper. Stir in shrimp. Transfer to two ungreased 3-quart rectangular baking dishes.

3 Bake, covered, in a 375°F oven about 35 minutes or until heated through, rotating baking dishes halfway through baking. Remove from oven; sprinkle with remaining 1 cup cheddar cheese. Let stand for 10 minutes before serving.

TO TOTE: Do not let stand after baking. Cover tightly. Transport in an insulated carrier.

Nutrition Facts per serving: 452 cal., 20 g total fat (11 g sat. fat), 205 mg chol., 1,274 mg sodium, 32 g carbo., 2 g fiber, 35 g pro.

Want to serve seafood that has a little zing? Try this Southwest-inspired recipe. It's studded with scallops, green onions, and crab for a tantalizing dish potluck guests will be talking about for weeks.

SOUTHWESTERN SEAFOOD CASSEROLE

1	pound dried penne pasta
1	pound bay scallops
1	tablespoon butter
⅓	cup butter
4	cloves garlic, minced
½	cup all-purpose flour
1⅓	cups milk
1	14-ounce can chicken broth
2	cups shredded Monterey Jack cheese with jalapeño peppers (8 ounces)
½	cup sliced green onions (4)
1	teaspoon dried basil, crushed
¼	teaspoon black pepper
1	6-ounce can crabmeat, drained, flaked, and cartilage removed
½	cup shredded Parmesan cheese (2 ounces)

PREP:
30 minutes
BAKE:
15 minutes
OVEN:
400°F
MAKES:
10 to 12 servings

1 Cook penne according to package directions; drain. Set aside. Rinse scallops; pat dry with paper towels. Meanwhile, in a large saucepan melt the 1 tablespoon butter over medium-high heat. Add scallops; cook and stir about 3 minutes or until scallops turn opaque. Remove scallops from saucepan; drain. Set aside.

2 Melt the ⅓ cup butter in the saucepan; add garlic and cook over medium-high heat for 1 minute. Add flour; cook and stir for 1 minute more. Add milk and broth all at once. Cook and stir until thickened and bubbly. Add Monterey Jack cheese, green onions, basil, and pepper. Cook and stir until cheese melts. Stir in cooked penne, scallops, and crabmeat. Transfer to an ungreased 3-quart casserole. Sprinkle with Parmesan cheese.

3 Bake, uncovered, in a 400°F oven for 15 to 20 minutes or until cheese is golden.

TO TOTE: Cover tightly. Transport in an insulated carrier.

Nutrition Facts per serving: 530 cal., 24 g total fat (13 g sat. fat), 92 mg chol., 925 mg sodium, 43 g carbo., 1 g fiber, 35 g pro.

Cheese-covered Brussels sprouts with crisp bacon and onion are sure to become a holiday favorite.

CHEESY BRUSSELS SPROUTS WITH BACON

PREP:

30 minutes

BAKE:

25 minutes

OVEN:

400°F

MAKES:

8 to 10 side-dish servings

1½   pounds Brussels sprouts (about 8 cups), quartered

3   slices bacon or 2 ounces pancetta, diced

½   cup chopped onion (1 medium)

2   cloves garlic, minced

1   16-ounce jar 4-cheese pasta sauce

1   cup soft bread crumbs*

⅓   cup shredded Parmesan cheese (1½ ounces)

2   tablespoons butter, melted

1 Cook Brussels sprouts in a small amount of boiling water for 5 minutes; drain (sprouts will not be tender). Set aside.

2 In a large skillet cook bacon over medium heat until crisp; remove with a slotted spoon, reserving drippings in skillet. Set bacon aside. Add onion and garlic to skillet; cook until onion is tender. In a large bowl combine Brussels sprouts, bacon, onion mixture, and cheese sauce. Toss to coat. Transfer to a greased 2-quart casserole.

3 In a small bowl combine bread crumbs, Parmesan cheese, and melted butter. Sprinkle over top of Brussels sprouts mixture.

4 Bake, uncovered, in a 400°F oven about 25 minutes or until heated through and topping is golden.

*NOTE: Use a blender or food processor to make fluffy soft bread crumbs. One slice yields ¾ cup crumbs.

TO TOTE: Cover tightly. Transport in an insulated carrier.

Nutrition Facts per serving: 309 cal., 22 g total fat (10 g sat. fat), 51 mg chol., 817 mg sodium, 15 g carbo., 4 g fiber, 14 g pro.

Combine canned soup—a longtime staple for making casseroles easier—with refrigerated diced potatoes and you have one of the easiest versions ever of this classic comfort food!

EASY SCALLOPED POTATOES & HAM

1	10¾-ounce can condensed cream of onion or cream of celery soup
½	cup milk
⅛	teaspoon black pepper
3	cups cubed cooked ham (about 1 pound)
1	20-ounce package refrigerated diced potatoes with onion
¾	cup shredded Swiss cheese or cheddar cheese (3 ounces)

1 In a large bowl combine soup, milk, and pepper. Stir in ham and potatoes. Transfer to an ungreased 2-quart rectangular baking dish.

2 Bake, covered, in a 350°F oven for 40 minutes. Stir mixture. Sprinkle with cheese. Bake, uncovered, for 5 to 10 minutes more or until heated through and cheese is melted. Let stand for 10 minutes before serving.

TO TOTE: Do not let stand after baking. Cover tightly. Transport in an insulated carrier.

Nutrition Facts per serving: 332 cal., 14 g total fat (6 g sat. fat), 64 mg chol., 1,613 mg sodium, 29 g carbo., 2 g fiber, 21 g pro.

PREP:
15 minutes
BAKE:
45 minutes
STAND:
10 minutes
OVEN:
350°F
MAKES:
6 to 8 servings

Although fresh vegetables of any kind are hard to beat, canned vegetables help out in a pinch. By using canned sweet potatoes, you'll cut your preparation time to just 10 minutes.

HAM WITH SWEET POTATOES & APPLES

PREP:
30 minutes

BAKE:
25 minutes

OVEN:
375°F

MAKES:
4 servings

4	medium sweet potatoes or one 18-ounce can sweet potatoes, drained
2	½-inch-thick slices cooked ham (about 12 ounces total)
2	medium apples
1	teaspoon finely shredded orange peel
¾	cup orange juice
2	teaspoons cornstarch
1	teaspoon reduced-sodium soy sauce
1	teaspoon grated fresh ginger
1	clove garlic, minced
	Snipped fresh parsley (optional)

1 Peel and quarter fresh sweet potatoes, if using. In a large covered saucepan cook potatoes in a small amount of boiling water for 15 minutes or until almost tender; drain. Set aside.

2 Cut each ham slice in half. Core apples and cut each apple into 8 wedges. Arrange drained sweet potatoes and apple wedges in an ungreased 2-quart rectangular baking dish. Arrange ham slices on top.

3 In a small saucepan combine orange peel, orange juice, cornstarch, soy sauce, ginger, and garlic. Cook and stir over medium heat until thickened and bubbly. Pour over ham in dish.

4 Bake, covered, in a 375°F oven for 15 minutes. Uncover. Bake about 10 minutes more or until potatoes and apples are just tender. If desired, sprinkle with parsley.

TO TOTE: Do not sprinkle with parsley. Cover tightly. Transport in an insulated carrier. If using parsley, transport separately in a self-sealing plastic bag. Sprinkle on casserole just before serving.

Nutrition Facts per serving: 376 cal., 8 g total fat (3 g sat. fat), 48 mg chol., 1,188 mg sodium, 59 g carbo., 10 g fiber, 18 g pro.

Think ahead! You can freeze leftover cooked ham for up to three months. Cube some and freeze it in 3-cup portions so the meat is measured and ready to thaw for this yummy bake.

HAM & BROCCOLI BAKE

½	cup chopped onion (1 medium)
2	tablespoons butter
2	10¾-ounce cans condensed cream of mushroom soup and/or cream of celery soup
1¼	cups milk
1	cup shredded cheddar cheese or Swiss cheese (4 ounces)
1	teaspoon Worcestershire sauce
3	cups cubed cooked ham (about 1 pound)
2	cups uncooked instant white rice
1	16-ounce package frozen cut broccoli, thawed

PREP:
25 minutes
BAKE:
1 hour
OVEN:
350°F
MAKES:
6 to 8 servings

1 In a small saucepan cook onion in hot butter over medium heat until tender.

2 In a large bowl combine soup, milk, cheese, and Worcestershire sauce. Stir in cooked onion, ham, rice, and broccoli. Transfer to an ungreased 2-quart rectangular baking dish.

3 Bake, covered, in a 350°F oven for 50 minutes. Uncover. Bake about 10 minutes more or until heated through and rice is tender.

TO TOTE: Cover tightly. Transport in an insulated carrier.

Nutrition Facts per serving: 516 cal., 25 g total fat (12 g sat. fat), 80 mg chol., 1,947 mg sodium, 44 g carbo., 3 g fiber, 26 g pro.

This is unlike any ordinary pork and beans you've had before. Green chiles and brown rice add lots of flavor. If you prefer a less spicy dish, reduce the green chiles to one can.

PORK & BEAN CASSEROLE

PREP:

25 minutes

BAKE:

30 minutes

OVEN:

375°F

MAKES:

6 servings

1½ to 1¾ pounds boneless pork shoulder roast, trimmed of fat

1 tablespoon cooking oil

1 15-ounce can black beans or pinto beans, rinsed and drained

1 10¾-ounce can condensed cream of chicken soup

2 4-ounce cans diced green chile peppers, drained

1 cup uncooked quick-cooking brown rice

¼ cup water

¼ cup purchased salsa

1 teaspoon ground cumin

½ cup shredded cheddar cheese (2 ounces)

1 Cut pork into bite-size strips. In a large skillet stir-fry pork, half at a time, in hot oil over medium-high heat until no longer pink. Drain. Return all meat to skillet. Stir in beans, soup, chile peppers, uncooked rice, the water, salsa, and cumin. Heat and stir just until bubbly; pour into an ungreased 2-quart casserole.

2 Bake, covered, in a 375°F oven for 25 minutes or until rice is tender. Sprinkle with cheese. Bake about 5 minutes more or until cheese is melted.

TO TOTE: Cover tightly. Transport in an insulated carrier.

Nutrition Facts per serving: 379 cal., 17 g total fat (6 g sat. fat), 87 mg chol., 833 mg sodium, 27 g carbo., 5 g fiber, 33 g pro.

This is it: that creamy, potato-chip-topped casserole that has been popular for years at bridge parties and luncheons. As always, it's a pleasing choice when serving a crowd.

HOT CHICKEN SALAD

1	cup coarsely crushed potato chips
⅔	cup finely chopped almonds
6	cups cubed cooked chicken (about 2 pounds)
3	cups chopped celery (6 stalks)
2	cups shredded mozzarella cheese (8 ounces)
2	8-ounce cartons dairy sour cream or plain yogurt
1	10¾-ounce can condensed cream of chicken soup
¼	cup chopped onion
1	teaspoon dried thyme or basil, crushed
4	hard-cooked eggs, chopped

1 In a small bowl combine potato chips and almonds; set aside. In a large bowl combine chicken, celery, cheese, sour cream, soup, onion, and thyme. Gently fold in hard-cooked eggs. Transfer to an ungreased 3-quart rectangular baking dish. Sprinkle with potato chip mixture.

2 Bake, uncovered, in a 400°F oven for 30 to 35 minutes or until heated through. Let stand for 10 minutes before serving.

TO TOTE: Do not let stand after baking. Cover tightly. Transport in an insulated carrier.

Nutrition Facts per serving: 398 cal., 25 g total fat (10 g sat. fat), 168 mg chol., 437 mg sodium, 9 g carbo., 2 g fiber, 33 g pro.

PREP:
25 minutes
BAKE:
30 minutes
STAND:
10 minutes
OVEN:
400°F
MAKES:
12 servings

Tomato soup gives a pleasant sweetness to this dish, and the cheeses make it extra luscious.

BAKED BEEF RAVIOLI

PREP:
15 minutes

BAKE:
20 minutes

OVEN:
375°F

MAKES:
8 to 10 servings

2   9-ounce packages refrigerated 4-cheese ravioli

1½   pounds ground beef

1   cup chopped onion (1 large)

6   cloves garlic, minced

1   14-ounce can diced tomatoes, undrained

1   10¾-ounce can condensed tomato soup

1   teaspoon dried basil, crushed

1   teaspoon dried oregano, crushed

1½   cups shredded mozzarella cheese (6 ounces)

½   cup shredded Parmesan cheese (2 ounces)

1 Cook ravioli according to package directions; drain. Set aside and keep warm.

2 Meanwhile, in a large skillet cook ground beef, onion, and garlic over medium heat until meat is brown and onion is tender; drain. Stir in undrained tomatoes, soup, basil, and oregano. Gently stir in cooked ravioli. Transfer to an ungreased 3-quart rectangular baking dish. Sprinkle with mozzarella cheese and Parmesan cheese.

3 Bake, uncovered, in a 375°F oven about 20 minutes or until mixture is heated through.

TO TOTE: Cover tightly. Transport in an insulated carrier.

Nutrition Facts per serving: 503 cal., 20 g total fat (9 g sat. fat), 113 mg chol., 854 mg sodium, 40 g carbo., 3 g fiber, 40 g pro.

Veal isn't a typical partner for stuffing—but in this case, the veal adds a delicate flavor and fine texture.

VEAL-STUFFING BAKE

1	tablespoon finely chopped shallot or green onion
4	cloves garlic, minced
1	tablespoon olive oil
1	pound boneless veal or boneless pork loin, cut into ½-inch cubes
2	cups sliced fresh shiitake or button mushrooms (6 ounces)
¼	cup butter
¼	cup brandy or water
¾	cup purchased beef gravy
1	tablespoon tomato paste
3	cups herbed stuffing mix
1	cup reduced-sodium chicken broth
¼	cup butter, melted

PREP:
30 minutes
BAKE:
30 minutes
OVEN:
350°F
MAKES:
4 servings

1 In a large skillet cook shallot and garlic in hot oil over medium heat until tender. Add half of the veal and cook about 3 minutes or until no longer pink. Remove veal mixture from skillet. Repeat with remaining veal. Set aside.

2 In the same skillet cook mushrooms in ¼ cup hot butter over medium heat until golden. Remove from heat. Carefully stir in brandy. Return to heat. Cook and stir about 2 minutes or until sauce is reduced by half. Stir in gravy and tomato paste; heat through. Stir in veal mixture. Transfer veal mixture to an ungreased 1½-quart casserole; set aside.

3 In a medium bowl combine stuffing mix, broth, and ¼ cup melted butter; toss to combine. Spoon stuffing mixture over veal mixture in dish.

4 Bake, uncovered, in a 350°F oven for 30 minutes or until the stuffing is golden.

TO TOTE: Cover tightly. Transport in an insulated carrier.

Nutrition Facts per serving: 649 cal., 32 g total fat (14 g sat. fat), 154 mg chol., 1,224 mg sodium, 48 g carbo., 5 g fiber, 33 g pro.

If you love sweet potatoes, you'll enjoy this dish. Take it along to your next holiday gathering. The pecan topper is simply delightful.

SWEET POTATO CASSEROLE

PREP:

20 minutes

BAKE:

35 minutes

OVEN:

350°F

MAKES:

8 side-dish servings

2	beaten eggs
½	cup granulated sugar
¼	cup butter, melted and cooled slightly
1	teaspoon vanilla
½	teaspoon salt
4	cups cooked, mashed sweet potatoes
½	cup raisins
½	cup packed brown sugar
¼	cup all-purpose flour
2	tablespoons cold butter
½	cup chopped pecans

1 In a large bowl combine eggs, granulated sugar, melted butter, vanilla, and salt. Stir in cooked sweet potatoes and raisins. Spread sweet potato mixture evenly into an ungreased 2-quart square baking dish.

2 For topping, in a small bowl combine brown sugar and flour. Using a pastry blender, cut in the cold butter until mixture resembles coarse crumbs; stir in pecans. Sprinkle over potato mixture. Bake, uncovered, in a 350°F oven for 35 to 40 minutes or until heated through.

TO TOTE: **Cover tightly. Transport in an insulated carrier.**

Nutrition Facts per serving: 460 cal., 16 g total fat (7 g sat. fat), 78 mg chol., 282 mg sodium, 77 g carbo., 4 g fiber, 6 g pro.

Worcestershire sauce for chicken keeps the color of this dish light and appetizing.

CREAMY BROCCOLI BAKE

1½   pounds broccoli, cut up (6 cups)

1   10¾-ounce can condensed cream of broccoli
or golden mushroom soup

½   cup shredded sharp cheddar cheese (2 ounces)

⅓   cup dairy sour cream

2   teaspoons Worcestershire sauce for chicken

PREP:
15 minutes

BAKE:
25 minutes

OVEN:
350°F

MAKES:
6 to 8 side-dish servings

1 In a large covered saucepan cook broccoli in a small amount of boiling salted water for 2 minutes; drain well (broccoli will not be crisp-tender). Transfer to an ungreased 1½-quart casserole. In a medium bowl combine soup, cheese, sour cream, and Worcestershire sauce. Pour over broccoli.

2 Bake, covered, in a 350°F oven about 25 minutes or until broccoli is tender and sauce is heated through.

TO TOTE: Cover tightly. Transport in an insulated carrier.

Nutrition Facts per serving: 129 cal., 8 g total fat (4 g sat. fat), 16 mg chol., 428 mg sodium, 9 g carbo., 3 g fiber, 6 g pro.

No peeling or chopping the vegetables! An easy-to-use bag of frozen vegetables goes gourmet with a buttery walnut topping.

VEGETABLE MEDLEY AU GRATIN

PREP:

20 minutes

BAKE:

1 hour 5 minutes

OVEN:

300°F/375°F

MAKES:

10 side-dish servings

1	10¾-ounce can condensed cream of chicken and mushroom soup
½	cup dairy sour cream
½	teaspoon dried dillweed
2	16-ounce packages loose-pack frozen broccoli, cauliflower, and carrots, thawed
⅔	cup crushed stone-ground wheat crackers (about 15 crackers)
⅓	cup finely chopped walnuts
¼	cup shredded Parmesan cheese
2	tablespoons butter, melted

1 In a large bowl combine soup, sour cream, and dillweed; stir in thawed vegetables. Transfer to an ungreased 2-quart rectangular baking dish. Bake, covered, in a 300°F oven for 50 minutes.

2 In a small bowl combine crackers, walnuts, cheese, and melted butter. Sprinkle mixture over vegetable mixture. Increase oven temperature to 375°F. Bake, uncovered, about 15 minutes more or until topping is brown.

MAKE-AHEAD DIRECTIONS: Assemble as directed. Cover and chill unbaked casserole and crumb mixture separately overnight. Bake as directed.

TO TOTE: Cover tightly. Transport in an insulated carrier.

Nutrition Facts per serving: 157 cal., 10 g total fat (4 g sat. fat), 16 mg chol., 452 mg sodium, 11 g carbo., 3 g fiber, 5 g pro.

Don't know where to find Gruyère cheese? Check the speciality cheese section of your supermarket. This cow's-milk cheese from Switzerland has a sweet nutty flavor similar to Swiss cheese.

GRUYÈRE, BACON & CARAMELIZED ONION GRITS

5	slices bacon (about ¼ pound), chopped
1	large onion, halved and thinly sliced (about 3 cups)
4	cups milk
¼	cup butter, cut up
½	teaspoon salt
1	cup uncooked quick-cooking grits
1½	cups shredded Gruyère cheese (6 ounces)
	Several dashes bottled hot pepper sauce or ¼ teaspoon cayenne pepper (optional)
2	tablespoons grated Parmesan cheese

PREP:
30 minutes
BAKE:
20 minutes
OVEN:
350°F
MAKES:
10 side-dish servings

1 In a large skillet cook bacon over medium heat until crisp. Remove bacon with a slotted spoon, reserving 2 tablespoons drippings in skillet. Drain bacon on paper towels; set aside. Cook onion slices, covered, in reserved drippings over medium heat for 15 minutes or until tender and golden. Set aside.

2 In a large saucepan combine milk, butter, and salt. Bring mixture almost to boiling over medium heat, stirring occasionally. (Watch carefully to prevent boiling over.) Gradually stir in grits; cook and stir with a long-handled wooden spoon until mixture just comes to boiling. Stir 2 minutes more or until thickened. (Reduce heat, if necessary.) Remove from heat; stir in bacon, onion, 1 cup of the Gruyère cheese, and, if desired, hot pepper sauce.

3 Spread grits mixture evenly into a greased 2-quart square baking dish. Sprinkle with remaining ½ cup Gruyère cheese and the Parmesan cheese. Bake, uncovered, in a 350°F oven for 20 to 25 minutes or until heated through.

TO TOTE: Cover tightly. Transport in an insulated carrier.

Nutrition Facts per serving: 283 cal., 17 g total fat (8 g sat. fat), 46 mg chol., 334 mg sodium, 21 g carbo., 1 g fiber, 12 g pro.

In this family favorite, lean Canadian bacon, sliced potatoes, and leeks are baked with chicken broth and just a sprinkling of freshly grated Parmesan cheese.

POTATO GRATIN WITH CANADIAN BACON

PREP:

35 minutes

BAKE:

1 hour

OVEN:

425°F

MAKES:

8 servings

3	cups sliced leeks or thinly sliced onions
¼	cup butter
4	large baking potatoes (about 2½ pounds)
1	teaspoon dried thyme, crushed
½	teaspoon black pepper
1	pound sliced Canadian-style bacon, chopped
¼	cup chicken broth
½	cup shredded Parmesan cheese (2 ounces)

1 In a large skillet cook leeks in hot butter over medium heat until tender.

2 Meanwhile, thinly slice potatoes. Combine thyme and pepper. Arrange alternate layers of potatoes, thyme mixture, bacon, and cooked leeks in an ungreased 3-quart rectangular baking dish. Drizzle with broth.

3 Bake, covered, in a 425°F oven for 40 minutes. Uncover. Bake for 15 minutes more. Sprinkle with cheese and bake about 5 minutes more or until cheese is golden.

TO TOTE: Cover tightly. Transport in an insulated carrier.

Nutrition Facts per serving: 292 cal., 12 g total fat (5 g sat. fat), 48 mg chol., 974 mg sodium, 30 g carbo., 3 g fiber, 17 g pro.

This is a streamlined version of the classic Mexican dish, chiles rellenos. Filled with gooey cheese and mild peppers, it's a winner for dinner or brunch.

CASSEROLE-STYLE CHILES RELLENOS

4	large poblano chile peppers* or green sweet peppers (1 pound)
2	cups shredded Monterey Jack cheese with jalapeño peppers (8 ounces)
6	eggs
½	cup milk
⅔	cup all-purpose flour
1	teaspoon baking powder
½	teaspoon cayenne pepper
¼	teaspoon salt
1½	cups shredded cheddar cheese (6 ounces)
1	cup purchased picante sauce
½	cup dairy sour cream

PREP:
25 minutes

BAKE:
17 minutes

STAND:
5 minutes

OVEN:
450°F

MAKES:
8 servings

1 Quarter peppers and remove stems, seeds, and veins. Immerse peppers in boiling water for 3 minutes. Drain. Invert peppers onto paper towels to drain well. Place peppers, cut sides up, into a well-greased 3-quart square baking dish. Top with Monterey Jack cheese.

2 In a medium bowl whisk together eggs and milk. Add flour, baking powder, cayenne pepper, and salt. Whisk until smooth. Pour egg mixture over peppers and cheese in dish.

3 Bake, uncovered, in a 450°F oven for 15 to 20 minutes or until a knife inserted near the center comes out clean. Sprinkle with cheddar cheese. Bake for 2 to 3 minutes more or until cheese melts. Let stand for 5 minutes. Serve with picante sauce and sour cream.

*NOTE: Because hot chile peppers contain volatile oils that can burn your skin and eyes, avoid direct contact with chiles as much as possible. When working with chile peppers, wear plastic or rubber gloves. If your bare hands do touch the chile peppers, wash your hands well with soap and water.

TO TOTE: Do not let stand after baking. Cover tightly. Transport in an insulated carrier. Transport picante sauce and dairy sour cream in tightly covered containers in a separate insulated carrier.

Nutrition Facts per serving: 347 cal., 23 g total fat (13 g sat. fat), 212 mg chol., 706 mg sodium, 16 g carbo., 0 g fiber, 20 g pro.

Yukon gold potatoes and cheese give these potatoes their eye-popping color and down-home taste.

GOLDEN CHEESY POTATOES

PREP:
15 minutes
BAKE:
15 minutes
OVEN:
350°F
MAKES:
4 side-dish servings

2   pounds Yukon gold or other potatoes, peeled and cut up

¼   teaspoon salt

⅛   teaspoon black pepper

     Milk (optional)

½   cup whipping cream

⅓   cup shredded American or cheddar cheese (1½ ounces)

1 In a large saucepan cook potatoes, covered, in a large amount of boiling water for 15 to 20 minutes or until tender. Drain. Mash with a potato masher or beat with an electric mixer on low speed. Stir in salt and pepper. If necessary, add a small amount of milk to make potatoes desired consistency. Spoon mashed potatoes into a 1-quart casserole or four greased 10-ounce casseroles or custard cups. Set aside.

2 In a chilled medium mixing bowl beat whipping cream with chilled beaters of an electric mixer on medium speed until soft peaks form (tips curl); fold in cheese. Spoon cheese mixture over potatoes. Bake, uncovered, in a 350°F oven for 15 to 20 minutes or until slightly brown.

TO TOTE: Cover tightly. Transport in an insulated carrier.

Nutrition Facts per serving: 366 cal., 15 g total fat (9 g sat. fat), 52 mg chol., 340 mg sodium, 51 g carbo., 2 g fiber, 8 g pro.

Water chestnuts and chow mein noodles add a decidedly Chinese edge and crunch to green beans.

GOLDEN GREEN BEAN CRUNCH

1 16-ounce package frozen French-cut green beans

1 10¾-ounce can condensed golden mushroom soup

1 8-ounce can sliced water chestnuts, drained (optional)

1 cup chow mein noodles or ½ of a 2.8-ounce can french-fried onions (about ¾ cup)

1 Cook frozen beans according to package directions; drain well. In an ungreased 1½-quart casserole combine beans, soup, and, if desired, water chestnuts.

2 Bake, uncovered, in a 350°F oven about 25 minutes or until bubbly around edges. Sprinkle with noodles or onions. Bake about 5 minutes more or until heated through.

TO TOTE: Cover tightly. Transport in an insulated carrier.

Nutrition Facts per serving: 188 cal., 6 g total fat (1 g sat. fat), 3 mg chol., 719 mg sodium, 27 g carbo., 5 g fiber, 5 g pro.

PREP:

15 minutes

BAKE:

30 minutes

OVEN:

350°F

MAKES:

4 to 6 side-dish servings

*Prosciutto (proh-SHOO-toh) is a spicy, cured ham, originally made in Italy.
You can substitute cooked lean ham, if you like.*

PROSCIUTTO, SPINACH & PASTA CASSEROLE

PREP:

25 minutes

BAKE:

25 minutes

STAND:

5 minutes

OVEN:

350°F

MAKES:

6 servings

8	ounces packaged dried orecchiette, mostaccioli, or ziti pasta
2	medium onions, cut into thin wedges, or 5 medium leeks, sliced
2	cloves garlic, minced
1	tablespoon butter
¼	cup all-purpose flour
½	teaspoon anise seeds, crushed
1¾	cups milk
1½	cups chicken broth
¼	cup grated Parmesan cheese
1	10-ounce package frozen chopped spinach, thawed and drained well
2	ounces prosciutto, cut into thin bite-size strips
½	cup chopped seeded tomato (1 medium)

1 Cook pasta according to package directions; drain. Rinse with cold water; drain well.

2 In a large saucepan cook onions and garlic, covered, in hot butter over medium heat about 5 minutes or until onions are tender, stirring occasionally. Stir in flour and anise seeds. Add milk and broth all at once. Cook and stir until thickened and bubbly. Stir in Parmesan cheese. Stir in cooked pasta, spinach, and prosciutto. Transfer to an ungreased 2-quart casserole.

3 Bake, covered, in a 350°F oven for 25 to 30 minutes or until heated through. Let stand for 5 minutes before serving. To serve, stir gently and top with tomato.

TO TOTE: Do not let stand after baking. Cover tightly. Transport in an insulated carrier. Transport tomato separately in a self-sealing plastic bag. Top casserole with tomato just before serving.

Nutrition Facts per serving: 276 cal., 6 g total fat (3 g sat. fat), 21 mg chol., 667 mg sodium, 41 g carbo., 3 g fiber, 14 g pro.

POULTRY

8

Smoked chicken and cheese distinguish this creamy casserole. Frozen hash browns, croutons, and canned cream of chicken soup make preparation a snap.

SMOKY CHICKEN & CHEESY POTATO CASSEROLE

PREP:
20 minutes

BAKE:
40 minutes

OVEN:
350°F

MAKES:
6 servings

1   10¾-ounce can condensed cream of chicken
    with herbs soup

1   8-ounce carton dairy sour cream

1½ cups shredded smoked cheddar cheese (6 ounces)

1   28-ounce package loose-pack frozen diced hash brown
    potatoes with onion and peppers, thawed

1   pound smoked or roasted chicken or turkey,
    cut into bite-size strips (3 cups)

1   cup crushed croutons

1   tablespoon butter, melted

1 In a large bowl combine soup, sour cream, and cheese. Stir in frozen potatoes and chicken. Transfer to a lightly greased 3-quart rectangular baking dish. In a small bowl, combine crushed croutons and melted butter. Sprinkle over potato mixture in dish.

2 Bake, uncovered, in 350°F oven for 40 to 50 minutes or until mixture is heated through.

Nutrition Facts per serving: 461 cal., 24 g total fat (13 g sat. fat), 89 mg chol., 1,468 mg sodium, 36 g carbo., 3 g fiber, 27 g pro.

If you're short on time, you can substitute one folded refrigerated unbaked piecrust for the Pastry Topper. Just put the chicken mixture in a 2-quart round casserole and top with the piecrust. Flute, brush, and bake as the recipe directs.

DEEP-DISH CHICKEN PIE

1	recipe Pastry Topper
1	cup sliced leeks (3 medium) or 1 cup chopped onion (1 large)
1	cup sliced fresh mushrooms
¾	cup sliced celery (1½ stalks)
½	cup chopped red sweet pepper (1 small)
2	tablespoons butter
⅓	cup all-purpose flour
1	teaspoon poultry seasoning
¼	teaspoon salt
1½	cups chicken broth
1	cup half-and-half, light cream, or milk
2½	cups chopped cooked chicken (about 13 ounces)
1	cup frozen peas
1	beaten egg

PREP:
50 minutes
BAKE:
30 minutes
STAND:
20 minutes
OVEN:
400°F
MAKES:
6 servings

1 Prepare Pastry Topper; set aside. In a large saucepan cook leeks, mushrooms, celery, and sweet pepper in hot butter over medium heat for 4 to 5 minutes or until tender. Stir in flour, poultry seasoning, salt, and ¼ teaspoon *black pepper.* Add broth and half-and-half all at once. Cook and stir until thickened and bubbly. Stir in cooked chicken and frozen peas. Transfer to an ungreased 2-quart rectangular baking dish.

2 On a lightly floured surface, roll pastry into a 13×9-inch rectangle. Using a sharp knife, cut slits in pastry to allow steam to escape. If desired, use small cutters to cut shapes from pastry or use a fork to prick pastry; reserve cut-out shapes. Place rolled pastry on top of hot chicken mixture in dish. Turn pastry edges under; flute to the side of dish. Brush with beaten egg. If desired, top with reserved pastry shapes. Brush again with beaten egg.

3 Bake, uncovered, in a 400°F oven for 30 to 35 minutes or until crust is golden brown. Let stand about 20 minutes before serving.

PASTRY TOPPER: In a medium bowl combine 1¼ cups all-purpose flour and ¼ teaspoon salt. Using a pastry blender, cut in ⅓ cup shortening until pieces are the size of small peas. Sprinkle 1 tablespoon cold water over part of the mixture; gently toss with a fork. Push moistened dough to side of bowl. Sprinkle 3 to 4 tablespoons more cold water over remaining flour mixture, 1 tablespoon at a time, tossing with a fork until all dough is moistened. Form into a ball.

Nutrition Facts per serving: 471 cal., 26 g total fat (10 g sat. fat), 113 mg chol., 543 mg sodium, 33 g carbo., 3 g fiber, 26 g pro.

To add extra heat to this Mexican-inspired dish, use the hot and smoky jalapeño peppers.

CHICKEN & ORZO CASSEROLE

PREP:

15 minutes

BAKE:

20 minutes

STAND:

10 minutes

OVEN:

350°F

MAKES:

4 to 6 servings

2   teaspoons cumin seeds

1   14-ounce can chicken broth

1   14½-ounce can Mexican-style stewed tomatoes
or one 10-ounce can diced tomatoes and green
chile peppers, undrained

¼   cup oil-packed dried tomatoes, cut up

1   cup dried orzo pasta

2   9-ounce packages Southwest-flavored frozen cooked chicken
breast strips, thawed, or two 6-ounce packages refrigerated
Southwest-flavored cooked chicken breast strips

Seeded and chopped jalapeño or serrano chile peppers*
(optional)

Smoked paprika (optional)

1 Place cumin seeds in a large saucepan. Heat over medium heat for
3 to 4 minutes or until seeds are toasted and aromatic, shaking pan
occasionally. Carefully stir in broth, undrained tomatoes, dried tomatoes,
and uncooked orzo. Bring to boiling. Transfer to an ungreased 2-quart
baking dish. Top with chicken breast strips.

2 Bake, covered, in a 350°F oven about 20 minutes or until orzo is
tender. Let stand, covered, for 10 minutes before serving. If desired, top
with jalapeño peppers and smoked paprika.

*NOTE: Because hot chile peppers contain volatile oils that can burn your
skin and eyes, avoid direct contact with chiles as much as possible. When
working with chile peppers, wear plastic or rubber gloves. If your bare hands
do touch the chile peppers, wash your hands well with soap and water.

Nutrition Facts per serving: 388 cal., 7 g total fat (2 g sat. fat), 60 mg chol., 1,227 mg sodium,
44 g carbo., 3 g fiber, 35 g pro.

Next time your menu features grilled or broiled chicken breasts, cook a couple of extra breasts and make this hearty dish the next day.

DIJON-CHICKEN POTPIE

1½	cups loose-pack frozen broccoli, cauliflower, and carrots
1	11½-ounce package (8) refrigerated corn bread twists
1	1.8-ounce envelope white sauce mix
2	cups chopped cooked chicken breast (10 ounces)
2	tablespoons Dijon-style mustard
1	teaspoon instant chicken bouillon granules

1 Place frozen vegetables in a colander. Run hot water over vegetables just until thawed; drain well. Cut up any large pieces.

2 Meanwhile, unroll corn bread dough. Separate into 16 sticks. Set aside.

3 In a medium saucepan prepare white sauce mix according to package directions, except after mixture starts to boil, stir in vegetables, chicken, mustard, and bouillon granules. Return to boiling; reduce heat. Cook and stir for 1 minute more.

4 Transfer chicken mixture to an ungreased 2-quart rectangular baking dish. Arrange corn bread sticks in a single layer on top of chicken mixture.

5 Bake, uncovered, in a 375°F oven for 15 to 20 minutes or until corn bread sticks are golden.

Nutrition Facts per serving: 496 cal., 18 g total fat (6 g sat. fat), 50 mg chol., 1,875 mg sodium, 51 g carbo., 1 g fiber, 29 g pro.

PREP:
25 minutes
BAKE:
15 minutes
OVEN:
375°F
MAKES:
4 servings

Paella (pronounced pai-YAH-ah) is a Spanish specialty that usually marries meat and seafood in a saffron-infused rice. This easy version gets its flavor from a soup mix.

LAZY PAELLA

PREP:
25 minutes
BAKE:
45 minutes
STAND:
10 minutes
OVEN:
350°F
MAKES:
4 to 6 servings

2½ to 3 pounds chicken thighs, skinned

2 tablespoons cooking oil

1 14-ounce can chicken broth

1 cup uncooked long grain rice

1 cup frozen peas, thawed

1 cup cooked, peeled, and deveined medium shrimp

1 4-ounce can (drained weight) sliced mushrooms, drained

2 tablespoons dry onion soup mix

Salt

Black pepper

Paprika

1 In a large skillet brown chicken thighs in hot oil over medium heat, turning to brown evenly. In a large bowl combine broth, uncooked rice, peas, shrimp, mushrooms, and dry soup mix. Spread in a lightly greased 3-quart rectangular baking dish. Arrange chicken thighs on rice mixture. Sprinkle chicken lightly with salt, pepper, and paprika. Cover dish tightly with foil.

2 Bake in a 350°F oven about 45 minutes or until chicken is no longer pink (180°F). Let stand, covered, for 10 minutes before serving.

Nutrition Facts per serving: 500 cal., 12 g total fat (2 g sat. fat), 212 mg chol., 1,101 mg sodium, 47 g carbo., 3 g fiber, 49 g pro.

This recipe streamlines preparation by omitting the step of cooking the manicotti shells in boiling water. Instead, just spoon the filling into uncooked shells—they'll cook as they bake.

SHORTCUT CHICKEN MANICOTTI

1	egg
1	10-ounce package frozen chopped spinach, thawed and drained well
1	cup finely chopped cooked chicken or turkey (5 ounces)
½	cup ricotta cheese or cream-style cottage cheese, drained
½	cup grated Parmesan cheese
12	dried manicotti shells
1	10¾-ounce can condensed cream of chicken soup
1	8-ounce carton dairy sour cream
1	cup milk
½	teaspoon dried Italian seasoning, crushed
1	cup boiling water
1	cup shredded mozzarella cheese (4 ounces)
2	tablespoons snipped fresh parsley (optional)

PREP:
25 minutes
BAKE:
1 hour
STAND:
10 minutes
OVEN:
350°F
MAKES:
6 servings

1 For filling, in a medium bowl beat egg with a fork; stir in spinach, chicken, ricotta cheese, and Parmesan cheese. Gently spoon about ¼ cup of the filling into each uncooked manicotti shell. Arrange filled shells in an ungreased 3-quart rectangular baking dish, making sure shells do not touch each other.

2 For sauce, in another medium bowl combine soup, sour cream, milk, and Italian seasoning. Pour over manicotti shells, spreading to cover shells. Slowly pour boiling water around edge of baking dish. Cover dish tightly with foil.

3 Bake in a 350°F oven for 60 to 65 minutes or until manicotti shells are tender. Sprinkle with mozzarella cheese and, if desired, parsley. Let stand for 10 minutes before serving.

Nutrition Facts per serving: 463 cal., 23 g total fat (13 g sat. fat), 106 mg chol., 758 mg sodium, 35 g carbo., 3 g fiber, 27 g pro.

Serve this easy-to-make casserole with buttered peas, hearty dinner rolls, and a quick fruit salad.

CHEESY CHICKEN CASSEROLE

PREP:

20 minutes

BAKE:

45 minutes

STAND:

5 minutes

OVEN:

350°F

MAKES:

4 to 6 servings

8   ounces dried curly noodles (about 4 cups)

1   10¾-ounce can condensed cream of broccoli or
    cream of celery soup

1   cup milk

1   12-ounce carton (1½ cups) cream-style cottage cheese

2   cups chopped cooked chicken or turkey (10 ounces)

1   4-ounce can (drained weight) sliced mushrooms, drained

¾   cup shredded American or cheddar cheese (3 ounces)

1   teaspoon dried basil or thyme, crushed

1 Cook noodles according to package directions; drain. In a large bowl combine soup and milk. Stir in cooked noodles, cottage cheese, chicken, mushrooms, half of the American cheese, and the basil. Transfer to an ungreased 1½-quart casserole.

2 Bake, covered, in a 350°F oven for 45 to 50 minutes or until heated through. Uncover and sprinkle with remaining American cheese. Let stand about 5 minutes or until cheese is melted.

Nutrition Facts per serving: 613 cal., 23 g total fat (11 g sat. fat), 155 mg chol., 1,329 mg sodium, 53 g carbo., 3 g fiber, 47 g pro.

Chicken soup and long grain and wild rice mix give you a head start for this warming casserole.

CHICKEN & WILD RICE CASSEROLE

1	6-ounce package long grain and wild rice mix
½	cup chopped onion (1 medium)
½	cup chopped celery (1 stalk)
2	tablespoons butter
1	10¾-ounce can condensed chicken white and wild rice soup or cream of chicken soup
½	cup dairy sour cream
⅓	cup dry white wine or chicken broth
½	teaspoon dried basil, crushed
2	cups cubed cooked chicken or turkey (10 ounces)
⅓	cup shredded Parmesan cheese (1½ ounces)

PREP:
30 minutes
BAKE:
30 minutes
OVEN:
350°F
MAKES:
4 servings

1 Prepare rice mix according to package directions. Meanwhile, in a large skillet cook onion and celery in hot butter over medium heat until tender. Stir in soup, sour cream, wine, and basil. Stir in cooked rice mix and chicken. Transfer to an ungreased 2-quart rectangular baking dish.

2 Bake, uncovered, in a 350°F oven for 25 to 30 minutes or until heated through. Sprinkle with Parmesan cheese. Bake about 5 minutes more or until cheese is melted.

Nutrition Facts per serving: 479 cal., 20 g total fat (10 g sat. fat), 101 mg chol., 1,559 mg sodium, 42 g carbo., 2 g fiber, 30 g pro.

Here's a great-tasting one-dish meal. The chicken, rice, broccoli, and a savory soup-based sauce bake together for a true fix-and-forget favorite.

CHICKEN, BROCCOLI & RICE BAKE

PREP:

20 minutes

BAKE:

1 hour

STAND:

5 minutes

OVEN:

350°F

MAKES:

4 servings

1	10¾-ounce can condensed cream of broccoli or cream of chicken soup
½	cup dairy sour cream
½	cup milk
1	teaspoon dried basil, crushed
1	cup uncooked instant white rice
4	skinless, boneless chicken breast halves (about 1¼ pounds)
	Salt
	Black pepper
1	10-ounce package frozen broccoli spears, thawed
½	cup shredded Swiss cheese (2 ounces)

1 In a medium bowl combine soup, sour cream, milk, and basil. Set aside ½ cup of the soup mixture. Add uncooked rice to remaining soup mixture. Transfer to an ungreased 2-quart rectangular baking dish.

2 Sprinkle chicken lightly with salt and pepper. Arrange chicken and broccoli over rice mixture. Spoon reserved ½ cup soup mixture over top.

3 Bake, covered, in a 350°F oven for 60 to 70 minutes or until chicken is no longer pink (170°F) and broccoli is tender. Sprinkle with Swiss cheese. Let stand for 5 minutes before serving.

Nutrition Facts per serving: 452 cal., 16 g total fat (8 g sat. fat), 110 mg chol., 684 mg sodium, 32 g carbo., 3 g fiber, 44 g pro.

This version of the all-time favorite features cheese and sour cream for extra flavor and richness.

CHICKEN-NOODLE CASSEROLE

4	ounces dried medium noodles (2 cups)
1	cup sliced fresh mushrooms
1/2	cup chopped green or red sweet pepper (1 small)
3	tablespoons sliced green onions
2	tablespoons butter
2	cups chopped cooked chicken (10 ounces)
1	10¾-ounce can condensed cream of chicken or cream of broccoli soup
1	cup loose-pack frozen peas and carrots
1	cup shredded cheddar cheese (4 ounces)
1/2	cup dairy sour cream
1/8	teaspoon black pepper
1/3	cup fine dry bread crumbs
2	tablespoons grated Parmesan cheese
2	tablespoons butter, melted

PREP:
30 minutes
BAKE:
30 minutes
OVEN:
350°F
MAKES:
4 to 6 servings

1 Cook noodles according to package directions; drain. Set aside.

2 Meanwhile, in a large saucepan cook mushrooms, sweet pepper, and green onions in 2 tablespoons hot butter over medium heat until tender. Stir in chicken, soup, peas and carrots, cheddar cheese, sour cream, and black pepper. Bring to boiling over medium heat, stirring frequently. Gently fold in cooked noodles. Transfer to an ungreased 2-quart casserole.

3 In a small bowl combine bread crumbs, Parmesan cheese, and 2 tablespoons melted butter. Sprinkle crumb mixture over chicken mixture.

4 Bake, uncovered, in a 350°F oven for 30 to 35 minutes or until heated through and top is golden.

Nutrition Facts per serving: 659 cal., 40 g total fat (20 g sat. fat), 170 mg chol., 1,229 mg sodium, 38 g carbo., 3 g fiber, 38 g pro.

You'll love the make-ahead angle to this super-satisfying recipe. Assemble it in the morning or the night before. Then, when you get home after a hectic day, pop it into the oven and relax as it bakes!

SAUCY CHICKEN CASSEROLE

PREP:

20 minutes

CHILL:

3 to 24 hours

BAKE:

1 hour

OVEN:

375°F

MAKES:

6 servings

1	10¾-ounce can condensed cream of chicken soup
½	cup milk
1	tablespoon dried minced onion
¼	teaspoon dried basil or sage, crushed
⅛	teaspoon black pepper
4	1-ounce slices American cheese, torn into small pieces
1	9¾- or 10-ounce can chunk-style chicken, undrained
1	cup dried elbow macaroni
¼	cup chopped red sweet pepper or one 2-ounce jar sliced pimiento, drained

1 In an ungreased 1½-quart casserole combine soup, milk, dried onion, basil, and black pepper. Add cheese, undrained chicken, uncooked macaroni, and sweet pepper to soup mixture; mix well. Cover and chill for 3 to 24 hours.

2 Bake, covered, in a 375°F oven about 1 hour or until macaroni is tender, stirring once.

Nutrition Facts per serving: 265 cal., 12 g total fat (5 g sat. fat), 46 mg chol., 815 mg sodium, 22 g carbo., 1 g fiber, 19 g pro.

Reminiscent of dishes of years gone by, this biscuit-lined pie will no doubt become a new family favorite.

CREAMY TURKEY PIE

1   pound ground turkey sausage or ground raw turkey*

½   of an 8-ounce tub cream cheese with chive and onion

1   4½-ounce jar (drained weight) sliced mushrooms, drained

1   package (10) refrigerated biscuits

1   cup cream-style cottage cheese

1   egg

1   tablespoon all-purpose flour

    Chopped tomato (optional)

    Snipped fresh chives (optional)

PREP:
25 minutes
BAKE:
25 minutes
STAND:
10 minutes
OVEN:
350°F
MAKES:
6 servings

1 In a large skillet cook turkey sausage over medium heat until brown; drain. Stir in cream cheese until combined. Stir in mushrooms; set aside.

2 For the crust, unwrap and separate biscuits. Arrange biscuits in a lightly greased 9-inch pie plate; press onto bottom and up side of the plate, extending about ½ inch above the plate. With kitchen scissors, cut edges of biscuits at half-inch intervals. Spoon turkey mixture into the shell, spreading evenly.

3 In a blender or food processor combine cottage cheese, egg, and flour. Cover and blend or process until smooth. Pour over turkey mixture.

4 Bake, uncovered, in a 350°F oven for 25 to 30 minutes or until edges are brown and filling is set. Let stand for 10 minutes. If desired, garnish with tomato and chives.

*NOTE: **If using ground raw turkey, add ¼ teaspoon each salt and black pepper to the meat mixture.**

Nutrition Facts per serving: 382 cal., 22 g total fat (9 g sat. fat), 111 mg chol., 1,164 mg sodium, 26 g carbo., 0 g fiber, 22 g pro.

Serve this classic dish with warm rolls and a tossed salad. Fresh fruit makes a light, sweet dessert.

CREAMY CHICKEN & RICE BAKE

PREP:
20 minutes

BAKE:
50 minutes

OVEN:
375°F

MAKES:
4 servings

4   skinless, boneless chicken breast halves (about 1¼ pounds total)

1   tablespoon cooking oil

1   cup sliced fresh mushrooms

½   cup chopped onion (1 medium)

¼   cup chopped red sweet pepper

1   10¾-ounce can condensed cream of celery soup

1   cup milk

⅔   cup uncooked long grain rice

½   cup shredded carrot (1 medium)

½   teaspoon dried marjoram or oregano, crushed

⅛   teaspoon black pepper

1   cup frozen peas

   Salt

   Black pepper

1 In a large skillet cook chicken in hot oil over medium-high heat, turning to brown evenly. Remove chicken and set aside. Add mushrooms, onion, and sweet pepper to skillet; cook over medium heat just until vegetables are tender. Stir in soup, milk, uncooked rice, carrot, marjoram, and the ⅛ teaspoon black pepper. Bring mixture to boiling. Stir in peas.

2 Transfer mixture to a lightly greased 2-quart rectangular baking dish. Arrange chicken on top. Lightly sprinkle chicken with salt and black pepper. Cover tightly with foil.

3 Bake in a 375°F oven about 50 minutes or until chicken is no longer pink (170°F) and rice is tender.

Nutrition Facts per serving: 442 cal., 11 g total fat (3 g sat. fat), 90 mg chol., 805 mg sodium, 43 g carbo., 4 g fiber, 41 g pro.

In this Hungarian-style dish, chicken bakes on top of vegetables flavored with bacon and paprika. The tangy sour cream gravy adds richness and extraordinary flavor.

CHICKEN PAPRIKASH

4	cups dried medium noodles
3	slices bacon, chopped
1	cup chopped onion (1 large)
1	cup chopped carrots (2 medium)
1	cup chopped celery (2 stalks)
1	teaspoon paprika
½	teaspoon finely shredded lemon peel
¼	teaspoon salt
⅛	teaspoon black pepper
1	8-ounce carton dairy sour cream
⅓	cup all-purpose flour
1¾	cups milk
6	skinless, boneless chicken breast halves (2 to 2¼ pounds)
	Salt
	Black pepper
	Paprika

PREP:
30 minutes
BAKE:
35 minutes
OVEN:
375°F
MAKES:
6 servings

1 Cook noodles according to package directions; drain. Set aside. In a large skillet cook bacon over medium heat until crisp. Remove bacon with a slotted spoon, reserving drippings in skillet. Drain bacon on paper towels; set aside. In the same skillet cook onion, carrots, and celery in reserved drippings over medium heat for 5 minutes. Stir in the 1 teaspoon paprika, the lemon peel, the ¼ teaspoon salt, and the ⅛ teaspoon pepper.

2 Meanwhile in a medium bowl combine sour cream and flour until smooth. Gradually whisk in milk. Stir into vegetables in skillet; cook and stir until thickened and bubbly. Stir in cooked noodles and bacon.

3 Spoon vegetable mixture into an ungreased 3-quart rectangular baking dish. Arrange chicken on top of vegetable mixture. Sprinkle chicken lightly with salt, pepper, and additional paprika. Bake, uncovered, in a 375°F oven for 35 to 40 minutes or until chicken is no longer pink (170°F).

Nutrition Facts per serving: 493 cal., 19 g total fat (9 g sat. fat), 141 mg chol., 389 mg sodium, 33 g carbo., 2 g fiber, 45 g pro.

Andouille sausage, spicy Cajun seasoning, and luscious Alfredo sauce offer southern Louisiana flavor to this feed-a-crowd casserole.

CAJUN CHICKEN LASAGNA

PREP:

45 minutes

BAKE:

30 minutes

STAND:

15 minutes

OVEN:

350°F

MAKES:

6 servings

8	dried lasagna noodles (8 ounces)
8	ounces cooked andouille sausage or smoked pork sausage, quartered lengthwise and sliced
8	ounces skinless, boneless chicken breast halves, cut into ³⁄₄-inch pieces
1	to 1¹⁄₂ teaspoons Cajun seasoning
¹⁄₂	teaspoon dried sage, crushed
¹⁄₄	cup chopped onion
¹⁄₄	cup chopped celery
2	tablespoons chopped green sweet pepper
3	cloves garlic, minced
1	10-ounce container refrigerated Alfredo sauce
¹⁄₄	cup grated Parmesan cheese
³⁄₄	cup shredded mozzarella cheese (3 ounces)

1 Cook lasagna noodles according to package directions; drain. Rinse with cold water; drain well.

2 Meanwhile, in a medium bowl combine sausage, chicken, Cajun seasoning, and sage. In a large skillet cook and stir chicken mixture over medium-high heat about 8 minutes or until chicken is no longer pink. Using a slotted spoon, remove chicken mixture from skillet, reserving drippings in skillet. Set chicken mixture aside. In the same skillet cook onion, celery, sweet pepper, and garlic in reserved drippings over medium heat until vegetables are tender. Return chicken mixture to skillet; stir in half of the Alfredo sauce and the Parmesan cheese.

3 Place 2 of the lasagna noodles in the bottom of a lightly greased 2-quart square baking dish, cutting as necessary to fit. Spread with one-third of the chicken-vegetable mixture. Sprinkle with ¹⁄₄ cup of the mozzarella cheese. Repeat layers twice; top with remaining 2 noodles. Carefully spread remaining Alfredo sauce over all.

4 Bake, covered, in a 350°F oven for 30 to 35 minutes or until heated through. Let stand for 15 minutes before serving.

Nutrition Facts per serving: 507 cal., 31 g total fat (7 g sat. fat), 83 mg chol., 938 mg sodium, 27 g carbo., 1 g fiber, 29 g pro.

Easy to make—delicious to eat! Leftover chicken or turkey, succulent stuffing, and crunchy pecans make a satisfying supper. Just add your favorite vegetable to round out the meal.

CHICKEN & HERBED DRESSING CASSEROLE

3	cups sliced fresh mushrooms (8 ounces)
¾	cup sliced celery (1½ stalks)
¾	cup chopped onions (1½ medium)
¼	cup butter
2	teaspoons dried basil, crushed
¼	teaspoon black pepper
12	slices white or wheat bread, cut into ½-inch cubes (8 cups) and dried*
2	cups cubed cooked chicken or turkey (10 ounces)
1	to 1¼ cups chicken broth
½	cup chopped pecans

PREP:
30 minutes
BAKE:
50 minutes
STAND:
10 minutes
OVEN:
325°F
MAKES:
4 to 6 servings

1 In a large skillet cook mushrooms, celery, and onions in hot butter over medium heat for 5 minutes. Remove from heat; stir in basil and pepper. In a very large bowl combine mushroom mixture, bread cubes, and chicken. Add broth to moisten to desired consistency, tossing gently. Transfer to a lightly greased 2-quart casserole.

2 Bake, covered, in 325°F oven for 40 minutes. Uncover and sprinkle with nuts. Bake, uncovered, about 10 minutes more or until heated through. Let stand for 10 minutes before serving.

*NOTE: **To dry bread cubes, spread cubes in a 15×10×1-inch baking pan. Bake in a 300°F oven for 10 to 15 minutes or until bread cubes are dry, stirring once. Cool. (Bread cubes will continue to dry and crisp as they cool.) Or let bread cubes stand, loosely covered, at room temperature for 8 to 12 hours.**

Nutrition Facts per serving: 573 cal., 31 g total fat (9 g sat. fat), 95 mg chol., 924 mg sodium, 46 g carbo., 4 g fiber, 31 g pro.

A tried-and-true chicken and broccoli bake is a must for family gatherings. To tote, simply cover tightly and transport in an insulated carrier.

CREAMY CHICKEN-BROCCOLI BAKE

PREP:
30 minutes

BAKE:
45 minutes

OVEN:
350°F

MAKES:
6 servings

6   ounces dried medium noodles

Nonstick cooking spray

12   ounces skinless, boneless chicken breast halves, cut into bite-size pieces

1½   cups sliced fresh mushrooms (4 ounces)

½   cup sliced green onions (4)

½   cup chopped red sweet pepper

1   10¾-ounce can condensed cream of broccoli soup

1   8-ounce carton dairy sour cream

¼   cup chicken broth

1   teaspoon dry mustard

⅛   teaspoon black pepper

1   10-ounce package frozen chopped broccoli, thawed and drained

¼   cup fine dry bread crumbs

1   tablespoon butter, melted

1 Cook noodles according to package directions; drain. Rinse with cold water; drain well. Set aside. Meanwhile, coat a large skillet with nonstick cooking spray. Heat over medium heat. Add chicken to skillet. Cook and stir about 3 minutes or until chicken is no longer pink. Transfer chicken to a large bowl.

2 Add mushrooms, green onions, and sweet pepper to skillet. Cook and stir over medium heat until vegetables are tender. (If necessary, add 1 tablespoon cooking oil to skillet). Transfer vegetables to bowl with chicken. Stir in soup, sour cream, broth, mustard, and black pepper. Gently stir in cooked noodles and broccoli.

3 Transfer chicken mixture to a greased 2-quart square baking dish. Combine bread crumbs and melted butter; sprinkle over chicken mixture. Bake, covered, in a 350°F oven for 30 minutes. Uncover and bake about 15 minutes more or until heated through.

Nutrition Facts per serving: 352 cal., 15 g total fat (7 g sat. fat), 83 mg chol., 558 mg sodium, 33 g carbo., 3 g fiber, 22 g pro.

Patterned after a popular Texas recipe, this irresistible main dish includes cooked chicken layered with tortillas, a chile-sour cream sauce, and cheese.

LAYERED CHICKEN & CHILE CASSEROLE

1	tomatillo
½	cup chopped onion (1 medium)
2	teaspoons chili powder
1	clove garlic, minced
1	tablespoon cooking oil
1	10¾-ounce can condensed cream of chicken soup
1	4-ounce can diced green chile peppers, drained
1	4-ounce jar diced pimiento, drained
¼	cup dairy sour cream
6	6-inch corn tortillas, torn
1½	cups cubed cooked chicken (about 8 ounces)
1	cup shredded Monterey Jack cheese (4 ounces)
	Purchased salsa verde (optional)

PREP:
20 minutes

BAKE:
35 minutes

STAND:
10 minutes

OVEN:
350°F

MAKES:
6 servings

1 Remove and discard the thin, brown, papery husks from the tomatillo. Rinse tomatillo; finely chop (you should have about ¼ cup). For sauce, in a medium saucepan cook tomatillo, onion, chili powder, and garlic in hot oil over medium heat until vegetables are tender. Remove from heat; stir in soup, chile peppers, pimiento, and sour cream.

2 Spread ½ cup of the sauce into the bottom of an ungreased 2-quart square baking dish. Arrange 3 of the tortillas over the sauce. Layer with half of the chicken, half of the remaining sauce, and half of the Monterey Jack cheese. Repeat layers.

3 Bake, covered, in a 350°F oven for 35 to 40 minutes or until heated through. Let stand for 10 minutes before serving. If desired, serve with salsa verde.

Nutrition Facts per serving: 297 cal., 16 g total fat (7 g sat. fat), 55 mg chol., 663 mg sodium, 20 g carbo., 3 g fiber, 19 g pro.

With layers of tortilla strips, chicken, a creamy sauce, and cheddar cheese, this casserole will delight Mexican food fans.

MEXICAN-STYLE CHICKEN

PREP:

20 minutes

BAKE:

35 minutes

STAND:

10 minutes

OVEN:

350°F

MAKES:

4 servings

1	10¾-ounce can reduced-sodium condensed cream of chicken soup
½	of a 10-ounce can (½ cup) diced tomatoes with green chiles, undrained
⅓	cup chopped green sweet pepper
¼	cup chopped onion
¾	teaspoon chili powder
⅛	teaspoon black pepper
6	6-inch corn tortillas, cut into thin bite-size strips
1½	cups cubed cooked chicken (about 8 ounces)
1	cup shredded cheddar cheese (4 ounces)
	Tomato slices (optional)
	Sliced green onions (optional)

1 Combine soup, undrained tomatoes with chiles, sweet pepper, onion, chili powder, and black pepper; set aside.

2 To assemble, sprinkle about one-third of the tortilla strips over the bottom of an ungreased 2-quart square baking dish. Layer half of the chicken over tortilla strips; spoon half of soup mixture on top. Sprinkle half of the cheese and another one-third of the tortilla strips over the soup mixture. Layer with remaining chicken, soup mixture, and tortilla strips.

3 Bake, uncovered, in a 350°F oven about 35 minutes or until bubbly around edges and center is hot. Sprinkle with remaining cheese. Let stand for 10 minutes before serving. If desired, top with sliced tomatoes and green onions.

Nutrition Facts per serving: 380 cal., 16 g total fat (7 g sat. fat), 83 mg chol., 702 mg sodium, 33 g carbo., 2 g fiber, 27 g pro.

If you enjoy nachos with all the fixings, you'll love this no-fuss casserole.

NACHO TURKEY CASSEROLE

5	cups slightly crushed tortilla chips
4	cups cubed cooked turkey or chicken (about 1¼ pounds)
2	16-ounce jars salsa
1	10-ounce package frozen whole kernel corn
½	cup dairy sour cream
2	tablespoons all-purpose flour
1	cup shredded Monterey Jack cheese with jalapeño peppers or mozzarella cheese (4 ounces)

PREP:
15 minutes
BAKE:
30 minutes
OVEN:
350°F
MAKES:
8 servings

1 Place 3 cups of the tortilla chips in bottom of a lightly greased 3-quart rectangular baking dish. In a large bowl combine turkey, salsa, corn, sour cream, and flour; spoon over tortilla chips.

2 Bake, uncovered, in a 350°F oven for 25 minutes. Sprinkle with the remaining 2 cups tortilla chips and the cheese. Bake for 5 to 10 minutes more or until heated through.

Nutrition Facts per serving: 444 cal., 17 g total fat (7 g sat. fat), 74 mg chol., 1,127 mg sodium, 46 g carbo., 4 g fiber, 29 g pro.

Rice and vermicelli mix simplifies this crowd-pleaser. The supporting cast of ingredients, including chile peppers, chili powder, and cumin, contributes to the pleasing Tex-Mex flavor.

TEX-MEX CHICKEN 'N' RICE CASSEROLE

PREP:

20 minutes

BAKE:

25 minutes

STAND:

5 minutes

OVEN:

425°F

MAKES:

6 servings

½	cup chopped onion (1 medium)
1	tablespoon olive oil
1	6.9-ounce package chicken-flavored rice and vermicelli mix
1	14-ounce can chicken broth
2	cups water
2	cups chopped cooked chicken (10 ounces)
1	cup chopped seeded tomatoes (2 medium)
3	tablespoons canned diced green chile peppers, drained
1	teaspoon dried basil, crushed
1½	teaspoons chili powder
⅛	teaspoon ground cumin
⅛	teaspoon black pepper
½	cup shredded cheddar cheese (2 ounces)

1 In a medium saucepan cook onion in hot oil over medium heat until tender. Stir in rice and vermicelli mix (including seasoning package). Cook and stir for 2 minutes. Stir in broth and the water. Bring to boiling; reduce heat. Cover and simmer for 20 minutes (liquid will not be fully absorbed).

2 Transfer the rice mixture to a large bowl. Stir in chicken, tomatoes, chile peppers, basil, chili powder, cumin, and black pepper. Transfer to an ungreased 2-quart casserole.

3 Bake, covered, in a 425°F oven for 25 minutes. Sprinkle with cheese. Let stand for 5 minutes before serving.

MAKE-AHEAD DIRECTIONS: Assemble as directed. Cover and chill unbaked casserole up to 24 hours. Bake, covered, in a 425°F oven about 40 minutes or until heated through. Uncover and sprinkle with cheese. Let stand for 5 minutes before serving.

Nutrition Facts per serving: 323 cal., 14 g total fat (4 g sat. fat), 53 mg chol., 971 mg sodium, 30 g carbo., 2 g fiber, 21 g pro.

Who can resist potpie, the ultimate in home cooking?
Dried tomatoes update the flavor of this classic.

TOMATO-MUSHROOM CHICKEN POTPIE

1	recipe Potpie Pastry
1	cup chopped onion (1 large)
2	tablespoons butter or margarine
3	cups sliced fresh mushrooms (8 ounces)
¼	cup all-purpose flour
½	teaspoon dried oregano, crushed
¼	teaspoon black pepper
1½	cups chicken broth
2	cups chopped cooked chicken (10 ounces)
½	of a 14½-ounce can (¾ cup) diced tomatoes, drained
⅓	cup sliced oil-packed dried tomatoes, drained
1	teaspoon milk
1	tablespoon grated Parmesan cheese

PREP:
45 minutes
BAKE:
25 minutes
STAND:
15 minutes
OVEN:
425°F
MAKES:
6 servings

1 Prepare Pot Pie Pastry; set aside.

2 In a large skillet cook onion in hot butter over medium heat for 2 minutes. Add mushrooms; cook for 3 to 4 minutes more or until tender. Stir in flour, oregano, and pepper. Add broth all at once. Cook and stir until thickened and bubbly. Add chicken and tomatoes; heat through. Transfer to an ungreased 1½-quart casserole.

3 On a lightly floured surface, roll pastry into a 9-inch circle. If desired, use small cutters to cut shapes from pastry or use a fork to prick pastry. Place rolled pastry on top of chicken mixture in casserole; trim to ½ inch beyond rim of casserole. Turn pastry edges under and flute to the side of casserole. Brush with milk. If desired, top with cutouts. Brush again with milk. Sprinkle with Parmesan cheese.

4 Place casserole on a baking sheet. Bake, uncovered, in a 425°F oven about 25 minutes or until golden. Let stand for 15 minutes before serving.

POTPIE PASTRY: In a bowl combine 2 cups all-purpose flour, 2 tablespoons yellow cornmeal, 2 tablespoons grated Parmesan cheese, and ½ teaspoon salt. Cut in ⅔ cup shortening until pieces are the size of small peas. Sprinkle 1 tablespoon cold water over part of the mixture; gently toss with a fork. Push moistened dough to side of bowl. Repeat with 5 to 7 tablespoons more cold water over remaining flour mixture, 1 tablespoon at a time, tossing with a fork until all dough is moistened. Form into a ball.

Nutrition Facts per serving: 557 cal., 34 g total fat (9 g sat. fat), 56 mg chol., 623 mg sodium, 43 g carbo., 3 g fiber, 22 g pro.

This cheesy, yet healthful lasagna is bound to become a family favorite. It's full of spinach, tomatoes, and carrots, and best of all—it's an intriguing twist on typical pasta fare.

VEGETABLE CHICKEN LASAGNA

PREP:

45 minutes

BAKE:

40 minutes

STAND:

10 minutes

OVEN:

350°F

MAKES:

8 to 10 servings

1	15-ounce carton ricotta cheese
1	10-ounce package frozen chopped spinach, thawed and drained well
1	slightly beaten egg
2	teaspoons dried Italian seasoning, crushed
1	pound skinless, boneless chicken breast halves, cut into $\frac{1}{2}$-inch pieces
3	cups sliced fresh mushrooms (8 ounces)
$\frac{1}{2}$	cup chopped onion (1 medium)
1	tablespoon olive oil
2	$14\frac{1}{2}$-ounce cans diced tomatoes, undrained
1	8-ounce can tomato sauce
2	cups shredded carrots (4 medium)
$\frac{1}{2}$	teaspoon black pepper
9	dried lasagna noodles
2	cups shredded mozzarella cheese (8 ounces)

1 For cheese filling, in a medium bowl combine ricotta cheese, spinach, egg, and 1 teaspoon of the Italian seasoning. Cover and chill until ready to assemble lasagna.

2 For sauce, in a large skillet cook chicken, mushrooms, onion, and the remaining 1 teaspoon Italian seasoning in hot oil over medium-high heat for 4 to 5 minutes or until chicken is no longer pink. Stir in undrained tomatoes, the tomato sauce, carrots, and pepper. Bring to boiling; reduce heat. Simmer, uncovered, about 15 minutes or until mixture is slightly thickened, stirring occasionally.

3 Meanwhile, cook lasagna noodles according to package directions; drain. Rinse with cold water; drain well.

4 Place 3 of the lasagna noodles in a lightly greased 3-quart rectangular baking dish. Spread half of the ricotta cheese mixture over the noodles. Spread one-third of the chicken mixture on top. Sprinkle with $\frac{1}{2}$ cup of the mozzarella cheese. Repeat layers. Top with remaining 3 noodles and remaining chicken mixture. Sprinkle with remaining 1 cup mozzarella cheese.

5 Bake, covered, in a 350°F oven for 35 minutes. Uncover and bake for 5 to 10 minutes more or until cheese is bubbly. Let stand for 10 minutes before serving.

Nutrition Facts per serving: 400 cal., 16 g total fat (8 g sat. fat), 102 mg chol., 552 mg sodium, 31 g carbo., 4 g fiber, 33 g pro.

These chicken-and-cheese-filled rolls fall somewhere between lasagna and stuffed manicotti. Warm crusty bread and steamed asparagus complete the meal.

CHEESY CHICKEN BUNDLES

8   dried lasagna noodles

1   15-ounce carton ricotta cheese

1½ cups finely chopped cooked chicken (about 8 ounces)

1   beaten egg

½   teaspoon dried basil, crushed

2   tablespoons butter

2   tablespoons all-purpose flour

½   teaspoon dry mustard

¼   teaspoon salt

⅛   teaspoon black pepper

1½ cups milk

1½ cups shredded process Swiss cheese (6 ounces)

PREP:
30 minutes

BAKE:
30 minutes

STAND:
10 minutes

OVEN:
375°F

MAKES:
8 servings

1 Cook lasagna noodles according to package directions; drain. Rinse with cold water; drain well. For filling, in a medium bowl combine ricotta cheese, chicken, egg, and basil.

2 Spread about ⅓ cup of the filling over each lasagna noodle. Roll up noodles and place bundles, seam sides down, into an ungreased 2-quart rectangular baking dish. Set aside.

3 For sauce, in a medium saucepan melt butter over medium heat. Stir in flour, mustard, salt, and pepper. Add milk all at once. Cook and stir until thickened and bubbly. Gradually add cheese, stirring until melted after each addition. Pour sauce over bundles. Cover dish with foil.

4 Bake in a 375°F oven for 30 to 35 minutes or until heated through. Let stand for 10 minutes. Spoon sauce over each roll when serving.

Nutrition Facts per serving: 369 cal., 19 g total fat (10 g sat. fat), 106 mg chol., 522 mg sodium, 25 g carbo., 1 g fiber, 24 g pro.

With just a few flavorful touches, including toasted almonds, rich Parmesan cheese, and a little ham, this quick chicken-and-rice casserole becomes a dinnertime event worth repeating.

PARMESAN CHICKEN & BROCCOLI

PREP:

25 minutes

BAKE:

25 minutes

OVEN:

350°F

MAKES:

6 servings

1	cup uncooked parboiled (converted) rice
½	cup sliced green onions (4)
1¼	pounds skinless, boneless chicken breast halves, cut into strips
1	tablespoon cooking oil
1	teaspoon dried Italian seasoning, crushed
2	cloves garlic, minced
4	teaspoons cornstarch
2¾	cups milk
½	of an 8-ounce package cream cheese, cut up
1½	cups loose-pack frozen cut broccoli
½	cup grated Parmesan cheese
⅓	cup diced fully cooked ham (2 ounces)
2	tablespoons sliced almonds, toasted

1 Cook rice according to package directions; remove from heat and stir in ¼ cup of the green onions. Transfer to a greased 2-quart rectangular baking dish, spreading evenly. Set aside.

2 In a large skillet cook half the chicken strips in hot oil over medium heat about 6 minutes or until chicken is no longer pink. Remove from skillet. Add remaining chicken strips, the Italian seasoning, and garlic to the pan. Cook about 6 minutes or until chicken is no longer pink. Remove from skillet; reserve drippings.

3 Cook remaining ¼ cup green onions in reserved drippings in skillet over medium heat until tender, adding more oil as necessary. Stir in cornstarch. Add milk all at once. Cook and stir until slightly thickened and bubbly. Reduce heat; stir in cream cheese until nearly smooth. Remove sauce from heat; stir in chicken, broccoli, Parmesan cheese, and ham. Spoon over rice in baking dish; sprinkle with *salt* and *black pepper*.

4 Bake, covered, in a 350°F oven for 25 to 30 minutes or until heated through. Sprinkle with almonds.

MAKE-AHEAD DIRECTIONS: Assemble as directed. Cover unbaked casserole with heavy foil; seal, label, and freeze for up to 3 months. Thaw covered frozen casserole in the refrigerator overnight (casserole may still be icy). Bake casserole, covered, in a 350°F oven for 1 hour. Uncover. Bake for 20 to 25 minutes more or until heated through. Sprinkle with almonds.

Nutrition Facts per serving: 455 cal., 17 g total fat (8 g sat. fat), 95 mg chol., 448 mg sodium, 37 g carbo., 3 g fiber, 37 g pro.

An adaptation of Spanish paella, this dish features meaty chicken thighs instead of seafood.

CARIBBEAN CHICKEN & RICE CASSEROLE

4	skinless, boneless chicken thighs (about 12 ounces)
2	tablespoons cooking oil
¾	cup chopped green sweet pepper (1 medium)
½	cup chopped onion (1 medium)
1	10-ounce package Spanish yellow rice mix
2½	cups water
1	cup frozen peas
½	cup diced cooked ham (2½ ounces)
½	cup sliced pimiento-stuffed green olives (optional)

PREP:
25 minutes
BAKE:
35 minutes
OVEN:
350°F
MAKES:
4 servings

1 In a large skillet cook chicken in hot oil over medium-high heat about 5 minutes, turning once. Remove chicken from skillet. Add sweet pepper and onion to drippings in skillet. Cook and stir for 3 to 5 minutes or until tender. Stir in the rice mix and the water (or the amount of water recommended in the package directions); bring to boiling. Carefully transfer to an ungreased 2-quart casserole. Arrange chicken on top.

2 Bake, covered, in a 350°F oven about 25 minutes or until most of the liquid is absorbed. Remove from oven and stir in peas, ham, and, if desired, green olives. Bake, covered, about 10 minutes more or until heated through.

Nutrition Facts per serving: 476 cal., 13 g total fat (2 g sat. fat), 78 mg chol., 1,334 mg sodium, 63 g carbo., 5 g fiber, 27 g pro.

Proscuitto and capers bring a gourmet touch to this dish that's based on two refrigerated pasta sauces. You can find proscuitto in Italian specialty markets or at deli counters.

CHICKEN & PROSCIUTTO PASTA

PREP:

30 minutes

BAKE:

25 minutes

OVEN:

350°F

MAKES:

6 servings

6	ounces dried penne pasta (about 3 cups)
1	tablespoon olive oil
12	ounces skinless, boneless chicken breast halves, cut into 1/2-inch-wide strips
2	cloves garlic, minced
1	cup coarsely chopped sliced prosciutto or ham (5 ounces)
1/2	of a medium green sweet pepper, cut into bite-size strips
1/2	of a medium yellow sweet pepper, cut into bite-size strips
1	teaspoon dried basil, crushed
1	tablespoon capers, drained (optional)
1	15-ounce container refrigerated marinara sauce
1	10-ounce container refrigerated Alfredo sauce
1/3	cup shredded Parmesan cheese (1 1/2 ounces)

1 Cook penne according to package directions; drain. Return penne to pan; set aside.

2 Meanwhile, in large skillet heat oil over medium-high heat. Add chicken and garlic; cook and stir for 2 minutes. Add prosciutto, sweet pepper strips, basil, and capers (if desired). Cook and stir for 2 to 3 minutes longer or until chicken is no longer pink and peppers are crisp-tender. Add to penne in saucepan; mix well.

3 Spread half of the penne mixture into a greased 2-quart casserole. Top with 1 cup of the marinara sauce. Top with the remaining penne mixture; add Alfredo sauce. Drizzle with remaining marinara sauce. Sprinkle with Parmesan cheese.

4 Bake, uncovered, in a 350°F oven for 25 to 35 minutes or until heated through.

Nutrition Facts per serving: 540 cal., 29 g total fat (6 g sat. fat), 91 mg chol., 1,445 mg sodium, 31 g carbo., 1 g fiber, 37 g pro.

Elegant additions, like white wine, tarragon, shallots, and a golden-brown pastry that magically puffs as it cooks, raise a humble potpie to new gourmet heights.

CHICKEN POTPIE IN PUFF PASTRY

1	sheet frozen puff pastry (½ of a 17¼-ounce package)
2	tablespoons butter
12	ounces skinless, boneless chicken breast halves, cut into ¾-inch pieces
¼	cup chopped red sweet pepper (optional)
2	medium shallots, thinly sliced
2	tablespoons all-purpose flour
¾	teaspoon salt
½	teaspoon dried tarragon, crushed
¼	teaspoon black pepper
1¼	cups milk
⅓	cup dry white wine or chicken broth
½	cup frozen peas

PREP:
30 minutes
BAKE:
20 minutes
OVEN:
425°F
MAKES:
4 servings

1 Thaw puff pastry according to package directions. Meanwhile, in a large skillet melt butter over medium-high heat. Add chicken, sweet pepper (if using), and shallots. Cook for 4 to 5 minutes or until chicken is no longer pink, stirring frequently. Stir in flour, salt, tarragon, and black pepper. Add milk all at once. Cook and stir until thickened and bubbly. Stir in wine and peas; heat through. Keep warm while preparing topper.

2 For topper, unfold and roll puff pastry sheet into an 11-inch square. Cut out a 10-inch circle from pastry.* Transfer the hot chicken mixture to a 1½-quart casserole. Place pastry over the hot chicken mixture in casserole. Turn edges of pastry under; flute to the edges of casserole. Cut slits in pastry to allow steam to escape.

3 Bake in a 425°F oven for 20 to 25 minutes or until crust is puffed and golden brown.

*NOTE: Scraps of puff pastry may be trimmed into cutout shapes or discarded. If using cutouts, moisten with a little water and place on top of pastry before baking.

Nutrition Facts per serving: 504 cal., 28 g total fat (4 g sat. fat), 72 mg chol., 825 mg sodium, 32 g carbo., 1 g fiber, 26 g pro.

Chipotle chile peppers are smoked jalapeño peppers. Look for canned chipotles in adobo sauce in the ethnic food aisle of your supermarket or at Hispanic food stores.

CHIPOTLE-CHICKEN CASSEROLE

PREP:

20 minutes

BAKE:

20 minutes

OVEN:

375°F

MAKES:

4 servings

Nonstick cooking spray

3　cups loose-pack frozen diced hash brown potatoes

2　cups frozen or fresh whole kernel corn

1　14½-ounce can diced tomatoes with basil, garlic, and oregano, undrained

1　to 2 chipotle peppers in adobo sauce, chopped*

½　teaspoon chili powder

½　teaspoon ground cumin

½　teaspoon dried oregano, crushed

4　skinless, boneless chicken breast halves (about 1¼ pounds total)

¼　teaspoon salt

¼　teaspoon chili powder

¼　teaspoon ground cumin

1　tablespoon olive oil

¾　cup shredded Monterey Jack cheese (3 ounces)

1 Coat a large nonstick skillet with cooking spray. Heat skillet over medium-high heat. Add potatoes and corn; cook and stir for 5 to 8 minutes or until vegetables begin to brown. Stir in undrained tomatoes, the chipotle peppers, the ½ teaspoon chili powder, the ½ teaspoon cumin, and the oregano. Remove from heat. Transfer to a greased 2-quart casserole; set aside.

2 Sprinkle chicken evenly with salt, the ¼ teaspoon chili powder, and the ¼ teaspoon cumin. Wipe skillet clean. In skillet cook chicken in hot oil over medium-high heat about 6 minutes, turning once. Place chicken on top of potato mixture in casserole.

3 Bake, uncovered, in a 375°F oven for 20 to 25 minutes or until bubbly and chicken is no longer pink (170°F). Sprinkle with cheese. Serve with a slotted spoon.

*NOTE: Because hot chile peppers contain volatile oils that can burn your skin and eyes, avoid direct contact with chiles as much as possible. When working with chile peppers, wear plastic or rubber gloves. If your bare hands do touch the chile peppers, wash your hands well with soap and water.

Nutrition Facts per serving: 460 cal., 15 g total fat (6 g sat. fat), 79 mg chol., 939 mg sodium, 50 g carbo., 4 g fiber, 33 g pro.

Quinoa (pronounced KEEN-wah) is a staple of the South American diet because of its high protein content. It cooks like rice but has a light nutty flavor that is similar to couscous.

CHICKEN SAUSAGE & QUINOA CASSEROLE

3	cups sliced fresh mushrooms
½	cup chopped onion (1 medium)
2	tablespoons butter
1½	pounds cooked chicken sausage links (about 10 links) or smoked turkey sausage
3	cups cooked quinoa*
1	10¾-ounce can condensed cream of chicken soup with herbs
1	cup milk
1½	cups shredded Monterey Jack cheese (6 ounces)

PREP:
30 minutes
BAKE:
1 hour 5 minutes
OVEN:
350°F
MAKES:
8 servings

1 In a large skillet cook mushrooms and onion in hot butter over medium heat for 5 minutes or until onion is tender. Meanwhile, slice sausage into ½-inch-thick pieces. In a very large bowl combine sausage, mushroom mixture, quinoa, soup, milk, and ¾ cup of the cheese. Transfer to an ungreased 3-quart casserole.

2 Bake, covered, in a 350°F oven for 1 hour. Sprinkle with remaining ¾ cup cheese. Bake, uncovered, for 5 to 10 minutes more or until mixture is heated through.

***NOTE:** For 3 cups cooked quinoa, rinse 1 cup uncooked quinoa well under cold water; drain. In a medium saucepan combine rinsed quinoa, 2 cups water, and ½ teaspoon salt. Bring to boiling; reduce heat. Cover and simmer about 15 minutes or until quinoa is tender. Drain, if necessary.*

Nutrition Facts per serving: 391 cal., 25 g total fat (10 g sat. fat), 55 mg chol., 999 mg sodium, 21 g carbo., 2 g fiber, 23 g pro.

To keep the sodium in check, opt for a salt-free Cajun seasoning.

CAJUN CHICKEN PASTA

PREP:

50 minutes

BAKE:

25 minutes

OVEN:

350°F

MAKES:

8 to 10 servings

1	pound dried bow tie or rotini pasta
1½	pounds skinless, boneless chicken breast halves, cut into 2-inch pieces
2	tablespoons all-purpose flour
2	tablespoons salt-free Cajun seasoning
1	tablespoon cooking oil
2	cups whipping cream
2	cups shredded cheddar and Monterey Jack cheese blend (8 ounces)
½	teaspoon salt
3	cups seeded, diced tomatoes (6 medium)
¼	cup sliced green onions (2)
	Bottled hot pepper sauce (optional)

1 Cook bow tie pasta according to package directions; drain. Place in a very large bowl; set aside.

2 Place chicken, flour, and 1 tablespoon of the Cajun seasoning in a large self-sealing plastic bag; seal and toss to coat. Heat oil in a large skillet over medium-high heat. Add chicken; cook and stir until chicken is no longer pink. Place in bowl with bow tie pasta.

3 For sauce, bring cream just to boiling in a medium saucepan over medium heat, stirring occasionally. Remove from heat. Whisk in 1 cup of the cheese, the remaining 1 tablespoon Cajun seasoning, and the salt until cheese is melted and mixture is smooth.

4 Add sauce, tomatoes, and the remaining 1 cup cheese to bowl with chicken and bow tie pasta; toss to combine. Transfer to a greased 3-quart rectangular baking dish.

5 Cover and bake in a 350°F oven for 25 to 30 minutes or until mixture is heated through. Sprinkle with green onions before serving. If desired, serve with hot pepper sauce.

MAKE-AHEAD DIRECTIONS: Assemble as directed. Cover unbaked casserole with plastic wrap, then foil, and chill up to 24 hours. Remove plastic wrap. Bake, covered with foil, in a 350°F oven for 35 to 40 minutes or until mixture is heated through.

Nutrition Facts per serving: 656 cal., 37 g total fat (21 g sat. fat), 207 mg chol., 395 mg sodium, 47 g carbo., 2 g fiber, 34 g pro.

This dinner party favorite features chicken breasts stuffed with crab, laced with a wine sauce, and finished with a sheen of rich Swiss cheese.

CRAB-STUFFED CHICKEN

8	skinless, boneless chicken breast halves (about 2½ pounds total)
3	tablespoons butter
¼	cup all-purpose flour
¾	cup milk
¾	cup chicken broth
⅓	cup dry white wine
1	cup chopped fresh mushrooms
¼	cup chopped onion
1	tablespoon butter
1	6¼-ounce can crabmeat, drained, flaked, and cartilage removed
½	cup coarsely crushed saltine crackers (10 crackers)
2	teaspoons dried parsley flakes, crushed
2	tablespoons butter
1	cup shredded Swiss cheese (4 ounces)
½	teaspoon paprika

PREP:
45 minutes
BAKE:
37 minutes
OVEN:
350°F
MAKES:
8 servings

1 Place a chicken breast half between 2 pieces of plastic wrap. Using the flat side of a meat mallet and working from the center out, pound meat lightly into a rectangle about ⅛ inch thick. Remove plastic wrap. Repeat with remaining chicken. Set aside. For sauce, in a medium saucepan melt the 3 tablespoons butter over medium heat; stir in flour. Add milk, broth, and wine all at once. Cook and stir until thickened and bubbly. Set aside.

2 In a medium skillet cook mushrooms and onion in the 1 tablespoon butter over medium heat until tender but not brown. Stir in crabmeat, cracker crumbs, parsley, ½ teaspoon *salt,* and dash *black pepper.* Stir in 2 tablespoons of the sauce. Top each chicken piece with about ¼ cup of the mixture. Fold in sides; roll up. Secure with wooden toothpicks, if necessary. In a large skillet cook the chicken rolls, half at a time, in the 2 tablespoons hot butter over medium heat until brown on all sides. Place chicken rolls, seam sides down, in an ungreased 3-quart rectangular baking dish. Pour remaining sauce over rolls.

3 Bake, covered, in a 350°F oven about 35 minutes or until chicken is no longer pink (170°F). Sprinkle with Swiss cheese and paprika. Bake, uncovered, about 2 minutes more or until cheese is melted. Transfer chicken to a platter. Whisk mixture in baking dish and pass with chicken.

Nutrition Facts per serving: 371 cal., 17 g total fat (8 g sat. fat), 141 mg chol., 541 mg sodium, 8 g carbo., 0 g fiber, 43 g pro.

Arroz con Pollo means "chicken with rice." Traditionally it is made with rice, chicken, tomatoes, sweet pepper, and saffron as is this casserole version.

ARROZ CON POLLO

PREP:
40 minutes
BAKE:
40 minutes
OVEN:
350°F
MAKES:
4 to 6 servings

2½ to 3 pounds meaty chicken pieces (breasts, thighs, and drumsticks)
Salt
Black pepper
2 tablespoons olive oil or cooking oil
¾ cup coarsely chopped green sweet pepper (1 medium)
½ cup chopped onion (1 medium)
3 cloves garlic, minced
1 cup coarsely chopped tomatoes (2 medium)
1 14-ounce can chicken broth
¼ cup dry white wine
2 tablespoons tomato paste
½ teaspoon salt
¼ teaspoon thread saffron or ground turmeric
⅛ teaspoon black pepper
1 cup uncooked long grain rice
1 cup frozen peas

1 Skin chicken. Sprinkle chicken lightly with salt and black pepper. In a large skillet cook chicken in hot oil over medium heat about 10 minutes or until brown, turning to brown evenly. Remove chicken; set aside.

2 Add sweet pepper, onion, and garlic to skillet; cook about 3 minutes or until vegetables are tender. Stir in tomatoes, broth, wine, tomato paste, the ½ teaspoon salt, the saffron, and the ⅛ teaspoon black pepper. Bring to boiling. Stir in rice and peas; return to boiling. Transfer to an ungreased 3-quart casserole; top with chicken.

3 Bake, covered, in a 350°F oven for 40 to 50 minutes or until rice is tender and chicken is no longer pink (170°F for breasts; 180°F for thighs and drumsticks).

Nutrition Facts per serving: 549 cal., 17 g total fat (4 g sat. fat), 116 mg chol., 926 mg sodium, 51 g carbo., 4 g fiber, 45 g pro.

Adding barley to everyone's favorite chicken gives this meal out-of-the-ordinary taste and texture.

CHICKEN & BARLEY BAKE

1	cup water
1	cup chopped onion (1 large)
¾	cup chopped carrots (2 small)
½	cup uncooked pearl barley
1½	teaspoons instant chicken bouillon granules
1	teaspoon dried parsley flakes, crushed
1	clove garlic, minced
½	teaspoon poultry seasoning
1	to 1¼ pounds chicken thighs, skinned
	Salt
	Black pepper

PREP:

20 minutes

BAKE:

30 minutes

OVEN:

350°F

MAKES:

4 servings

1 In a medium saucepan combine the water, onion, carrots, barley, bouillon granules, parsley, garlic, and poultry seasoning. Bring to boiling; reduce heat. Cover and simmer for 10 minutes.

2 Transfer hot barley mixture to an ungreased 2-quart square baking dish. Place chicken on top of barley mixture. Sprinkle chicken with salt and pepper.

3 Bake, covered, in a 350°F oven for 30 to 35 minutes or until barley is tender and chicken is no longer pink (180°F).

Nutrition Facts per serving: 192 cal., 3 g total fat (1 g sat. fat), 57 mg chol., 434 mg sodium, 24 g carbo., 5 g fiber, 17 g pro.

Tangy-tart cranberry sauce lends new dimension to this captivating casserole.

CRANBERRY SWEET & SOUR CHICKEN

PREP:

20 minutes

BAKE:

35 minutes

OVEN:

350°F

MAKES:

4 to 6 servings

4 cups shredded cooked chicken (about 1¼ pounds)

1 8-ounce can pineapple chunks (juice pack)

1 medium green sweet pepper, cut into bite-size strips

1 medium red sweet pepper, cut into bite-size strips

2 cups cooked white rice

2 tablespoons cornstarch

2 tablespoons packed brown sugar

1 16-ounce can whole cranberry sauce

3 tablespoons frozen orange juice concentrate, thawed

3 tablespoons rice vinegar or cider vinegar

2 tablespoons dry sherry or water

2 tablespoons soy sauce

½ teaspoon ground ginger

¼ cup slivered almonds

1 Place chicken in a large bowl. Drain pineapple well, reserving juice (you should have ⅓ cup juice). Add pineapple, sweet pepper strips, and rice to the chicken; set aside.

2 In a small saucepan combine cornstarch and brown sugar; add reserved pineapple juice, the cranberry sauce, orange juice concentrate, vinegar, sherry, soy sauce, and ginger. Cook and stir over medium heat until thickened and bubbly. Add to chicken mixture; stir to coat. Transfer to an ungreased 2-quart square baking dish.

3 Bake, covered, in a 350°F oven for 30 minutes. Sprinkle with almonds. Bake, uncovered, for 5 minutes more.

Nutrition Facts per serving: 727 cal., 15 g total fat (3 g sat. fat), 125 mg chol., 608 mg sodium, 96 g carbo., 5 g fiber, 46 g pro.

The tomatillos in this dish add a flavor that is reminiscent of a mix of lemon, apples, and herbs. To choose excellent tomatillos, look for fruit with dry, tight-fitting husks. You can store them in a brown paper bag for up to a month before using.

SOUTHWEST CHICKEN & TOMATILLOS

1	cup chopped onion (1 medium)
1	cup chopped red sweet pepper (1 large)
2	tomatillos, husks removed, rinsed, and finely chopped (about ½ cup)
2	tablespoons cooking oil
1	4½-ounce can diced green chile peppers, drained
2	tablespoons finely chopped, seeded jalapeño peppers* (about 2 peppers)
¼	cup butter
¼	cup all-purpose flour
4	teaspoons chili powder
¼	teaspoon salt
2	cups chicken broth
1	8-ounce carton dairy sour cream
10	6-inch tostada shells, coarsely broken
3	cups chopped cooked chicken (about 1 pound)
2	cups crumbled white Mexican cheese (queso fresco) or shredded Monterey Jack cheese (8 ounces)

PREP:
30 minutes

BAKE:
35 minutes

STAND:
10 minutes

OVEN:
350°F

MAKES:
8 servings

1 In a large skillet cook onion, sweet pepper, and tomatillos in hot oil over medium heat until tender. Remove from heat; stir in green chile peppers and jalapeño peppers. Set aside.

2 For sauce, in a medium saucepan melt butter over medium heat. Stir in flour, chili powder, and salt. Add broth all at once. Cook and stir until thickened and bubbly. Remove from heat. Stir in sour cream.

3 Arrange half of the broken tostada shells in the bottom of an ungreased 3-quart rectangular baking dish. Layer with half of the chicken, half of the vegetables, half of the sauce, and half of the cheese. Repeat layers.

4 Cover loosely with foil. Bake, covered, in a 350°F oven for 35 to 40 minutes or until heated through. Let stand for 10 minutes.

NOTE: **Because hot chile peppers contain volatile oils that can burn your skin and eyes, avoid direct contact with chiles as much as possible. When working with chile peppers, wear plastic or rubber gloves. If your bare hands do touch the chile peppers, wash your hands well with soap and water.**

Nutrition Facts per serving: 408 cal., 26 g total fat (10 g sat. fat), 85 mg chol., 631 mg sodium, 23 g carbo., 3 g fiber, 23 g pro.

Greek seasoning varies from brand to brand, but most include a great variety of herbs and spices, including parsley, oregano, onion powder, nutmeg, and pepper. The product makes bringing a load of flavor to a recipe easy—without a lengthy ingredient list.

GREEK CHICKEN & PITA BAKE

PREP:

20 minutes

BAKE:

50 minutes

OVEN:

350°F

MAKES:

4 servings

1   10¾-ounce can condensed cream of chicken soup

4   cups chopped cooked chicken (about 1¼ pounds)

2   medium zucchini, halved lengthwise and sliced into ½-inch pieces (4 cups)

½   cup chicken broth

½   cup chopped red onion (1 medium)

2   cloves garlic, minced

½   teaspoon Greek seasoning

3   6-inch pita breads, torn into bite-size pieces

1   cup crumbled feta cheese (4 ounces)

½   cup pitted kalamata olives, sliced

2   tablespoons olive oil

2   cups chopped roma tomatoes (4 large)

1 In a large bowl combine soup, chicken, zucchini, broth, onion, garlic, and Greek seasoning; mix well. Transfer to an ungreased 3-quart rectangular baking dish. Bake, covered, in a 350°F oven about 30 minutes or until vegetables are almost tender. Stir.

2 In a medium bowl toss together pita bread pieces, cheese, olives, and oil. Sprinkle pita mixture and tomatoes over chicken mixture. Bake, uncovered, about 20 minutes more or until top is golden.

Nutrition Facts per serving: 468 cal., 22 g total fat (8 g sat. fat), 109 mg chol., 1,118 mg sodium, 30 g carbo., 3 g fiber, 36 g pro.

There's something undeniably delightful about being served your own personal-size casserole. That's part of the beauty of this dish.

MONTEREY TORTILLA CASSEROLES

Nonstick cooking spray

6   6-inch corn tortillas, each cut into six wedges

2   cups cubed cooked chicken (10 ounces)

1   cup frozen whole kernel corn

1   16-ounce jar salsa verde

3   tablespoons dairy sour cream

1   tablespoon dried cilantro, crushed

1   tablespoon all-purpose flour

1   cup crumbled or shredded Chihuahua cheese
    or farmer cheese (4 ounces)

Dairy sour cream, thinly sliced fresh jalapeño pepper*,
and/or chopped tomato (optional)

1 Lightly coat four 10- to 12-ounce baking dishes with cooking spray. Line the bottom and side of each dish with 5 tortilla wedges; set aside. Place remaining tortilla pieces on a baking sheet. Bake in a 350°F oven about 10 minutes or until crisp and golden.

2 Meanwhile, in a large bowl combine chicken, corn, salsa verde, the 3 tablespoons sour cream, the cilantro, and flour. Divide mixture evenly among baking dishes.

3 Bake, uncovered, in a 350°F oven for 20 minutes. Arrange baked tortilla pieces on top of casseroles. Top with crumbled cheese. Bake for 5 to 10 minutes more or until heated through. If desired, garnish with additional sour cream, jalapeño pepper, and/or chopped tomato.

*NOTE: Because hot chile peppers contain volatile oils that can burn your skin and eyes, avoid direct contact with chiles as much as possible. When working with chile peppers, wear plastic or rubber gloves. If your bare hands do touch the chile peppers, wash your hands well with soap and water.

Nutrition Facts per serving: 418 cal., 18 g total fat (8 g sat. fat), 96 mg chol., 467 mg sodium, 36 g carbo., 3 g fiber, 31 g pro.

PREP:
30 minutes
BAKE:
25 minutes
OVEN:
350°F
MAKES:
4 servings

A mix of butter and black beans makes this chicken and turkey-sausage combo as eye-catching as it is scrumptious.

TWO-BEAN CASSOULET

PREP:

25 minutes

BAKE:

25 minutes

OVEN:

350°F

MAKES:

6 servings

6   skinless, boneless chicken thighs (about 1¼ pounds)

1   tablespoon olive oil or cooking oil

1½   cups thinly sliced carrots (3 medium)

½   cup chopped onion (1 medium)

2   cloves garlic, minced

1   15-ounce can butter beans, rinsed and drained

1   15-ounce can black beans, rinsed and drained

1   8-ounce can tomato sauce

¼   cup dry red wine

1   teaspoon dried thyme, crushed

¼   teaspoon ground allspice

8   ounces smoked turkey sausage, cut into ½-inch slices

     Chopped seeded tomatoes (optional)

     Snipped fresh parsley (optional)

1 In a large skillet brown chicken in hot oil over medium-low heat about 10 minutes, turning occasionally. Remove chicken from skillet, reserving drippings. Add carrots, onion, and garlic to drippings in skillet. Cover and cook about 10 minutes or just until carrots are tender, stirring occasionally.

2 Stir in drained beans, tomato sauce, wine, thyme, and allspice. Stir in sausage. Transfer to an ungreased 2-quart casserole. Place chicken on top.

3 Bake, uncovered, in a 350°F oven for 25 to 30 minutes or until chicken is no longer pink (180°F). If desired, sprinkle with tomatoes and parsley. Bake about 5 minutes more or just until tomatoes are heated through.

Nutrition Facts per serving: 331 cal., 10 g total fat (2 g sat. fat), 101 mg chol., 1,030 mg sodium, 27 g carbo., 7 g fiber, 34 g pro.

Use refrigerated—not dried—tortellini for this chicken-pasta bake. Cream cheese and a little lemon juice add a slight tang to the creamy sauce.

TORTELLINI & GARDEN VEGETABLE CASSEROLE

2	9-ounce packages refrigerated tortellini
1½	cups sugar snap peas, trimmed and halved crosswise
½	cup thinly sliced carrot (1 medium)
1	tablespoon butter
1	pound skinless, boneless chicken breast halves, cut into bite-size pieces
1	cup sliced fresh mushrooms
⅓	cup chicken broth
2	teaspoons all-purpose flour
1½	teaspoons dried oregano, crushed
½	teaspoon garlic salt
½	teaspoon black pepper
1	cup milk
1	8-ounce package cream cheese, cubed and softened
1	tablespoon lemon juice
1	cup quartered cherry tomatoes
½	cup coarsely chopped red or green sweet pepper (1 small)
2	tablespoons grated Parmesan cheese

PREP:
30 minutes
BAKE:
30 minutes
OVEN:
350°F
MAKES:
8 servings

1 Cook tortellini according to package directions, adding snap peas and carrot during the last 1 minute of cooking; drain well. Set aside.

2 Meanwhile, in a large skillet melt butter over medium heat. Add chicken and mushrooms; cook and stir about 5 minutes or until chicken is no longer pink. Remove from skillet.

3 In a screw-top jar combine broth, flour, oregano, garlic salt, and black pepper. Cover and shake well. Add to skillet along with milk. Cook and stir until thickened and bubbly. Add cream cheese. Cook and stir until cream cheese is melted. Remove from heat; stir in lemon juice. Stir in tortellini mixture, chicken mixture, tomatoes, and sweet pepper. Transfer to an ungreased 3-quart rectangular baking dish.

4 Bake, covered, in a 350°F oven about 30 minutes or until heated through. Sprinkle with Parmesan cheese.

Nutrition Facts per serving: 420 cal., 18 g total fat (10 g sat. fat), 101 mg chol., 501 mg sodium, 37 g carbo., 1 g fiber, 28 g pro.

Busy week ahead? Stock up on these ingredients now and you'll be less than half an hour away from an incredibly satisfying supper when you need it most.

TURKEY-BISCUIT PIE

PREP:

15 minutes

BAKE:

12 minutes

OVEN:

450°F

MAKES:

4 servings

1	10¾-ounce can condensed cream of chicken soup
½	cup milk
¼	cup dairy sour cream
1	cup cubed cooked turkey breast (5 ounces)
1½	cups loose-pack frozen mixed vegetables
½	teaspoon dried basil, crushed
⅛	teaspoon black pepper
1	package (5 or 6) refrigerated biscuits, quartered

1 In a medium saucepan combine soup, milk, and sour cream. Stir in turkey, mixed vegetables, basil, and pepper. Cook and stir over medium heat until boiling. Transfer to a lightly greased 1½-quart casserole. Top with quartered biscuits.

2 Bake, uncovered, in a 450°F oven for 12 to 15 minutes or until biscuits are browned.

Nutrition Facts per serving: 335 cal., 14 g total fat (5 g sat. fat), 49 mg chol., 1,049 mg sodium, 33 g carbo., 3 g fiber, 20 g pro.

Tailor the vegetables to your family's tastes. For this recipe, you can use just about any combination of mixed vegetables or simply use all peas.

POTATO-TOPPED TURKEY PIE

1	pound uncooked ground turkey or chicken
½	cup chopped onion (1 medium)
1	10¾-ounce can condensed golden mushroom soup
1	10-ounce package frozen peas and carrots, thawed
¼	cup water
½	teaspoon salt
⅛	teaspoon black pepper
1	20-ounce package refrigerated mashed potatoes
1	cup shredded cheddar cheese (4 ounces)

PREP:
25 minutes
BAKE:
40 minutes
OVEN:
350°F
MAKES:
4 to 6 servings

1 In a large skillet cook ground turkey and onion over medium heat until turkey is brown and onion is tender. Stir in soup, peas and carrots, the water, salt, and pepper. Transfer to an ungreased 1½-quart casserole.

2 In a medium bowl combine mashed potatoes and ½ cup of the cheese. Drop potato mixture in mounds on top of turkey mixture in casserole. Sprinkle with remaining ½ cup cheese.

3 Bake, uncovered, in a 350°F oven for 40 to 45 minutes or until mixture is heated through.

Nutrition Facts per serving: 491 cal., 23 g total fat (9 g sat. fat), 123 mg chol., 1,406 mg sodium, 36 g carbo., 4 g fiber, 34 g pro.

This quick casserole is perfect to use up leftover turkey after Thanksgiving. With a combined cook and prep time of less than 30 minutes, it's ready in no time—a satisfying busy-night standby.

QUICK TURKEY TETRAZZINI

PREP:

15 minutes

BAKE:

12 minutes

OVEN:

425°F

MAKES:

4 servings

6   ounces uncooked spaghetti

1   19-ounce can ready-to-serve chunky creamy chicken with mushroom soup

1   cup chopped cooked turkey breast (5 ounces)

½   cup shredded Parmesan cheese (2 ounces)

2   tablespoons sliced almonds

1 Cook spaghetti according to package directions; drain. Return spaghetti to pan. Add soup, turkey, and ¼ cup of the cheese; heat through over medium heat. Transfer to a lightly greased 2-quart square baking dish. Sprinkle with almonds and remaining ¼ cup cheese.

2 Bake, uncovered, in a 425°F oven for 12 to 15 minutes or until top is golden and mixture is heated through.

Nutrition Facts per serving: 413 cal., 13 g total fat (5 g sat. fat), 59 mg chol., 752 mg sodium, 43 g carbo., 2 g fiber, 28 g pro.

Rice and vegetables win an encore for the last of the holiday turkey. This creamy main dish gives leftover turkey or chicken a good name.

TURKEY & VEGETABLE RICE BAKE

2	cups sliced fresh mushrooms (8 ounces)
¾	cup chopped red or yellow sweet pepper (1 medium)
½	cup chopped onion (1 medium)
2	cloves garlic, minced
2	tablespoons butter
¼	cup all-purpose flour
¾	teaspoon salt
½	teaspoon dried thyme, crushed
¼	teaspoon black pepper
2	cups fat-free milk
1	10-ounce package frozen chopped spinach, thawed and drained well
2	cups cooked brown rice
2	cups chopped cooked turkey or chicken (10 ounces)
½	cup shredded Parmesan cheese (2 ounces)

PREP:
35 minutes

BAKE:
30 minutes

STAND:
15 minutes

OVEN:
350°F

MAKES:
6 servings

1 In a 12-inch skillet cook mushrooms, sweet pepper, onion, and garlic in hot butter over medium heat until tender. Stir in flour, salt, thyme, and black pepper. Add milk all at once. Cook and stir until thickened and bubbly. Stir in spinach, cooked rice, turkey, and ¼ cup of the Parmesan cheese. Transfer to an ungreased 2-quart rectangular baking dish. Sprinkle with remaining ¼ cup Parmesan cheese.

2 Bake, covered, in a 350°F oven for 20 minutes. Uncover and bake about 10 minutes more or until heated through. Let stand for 15 minutes before serving.

Nutrition Facts per serving: 297 cal., 10 g total fat (5 g sat. fat), 53 mg chol., 602 mg sodium, 28 g carbo., 3 g fiber, 24 g pro.

Stash away some cooked turkey in the freezer—in 1 1/2-cup portions—so you'll have the meat on hand for this lively bake. You can freeze cooked turkey for up to 4 months.

MEXICAN TURKEY CASSEROLE

PREP:

20 minutes

BAKE:

35 minutes

OVEN:

375°F

MAKES:

4 to 6 servings

1½   cups chopped cooked turkey or chicken (about 8 ounces)

1   10¾-ounce can condensed cream of chicken or cream of mushroom soup

½   cup dairy sour cream

1   4-ounce can diced green chile peppers, undrained

1   2¼-ounce can sliced pitted ripe olives, undrained

¼   cup sliced green onions (2)

1½   cups coarsely crushed tortilla chips or corn chips

1½   cups shredded Monterey Jack cheese with jalapeño peppers or Monterey Jack cheese (6 ounces)

1   cup chopped tomatoes (2 medium)

1 In a large bowl combine turkey, soup, sour cream, undrained chile peppers, undrained olives, and the green onions.

2 Sprinkle ½ cup of the chips over the bottom of a greased 2-quart square baking dish. Spoon half of the turkey mixture over chips. Top with ¾ cup of the cheese. Repeat layers, ending with a layer of chips.

3 Bake, uncovered, in a 375°F oven about 35 minutes or until mixture is heated through. Sprinkle with tomatoes just before serving.

Nutrition Facts per serving: 487 cal., 32 g total fat (15 g sat. fat), 87 mg chol., 1,413 mg sodium, 26 g carbo., 3 g fiber, 27 g pro.

Curry is a pulverized blend of up to 20 spices, herbs, and seeds. The mixture lends a spicy flair to transform just another turkey casserole into a dynamite entrée.

TURKEY CURRY BAKE

1½   cups herb-seasoned stuffing mix

¼   cup butter, melted

2   tablespoons water

1   10¾-ounce can condensed cream of celery soup

½   cup milk

1½   cups cubed cooked turkey (about 8 ounces)

1   cup chopped red apple (1 large)

¼   cup golden raisins

1   tablespoon finely chopped onion

1   to 2 teaspoons curry powder

PREP:
20 minutes

BAKE:
30 minutes

OVEN:
375°F

MAKES:
4 servings

1 In a small bowl combine stuffing mix, melted butter, and the water. Reserve ½ cup of the stuffing mixture. Press remaining stuffing mixture into the bottom of an ungreased 1½-quart casserole.

2 In a medium bowl combine soup and milk. Stir in turkey, apple, raisins, onion, and curry powder. Spoon turkey mixture on top of stuffing mixture in casserole. Sprinkle reserved stuffing mixture on top. Bake, uncovered, in a 375°F oven for 30 to 35 minutes or until mixture is heated through.

Nutrition Facts per serving: 411 cal., 21 g total fat (9 g sat. fat), 76 mg chol., 993 mg sodium, 37 g carbo., 4 g fiber, 21 g pro.

These creamy, turkey-filled rolls give a twist to typical chicken- or beef-filled enchiladas. This dish is perfect for six, but any more than that and you'll be fighting over seconds.

TURKEY ENCHILADAS

PREP:

40 minutes

BAKE:

45 minutes

OVEN:

350°F

MAKES:

12 enchiladas

½ cup chopped onion

½ of an 8-ounce package reduced-fat cream cheese (Neufchâtel), softened

1 tablespoon water

1 teaspoon ground cumin

¼ teaspoon black pepper

⅛ teaspoon salt

4 cups chopped cooked turkey or chicken breast (about 1¼ pounds)

¼ cup chopped pecans, toasted

12 7- to 8-inch flour tortillas

1 10¾-ounce can reduced-fat and reduced-sodium condensed cream of chicken soup

1 8-ounce carton light dairy sour cream

1 cup fat-free milk

2 to 4 tablespoons finely chopped, pickled jalapeño chile peppers*

½ cup shredded reduced-fat sharp cheddar cheese (2 ounces)

1 For filling, in a small covered saucepan cook onion in a small amount of boiling water until tender; drain. In a medium bowl combine cream cheese, the 1 tablespoon water, the cumin, black pepper, and salt. Stir in cooked onion, turkey, and pecans; set aside. Wrap the tortillas in foil. Heat in a 350°F oven about 10 minutes or until softened.

2 For each enchilada, spoon about ¼ cup of the filling onto a tortilla; roll up. Place enchilada, seam side down, into a greased 3-quart rectangular baking dish. Repeat with the remaining filling and tortillas.

3 For sauce, in a medium bowl combine soup, sour cream, milk, and jalapeño peppers. Pour sauce over enchiladas.

4 Bake, covered, in a 350°F oven about 40 minutes or until heated through. Sprinkle with cheddar cheese. Bake, uncovered, about 5 minutes more.

*NOTE: Because hot chile peppers contain volatile oils that can burn your skin and eyes, avoid direct contact with chiles as much as possible. When working with chile peppers, wear plastic or rubber gloves. If your bare hands do touch the chile peppers, wash your hands well with soap and water.

Nutrition Facts per enchilada: 273 cal., 11 g total fat (4 g sat. fat), 55 mg chol., 417 mg sodium, 21 g carbo., 1 g fiber, 21 g pro.

Another time, try this mushroom- and rice-laced casserole using the meat from a roasted chicken you've picked up at your supermarket's deli counter.

HEARTY TURKEY & MUSHROOM CASSEROLE

1 cup chopped onion (1 large)

6 cloves garlic, minced

1 tablespoon olive oil

1 cup uncooked brown rice

1 14-ounce can chicken broth

½ cup water

½ teaspoon ground sage

6 cups sliced fresh white button and/or shiitake mushrooms (1 pound)

1 tablespoon butter

3 cups chopped, cooked turkey (about 1 pound)

1 10¾-ounce can condensed cream of mushroom soup

¼ cup dry sherry

¼ teaspoon salt

¼ teaspoon black pepper

¼ cup snipped fresh parsley (optional)

PREP:
50 minutes
BAKE:
25 minutes
OVEN:
350°F
MAKES:
6 servings

1 In a medium saucepan cook onion and garlic in hot oil over medium heat until tender. Stir in rice. Add broth, ¼ cup of the water, and the sage. Bring to boiling; reduce heat. Cover and simmer about 40 minutes or until rice is tender and liquid is absorbed.

2 Meanwhile, in a large skillet cook mushrooms in hot butter over medium heat about 5 minutes or until tender. Stir in turkey, soup, sherry, remaining ¼ cup water, the salt, and pepper.

3 Spread rice mixture evenly into the bottom of a lightly greased 2-quart rectangular baking dish. Spread turkey mixture over rice mixture. Bake, covered, in a 350°F oven for 25 to 30 minutes or until mixture is heated through. If desired, sprinkle with parsley before serving.

Nutrition Facts per serving: 368 cal., 13 g total fat (4 g sat. fat), 60 mg chol., 796 mg sodium, 35 g carbo., 3 g fiber, 27 g pro.

For a change of pace, substitute ground beef or sausage for the turkey and add different cheeses or veggie toppers that make your family smile.

MEXICAN TURKEY PIE

PREP:

25 minutes

BAKE:

24 minutes

OVEN:

400°F

MAKES:

6 servings

1	8½-ounce package corn muffin mix
1	cup all-purpose flour
1	9-ounce can plain bean dip
½	cup bottled thick-and-chunky salsa
2	cups chopped cooked turkey breast (10 ounces)
1	4-ounce can diced green chile peppers, drained
1	2¼-ounce can sliced pitted ripe olives, drained
1	cup shredded sharp American cheese (4 ounces)
	Bottled thick-and-chunky salsa (optional)

1 For crust, prepare corn muffin mix according to package directions, except stir in ¾ cup of the flour with the dry corn muffin mix. Using a wooden spoon, stir in as much of the remaining ¼ cup flour as you can. Turn dough out onto a lightly floured surface. Knead in any remaining flour to make a moderately soft dough. Shape dough into a ball. Roll into a 13-inch circle. Carefully transfer the dough to a greased 12-inch pizza pan, building up edge slightly.

2 Bake in a 400°F oven about 12 minutes or until golden.

3 Meanwhile, in a small bowl combine bean dip and the ½ cup salsa. Spread over hot crust. Top with turkey, chile peppers, and olives. Sprinkle with cheese. Bake for 12 to 15 minutes more or until mixture is heated through. If desired, serve with additional salsa.

Nutrition Facts per serving: 435 cal., 14 g total fat (4 g sat. fat), 71 mg chol., 1,505 mg sodium, 54 g carbo., 3 g fiber, 22 g pro.

Enjoy dumplings? Then you and your family will love this biscuit-topped casserole.

ONE-DISH TURKEY & BISCUITS

1	cup chicken broth
½	cup finely chopped onion (1 medium)
½	cup finely chopped celery (1 stalk)
1½	cups loose-pack frozen peas and carrots
1	cup milk
3	tablespoons all-purpose flour
2	cups cubed cooked turkey breast (10 ounces)
½	teaspoon dried sage, crushed
⅛	teaspoon black pepper
1¼	cups packaged biscuit mix
½	cup milk
2	teaspoons dried parsley flakes, crushed

PREP:
30 minutes
BAKE:
20 minutes
OVEN:
425°F
MAKES:
4 servings

1 In a medium saucepan combine broth, onion, and celery. Bring to boiling; reduce heat. Cover and simmer for 5 minutes. Add peas and carrots; return to boiling.

2 In a small bowl stir the 1 cup milk into flour until well mixed; stir into vegetable mixture in saucepan. Cook and stir until thickened and bubbly. Stir in turkey, sage, and pepper. Transfer to an ungreased 2-quart casserole.

3 In a small bowl combine biscuit mix, the ½ cup milk, and the parsley. Stir with a fork just until moistened. Spoon into 8 mounds on top of the hot turkey mixture in casserole.

4 Bake, uncovered, in a 425°F oven for 20 to 25 minutes or until biscuits are golden brown.

Nutrition Facts per serving: 356 cal., 8 g total fat (3 g sat. fat), 67 mg chol., 844 mg sodium, 41 g carbo., 3 g fiber, 30 g pro.

Your family or guests will feel truly treated to something special when they taste this Cajun-inspired masterpiece chock-full of crisp-tender veggies.

SMOKED TURKEY JAMBALAYA

PREP:
30 minutes
BAKE:
55 minutes
OVEN:
350°F
MAKES:
6 servings

2   cups water

1   cup uncooked long grain rice

1   14½-ounce can diced tomatoes with green pepper, celery, and onions, undrained

1   10-ounce can diced tomatoes and green chiles, undrained

1   16-ounce package frozen peppers and onion stir-fry vegetables

8   ounces turkey kielbasa or other smoked turkey sausage, cut into ¼-inch rounds (1½ cups)

½   cup sliced green onions (4)

½   teaspoon Cajun seasoning

1   clove garlic, minced

    Bottled hot pepper sauce

1   In a medium saucepan combine the water and rice. Bring to boiling; reduce heat. Cover and simmer for 15 to 18 minutes or until rice is tender and water is absorbed.

2   In a large bowl combine rice, undrained tomatoes, frozen vegetables, kielbasa, green onions, Cajun seasoning, and garlic. Mix well. Transfer to an ungreased 2-quart square baking dish.

3   Bake, uncovered, in a 350°F oven about 55 minutes or until mixture is heated through, stirring once. Serve with hot pepper sauce.

Nutrition Facts per serving: 219 cal., 3 g total fat (0 g sat. fat), 0 mg chol., 842 mg sodium, 35 g carbo., 3 g fiber, 12 g pro.

Don't turn the page because of the short ingredient list—this easy dish packs a load of cheesy-good flavor because of the addition of the quick-and-easy julienne potato mix.

TURKEY-POTATO BAKE

2¼ cups water

1 4.6- to 5-ounce package dry julienne potato mix

2 cups cubed cooked turkey breast (10 ounces)

1 cup shredded cheddar cheese (4 ounces)

1 teaspoon dried parsley flakes, crushed

⅔ cup milk

1 Bring the water to boiling. Meanwhile, in an ungreased 2-quart square baking dish combine dry potatoes and sauce mix from potato mix. Stir in turkey, ½ cup of the cheese, and the parsley. Stir in boiling water and milk.

2 Bake, uncovered, in a 400°F oven for 30 to 35 minutes or until potatoes are tender. Sprinkle with remaining ½ cup cheese. Let stand for 10 minutes before serving (mixture will thicken on standing).

Nutrition Facts per serving: 373 cal., 15 g total fat (8 g sat. fat), 87 mg chol., 994 mg sodium, 27 g carbo., 1 g fiber, 32 g pro.

PREP:

15 minutes

BAKE:

30 minutes

STAND:

10 minutes

OVEN:

400°F

MAKES:

4 servings

Stop racking your brain for ideas to use leftover ham and turkey. Try this creamy main dish.

TURKEY-STUFFED MANICOTTI

PREP:

45 minutes

BAKE:

20 minutes

STAND:

5 minutes

OVEN:

400°F

MAKES:

8 servings

8	dried manicotti shells
¼	cup finely chopped onion
¼	cup butter
3	tablespoons all-purpose flour
¼	teaspoon salt
2	cups whole milk
1¼	cups grated Parmesan cheese
1	15-ounce container ricotta cheese
1	cup shredded cooked turkey (5 ounces)
½	cup chopped cooked ham (2½ ounces)
1	egg yolk
½	teaspoon ground nutmeg
	Ground nutmeg (optional)

1 Cook manicotti shells according to package directions; drain. Rinse with cold water; drain well. Set aside.

2 For sauce, in a medium saucepan cook onion in hot butter over medium heat about 4 minutes or until tender. Stir in flour and salt. Add milk all at once. Cook and stir until thickened and bubbly. Remove from heat; set aside.

3 For filling, in a medium bowl combine 1 cup of the Parmesan cheese, the ricotta cheese, turkey, ham, egg yolk, and the ½ teaspoon nutmeg. Spread about ½ cup of the sauce into the bottom of a buttered 2-quart rectangular baking dish.

4 Use a pastry tube fitted with the largest tip to pipe the filling into each end of the cooked manicotti shells. (Or carefully spoon about ⅓ cup of the filling into each shell.) Arrange filled manicotti in a single layer on sauce in baking dish. Pour the remaining sauce over the manicotti. Sprinkle with the remaining ¼ cup Parmesan cheese.

5 Bake, uncovered, in a 400°F oven about 20 minutes or until manicotti are golden and heated through. Let stand for 5 to 10 minutes before serving. If desired, garnish with a sprinkling of nutmeg.

MAKE-AHEAD DIRECTIONS: Assemble as directed. Cover and chill unbaked casserole up to 24 hours. Bake, uncovered, in a 400°F oven for 25 to 30 minutes or until manicotti are golden and heated through. Let stand for 5 to 10 minutes before serving. If desired, garnish with nutmeg.

Nutrition Facts per serving: 370 cal., 22 g total fat (13 g sat. fat), 108 mg chol., 572 mg sodium, 20 g carbo., 1 g fiber, 23 g pro.

Use turkey sausage as the recipe suggests—or change things up a bit by substituting pork sausage. Creamed corn, onion, and sweet pepper add to this dish's delightful flavor.

HERBED SAUSAGE & STUFFING CASSEROLE

2½   cups herb-seasoned stuffing mix

2   tablespoons butter, melted

1   pound uncooked bulk turkey sausage

1   cup chopped onion (1 large)

1   cup chopped green or red sweet pepper (1 large)

2   15-ounce cans cream-style corn

1   teaspoon dried parsley flakes, crushed

1 In a small bowl combine ½ cup of the stuffing mix and melted butter; set aside.

2 In a large skillet cook sausage, onion, and sweet pepper until meat is brown and vegetables are tender; drain. Transfer to a large bowl. Add corn and parsley. Stir in remaining 2 cups stuffing mix. Transfer to a greased 2-quart casserole. Sprinkle the buttered stuffing mix on top.

3 Bake, uncovered, in a 375°F oven about 35 minutes or until the mixture is brown and bubbly around the edges. Let stand for 5 minutes before serving.

Nutrition Facts per serving: 481 cal., 18 g total fat (7 g sat. fat), 47 mg chol., 1,618 mg sodium, 58 g carbo., 5 g fiber, 26 g pro.

PREP:
20 minutes

BAKE:
35 minutes

STAND:
5 minutes

OVEN:
375°F

MAKES:
5 or 6 servings

This easygoing, layered casserole provides the wonderful flavor of tamales without all the work of filling, wrapping, and steaming that a traditional recipe requires.

EASY OVEN TURKEY TAMALES

PREP:

30 minutes

BAKE:

27 minutes

STAND:

5 minutes

OVEN:

350°F

MAKES:

6 to 8 servings

1   pound uncooked ground turkey

2   cloves garlic, minced

1   14- to 17-ounce can cream-style corn

1   10½-ounce can chili without beans

2   teaspoons dried oregano, crushed

½   teaspoon ground cumin

¼   teaspoon salt

½   cup chicken broth

1   2¼-ounce can sliced pitted ripe olives, drained

8   6-inch corn tortillas

1   cup shredded cheddar cheese (4 ounces)

    Dairy sour cream (optional)

    Thinly sliced green onions (optional)

1 In a large skillet cook turkey and garlic over medium heat until turkey is brown; drain. Stir in corn, chili, oregano, cumin, and salt. Bring to boiling; reduce heat. Cover and simmer for 5 minutes. Stir in broth and olives. Remove from heat; set aside.

2 Stack tortillas; cut into 6 wedges. In an ungreased 2-quart rectangular baking dish layer 2 cups of the turkey mixture and half of the tortilla wedges. Repeat layers. Top with remaining turkey mixture, spreading to cover tortilla wedges.

3 Bake, uncovered, in a 350°F oven about 25 minutes or until heated through. Sprinkle cheese on top. Bake for 2 minutes more. Let stand for 5 minutes before serving. If desired, top each serving with sour cream and green onions.

Nutrition Facts per serving: 454 cal., 22 g total fat (9 g sat. fat), 93 mg chol., 944 mg sodium, 36 g carbo., 3 g fiber, 27 g pro.

Cook this surefire pleaser until the cheese sprinkled on top bubbles and turns slightly golden brown. For a delectable, rich vegetarian dish, skip the turkey or ham.

THREE-CHEESE & ARTICHOKE LASAGNA

9	dried lasagna noodles (8 ounces)
1	9-ounce package frozen artichoke hearts, thawed, or one 14-ounce can artichoke hearts, drained
1	cup finely chopped red onion (1 large)
4	cloves garlic, minced
1	tablespoon butter or olive oil
½	cup dry white wine
2	cups milk
3	tablespoons all-purpose flour
2	teaspoons finely shredded lemon peel
¼	teaspoon salt
¼	teaspoon black pepper
1	15-ounce container ricotta cheese
¾	cup shredded Parmigiano-Reggiano cheese, Asiago cheese, or Parmesan cheese (3 ounces)
½	teaspoon dried tarragon, crushed
1½	cups shredded Gruyère cheese or Swiss cheese (6 ounces)
1	cup cubed smoked turkey or ham (5 ounces)

PREP:
40 minutes
BAKE:
40 minutes
STAND:
10 minutes
OVEN:
375°F
MAKES:
8 servings

1 Cook lasagna noodles according to package directions; drain. Rinse with cold water; drain well. Set aside. Quarter artichoke hearts lengthwise and pat dry with paper towels; set aside.

2 Meanwhile, for sauce, in a large saucepan cook onion and garlic in hot butter or oil over medium heat until tender. Add wine; cook for 3 minutes more. In a small bowl stir milk into flour until smooth; stir into onion mixture. Cook and stir until thickened and bubbly. Stir in artichoke hearts, lemon peel, salt, and pepper; set aside.

3 In a small bowl combine ricotta cheese, ¼ cup of the Parmigiano-Reggiano cheese, and the tarragon; set aside.

4 In a lightly greased 2-quart rectangular baking dish layer 1 cup of the sauce, 3 noodles, ¾ cup of the Gruyère cheese, and ½ cup of the turkey. Spoon half of the ricotta cheese mixture on top. Repeat layering. Top with remaining 3 noodles and the remaining sauce. Cover dish with foil.

5 Bake in a 375°F oven for 20 minutes. Sprinkle with the remaining ½ cup Parmigiano-Reggiano cheese. Bake, uncovered, about 20 minutes more or until bubbly and golden. Let stand for 10 minutes before serving.

Nutrition Facts per serving: 581 cal., 31 g total fat (19 g sat. fat), 106 mg chol., 1,242 mg sodium, 30 g carbo., 3 g fiber, 41 g pro.

Next time you're shopping for a holiday meal, pick up these ingredients when you pick up your turkey. That way, you'll have the fixings for serving leftovers at the ready.

TURKEY-BROCCOLI CASSEROLE

PREP:

25 minutes

BAKE:

35 minutes

OVEN:

350°F

MAKES:

6 servings

2 cups dried medium noodles (4 ounces)

2 cups loose-pack frozen cut broccoli

1 10¾-ounce can condensed cream of onion or cream of celery soup

1 8-ounce carton dairy sour cream

½ cup milk

2 cups chopped cooked turkey or chicken (about 10 ounces)

1 8-ounce can sliced water chestnuts, drained

½ cup shredded Swiss cheese (2 ounces)

⅓ cup fine dry bread crumbs

2 tablespoons butter, melted

1 Cook noodles according to package directions, adding the broccoli during the last 2 minutes of cooking; drain. Set aside.

2 In a large bowl combine soup, sour cream, and milk. Stir in turkey, water chestnuts, Swiss cheese, and noodle mixture. Transfer to an ungreased 2-quart square baking dish.

3 In a small bowl combine bread crumbs and melted butter. Sprinkle over noodle mixture.

4 Bake, uncovered, in a 350°F oven about 35 minutes or until mixture is heated through.

Nutrition Facts per serving: 441 cal., 23 g total fat (11 g sat. fat), 100 mg chol., 656 mg sodium, 38 g carbo., 3 g fiber, 24 g pro.

This hearty stuffing casserole cuts into neat squares for serving.

TURKEY-STUFFING BAKE

1 cup water

1 cup chopped red sweet pepper (1 large)

½ cup uncooked long grain rice

½ cup chopped onion (1 medium)

1 8-ounce package herb-seasoned stuffing mix

2 cups water

4 cups diced cooked turkey or chicken (about 1¼ pounds)

3 beaten eggs

1 10¾-ounce can condensed cream of chicken soup

½ cup dairy sour cream

¼ cup milk

2 teaspoons dry sherry

PREP:

35 minutes

BAKE:

35 minutes

STAND:

5 minutes

OVEN:

350°F

MAKES:

8 servings

1 In a medium saucepan bring the 1 cup water to boiling. Stir in sweet pepper, rice, and onion. Reduce heat to low. Cover and simmer about 20 minutes or until rice and vegetables are tender and water is absorbed.

2 In a large bowl combine stuffing mix and the 2 cups water. Stir in turkey, eggs, and half of the soup. Stir in cooked rice mixture. Transfer to a greased 3-quart rectangular baking dish.

3 Bake, uncovered, in a 350°F oven for 35 to 40 minutes or until mixture is heated through.

4 Meanwhile, for sauce, in a small saucepan combine remaining soup, the sour cream, and milk. Cook over low heat until heated through. Stir in sherry.

5 Let casserole stand for 5 minutes before serving. Spoon sauce over individual servings.

Nutrition Facts per serving: 383 cal., 12 g total fat (4 g sat. fat), 142 mg chol., 765 mg sodium, 38 g carbo., 3 g fiber, 29 g pro.

For a potluck or party, use a large baking dish. For a smaller party or intimate dinners at home, try au gratin dishes—they're simply more elegant.

TURKEY-SPINACH CASSEROLE

PREP:
30 minutes

BAKE:
25 minutes

OVEN:
350°F

MAKES:
8 servings

2   10-ounce packages frozen chopped spinach
     or chopped broccoli

2   10¾-ounce cans reduced-fat and reduced-sodium condensed
     cream of celery, chicken, mushroom, or broccoli soup

2   cups water

¼   cup butter

6   cups herb-seasoned stuffing mix

4   cups chopped cooked turkey or chicken (about 1¼ pounds)

⅔   cup milk

2   tablespoons grated Parmesan cheese

1 In a large saucepan combine spinach, half of the soup, the water, and butter. Bring to boiling. (If using spinach, separate it with a fork.) Cover and simmer for 5 minutes. Add stuffing mix to saucepan; stir to moisten. Spread into an ungreased 3-quart rectangular baking dish or eight 10-ounce au gratin dishes; top with turkey.

2 Stir milk into remaining soup; pour over turkey. Sprinkle with Parmesan cheese. Bake, uncovered, in a 350°F oven about 25 minutes or until heated through.

Nutrition Facts per serving: 375 cal., 12 g total fat (5 g sat. fat), 65 mg chol., 1,065 mg sodium, 44 g carbo., 5 g fiber, 23 g pro.

SIDE DISH

9

A medley of vegetables seasoned with herbs hides under a blanket of cheese in this serve-along.

ROASTED VEGETABLE CASSEROLE

PREP:

45 minutes

BAKE:

35 minutes

OVEN:

425°F

MAKES:

8 to 10 servings

2	14½-ounce cans Italian-style stewed tomatoes
1	medium eggplant (1 pound), peeled, if desired, and cut into 1-inch pieces (5½ cups)
4½	cups fresh mushrooms, halved (12 ounces)
2	medium zucchini, cut into 1-inch pieces (3½ cups)
1	cup chopped onion (1 large)
2	tablespoons olive oil
2	teaspoons dried basil, crushed
1	teaspoon salt
¾	teaspoon dried oregano, crushed
½	teaspoon black pepper
½	cup shredded mozzarella cheese (2 ounces)
½	cup shredded Parmesan cheese (2 ounces)

1 Drain tomatoes in a colander while preparing recipe (do not chill). Place eggplant, mushrooms, zucchini, and onion into an ungreased 3-quart rectangular baking dish. Sprinkle with olive oil, basil, salt, oregano, and pepper, tossing to coat.

2 Roast vegetables in a 425°F oven about 30 minutes or until vegetables are tender, stirring twice. Stir in tomatoes. Sprinkle with cheeses. Bake about 5 minutes more or until cheeses are melted.

Nutrition Facts per serving: 274 cal., 16 g total fat (7 g sat. fat), 28 mg chol., 1,127 mg sodium, 17 g carbo., 4 g fiber, 18 g pro.

This is family comfort food at its best. Flavored with fragrant garlic and onion and earthy mushrooms, it's terrific with grilled pork chops.

CREAMY MUSHROOM-POTATO CASSEROLE

3   large potatoes, peeled and halved (about 1½ pounds)

6   cups sliced fresh mushrooms (1 pound)

¼   cup chopped onion

1   clove garlic, minced

2   tablespoons butter

1   cup milk

2   eggs

2   tablespoons all-purpose flour

½   teaspoon salt

¼   teaspoon black pepper

¾   cup soft bread crumbs*

1   tablespoon butter, melted

PREP:
50 minutes
BAKE:
35 minutes
OVEN:
350°F
MAKES:
6 servings

1 In a large saucepan cook potatoes in boiling salted water for 20 to 25 minutes or until tender; drain and slice. In a large skillet cook mushrooms, onion, and garlic in the 2 tablespoons butter over medium heat about 10 minutes or until liquid is almost evaporated.

2 Layer half of the potatoes and half of the mushroom mixture in a buttered 2-quart square baking dish. Repeat layers. Whisk together milk, eggs, flour, salt, and pepper; pour over vegetables in the baking dish. In a small bowl combine bread crumbs and the 1 tablespoon melted butter. Sprinkle over vegetable mixture.

3 Bake, uncovered, in a 350°F oven about 35 minutes or until set.

*NOTE: **Use a blender or food processor to make fluffy soft bread crumbs. One slice yields ¾ cup crumbs.**

Nutrition Facts per serving: 214 cal., 10 g total fat (4 g sat. fat), 90 mg chol., 326 mg sodium, 25 g carbo., 2 g fiber, 8 g pro.

This hearty side dish is an enticing mix of fresh mushrooms, onion, and barley.

MUSHROOM-BARLEY CASSEROLE

PREP:

20 minutes

BAKE:

1 hour 15 minutes

STAND:

15 minutes

OVEN:

350°F

MAKES:

10 to 12 servings

1 cup chopped onion (1 large)

2 tablespoons butter

5 cups sliced fresh mushrooms (such as cremini, button, and/or shiitake)

2 cloves garlic, minced

4 cups water

1 cup uncooked regular barley

1 envelope (½ of a 1.8-ounce box) onion mushroom soup mix

1 teaspoon dried thyme, crushed

½ teaspoon salt

1 In a large skillet cook onion in hot butter over medium heat until tender. Add mushrooms and garlic. Cook about 5 minutes or until mushrooms are tender, stirring occasionally. Transfer to a greased 3-quart casserole. Stir in the water, barley, dry soup mix, thyme, and salt.

2 Bake, covered, in a 350°F oven about 1 hour 15 minutes or until barley is tender and most of the liquid is absorbed, stirring once or twice. Let stand, covered, for 15 minutes before serving.

Nutrition Facts per serving: 115 cal., 4 g total fat (1 g sat. fat), 6 mg chol., 276 mg sodium, 18 g carbo., 4 g fiber, 4 g pro.

Sweet onion varieties, such as Vadalia, Maui, or Walla Walla—full of succulent sweetness and pungent flavor—update this long-time favorite vegetable dish.

GREEN BEAN & SWEET ONION GRATIN

2	medium sweet onions, halved and thinly sliced (about 2 cups)
¼	cup butter
⅓	cup all-purpose flour
½	teaspoon salt
¼	teaspoon black pepper
⅛	teaspoon ground nutmeg
1	cup chicken broth
1	cup reduced-fat milk
2	16-ounce packages frozen cut green beans, thawed
1½	cups soft bread crumbs*
2	tablespoons butter, melted

PREP:
25 minutes
BAKE:
35 minutes
STAND:
10 minutes
OVEN:
325°F
MAKES:
10 to 12 servings

1 In a large skillet cook onion slices in the ¼ cup butter over medium heat until tender. Stir in flour, salt, pepper, and nutmeg. Add broth and milk all at once. Cook and stir until mixture is thickened and bubbly.

2 Place beans into an ungreased 3-quart au gratin or baking dish. Top with onion mixture. In a small bowl combine bread crumbs and the 2 tablespoons melted butter; sprinkle over mixture in dish.

3 Bake, uncovered, in a 325°F oven about 35 minutes or until heated through. Let stand for 10 minutes before serving.

*NOTE: Use a blender or food processor to make fluffy soft bread crumbs. One slice yields ¾ cup crumbs.

MAKE-AHEAD DIRECTIONS: Assemble as directed, except do not top with the bread crumb mixture. Cover unbaked casserole; wrap bread crumb mixture separately. Chill up to 24 hours. Sprinkle casserole with bread crumb mixture. Bake, uncovered, in a 325°F oven for 40 to 45 minutes or until heated through.

Nutrition Facts per serving: 150 cal., 8 g total fat (5 g sat. fat), 22 mg chol., 333 mg sodium, 17 g carbo., 3 g fiber, 4 g pro.

Similar to Mexican and Spanish rice recipes, this Southern speciality kicks up the flavor with hot pepper sauce. Add cooked ground beef to serve as a main dish.

SAVANNAH RED RICE

PREP:

20 minutes

BAKE:

1 hour

OVEN:

350°F

MAKES:

12 servings

½   cup chopped onion (1 medium)

½   cup chopped celery (1 stalk)

¼   cup chopped green sweet pepper

¼   cup chopped red sweet pepper

1   tablespoon olive oil

2   14½-ounce cans diced tomatoes, undrained

2   cups uncooked long grain rice

½   cup water

1   teaspoon sugar

1   teaspoon salt

¼   teaspoon black pepper

     Several dashes bottled hot pepper sauce

1 In a large saucepan cook onion, celery, and sweet peppers in hot oil over medium heat for 5 minutes or until tender. Stir in undrained tomatoes, the uncooked rice, the water, sugar, salt, black pepper, and pepper sauce. Bring mixture to boiling; reduce heat. Simmer, uncovered, for 10 minutes, stirring frequently.

2 Transfer rice mixture to a greased 2-quart casserole. Bake, covered, in a 350°F oven about 1 hour or until rice is tender.

Nutrition Facts per serving: 146 cal., 1 g total fat (0 g sat. fat), 0 mg chol., 312 mg sodium, 30 g carbo., 1 g fiber, 3 g pro.

The canned corn speeds getting this casserole to the oven—and you also can use chopped frozen onion for a faster prep time.

SQUASH CASSEROLE

2	pounds butternut or acorn squash, peeled, seeded, and cubed
6	slices white bread, toasted
½	cup butter, melted
6	lightly beaten eggs
1⅓	cups milk
1	teaspoon salt
½	teaspoon black pepper
2	15¼-ounce cans whole kernel corn, drained
1	cup finely chopped onion (1 large)

PREP:
40 minutes
BAKE:
40 minutes
STAND:
10 minutes
OVEN:
350°F
MAKES:
10 to 12 servings

1 In a large saucepan cook squash in boiling lightly salted water for 20 minutes or until tender; drain. Set aside.

2 Place bread, half at a time, in a food processor, tearing to fit. Cover and process to fine crumbs (you should have 1⅔ cups total). Set aside. Place melted butter into an ungreased 3-quart rectangular baking dish. Set aside. In a large bowl whisk together eggs, milk, salt, and pepper. Stir in corn, onion, drained squash, and bread crumbs. Transfer to baking dish.

3 Bake, uncovered, in a 350°F oven about 40 minutes or until center is set and edges are slightly puffed. Let stand for 10 minutes before serving.

Nutrition Facts per serving: 270 cal., 14 g total fat (6 g sat. fat), 155 mg chol., 648 mg sodium, 30 g carbo., 3 g fiber, 9 g pro.

This mushroom-and-leek combo earns the title "Milanese" because it's topped with a blend of bread crumbs and shredded Parmesan cheese.

LEEK CASSEROLE MILANESE

PREP:

27 minutes

BAKE:

20 minutes

OVEN:

400°F

MAKES:

6 servings

5   to 6 leeks (about 1½ pounds)

2   teaspoons cooking oil

½   cup sliced fresh oyster mushrooms or button mushrooms

½   cup dry white wine

¾   cup whipping cream

¼   to ½ teaspoon salt
    Dash ground nutmeg

¼   cup soft bread crumbs*

¼   cup shredded Parmesan cheese (1 ounce)

1 Bias-cut leeks into ¼-inch slices. Rinse slices under cold running water to remove any remaining sand; drain well. Set aside (you should have about 3 cups sliced leeks).

2 In a large skillet heat oil over medium heat. Add leeks. Cook and stir for 2 to 3 minutes or just until tender.

3 Remove leeks from skillet; set aside. In the same skillet cook mushrooms over medium heat for 3 to 5 minutes or just until tender. Add wine. Bring mixture just to boiling; reduce heat. Cook for 4 to 5 minutes or until most of the liquid has evaporated, stirring occasionally. Add cream, salt, and nutmeg. Return to boiling.

4 Cook and stir mushroom mixture for 3 minutes or until slightly thickened (you should have about ¾ cup). Add leeks to mushroom mixture. Transfer to a lightly greased 1-quart casserole. Top with bread crumbs and cheese.

5 Bake, uncovered, in a 400°F oven for 20 to 25 minutes or until heated through and topping is golden. Serve immediately.

*NOTE: **Use a blender or food processor to make fluffy soft bread crumbs. One slice yields ¾ cup crumbs.**

Nutrition Facts per serving: 187 cal., 14 g total fat (7 g sat. fat), 44 mg chol., 175 mg sodium, 10 g carbo., 3 g fiber, 3 g pro.

Cream of onion soup is the base for the creamy sauce that goes over this tasty side dish.

BROCCOLI BREAD BAKE

2	10-ounce packages frozen cut broccoli, thawed
1	slightly beaten egg
1	10¾-ounce can condensed cream of onion soup
¼	cup finely chopped celery
1	teaspoon dried parsley flakes, crushed
¼	teaspoon dried tarragon, crushed
	Dash black pepper
1	package (6 or 8) refrigerated dinner rolls
¼	cup milk

PREP:
15 minutes
BAKE:
20 minutes
OVEN:
350°F
MAKES:
6 servings

1 Spread broccoli into the bottom of an ungreased 2-quart square baking dish; set aside. In a medium bowl combine egg, half of the soup, the celery, parsley, tarragon, and pepper. Spoon soup mixture over broccoli; set aside. Separate dinner rolls; snip each roll into quarters. Arrange roll quarters on top of broccoli mixture.

2 Bake, uncovered, in a 350°F oven for 20 to 25 minutes or until rolls are golden.

3 Meanwhile, for sauce, in a small saucepan combine remaining soup and the milk; heat through. Serve sauce over baked casserole.

Nutrition Facts per serving: 200 cal., 5 g total fat (1 g sat. fat), 42 mg chol., 698 mg sodium, 28 g carbo., 3 g fiber, 9 g pro.

This all-American vegetable classic is full of flavor—earthy mushroom soup, luscious cheese, and buttery bread crumb topping make it so!

BROCCOLI-CAULIFLOWER BAKE

PREP:

20 minutes

BAKE:

15 minutes

OVEN:

375°F

MAKES:

10 servings

4	cups broccoli florets*
3	cups cauliflower florets*
1	10¾-ounce can condensed cream of mushroom soup or cream of chicken soup
¾	cup torn American cheese or process Swiss cheese (3 ounces)
1	tablespoon dried minced onion
½	teaspoon dried basil, thyme, or marjoram, crushed
¾	cup soft bread crumbs**
1	tablespoon butter, melted

1 In a large covered saucepan cook broccoli and cauliflower in a small amount of boiling lightly salted water for 6 to 8 minutes or until vegetables are almost crisp-tender. Drain well; remove from pan.

2 In the same saucepan combine soup, cheese, onion, and basil. Cook and stir over medium heat until bubbly. Stir in cooked broccoli and cauliflower. Transfer mixture to an ungreased 1½-quart casserole.

3 In a small bowl combine bread crumbs and melted butter; sprinkle over vegetable mixture. Bake in a 375°F oven about 15 minutes or until heated through.

*NOTE: **If desired, substitute loose-pack frozen broccoli and cauliflower, thawed, for the fresh broccoli and cauliflower florets. Bake in a 375°F oven about 35 minutes or until heated through.**

NOTE: **Use a blender or food processor to make fluffy soft bread crumbs. One slice yields ¾ cup crumbs.

Nutrition Facts per serving: 100 cal., 6 g total fat (3 g sat. fat), 12 mg chol., 376 mg sodium, 7 g carbo., 2 g fiber, 4 g pro.

Here's an easy-to-make casserole to remember for upcoming party meals.

CARROTS AU GRATIN

1	pound carrots, sliced ½ inch thick (about 3 cups)
¼	cup fine dry bread crumbs
1	tablespoon butter, melted
1	10¾-ounce can condensed cream of celery soup or reduced-fat condensed cream of celery soup
1	cup shredded cheddar cheese (4 ounces)
1	teaspoon dried parsley flakes, crushed
½	teaspoon dried rosemary, crushed

PREP:
15 minutes
COOK:
20 minutes
OVEN:
350°F
MAKES:
6 servings

1 In a medium covered saucepan cook carrot slices in a small amount of boiling water for 10 to 12 minutes or just until tender. Drain well. Meanwhile, in a small bowl combine bread crumbs and butter; set aside.

2 In a medium bowl combine cooked carrots, soup, cheese, parsley, and rosemary. Transfer to a greased 1-quart casserole. Sprinkle with bread crumb mixture. Bake, uncovered, in a 350°F oven for 20 to 25 minutes or until heated through.

Nutrition Facts per serving: 177 cal., 11 g total fat (6 g sat. fat), 31 mg chol., 598 mg sodium, 14 g carbo., 3 g fiber, 7 g pro.

A little bit exotic, but still as comforting as a casserole can be, this recipe calls on curry powder and dried cherries to add a touch of intrigue.

CURRIED RICE-VEGETABLE BAKE

PREP:

30 minutes

BAKE:

35 minutes

OVEN:

350°F

MAKES:

6 servings

1	cup water
½	cup uncooked long grain rice
2	cups loose-pack frozen broccoli, cauliflower, and carrots
1	10¾-ounce can condensed cream of celery soup
½	cup milk
1	3-ounce package cream cheese, cut up
1	to 1½ teaspoons curry powder
1	teaspoon dried minced onion
¼	cup snipped dried tart cherries or golden raisins
⅓	cup chopped peanuts

1 In a small saucepan bring the water to boiling. Add rice. Return to boiling; reduce heat. Cover and simmer about 15 minutes or until rice is tender and most of the water is absorbed. Let stand, covered, for 5 minutes. Meanwhile, cook vegetables according to package directions; drain well.

2 In an ungreased 1½-quart casserole combine soup, milk, cream cheese, curry powder, and dried onion. Stir in cooked rice, drained vegetables, and cherries.

3 Bake, covered, in a 350°F oven for 25 minutes. Uncover. Bake for 10 to 15 minutes more or until heated through. Sprinkle with peanuts.

Nutrition Facts per serving: 228 cal., 12 g total fat (5 g sat. fat), 23 mg chol., 546 mg sodium, 25 g carbo., 2 g fiber, 6 g pro.

Traditional risotto requires a lot of hands-on stirring. This one, which goes straight into the oven and is just stirred twice, is designed for people with better things to do!

EASY OVEN RISOTTO

3¼	cups water
1	10¾-ounce can condensed cream of chicken and herbs, cream of chicken, or cream of celery soup
1¼	cups uncooked Arborio or medium grain white rice
⅓	cup coarsely shredded carrot (1 small)
¼	teaspoon salt
¼	teaspoon black pepper
½	cup frozen pea pods, thawed and bias-cut in half
½	cup shredded Parmesan cheese (2 ounces)

PREP:
10 minutes
BAKE:
55 minutes
STAND:
10 minutes
OVEN:
375°F
MAKES:
6 servings

1 In an ungreased 2-quart casserole combine the water, soup, uncooked rice, carrot, salt, and pepper. Bake, covered, in a 375°F oven for 55 to 60 minutes or until rice is tender, stirring twice during baking.

2 Remove casserole from oven; gently stir in pea pods and Parmesan cheese. Let the risotto stand for 10 minutes before serving.

Nutrition Facts per serving: 137 cal., 4 g total fat (2 g sat. fat), 9 mg chol., 605 mg sodium, 21 g carbo., 1 g fiber, 6 g pro.

Frozen vegetables are lifesavers in this easy-fixing side dish. Choose the mixture of vegetables that you and your family enjoy most.

SWISS VEGETABLE MEDLEY

PREP:

15 minutes

BAKE:

35 minutes

OVEN:

350°F

MAKES:

6 servings

1 16-ounce package loose-pack frozen broccoli, cauliflower, and carrots, thawed

1 10¾-ounce can condensed cream of mushroom soup

1 cup shredded Swiss cheese (4 ounces)

⅓ cup dairy sour cream

¼ teaspoon black pepper

1 2.8-ounce can french-fried onions

1 In a large bowl combine vegetables, soup, ½ cup of the Swiss cheese, the sour cream, and pepper. Stir in half of the french-fried onions. Transfer to an ungreased 2-quart square baking dish.

2 Bake, covered, in a 350°F oven for 30 minutes. Uncover. Sprinkle with the remaining ½ cup cheese and remaining french-fried onions. Bake about 5 minutes more or until heated through.

Nutrition Facts per serving: 249 cal., 17 g total fat (6 g sat. fat), 22 mg chol., 589 mg sodium, 14 g carbo., 3 g fiber, 9 g pro.

At eight servings, this double-cheese combo makes the perfect side dish for roasted meats or poultry, but you also can serve it as a hearty meatless main dish for four.

SPINACH & FETA CASSEROLE

2 cups cottage cheese

1 10-ounce package frozen chopped spinach, thawed and drained well

⅓ cup crumbled feta cheese

3 beaten eggs

¼ cup butter

3 tablespoons all-purpose flour

2 teaspoons dried minced onion

Dash ground nutmeg

PREP:
20 minutes
BAKE:
45 minutes
OVEN:
350°F
MAKES:
8 servings

1 In a large bowl combine cottage cheese, spinach, feta cheese, eggs, butter, flour, dried onion, and nutmeg; mix well. Transfer to a greased 1½-quart casserole.

2 Bake, uncovered, in a 350°F oven about 45 minutes or until center is almost set (an instant-read thermometer inserted in the center should register 160°F).

Nutrition Facts per serving: 172 cal., 12 g total fat (7 g sat. fat), 109 mg chol., 392 mg sodium, 6 g carbo., 1 g fiber, 11 g pro.

If you prefer not to use the wax beans, add another package or can of green beans to fill out this sumptuous twist on the traditional green bean casserole.

HOME-STYLE GREEN BEAN BAKE

PREP:

15 minutes

BAKE:

40 minutes

OVEN:

350°F

MAKES:

6 servings

1   10¾-ounce can condensed cream of celery soup or cream of mushroom soup

½   cup shredded cheddar cheese or American cheese (2 ounces)

1   2-ounce jar diced pimiento, drained (optional)

2   9-ounce packages frozen French-cut green beans, thawed and drained, or two 16-ounce cans French-cut green beans, drained

1   16-ounce can cut wax beans, drained

½   of a 2.8-ounce can (¾ cup) french-fried onions

1 In a large bowl combine soup, cheese, and, if desired, pimiento. Stir in green beans and wax beans. Transfer to an ungreased 1½-quart casserole.

2 Bake, uncovered, in a 350°F oven for 35 minutes. Remove from oven and stir; sprinkle with french-fried onions. Bake about 5 minutes more or until heated through.

Nutrition Facts per serving: 155 cal., 8 g total fat (3 g sat. fat), 15 mg chol., 686 mg sodium, 14 g carbo., 3 g fiber, 5 g pro.

Wonderful as a side dish, this sensational spinach-and-artichoke duet becomes an appetizer dip when you top it with picante sauce and sour cream and serve it with tortilla chips.

SPINACH & ARTICHOKE CASSEROLE

1	10¾-ounce can reduced-fat condensed cream of mushroom soup
1	8-ounce package reduced-fat cream cheese (Neufchâtel), cubed
2	10-ounce packages frozen chopped spinach, thawed and drained well
1	14-ounce can artichoke hearts, drained and coarsely chopped
1	2.8-ounce can french-fried onions, coarsely crushed
⅔	cup crushed crackers (such as rich round or saltine crackers)
2	tablespoons butter, melted

PREP:
20 minutes

BAKE:
40 minutes

OVEN:
350°F

MAKES:
8 servings

1 In a large saucepan combine soup and cream cheese. Cook and stir over medium heat until cream cheese is melted. Remove from heat. Stir in spinach, artichokes, and french-fried onions. Transfer to a greased 2-quart casserole.

2 In a small bowl combine crushed crackers and melted butter. Sprinkle over top of spinach mixture.

3 Bake, uncovered, in a 350°F oven about 40 minutes or until mixture is heated through.

Nutrition Facts per serving: 247 cal., 17 g total fat (7 g sat. fat), 33 mg chol., 637 mg sodium, 17 g carbo., 4 g fiber, 7 g pro.

Served alongside a Sunday roast, a holiday bird, or an everyday meat loaf, this versatile dish could easily become a family favorite.

SPINACH-CHEESE CASSEROLE

PREP:

20 minutes

BAKE:

30 minutes

STAND:

5 minutes

OVEN:

375°F

MAKES:

6 servings

½   cup chopped carrot (1 medium)

¼   cup chopped onion

1   tablespoon butter

1   10¾-ounce can condensed cream of onion soup

1   10-ounce package frozen chopped spinach, thawed and drained well

¾   cup uncooked instant white rice

½   cup milk

½   cup shredded Parmesan cheese (2 ounces)

1 In a 2-quart saucepan cook carrot and onion in hot butter over medium heat until tender. Remove from heat. Stir in soup, spinach, uncooked rice, milk, and ¼ cup of the cheese. Transfer to an ungreased 1-quart casserole.

2 Bake, covered, in a 375°F oven about 30 minutes or until rice is tender. Sprinkle with remaining ¼ cup cheese. Let stand for 5 minutes before serving.

Nutrition Facts per serving: 175 cal., 7 g total fat (4 g sat. fat), 20 mg chol., 647 mg sodium, 19 g carbo., 2 g fiber, 8 g pro.

When you've got a bumper crop of zucchini, serve this.

SUMMER SQUASH CASSEROLE

6   medium zucchini and/or yellow summer squash
    (about 2 pounds), halved lengthwise and cut
    into ⅜-inch slices (about 7 cups)

¼   cup chopped onion

1   10¾-ounce can condensed cream of onion or cream
    of mushroom soup

1   8-ounce carton dairy sour cream

1   cup shredded carrots (2 medium)

2   cups herb-seasoned stuffing mix (about ½ of
    an 8-ounce package)

¼   cup butter, melted

PREP:
25 minutes

BAKE:
25 minutes

OVEN:
350°F

MAKES:
8 to 10 servings

1 In a large saucepan cook zucchini and onion in a small amount of boiling water for 3 to 5 minutes or until crisp-tender; drain. In a large bowl combine soup and sour cream; stir in carrots. Fold in zucchini mixture. Set aside.

2 In a medium bowl toss together stuffing mix and melted butter. Sprinkle half of the stuffing mixture into an ungreased 2-quart rectangular baking dish. Spoon vegetable mixture on top. Sprinkle with remaining stuffing mixture.

3 Bake, uncovered, in a 350°F oven for 25 to 30 minutes or until mixture is heated through.

Nutrition Facts per serving: 228 cal., 15 g total fat (8 g sat. fat), 35 mg chol., 574 mg sodium, 21 g carbo., 3 g fiber, 5 g pro.

This vegetable and rice dish is a colorful side for baked chicken or grilled steaks.

CALIFORNIA VEGETABLE CASSEROLE

PREP:

15 minutes

BAKE:

1 hour 10 minutes

OVEN:

350°F

MAKES:

8 servings

1	10¾-ounce can condensed cream of mushroom soup
1	cup uncooked instant white rice
½	of a 15-ounce jar cheese dip (about ¾ cup)
1	cup milk
⅓	cup chopped onion (1 small)
¼	teaspoon dried oregano, crushed
1	16-ounce package frozen loose-pack cauliflower, broccoli, and carrots

1 In a large bowl combine soup, uncooked rice, cheese dip, milk, onion, and oregano. Stir in frozen vegetables. Transfer to an ungreased 1½-quart casserole.

2 Bake, covered, in a 350°F oven about 1 hour 10 minutes or until heated through, stirring once. Stir before serving.

Nutrition Facts per serving: 179 cal., 8 g total fat (4 g sat. fat), 26 mg chol., 723 mg sodium, 21 g carbo., 2 g fiber, 6 g pro.

A "gratin" is a casserole that's topped with bread crumbs and cheese.

SUMMER VEGETABLE GRATIN

1¼   cups sliced zucchini (1 medium)

1¼   cups sliced yellow summer squash (1 medium)

1   cup sliced leeks (2 large)

2   tablespoons olive oil

Salt

Black pepper

2   tablespoons fine dry bread crumbs

2   tablespoons shredded Parmesan cheese (1 ounce)

¾   teaspoon dried thyme, crushed

1   clove garlic, minced

1 In a medium bowl combine zucchini, yellow squash, leeks, and 1 tablespoon of the oil. Sprinkle with salt and pepper. Transfer to a greased 2-quart square baking dish.

2 In a small bowl combine bread crumbs, Parmesan cheese, thyme, garlic, and remaining 1 tablespoon oil. Sprinkle crumb mixture over vegetables. Bake, uncovered, in a 425°F oven for 20 to 25 minutes or until vegetables are tender.

Nutrition Facts per serving: 117 cal., 8 g total fat (1 g sat. fat), 2 mg chol., 104 mg sodium, 10 g carbo., 3 g fiber, 3 g pro.

PREP:
15 minutes
BAKE:
20 minutes
OVEN:
425°F
MAKES:
4 servings

For a meal that's kissed with a touch of the Irish, team these cheddary spuds with corned beef.

POTATO-CABBAGE CASSEROLE

PREP:

25 minutes

BAKE:

30 minutes

OVEN:

350°F

MAKES:

6 servings

1	pound unpeeled potatoes, sliced
1/3	cup chopped onion (1 small)
2	tablespoons butter
8	cups shredded cabbage (1 medium)
1	10¾-ounce can condensed cream of mushroom soup
¾	cup milk
½	cup shredded cheddar cheese (2 ounces)
½	teaspoon black pepper
¼	teaspoon dried rosemary, crushed
⅛	teaspoon garlic salt
1	cup soft bread crumbs*
2	tablespoons butter, melted

1 Place potatoes in a large saucepan; add enough water to cover. Bring to boiling; reduce heat. Cover and simmer about 10 minutes or just until tender. Drain; set aside.

2 Meanwhile, in a large saucepan or Dutch oven cook onion in the 2 tablespoons butter over medium heat until tender. Add cabbage; cover and cook about 5 minutes or just until cabbage wilts. Stir in soup, milk, cheese, pepper, rosemary, and garlic salt. Cook and stir until cheese melts. Carefully stir in potatoes.

3 Transfer potato mixture to a lightly greased 2-quart square baking dish. Combine bread crumbs and the 2 tablespoons melted butter; sprinkle over potatoes. Bake, uncovered, in a 350°F oven for 30 minutes.

*NOTE: Use a blender or food processor to make fluffy soft bread crumbs. One slice yields ¾ cup crumbs.

Nutrition Facts per serving : 275 cal., 15 g total fat (8 g sat. fat), 37 mg chol., 590 mg sodium, 27 g carbo., 4 g fiber, 8 g pro.

Serve these fiery grits with a Southern favorite, such as barbecued ribs or fried chicken.

SOUTHERN GRITS CASSEROLE

4	cups water
1	cup uncooked quick-cooking grits
4	beaten eggs
2	cups shredded cheddar cheese (8 ounces)
½	cup milk
¼	cup sliced green onions (2)
1	or 2 jalapeño chile peppers, seeded and finely chopped*
½	teaspoon garlic salt
¼	teaspoon ground white pepper
	Sliced green onions (optional)

1 In a large saucepan bring the water to boiling. Slowly stir in grits. Gradually stir about 1 cup of the hot mixture into the eggs. Return to saucepan. Stir in cheese, milk, the ¼ cup green onions, jalapeño peppers, garlic salt, and white pepper. Transfer to a greased 2-quart casserole.

2 Bake, uncovered, in a 350°F oven for 45 to 50 minutes or until a knife inserted near the center comes out clean. If desired, sprinkle with additional green onions.

*NOTE: Because hot chile peppers contain volatile oils that can burn your skin and eyes, avoid direct contact with chiles as much as possible. When working with chile peppers, wear plastic or rubber gloves. If your bare hands do touch the chile peppers, wash your hands well with soap and water.

Nutrition Facts per serving: 221 cal., 12 g total fat (7 g sat. fat), 137 mg chol., 281 mg sodium, 16 g carbo., 1 g fiber, 12 g pro.

PREP:
25 minutes
BAKE:
45 minutes
OVEN:
350°F
MAKES:
8 to 10 servings

These easy, cheesy Mexican potatoes are a super-simple side to serve alongside roasted meats.

FIESTA POTATO BAKE

PREP:
15 minutes

BAKE:
45 minutes

OVEN:
350°F

MAKES:
6 servings

1   10¾-ounce can condensed cream of onion or cream of chicken soup

½   cup dairy sour cream

1   4-ounce can diced green chile peppers, undrained

4   cups loose-pack frozen diced hash brown potatoes with onion and peppers

1   cup shredded Colby and Monterey Jack cheese or Mexican-style cheese blend (4 ounces)

① In a large bowl combine soup, sour cream, and undrained chile peppers. Stir in hash browns and ½ cup of the cheese. Transfer to an ungreased 2-quart square baking dish.

② Bake, covered, in a 350°F oven for 40 minutes. Stir. Sprinkle with remaining ½ cup cheese. Bake, uncovered, about 5 minutes more or until mixture is heated through.

Nutrition Facts per serving: 212 cal., 13 g total fat (7 g sat. fat), 32 mg chol., 583 mg sodium, 19 g carbo., 2 g fiber, 7 g pro.

Here's a version of those great cheesy scalloped potatoes that everyone loves, including the cook, as they're easy as can be.

SHORTCUT POTATO SCALLOP

1	20-ounce package refrigerated diced potatoes with onion
1	4-ounce can (drained weight) sliced mushrooms, drained (optional)
1	10¾-ounce can condensed cheddar cheese soup
½	cup dairy sour cream
¼	teaspoon black pepper
½	cup finely crushed cornflakes
1	tablespoon butter, melted

PREP:
15 minutes

BAKE:
45 minutes

OVEN:
350°F

MAKES:
6 servings

1 In a large bowl combine potatoes, mushrooms (if desired), soup, sour cream, and pepper. Transfer to a greased 2-quart square baking dish. Bake, covered, in a 350°F oven for 25 minutes.

2 Meanwhile, in a small bowl combine crushed cornflakes and melted butter. Uncover potato mixture. Sprinkle with cornflakes mixture. Bake, uncovered, about 20 minutes more or until heated through.

Nutrition Facts per serving: 194 cal., 9 g total fat (5 g sat. fat), 19 mg chol., 649 mg sodium, 29 g carbo., 3 g fiber, 5 g pro.

With a sprinkling of walnuts and a snipping of sage, this traditional French side dish becomes more magnifique than ever.

WALNUT-SAGE POTATOES AU GRATIN

PREP:

30 minutes

BAKE:

1 hour 10 minutes

STAND:

10 minutes

OVEN:

350°F

MAKES:

8 servings

6	medium potatoes (2 pounds)
½	cup chopped onion (1 medium)
2	cloves garlic, minced
2	tablespoons walnut oil or cooking oil
3	tablespoons all-purpose flour
1	tablespoon dried sage, crushed
¾	teaspoon salt
¼	teaspoon black pepper
2½	cups milk
1	cup shredded Gruyère cheese (4 ounces)
⅓	cup broken walnut pieces, toasted

1 Peel potatoes, if desired, and thinly slice (you should have 6 cups). Place slices into a colander. Rinse with cold water; set aside to drain.

2 For sauce, in a medium saucepan cook onion and garlic in hot oil over medium heat until onion is tender. Stir in flour, sage, salt, and pepper. Add milk all at once. Cook and stir over medium heat until thickened and bubbly. Remove from heat.

3 Layer half of the potatoes in a greased 2-quart casserole. Pour half of the sauce on top. Sprinkle with ½ cup of the cheese. Repeat layering with the potatoes and sauce. (Cover and chill remaining cheese until needed.)

4 Bake, covered, in a 350°F oven for 45 minutes. Uncover. Bake for 25 to 30 minutes more or just until potatoes are tender. Sprinkle remaining ½ cup cheese and the walnuts on top. Let stand for 10 minutes.

MAKE-AHEAD DIRECTIONS: **Peel potatoes, if desired, and thinly slice (you should have 6 cups). Cook potatoes in boiling salted water for 5 minutes; drain. Continue as directed through step 3. Cover and chill unbaked casserole up to 24 hours. Bake as directed.**

Nutrition Facts per serving: 285 cal., 13 g total fat (4 g sat. fat), 21 mg chol., 310 mg sodium, 33 g carbo., 2 g fiber, 10 g pro.

Dill, cheddar cheese, and pimiento bring flavor to this great-tasting potato dish. A cracker crumb topper adds the crunch.

AU GRATIN POTATOES & PEAS

1	pound potatoes, peeled and cut into ½-inch cubes
½	cup coarsely crushed rich round crackers or shredded wheat wafers
1	tablespoon butter, melted
¼	cup butter
¼	cup all-purpose flour
¾	teaspoon dried dillweed
½	teaspoon salt
⅛	teaspoon black pepper
1¾	cups milk
1	cup shredded sharp cheddar cheese (4 ounces)
1	10-ounce package frozen peas, thawed
1	2-ounce jar diced pimiento, drained

PREP:
35 minutes
BAKE:
30 minutes
OVEN:
350°F
MAKES:
6 servings

1 Place potatoes in a large saucepan; add enough water to cover. Bring to boiling. Cook, covered, for 3 minutes. Drain; set aside. In a small bowl combine crushed crackers and the 1 tablespoon melted butter; set aside.

2 For sauce, in a medium saucepan melt the ¼ cup butter over medium heat. Stir in flour, dillweed, salt, and pepper. Add milk all at once. Cook and stir until thickened and bubbly. Remove from heat. Stir in cheese until melted.

3 Combine potatoes, peas, and pimiento in a greased 2-quart rectangular baking dish; pour sauce over all. Sprinkle with cracker mixture. Bake, uncovered, in a 350°F oven about 30 minutes or until potatoes are tender.

Nutrition Facts per serving: 329 cal., 19 g total fat (10 g sat. fat), 52 mg chol., 519 mg sodium, 28 g carbo., 3 g fiber, 12 g pro.

Yukon gold and Finnish yellow potatoes contain more moisture than high-starch potatoes such as russets. They're a good choice for gratins and casseroles because they retain their shape.

CHEESE & GARLIC POTATO GRATIN

PREP:
15 minutes

BAKE:
1 hour 15 minutes

OVEN:
350°F

MAKES:
6 to 8 servings

1½ pounds Yukon gold or other yellow-fleshed potatoes, thinly sliced (about 5 cups)

⅓ cup sliced green onions (about 3)

1½ cups shredded Swiss cheese (6 ounces)

4 cloves garlic, minced

1 teaspoon salt

¼ teaspoon black pepper

1 cup whipping cream

1 Layer half of the potatoes and half of the green onions in a greased 2-quart square baking dish. Sprinkle with half of the cheese, half of the garlic, half of the salt, and half of the pepper. Repeat layers. Pour whipping cream over all.

2 Bake, covered, in a 350°F oven for 1 hour. Uncover. Bake for 15 to 20 minutes more or until potatoes are tender and top is golden brown.

Nutrition Facts per serving: 365 cal., 23 g total fat (14 g sat. fat), 80 mg chol., 454 mg sodium, 30 g carbo., 1 g fiber, 12 g pro.

Whether at a potluck or at home, expect requests for second helpings of this delicious classic.

CHEESY POTATOES

1   10¾-ounce can condensed cream of chicken soup

1   8-ounce carton dairy sour cream

1   cup shredded cheddar cheese (4 ounces)

¼   teaspoon black pepper

1   28-ounce package frozen loose-pack diced potatoes
     with onion and peppers, thawed

1   cup crushed cornflakes

2   tablespoons butter or margarine, melted

1 In a large bowl combine soup, sour cream, cheese, and pepper. Stir in potatoes. Transfer to an ungreased 2-quart rectangular baking dish. Combine crushed cornflakes and melted butter; sprinkle over the potato mixture.

2 Bake, uncovered, in a 375°F oven about 35 minutes or until bubbly and golden brown.

Nutrition Facts per serving: 286 cal., 16 g total fat (9 g sat. fat), 39 mg chol., 515 mg sodium, 27 g carbo., 2 g fiber, 8 g pro.

PREP:
15 minutes
BAKE:
35 minutes
OVEN:
375°F
MAKES:
8 servings

Spinach and red sweet pepper lend a colorful twist to scalloped potatoes.

SCALLOPED NEW POTATOES

PREP:

25 minutes

BAKE:

20 minutes

OVEN:

375°F

MAKES:

10 to 12 servings

2   pounds tiny new potatoes, sliced ¼ inch thick (about 7 cups)

1   cup chopped onion (1 large)

3   cloves garlic, minced

3   tablespoons olive oil

3   tablespoons all-purpose flour

1   teaspoon dried parsley flakes, crushed

½   teaspoon dried basil, crushed

½   teaspoon salt

¼   teaspoon black pepper

1¾   cups reduced-fat milk

6   cups torn fresh spinach

1   small red sweet pepper, cut into thin bite-size strips (¾ cup)

¼   cup fine dry bread crumbs

1 Place potatoes in a large saucepan; add enough water to cover. Bring to boiling; reduce heat. Cover and simmer about 8 minutes or just until tender. Drain and transfer to a very large bowl; set aside.

2 For sauce, in a medium saucepan cook onion and garlic in 2 tablespoons of the oil over medium heat about 5 minutes or just until tender. Stir in flour, parsley, basil, salt, and pepper. Add milk all at once. Cook and stir until thickened and bubbly. Remove from heat.

3 Add spinach and sweet pepper to potatoes. Toss gently to combine. Pour sauce over potato mixture; stir gently until coated. Transfer to a lightly greased 2-quart oval or rectangular baking dish.

4 In a small bowl combine bread crumbs and the remaining 1 tablespoon oil. Sprinkle over potato mixture. Bake, uncovered, in a 375°F oven about 20 minutes or until crumbs are golden and edges are bubbly.

Nutrition Facts per serving: 152 cal., 5 g total fat (1 g sat. fat), 3 mg chol., 221 mg sodium, 23 g carbo., 4 g fiber, 5 g pro.

Use the nacho cheese soup if you want a zestier dish. Either way, sprinkle with chives or green onion to add a little extra flavor and color.

CHEESY SCALLOPED POTATOES

6	medium potatoes (2 pounds)
1	10¾-ounce can condensed cheddar cheese or nacho cheese soup
½	cup dairy sour cream
½	cup milk
¼	teaspoon salt
¼	teaspoon black pepper
1	to 2 tablespoons snipped fresh chives or sliced green onion (optional)

PREP:
45 minutes
BAKE:
40 minutes
STAND:
10 minutes
OVEN:
375°F
MAKES:
6 servings

1 Place potatoes in a large saucepan; add enough salted water to cover. Bring to boiling; reduce heat. Cover and simmer for 20 to 25 minutes or just until tender. Drain; cool slightly. Peel and slice potatoes. In a small bowl combine soup, sour cream, milk, salt, and pepper. Place half of the potato slices in an ungreased 2-quart square baking dish. Top with half of the soup mixture. Repeat layers with remaining potatoes and soup mixture.

2 Bake, covered, in a 375°F oven for 25 minutes. Uncover. Bake about 15 minutes more or until heated through and potatoes are tender. Let stand for 10 minutes. If desired, sprinkle with chives before serving.

Nutrition Facts per serving: 193 cal., 7 g total fat (4 g sat. fat), 15 mg chol., 522 mg sodium, 29 g carbo., 3 g fiber, 7 g pro.

Chili sauce and vinegar give this version zing, while the brown sugar offers a sweet touch.

EASY BAKED BEANS

PREP:

20 minutes

BAKE:

1 hour

OVEN:

350°F

MAKES:

6 servings

2   16-ounce cans pork and beans in tomato sauce

½   cup chopped onion (1 medium)

¼   cup bottled chili sauce or ketchup

1   tablespoon packed brown sugar

1   tablespoon cider vinegar

3   slices bacon, crisp-cooked, drained, and crumbled

¼   teaspoon liquid smoke

1 Drain tomato sauce from one of the cans of beans. In a 1½-quart casserole combine drained beans, the can of undrained beans, onion, chili sauce, brown sugar, vinegar, cooked bacon, and liquid smoke.

2 Bake, uncovered, in a 350°F oven about 1 hour or until bubbly and heated through.

Nutrition Facts per serving: 197 cal., 4 g total fat (1 g sat. fat), 14 mg chol., 864 mg sodium, 36 g carbo., 8 g fiber, 9 g pro.

This hearty five-bean recipe is a true crowd-pleaser. Make it for your next summertime picnic to go with sizzling brats or hamburgers off the grill.

BAKED BEAN QUINTET

1 cup chopped onion (1 large)
1 clove garlic, minced
6 slices bacon, chopped
1 21-ounce can pork and beans in tomato sauce, undrained
1 15- to 16-ounce can butter or lima beans, drained
1 15- to 16-ounce can red kidney beans, rinsed and drained
1 15- to 19-ounce can cannellini beans, rinsed and drained
1 15-ounce can garbanzo beans (chickpeas), rinsed and drained
¾ cup ketchup
½ cup molasses
¼ cup packed brown sugar
1 tablespoon yellow mustard
1 tablespoon Worcestershire sauce

PREP:
25 minutes
BAKE:
1 hour
OVEN:
375°F
MAKES:
12 to 16 servings

1 In a large skillet cook onion, garlic, and bacon over medium heat until bacon is crisp and onion is tender; drain. In an ungreased 3-quart casserole combine onion mixture, undrained pork and beans, the butter beans, kidney beans, cannellini beans, garbanzo beans, ketchup, molasses, brown sugar, mustard, and Worcestershire sauce.

2 Bake, covered, in a 375°F oven about 1 hour or until mixture is bubbly and heated through.

Nutrition Facts per serving: 246 cal., 5 g total fat (2 g sat. fat), 9 mg chol., 842 mg sodium, 50 g carbo., 5 g fiber, 12 g pro.

Every great summer gathering needs a delicious batch of baked beans. Studded with pineapple tidbits, this version brings something unique to the table.

HAWAIIAN PINEAPPLE BAKED BEANS

PREP:
20 minutes
BAKE:
1 hour
OVEN:
350°F
MAKES:
8 to 10 servings

1	pound ground beef
½	cup chopped onion (1 medium)
½	cup ketchup
½	cup bottled hot-style barbecue sauce
2	tablespoons packed brown sugar
1	16-ounce can pork and beans in tomato sauce
1	15-ounce can chili beans with chili gravy
1	8-ounce can pineapple tidbits (juice pack), drained

1 In a large skillet cook ground beef and onion over medium heat until meat is brown and onion is tender; drain. Stir in ketchup, barbecue sauce, and brown sugar. Stir in pork and beans, chili beans, and pineapple. Transfer to an ungreased 2-quart casserole.

2 Bake, uncovered, in a 350°F oven about 1 hour or until mixture is bubbly and heated through.

Nutrition Facts per serving: 322 cal., 14 g total fat (5 g sat. fat), 41 mg chol., 833 mg sodium, 35 g carbo., 6 g fiber, 15 g pro.

When you buy the zucchini for this first-rate side dish, choose smaller zucchini, which will be younger, more tender, and thinner-skinned, making them all the better for baking.

ZUCCHINI BREAD PUDDING

2½	cups sliced zucchini (2 medium)
½	cup frozen whole kernel corn
2	tablespoons olive oil
½	cup chopped bottled roasted red sweet peppers
6	cloves garlic, minced
1	teaspoon dried basil, crushed
1	teaspoon dried parsley flakes, crushed
1	teaspoon dried sage, crushed
5	cups cubed sourdough or Italian bread (1-inch cubes)
1	cup shredded Swiss cheese (4 ounces)
3	tablespoons chopped toasted pecans
2	cups half-and-half or light cream
5	slightly beaten eggs
1	teaspoon salt
¼	teaspoon black pepper

PREP:
25 minutes
BAKE:
35 minutes
STAND:
10 minutes
OVEN:
350°F
MAKES:
6 servings

1 In a large skillet cook zucchini and corn in hot oil over medium heat for 3 minutes. Stir in sweet peppers, garlic, basil, parsley, and sage. Cook and stir for 2 minutes more or until zucchini is tender. Stir in bread.

2 Spoon half of the zucchini mixture into a greased 2-quart rectangular or oval baking dish. Sprinkle with ½ cup of the cheese. Repeat layers. Sprinkle nuts over top. In a medium bowl whisk together half-and-half, eggs, salt, and black pepper. Carefully pour over bread mixture, pressing lightly to thoroughly moisten the bread.

3 Bake, uncovered, in a 350°F oven about 35 minutes or until a knife inserted near the center comes out clean. Let stand for 10 minutes before serving.

MAKE-AHEAD DIRECTIONS: Assemble as directed. Cover and chill unbaked casserole for 2 to 24 hours. Bake in a 350°F oven about 45 minutes or until a knife inserted near the center comes out clean. Let stand for 10 minutes before serving.

Nutrition Facts per serving: 502 cal., 26 g total fat (11 g sat. fat), 224 mg chol., 886 mg sodium, 47 g carbo., 1 g fiber, 22 g pro.

This is classic comfort food that serves a crowd and will be a hit at any gathering.

BEST EVER CORN PUDDING

PREP:

20 minutes

BAKE:

40 minutes

OVEN:

325°F

MAKES:

8 servings

¼   cup butter

2   tablespoons granulated sugar

2   tablespoons all-purpose flour

4   eggs

½   cup half-and-half or light cream

1½   teaspoons baking powder

2   15-ounce cans yellow or white whole kernel corn, drained, or one 16-ounce bag frozen whole kernel corn, thawed and drained

2   tablespoons packed brown sugar

2   tablespoons butter, melted

¼   teaspoon ground cinnamon

1 In a large saucepan cook and stir the ¼ cup butter and granulated sugar over medium heat until the butter is melted. Remove from heat. Stir in flour. In a small bowl whisk together eggs, half-and-half, and baking powder. Stir into butter mixture. Stir in corn until combined. Transfer to a buttered 1½-quart casserole.

2 Bake, uncovered, in a 325°F oven for 35 minutes. Meanwhile, combine brown sugar, the 2 tablespoons melted butter, and the cinnamon. Sprinkle over the corn mixture. Bake about 5 minutes more or until a knife inserted near the center comes out clean.

Nutrition Facts per serving: 209 cal., 13 g total fat (7 g sat. fat), 132 mg chol., 345 mg sodium, 21 g carbo., 2 g fiber, 6 g pro.

This savory side dish combines basil with French bread, wild rice, and blueberries. Pair it with game, poultry, and meat dishes.

SAVORY WILD RICE BREAD CUSTARD

4	cups cubed French bread ($\frac{3}{4}$-inch cubes)
1	cup cooked wild rice
$\frac{1}{2}$	cup dried blueberries
$\frac{1}{2}$	cup finely chopped celery (1 stalk)
$\frac{1}{3}$	cup finely chopped onion (1 small)
$\frac{1}{2}$	teaspoon dried basil, crushed
$1\frac{3}{4}$	cups half-and-half or light cream
4	eggs
$\frac{1}{2}$	teaspoon salt
$\frac{1}{4}$	teaspoon black pepper

1 In a large bowl combine 3 cups of the bread cubes, the cooked rice, blueberries, celery, onion, and basil. Transfer to a greased 2-quart casserole.

2 Layer the remaining 1 cup bread cubes on top. In a medium bowl whisk together half-and-half, eggs, salt, and pepper. Pour egg mixture over bread mixture in dish, pressing lightly to thoroughly moisten the bread. Cover and chill for 30 to 60 minutes.

3 Bake, covered, in a 400°F oven for 30 minutes. Uncover. Bake about 10 minutes more or until a knife inserted near the center comes out clean. Let stand for 10 minutes before serving.

Nutrition Facts per serving: 231 cal., 9 g total fat (5 g sat. fat), 125 mg chol., 332 mg sodium, 29 g carbo., 1 g fiber, 8 g pro.

PREP:
25 minutes
CHILL:
30 minutes
BAKE:
40 minutes
STAND:
10 minutes
OVEN:
400°F
MAKES:
8 servings

Don't save sweet potatoes just for Thanksgiving. They're too tasty and pack a nutritious punch.

SWEET POTATO BREAD PUDDING

PREP:

15 minutes

BAKE:

30 minutes

OVEN:

325°F

MAKES:

6 servings

1 cup fat-free milk or vanilla-flavored soy milk

2 eggs

2 egg whites

1 cup mashed cooked sweet potato*

¼ cup packed brown sugar

1 teaspoon ground cinnamon

⅛ teaspoon ground nutmeg

4 slices whole-grain or raisin bread, cut into ½-inch cubes (3 cups) and dried**

⅓ cup golden raisins or snipped dried apricots

¼ cup chopped pecans, toasted

1 In a medium bowl whisk together milk, whole eggs, and egg whites. Whisk in sweet potato, brown sugar, cinnamon, and nutmeg.

2 Combine bread cubes, raisins, and pecans in an ungreased 2-quart square baking dish. Pour egg mixture over bread mixture in dish, pressing lightly to thoroughly moisten the bread.

3 Bake, uncovered, in a 325°F oven for 30 to 35 minutes or until a knife inserted near the center comes out clean. Serve warm.

*NOTE: For 1 cup mashed cooked sweet potato, peel and quarter one 12-ounce sweet potato. Place potato in a small saucepan; add enough water to cover. Bring to boiling; reduce heat. Cover and simmer about 25 minutes or until tender. Drain and mash.

**NOTE: To dry bread cubes, spread cubes in a 15×10×1-inch baking pan. Bake in a 300°F oven for 10 to 15 minutes or until bread cubes are dry, stirring once. Cool. (Bread cubes will continue to dry and crisp as they cool.) Or let bread cubes stand, loosely covered, at room temperature for 8 to 12 hours.

Nutrition Facts per serving: 283 cal., 7 g total fat (1 g sat. fat), 72 mg chol., 179 mg sodium, 48 g carbo., 4 g fiber, 9 g pro.

A savory twist on a favorite dessert, this bread pudding makes a tantalizing side for roasted chicken or pork. It's like having your own individual serving of stuffing.

SWEET PEPPER & ONION BREAD PUDDING

8	ounces crusty Italian bread
2	tablespoons butter, softened
1½	cups cups milk
3	eggs
1	12-ounce jar roasted red sweet peppers, drained well and coarsely chopped (about 1½ cups)
½	cup thinly sliced green onions (4)
2	teaspoons dried oregano, crushed
½	to 1 teaspoon bottled hot pepper sauce
¼	teaspoon salt
¼	teaspoon black pepper
1	cup shredded fontina cheese or provolone cheese (4 ounces)

PREP:
20 minutes

BAKE:
30 minutes

STAND:
10 minutes

OVEN:
350°F

MAKES:
8 servings

1 Cut the bread into 1-inch slices. Spread slices with butter, then tear bread into bite-size pieces. Set aside. In a large bowl whisk together milk and eggs. Stir in roasted sweet peppers, green onions, oregano, hot pepper sauce, salt, and black pepper. Add bread pieces and cheese, stirring well to coat bread.

2 Divide mixture among eight greased 6-ounce custard cups. (Or spoon into a greased 1½-quart soufflé dish.) Press mixture down lightly to thoroughly moisten bread.

3 Bake custard cups, uncovered, in a 350°F oven about 30 minutes or until golden and a knife inserted near the centers comes out clean. Let stand for 10 minutes before serving. (Or bake soufflé dish, uncovered, about 40 minutes or until golden and a knife inserted near the center comes out clean. Let stand for 15 minutes before serving.)

Nutrition Facts per serving: 225 cal., 11 g total fat (6 g sat. fat), 107 mg chol., 434 mg sodium, 20 g carbo., 2 g fiber, 11 g pro.

INDEX

METRIC INFORMATION

The charts on this page provide a guide for converting measurements from the U.S. customary system, which is used throughout this book, to the metric system.

Product Differences

Most of the ingredients called for in the recipes in this book are available in most countries. However, some are known by different names. Here are some common American ingredients and their possible counterparts:

- **All-purpose flour** is enriched, bleached or unbleached white household flour. When self-rising flour is used in place of all-purpose flour in a recipe that calls for leavening, omit the leavening agent (baking soda or baking powder) and salt.
- **Baking soda** is bicarbonate of soda.
- **Cornstarch** is cornflour.
- **Golden raisins** are sultanas.
- **Green, red, or yellow sweet peppers** are capsicums or bell peppers.
- **Light-colored corn syrup** is golden syrup.
- **Powdered sugar** is icing sugar.
- **Sugar** (white) is granulated, fine granulated, or castor sugar.
- **Vanilla** or vanilla extract is vanilla essence.

Volume and Weight

The United States traditionally uses cup measures for liquid and solid ingredients. The chart below shows the approximate imperial and metric equivalents. If you are accustomed to weighing solid ingredients, the following approximate equivalents will be helpful.

- 1 cup butter, castor sugar, or rice = 8 ounces = $\frac{1}{2}$ pound = 250 grams
- 1 cup flour = 4 ounces = $\frac{1}{4}$ pound = 125 grams
- 1 cup icing sugar = 5 ounces = 150 grams

Canadian and U.S. volume for a cup measure is 8 fluid ounces (237 ml), but the standard metric equivalent is 250 ml.

1 British imperial cup is 10 fluid ounces.

In Australia, 1 tablespoon equals 20 ml, and there are 4 teaspoons in the Australian tablespoon.

Spoon measures are used for smaller amounts of ingredients. Although the size of the tablespoon varies slightly in different countries, for practical purposes and for recipes in this book, a straight substitution is all that's necessary. Measurements made using cups or spoons always should be level unless stated otherwise.

Common Weight Range Replacements

Imperial / U.S.	Metric
$\frac{1}{2}$ ounce	15 g
1 ounce	25 g or 30 g
4 ounces ($\frac{1}{4}$ pound)	115 g or 125 g
8 ounces ($\frac{1}{2}$ pound)	225 g or 250 g
16 ounces (1 pound)	450 g or 500 g
$1\frac{1}{4}$ pounds	625 g
$1\frac{1}{2}$ pounds	750 g
2 pounds or $2\frac{1}{4}$ pounds	1,000 g or 1 Kg

Oven Temperature Equivalents

Fahrenheit Setting	Celsius Setting*	Gas Setting
300°F	150°C	Gas Mark 2 (very low)
325°F	160°C	Gas Mark 3 (low)
350°F	180°C	Gas Mark 4 (moderate)
375°F	190°C	Gas Mark 5 (moderate)
400°F	200°C	Gas Mark 6 (hot)
425°F	220°C	Gas Mark 7 (hot)
450°F	230°C	Gas Mark 8 (very hot)
475°F	240°C	Gas Mark 9 (very hot)
500°F	260°C	Gas Mark 10 (extremely hot)
Broil	Broil	Grill

*Electric and gas ovens may be calibrated using Celsius. However, for an electric oven, increase Celsius setting 10 to 20 degrees when cooking above 160°C. For convection or forced air ovens (gas or electric), lower the temperature setting 25°F/10°C when cooking at all heat levels.

Baking Pan Sizes

Imperial / U.S.	Metric
9×1$\frac{1}{2}$-inch round cake pan	22- or 23×4-cm (1.5 L)
9×1$\frac{1}{2}$-inch pie plate	22- or 23×4-cm (1 L)
8×8×2-inch square cake pan	20×5-cm (2 L)
9×9×2-inch square cake pan	22- or 23×4.5-cm (2.5 L)
11×7×1$\frac{1}{2}$-inch baking pan	28×17×4-cm (2 L)
2-quart rectangular baking pan	30×19×4.5-cm (3 L)
13×9×2-inch baking pan	34×22×4.5-cm (3.5 L)
15×10×1-inch jelly roll pan	40×25×2-cm
9×5×3-inch loaf pan	23×13×8-cm (2 L)
2-quart casserole	2 L

U.S. / Standard Metric Equivalents

$\frac{1}{8}$ teaspoon = 0.5 ml	
$\frac{1}{4}$ teaspoon = 1 ml	
$\frac{1}{2}$ teaspoon = 2 ml	
1 teaspoon = 5 ml	
1 tablespoon = 15 ml	
2 tablespoons = 25 ml	
$\frac{1}{4}$ cup = 2 fluid ounces = 50 ml	
$\frac{1}{3}$ cup = 3 fluid ounces = 75 ml	
$\frac{1}{2}$ cup = 4 fluid ounces = 125 ml	
$\frac{2}{3}$ cup = 5 fluid ounces = 150 ml	
$\frac{3}{4}$ cup = 6 fluid ounces = 175 ml	
1 cup = 8 fluid ounces = 250 ml	
2 cups = 1 pint = 500 ml	
1 quart = 1 litre